THE TELEVISION-RADIO AUDIENCE

AND RELIGION

STUDIES IN THE MASS MEDIA OF COMMUNICATION

Conducted by the

COMMUNICATIONS RESEARCH PROJECT

Supervised by

YALE UNIVERSITY DIVINITY SCHOOL

LISTON POPE, *Chairman, Administrative Committee*
EVERETT C. PARKER, *Project Director*

DAVID W. BARRY, *Research Consultant*
DALLAS W. SMYTHE, *Research Consultant*

STUDY REPORTS

The Television-Radio Audience and Religion
Film Use in the Church
Parents, Children and Television

A project of the Broadcasting and Film Commission

NATIONAL COUNCIL OF THE CHURCHES OF CHRIST IN THE U. S. A.

The TELEVISION-RADIO Audience and RELIGION

EVERETT C. PARKER

DAVID W. BARRY

DALLAS W. SMYTHE

HARPER & BROTHERS, PUBLISHERS

New York

To S. Franklin Mack, pioneer in the use
of the mass media of communication to
carry the Christian Gospel to the peoples
of the world

ACKNOWLEDGMENTS

The scope and size of the Communications Research Project have required the services of a large staff and many advisers. Most of the policy supervision and advisory assistance has been contributed as a service to co-operative religious broadcasting.

The Project was conducted under the supervision of Yale University Divinity School, and Liston Pope, dean of the Divinity School, acted as chairman of the Administrative Committee. Dr. Pope was the chief consultant to the staff and participated in all policy decisions. His friendship, support and advice were of inestimable value to the Director and the Project staff. Dr. Pope's knowledge of the mass media and his appreciation of research problems in communication greatly sharpened the focus of the studies. His leadership bore the Project over many serious and discouraging obstacles. The policies he recommended were always wise ones.

Other members of the Project's Administrative Committee were: Dr. Ronald Bridges, Dr. Truman B. Douglass, Dr. Clayton T. Griswold, Dr. F. Ernest Johnson, Miss Edith Lowry, Dr. S. Franklin Mack, Dr. Paul C. Payne, Dr. Stanley I. Stuber, Dr. Paul H. Vieth. This committee exercised close supervision over all phases of the work. Dr. Douglass deserves particular thanks for having originated the plan for the Project and steered it to approval by the board of managers of the Broadcasting and Film Commission of the National Council of Churches.

The Communications Research Project was sponsored and largely supported by the Broadcasting and Film Commission. Completion of the work of the Project was made possible by a generous grant from the Carnegie Corporation of New York. The Hazen Foundation and the Sneath Fund of the Yale University Divinity School similarly assisted the Project by granting funds to defray costs of preparing manuscripts for publication.

August B. Hollingshead, professor of sociology in Yale University, was one of the chief friends and consultants to the Project throughout its life. Professor Hollingshead graciously granted the Project staff access to the 5 per cent sample of the population of New Haven which has been the basic research resource for all of the studies that were conducted. This sample was drawn by Dr. Hollingshead for his own research use. He gave the Communications Research Project free access to all data that he had accumulated, assisted in the design of the research conducted by the Project and gave his services without stint to insure an accurate and a meaningful analysis of the sociological data gathered by the Project staff. Without Dr. Hollingshead's help, it would have been impossible to carry out the studies of the composition of audiences for the mass media.

Dr. Jerome K. Myers, Dr. Hollingshead's associate on the Yale sociology faculty, gave similar assistance in the analysis of data from the 5 per cent sample and gave his time to supervise the coding of data.

Professor Hollingshead and his associates, of course, are not responsible for the work of the Project staff, nor for the conclusions drawn from the sample data and detailed in this book.

Many advisers assisted in the design of the studies. Chief among them were Professor Samuel C. Kincheloe, Professor David Riesman, Professor Charles Glock and Professor Ross Snyder.

Hanan Selvin and Arnold Simmel, of the Columbia University Bureau of Applied Social Research, conducted the latent structure analysis reported in Chapter 9. Vernon Johns of Columbia University supervised mathematical and statistical tests to check the accuracy of all data gathered in the Project. Dr. J. J. Stein of the Veterans' Administration conducted preliminary analyses of personality types among the depth interview respondents.

The Project owes much of its success to Dr. Ronald Bridges and Dr. S. Franklin Mack, who acted successively as executive director of the Broadcasting and Film Commission during the life of the Project. Dr. Bridges and Dr. Mack were charged at various times with administrative supervision of the Project in behalf of the Commission and both took part in raising the necessary funds to pay for the Project.

Ultimately, of course, the success or failure of a large-scale research study depends upon the ability of the staff. The Communications Research Project was fortunate to have a staff devoted to the work, and highly competent. Mrs. John C. Temple acted as secretary for the Project and administrative co-ordinator. Mrs. Robert C. Nodine was chief of the research staff and acted as research co-ordinator. Mrs. Charles T. St. Clair was in charge of tabulating and analysis of statistical data. She was assisted by Mrs. Everett A. Sherwood and Mrs. W. Harold Denison. Mrs. Gordon Corbett supervised field interviewing and the tabulation of data in the study of the churches of New Haven. Rev. Edward Carroll, Mrs. Anne Lively and Miss Frances Potter assisted in the depth interviews.

The Project also wishes to acknowledge the co-operation and assistance it received from the ministers and the churches of New Haven. Rev. John W. Abbott, executive secretary, The New Haven Council of Churches, was especially helpful in providing information and co-operating in the experimental broadcasting program of the Project. The Connecticut Council of Churches also co-operated in the program of experimental broadcasting and Rev. Edwin H. Tuller, general secretary of the Council, and Miss Edith F. Welker, associate secretary, participated extensively in both the planning and the production of these programs.

The writers express sincere gratitude to the many organizations and individuals who made the Communications Research Project possible.

EVERETT C. PARKER
DAVID W. BARRY
DALLAS W. SMYTHE

New Haven
August 1, 1955

PREFACE

Religious broadcasting has been a part of the American scene almost as long as broadcasting itself. On January 2, 1921, only two months after KDKA's first transmission, the station broadcast the first religious program, carrying the regular Sunday service of the Calvary Episcopal Church of Pittsburgh.

Since that time, religious broadcasting has expanded greatly. It is no longer an isolated phenomenon to be heard rarely on a few radio stations. Instead, virtually every radio station in the country devotes portions of its broadcast time to religious programming. In addition, there are many network religious programs, sectarian and non-sectarian, sponsored and sustaining. And, as television has become a vital factor in American life, religious broadcasting has taken its place in this new medium.

Considering the importance that radio and television have assumed in the American social and cultural scene, it is surprising that up to now, no start has been made in describing the place of religious broadcasting in American life and in analyzing its effect. But, until now, church bodies, and church leaders—with a few notable exceptions—have not given religious broadcasting the serious consideration it merits. There are signs that this situation is changing, and this study is one of them. The authors of *The Television-Radio Audience and Religion* have made a remarkable beginning in this analysis of the function of religious broadcasting. The positive conclusions which they draw, with an eye toward policy formation in the churches and the ultimate improvement of religious programming on the air, can be studied with profit by broadcasters and church leaders alike.

The *Television-Radio Audience and Religion* also makes an important contribution to the field of research in the communications process. Psychology, sociology and anthropology, upon which communications research is heavily dependent, are still far from being precise sciences in the same sense as the physical sciences. Consequently, it is desirable in social science research to utilize and integrate a variety of research approaches to the same general problem. This the authors of *The Television-Radio Audience and Religion* have done.

In an effort to provide an overall picture of the role of religious broadcasting in New Haven, they have first considered the cultural, social, and religious environment in which such broadcasting takes place, and they have studied the potential audience for broadcasting, the availability of programs, and the program selections by the audience. In gathering this kind of background data, the authors have recognized that the effects of communication stimuli vary with the environment in which they operate. Hence, any complete study must include a study of this environment. Having taken this step, the authors proceed to study religious broadcasting itself, again using a variety of approaches such as the questionnaire interview, the non-directive interview and content analysis. Such a multi-pronged attack on a problem is all too rare in the research field and has been used by the authors with particular effectiveness.

Although this study was necessarily restricted to the City of New Haven, it surely contains the largest, most authoritative available body of research information on the subject of religious broadcasting and it seems certain that it points the way to conclusions of nationwide importance.

Oscar Katz
Director of Research
CBS Television

New York City
July 1, 1955

INTRODUCTION

This volume has grown out of the first serious effort to understand the effects of religious programs broadcast over radio and television. But it is also far more than that: because it undertakes to trace effects within the setting of a concrete community and in the lives of particular individuals, this study reveals a great deal about the total impact of newer methods of communication on an American city and its inhabitants. As such, it is a pioneering study of human response to the electronic age.

The miracles of electronics are now taken for granted in most American homes, and they seem much less awesome than the threats of the atomic era. Yet their potential import for the control and direction of human beings, and of nations, is perhaps greater than that of any weapon yet devised. Just after the First World War radio invaded most homes in the Western world and quickly changed the tactics of domestic politics in many nations, for good or ill. On the debit side must be placed the role played by radio in the rise of Hitler to power and in the emotional consolidation of the German people under his dictatorship.

Now, within a decade after the close of the Second World War, a new invasion has taken place in the form of television. Television antennas have changed the skyline of every American city and its environs. In New Haven, Connecticut, three families out of four had television sets when this study was made, and the percentage is higher now. The TV set is rapidly replacing the bathtub and the telephone as the principal household gadget.

Despite the obvious import of these new devices for entry into the privacy of the home and for influence on the minds and loyalties of human beings old and young, very little knowledge about their actual effects has been established. Psychologists, sociologists, and political scientists have produced a few notable studies verging on the question, with special reference to propaganda and the mechanisms of public opinion. The most extensive efforts have been made by business and advertising agencies interested in market research, and more is known about the best methods of selling soap on radio and TV than about teaching honesty or inspiring reverence.

From the advent of radio, religious agencies have used it in various ways in an effort to proclaim their message, and they have extended their interest more recently to include television. In the last few years sizable sums have been expended annually for religious programs and local stations and networks have contributed a significant though minor amount of time to this type of broadcasting. But the emphasis has been almost exclusively on the production of programs, and the producers have been too busy to ask about the results. Their attitude for the most part has been, and is, that of promotion rather than evaluation. To "get on the air" has sometimes been regarded as more important than to get something worth while on the air. It has been widely assumed that anything designated as "religious" or sponsored by a religious agency must by definition be worth while, at least in the eyes of loyal churchmen, even if the general public were suspected of taking a different view.

In the absence of any study of the effects of religious programs, a number of questions of practical import have gone unanswered, or the answers have been guessed at, often in very optimistic mood. Do religious programs on the air become a substitute for church attendance? Do they reach non-churchmen, and with what effect? Do they provide a valuable service for shut-ins? Do they help to build character, to improve society, to inspire reverence? Most important, do they convey the Christian Gospel faithfully, or is the Christian message distorted or falsified as it passes through these new media of communication?

Aware of these and kindred questions, the Broadcasting and Film Commission of the National Council of Churches launched a Communications Research Project late in 1951, and appointed the Rev. Everett C. Parker as its director. Mr. Parker has had extensive experience in the broadcasting industry and has carried primary responsibilities in the field of religious broadcasting. He had become acutely aware of the problems and dangers of untested programming. He quickly assembled a small but highly competent staff, and also obtained the consultative services of experts in research. The names of two of the latter appear with his own as authors of this volume, and acknowledgments of the services of others appear at appropriate places.

Dr. Barry was Director of the Central Department of Research and Survey of the National Council of Churches during the period of the study, and is at present the Director of the New York City Mission Society. Dr. Smythe, Research Professor of the Institute of Communications Research and Professor of Economics at the University of Illinois, was formerly head of the economics section of the Federal Communications Commission, and has pioneered in communications research.

Rather than studying the effects of religious broadcasting at random or through some procedure of national sampling, it was determined early that a particular American community should be chosen for intensive investigation. Concentration on one community would permit an accurate definition of radio and television audiences for various types of programs. More important, it would place these audiences and individuals within the setting of their total community, including their relation to local churches. Thereby the deeper dynamics of response to diverse programs could be studied, whether in sociological or psychological terms.

New Haven, Connecticut, and its adjacent suburbs were chosen as the laboratory, for various reasons. The resources of a large university were available there, including basic studies of the community made by graduate students and faculty members at Yale—background studies of invaluable significance for specialized research. Expert firsthand advice was available from university personnel, and the faculty of Yale Divinity School was willing to assume supervision of the project. The radio and television fare for the population of Metropolitan New Haven was as extensive as could be found in the country, as all major New York stations are available as well as New Haven's own stations.

New Haven provided a research tool of special importance in a 5 per cent sample of the total population carefully constructed and tested by Professor August B. Hollingshead and colleagues in the Department of Sociology at Yale. Professor Hollingshead generously made the sample, defined at considerable labor and expense, available to the Communications Research Project, though he is not responsible for the conclusions drawn from this particular use of it. This sample was far larger and more accurate than those used typically for audience measurement.

There has been no assumption that New Haven is a "typical" American community. Readers can measure its atypicality as compared with their own communities at numerous points in the pages that follow. In the extensive literature of community studies produced by American sociologists in the last thirty years it has become clear that there is no typical American town (except my own home town!), but that a careful study of one community can illuminate social patterns and personal problems that prevail in many others.

As will become apparent, the methods used in the research have been of many kinds, ranging over various social sciences and including some that may as yet only dubiously be designated as scientific or precise. They include efforts to classify people into groups by external characteristics such as income, education, occupation, et cetera. They include attempts to probe the hidden patterns of personality. They have brought forth gross statistics and refined tables and mathematical adumbrations likely to confuse the layman. They have explored the need-value systems of individuals, using all sorts of tools (including a modified version of the controversial F-Scale of T. W. Adorno) in an effort to understand why certain persons are susceptible to certain broadcasts, and with what effects. It is doubtful that any specialist will be pleased with all the methods employed, or impressed by all the results. But the design for the research intentionally included several different approaches to the same basic questions, all converging on the central question of "effects."

The research staff has not assumed that it was working in pure detachment, though it has undertaken to be scrupulously accurate. Studies involving effects, values, character-orientation and religious response always involve presuppositions for definition of these elusive qualities. In the case of the present study, the following policy statement was adopted at the outset:

The concern of the agencies initiating this project centers in the development and reinforcement of constructive character patterns, both personal and social. The research is concerned with value systems in American life, and with the effects of the mass media—for good or bad—on the structure of values. These aims require that, at the outset, the researchers define the ethical norms that will be used in measuring the constructive aspects of American character. These norms have been tentatively established as follows:

1. The ethical framework for this study will be the Judaeo-Christian tradition, as expressed in Protestant thought and action.

2. The principles and standards of this tradition are to be applied to concrete problems of practical and personal decisions.

3. In applying the Judaeo-Christian principles and standards to such problems, the freedom of the individual is to be recognized and the sanctity of the individual personality is to be respected.

4. The Judaeo-Christian belief and faith is that the Will of God is that which is ultimately authoritative. Each person has freedom of choice, but he lives under the responsibility of making choices and acting in accordance with the Will of God.

5. As a corollary, the Judaeo-Christian ethic forces upon the conscience of the individual the necessity of deciding with whom, or with what group he will take a stand, and what image of the desirable person and the desirable society he will defend and uphold. This ethic also requires that decisions be taken in council; that the religious man decides and acts under a mandate of responsibility to a community with standards he is committed to uphold.

The principal results of the study lie in the pages that follow. (Two other reports, much briefer and more specialized, have been published earlier; their titles are included on the summary page at the beginning of this volume.) They contain something for everybody. Indeed, in their diversity they rather resemble the disorder of an old-fashioned general store (there are still stores in Vermont that sell both nails and lingerie). Writing a brief summary of the results would be as difficult as drafting a terse advertisement for a general store. Billy Graham, Bishop Sheen, and other notables appear at some length, as do disguised individuals in the audiences who have never spoken on radio or television and were terrified by being asked to speak into a tape recorder.

Specialists interested in the theory of communications will find material for reflection. Radio and television practitioners may find clues for alteration in programs, though the more successful performers may conclude that the study only reveals what they had suspected all along. The people in the audiences may find many of their previous views upset and may be led to a new self-consciousness as they sit before the loudspeaker or screen.

And it may be that those responsible for the more effective utilization of radio and television for the support of the churches and the proclamation of the Gospel will find this volume an important source for future policy. This is only a "pilot study" so far as research is concerned, and it is hoped that it will help to stimulate many further studies. But it may turn out to be a pilot study also in that it points new directions for the broadcasting of religion with intelligence and integrity.

LISTON POPE

Grand Isle, Vermont
July 6, 1955

CONTENTS

TABLES

APPENDIX D

APPENDIX F

1. Comparison of Distribution of Respondents in Opinion Interview with Distribution of Householders in the Great Sample of
the Whole Population

2. Intra-group Comparison of Hopeful and Fearful Prognosticators

FIGURES

CHAPTER 11

CHAPTER 13

CHAPTER 14

PART I

Metropolitan New Haven, Its People and Its Religious Practices

CHAPTER 1

The Social History of
New Haven

New Haven was founded in 1638 by English Puritans under the leadership of John Davenport, a Church of England clergyman, and Theophilus Eaton, a merchant. The two men were close, lifelong friends. Davenport, the son of a merchant, had been persecuted in England for his Puritan beliefs. Both men despaired of reforming the Church of England from within. They turned to the "New Haven" in the New World.

Davenport and Eaton were opposed to the separation of Church and State. They conceived of New Haven as a church-state, the rule to be according to the Bible. Real democratic government was not considered. The elect were the electors. Church membership was a prerequisite for any participation in public life.[1]

Agriculture and trade with the Indians were planned as the economic bases of the new town. It was expected that later the harbor would make New Haven a port for coastwise and ocean trade.

New Haven existed as a small, rural town for more than 150 years. Its life was dominated by the religious principles and moral code of the founders. Its population was overwhelmingly British. The first United States census, in 1790, showed 97.3 per cent of the New Haven County population was white and 2.7 per cent Negro. Ninety-six per cent of the whites were English and Welsh, 3 per cent were Scotch and 1 per cent were Irish.

The year 1800 opened a new era as well as a new century for New Haven. In the next thirty years the town's character changed more than during the whole of its previous history. The population doubled, reaching 10,000 in 1830. The town prospered. Now the hope for commerce was realized. The West Indies furnished the prime market, where Connecticut farm products

[1] The first church was not formed immediately. Its formation was a solemn thing to be entered into only after a long period of prayer and planning. The company finally gathered on August 22, 1639, and organized the First Church. This church is the present Center Church, Congregational Christian, in New Haven.

were exchanged for molasses, sugar and rum. There was trade, also, in European manufactured goods and teas, silks and spices from the East.

But New Haven never achieved its dream of becoming a great home port for the clipper ships or the whalers. The competition from other ports was keen, and New Haven had a shallow harbor, cursed by progressive silting. New Haven was outranked by ten other Atlantic ports by 1830. From then, it lost ground rapidly. But even though New Haven lost in the general competition, the absolute volume of its ocean trade increased continuously until the War Between the States and brought profit to the community.

Social Change and Social Control

While New Haven was becoming a commercial center in the early 1800's, the social structure of the community changed little. Dependence on farming a poor soil had a leveling influence in eighteenth-century New Haven, but the town had always been more wealthy and aristocratic than other Connecticut towns. One striking illustration of this leadership was the proportion of Negroes in the population. Negroes in early Connecticut were the slaves or the servants of the wealthy and aristocratic whites. New Haven in 1790 had 2 per cent of Connecticut's population, but almost 4 per cent of its Negroes. By 1820 the population had increased to only 3 per cent of the state's total, but the town had 8 per cent of the Negroes.[2]

The founding of Yale and its official location in New Haven in 1718 had increased and consolidated the town's aristocratic tradition. The clergy had always exercised social dominance. In the early nineteenth century clerical and academic groups joined with the shipping merchants who were steering the town's commercial growth to form the upper class. This upper class combination controlled political life. Its members held the community's financial purse strings and dominated commercial ventures. They staffed the professions. They were, of course, dominant socially.

The ministers were especially influential in this social union. The Congregational churches enjoyed a majority in the state, although they had been forced by a union of sectarian opponents to grant toleration and yield political power. But the Congregationalists remained dominant, particularly in New Haven. "The ideal of equality was represented in the Calvinistic 'equality of sinfulness,' but was in practice modified by a 'doctrine of election' so strong that some New Haveners almost believed that with their

[2] Robert A. Warner, New Haven Negroes, A Social History (New Haven: Yale University Press, 1940), p. 5.

family fortune, social prominence, and political influence they had inherited *divine grace itself*."[3]

This small group of clergymen, merchants and academicians formed the upper layer of early nineteenth-century New Haven society. Beneath this group were the bulk of the white population, and at the bottom, then as now, were the Negroes.

The Coming of Industry

Social and economic change was accelerated from 1830 to 1860. The population increased fourfold to 40,000. Value of industries multiplied even more. Her commercial contacts with the world, the support of her agricultural hinterland and the skill of her artisans equipped New Haven to share in the industrial growth of the Northeast.

The railroad to Boston and New York began service in the Forties, opening new markets and sources of materials, and quickening population and industrial growth. The carriage industry developed in New Haven at this time, and the community was destined to become its national center. The manufacture of rubber goods, clocks, shirts, corsets and paper boxes became important. The community took on an urban character in the late Forties, and by the Fifties it was a full-fledged city.

The earlier commercial prosperity had been monopolized by the aristocracy. The new industrial prosperity benefited the artisans as well. They had operated in the guild tradition of masters, journeymen and apprentices. Factories were small and the masters worked with their journeymen. The new technology changed this pattern.[4] Masters were able to build bigger shops where they were bosses rather than bench workers. Profits soared. Many masters became wealthy and tried to live like the social leaders of the merchant-clerical group. In time they—or their children—succeeded in rising into the upper social stratum.

The new technology also helped some laborers to rise in the social system. The demand for artisans allowed able journeymen to step up, and enlarged the skilled working class. As manufacturing expanded, though, the old guild system lost importance. In the newer and larger factories, the great demand was for unskilled labor.

As early as the Forties, the growing industries of Connecticut were handicapped by a shortage of factory hands. Factory owners sent long black wag-

---

[3] *Ibid.*, p. 4.
[4] *Ibid.*, pp. 13–14.

ons, called "slavers," to scour the farm communities and lure young girls
to the mills.[5] A better source of cheap, abundant labor soon turned up in
European immigrants. First the Irish, then peasants from southern and eastern Europe flocked to the unskilled jobs, and in time changed the ethnic
and religious character of New Haven.

The first large group of Irish came in 1825 to work on the Farmington
Canal. Others followed, and by 1834 there were enough Irish in New Haven
to form a Roman Catholic church. They, and their fellows who fled the
potato famines in the Forties, were glad to do a hard day's work for fifty
cents or a dollar. By 1854 they had grown so much in numbers and in self-
assertion that they petitioned the town council of aristocratic New Haven
to appoint some of them constables.[6] The request was tabled, but the next
generation was to see not only the police force, but the city government itself dominated by the Irish.

Germans also came to New Haven at the same time the Irish did, but not
in as large numbers. Bavarian Jews were among the first German immigrants,
and by 1840 there were enough families to establish the Congregation
Mishkan Israel. The Jewish population increased slowly. By 1856 there were
fifty Jewish families. They took over the petty merchandising in the community.

The first political refugees from Germany came in 1849, following the
German revolution of 1848. In the days before the War Between the States,
German Lutherans and Catholics probably affiliated with existing Protestant
and Roman Catholic churches, since the German Lutheran and Catholic
congregations date from 1865 and 1868 respectively.[7]

English immigration to New Haven remained important throughout the
Fifties while the Irish and German influx was increasing.

The Great Ethnic and Religious Change

A great change in the ethnic and religious composition of the New Haven
population began toward the end of the 1850's. Ninety per cent of the population of Connecticut was native born in 1850. The Register surveyed New
Haven churches in 1855 and found that 25 of a total of 28 were Protestant.

[5] Samuel Koenig, Immigrant Settlements in Connecticut (Hartford: Connecticut Department of Education, 1938), p. 15.
[6] E. E. Atwater, The History of the City of New Haven (New York: W. W. Munsell
& Co., 1887), p. 464.
[7] Rollin G. Osterweis, Three Centuries of New Haven, 1638–1938 (New Haven: Yale
University Press, 1953), p. 286.

There were only two Roman Catholic churches and one Jewish congregation.[8]

Immigration practically ceased during the War Between the States, but as soon as it was over Irish and German settlers came to New Haven in greater numbers than ever before. At the same time, Swedes began to settle in New Haven and West Haven. By 1870, 28 per cent of the New Haven city population was foreign born, with Irish constituting 67 per cent of this group and Germans 17 per cent. Swedes and other Scandinavians came in increasing numbers in the Seventies. Then the source of immigration shifted to southern and eastern Europe.

There were about 500 Italians in New Haven in 1880, although the U.S. census lists only 102. There were even fewer Russian and Polish Jews.[9] Within a year though there were enough Jews to form a new congregation. In 1885 they bought the old Temple Street church for a synagogue. Russian and Polish Jews and Italians came in a mounting stream from 1890 to the outbreak of World War I. Near the turn of the century, Roman Catholic Poles also began to settle in New Haven in appreciable numbers.

The immigrants were attracted to New Haven by its industrial expansion after 1865. Sargent and Company, a leading hardware manufacturer today, opened its plant in 1864. The Winchester Repeating Arms Company began operations in 1867. The opening of large plants was accompanied by expansion in manufacturing of machine tools, clocks, corsets and cigars.

The New Haven population in 1900 was 108,027, 29 per cent of whom were foreign born and 35 per cent native born of foreign parentage. The Irish were still the largest ethnic group, but foreign-born Italians outnumbered first generation Germans, and the foreign-born Russian Jewish group was nearly as large. Many more Italians and Jews came to New Haven from 1900 to 1910.

New Haven's prosperity and growth were built on a diversified economic base. It was never a one-industry town. It was a local distribution center, a local coastwise shipping port, an educational center of national importance. But its chief economic resource was—and is—light manufacturing of various sorts. As the industries expanded, they attracted as laborers European immigrants who were, in turn, responsible for the community's population growth. When large-scale immigration stopped in the 1920's, the growth of the New Haven population slowed down. The city proper has not

[8] *Ibid.*, p. 218.
[9] Warner, *op. cit.*, p. 165.

grown since 1920, although its suburbs have continued to grow 20 per cent from 1930 to 1940 and 23 per cent from 1940 to 1950.

New Haven Today

Metropolitan New Haven is an industrial community of approximately a quarter of a million persons, most of whom are descendants of the immigrants of the past century. The metropolitan area includes the City of New Haven (population 164,443) and the suburbs of West Haven (32,010), Hamden (29,715), East Haven (12,212) and North Haven (9,444).

The population in 1940 was distributed among these ethnic groups: Italians, 33 per cent; Irish, 23 per cent; Russian, Polish and Austrian Jews, 16 per cent; British Americans, 13 per cent; Germans, 6 per cent; Poles, 4 per cent; Scandinavians, 2 per cent; Negroes, 3 per cent.[10] All of these people are very much aware of their ethnic origins. They cluster together, maintaining their national identification in the second and third generations. Social and political action are both built around ethnic grouping.

The Negro population has nearly doubled since 1940. This growth is the main population trend. There has been a steady flow of Negro laborers into the least skilled, lowest paid jobs in New Haven industry. In the period of high employment following World War II, Negroes have filled the dirty, heavy and least desirable jobs, formerly performed by European immigrants.

OCCUPATION AND ETHNIC GROUPS

The influx of immigrants in the nineteenth century began a tendency to associate particular occupations with ethnic groups.[11] This association began with the Irish who were welcomed as unskilled railroad laborers and factory hands. Southern and eastern Europeans also went into laboring jobs as they migrated to the community. Scandinavians, on the other hand, were mostly skilled craftsmen who quickly made a place for themselves as carpenters, cabinetmakers and carriage and boat builders.

German immigrants to New Haven provided a social pattern of their own that somewhat paralleled that of the community, yet was a separate entity. Many of them were refugees from the revolution of 1848 in their homeland and they were of various social classes. Some were well-to-do and

10 Ruby J. R. Kennedy, "Single or Triple Melting Pot? Intermarriage Trends in New Haven, 1870–1940," *American Journal of Sociology*, Vol. 39 (January, 1944), pp. 331–39.
11 August B. Hollingshead, "Trends in Social Stratification: A Case Study," *American Sociological Review*, Vol. 17 (December, 1952), pp. 679–86.

were able to establish businesses in their new home. Often they sent to the homeland for skilled workers. The result was a division of the German community into owners and workers.

The status pattern of immigrant groups followed the pattern that has been common in many parts of America. Each new ethnic group began at the bottom, in the least desirable and rewarding jobs, lived in the poorest housing, enjoyed the fewest privileges. The earlier migrants with their greater experience in the community were able to move upward as successive waves of newcomers appeared.

World War I stopped large-scale immigration. By then the New Haven community had become stratified economically and socially. The stratification and lack of assimilation were revealed in a study made by John McConnell in 1936,[12] in which he analyzed the nationality backgrounds and occupations of a random sample of 1,633 heads of households.

He found that approximately two-thirds of the British-American heads of households were in non-manual occupational pursuits, and exactly two-thirds of the Italians and Poles were in manual occupations. What was more striking was his finding that 64 per cent of the professionals and business executives were British-Americans, and less than four per cent were of Italian or Polish origin. The Irish were concentrated in public service jobs and white-collar clerical work. The Russian Jews showed a marked tendency to be retail proprietors. The Germans spread from the highest executive positions to the skilled crafts with very few in the semi-skilled and unskilled categories.[13]

A study of the assimilation of Italians in the community, made by Jerome K. Myers in 1948,[14] supported McConnell's findings by showing that the vast majority of Italians were still manual workers.

These studies reveal that the differential in the time each ethnic group has been in the community, coupled with the way the group was regarded by the "Old Yankee" elite, set the stage for the current system of stratification.[15]

The isolation and stratification of social groups is something more than an identification with an occupation or a class of occupation. The cleavage between ethnic groups is wide, and is not narrowing to any marked degree.

[12] John W. McConnell, The Influence of Occupation upon Social Stratification, unpublished Ph.D. thesis, Sterling Memorial Library, Yale University, 1937.
[13] Hollingshead, op. cit., p. 681.
[14] Jerome K. Myers, Jr., The Differential Time Factor in Assimilation: A Study of Aspects and Processes of Assimilation among the Italians of New Haven, unpublished Ph.D. thesis, Sterling Memorial Library, Yale University, 1949.
[15] Hollingshead, op. cit.

The Irish and the Italians—the two largest nationality groups—are particularly antithetic toward each other. Both groups are composed largely of Roman Catholics, but Irish will not willingly hear mass from an Italian priest, nor Italians from an Irish priest. Their rivalry is particularly keen in politics, where they conduct seesaw battles for control of the city administration and the office of mayor. (In state and national politics both groups are likely to be found voting the Democratic ticket.) Professional services are sought and rendered on an ethnic basis whenever possible, Italians going to Italian lawyers and doctors and vice versa. Each group also has its service agencies. Italians, in particular, have their grocery stores and other shops. Each group, within itself, also reflects the vertical status structure of the community from upper to lower classes, though in varying proportions at the various levels.

Poles, Lithuanians, Scandinavians and Germans also have vertical social structures, based upon ethnic origins. Negroes live in a world of their own, but it is patterned on the social structure of the white groups.

RELIGION

Religion plays a part in the complex compartmentalization of social life in New Haven. Negroes are mostly Protestants—or if unchurched, of Protestant background—but there is a developing Roman Catholic minority. White citizens are divided by their Protestant, Roman Catholic and Jewish backgrounds, and each faith group is subdivided on ethnic lines. The Jews, in particular, are separated from other groups on religious lines, largely maintaining a separate religious and social life from the Gentiles.

The religious composition of the population will be discussed at length in later chapters. Numerical religious dominance has shifted with the ethnic changes. Today, Roman Catholics have a two-to-one majority over Protestants in the population. The proportion of Jews in New Haven is about three times the national average, with Jewish population about one-sixth the size of the Roman Catholic population and less than one-third the Protestant.

Protestantism, although numerically a minority, still enjoys a prestige advantage in New Haven. People of other faiths, especially Roman Catholics, who wish to improve their social status, may turn to the Protestant churches as one of several symbols of upward class movement.[16]

16 At least, this is the testimony of a number of Protestant clergymen, supported by several illustrations in the depth interviews. This study did not attempt to examine motivations involved in changing church affiliations, except incidentally.

AMERICANISM

The ethnic subcultures of former immigrant groups in New Haven have not kept their members from assimilating American ideas and institutions, as has often happened in the large cities of the United States. On the contrary, the immigrant peoples have striven manfully and successfully to become active citizens on a par with their native-born fellow Americans.

Lack of numbers has caused the British-American Protestants to lose control of the political life of New Haven. For many decades the Irish were dominant. Now the Italians hold the balance of power.

August B. Hollingshead holds that the job and the school have been the most important factors in bringing New Haven's national groups under the influence of the dominant American culture. At any rate these people have, in fact, accepted fully the American belief in the equality of man and the equality of opportunity.

Even by 1900, the British-American Protestant group, representative of the founders of New Haven, had become a minority in the community. Today they are a small minority indeed, but they have managed to maintain financial control and social dominance. They have never lost sight of the fact that their forefathers wrested this community from the wilderness, established a pattern of living and handed down a faith and a tradition. The pattern and the tradition formed the "Yankee" culture, which has set the standards for the immigrant groups. Only a few of the "Yankees" have been willing to grant the immigrants social equality, but they have managed to make the attainment of their cultural standards the principal test of the achievement of "Americanism" by the immigrants.

What has been the result of the imposition of the Yankee cultural mold on the population of New Haven? It has made social mobility, in the traditional American sense, difficult to achieve. It has intensified social distance, separated the community into a series of almost self-contained subcultures and subsocieties. Hollingshead sums up the situation in a succinct sentence. "In short, a major trend in the social structure of the New Haven community during the last half-century has been the development of *parallel class structures* within the limits of race, ethnic origin, and religion."[17]

Hollingshead goes on to point out:

This development may be illustrated by the fact that there are seven different Junior Leagues in the white segment of the community for appropriately affiliated upper class young women. The top ranking organization is the Junior League of New Haven which draws its membership from "Old Yankee" Protes-

[17] Hollingshead, *op. cit.*, p. 686.

tant families whose daughters have been educated in private schools. The Catholic Charity League is next in rank and age—its membership is drawn from Irish-American families. In addition to this organization there are Italian and Polish Junior Leagues within the Catholic division of the society. The Swedish and Danish Junior Leagues are for properly connected young women in these ethnic groups, but they are Protestant. Then too, the upper class Jewish families have their Junior League. The Negroes have a Junior League for their top-drawer young women. This principle of parallel structures for a given class level, by religious, ethnic and racial groups, proliferates throughout the community.[18]

Marriage practices offer a good index of the narrow limits of choice in this type of social structure.[19] Hollingshead and his associates interviewed a 50 per cent sample of couples who were married in New Haven during 1948, 1949 and 1950. All couples were stratified by the use of an Index of Social Position[20] into classes. The data were analyzed in the light of the concept of parallel social structure. They showed that 91 per cent of all white marriages were within the same religious group, and that 93 per cent were within the same social level. Hollingshead concluded from the figures that "the community is tightly compartmentalized vertically by race and religion, and horizontally by status, class or social level."[21]

What of the Future?

What of the future social structure of New Haven? Will present social barriers be broken and a more fluid society develop in which movement from one ethnic and social group to another is both acceptable and easy? Hollingshead from his detailed study of New Haven concludes that social mobility from group to group will become even more difficult than it is now, that the "compartmentalization is becoming more rigid with the passage of time."[22] The people of New Haven seem destined to remain within the fences of culture and class that they have built to divide the community.

[18] *Ibid.* For an exhaustive analysis of this principle as it applies to women's organizations, see Mhyra S. Minnis, *The Relationship of Women's Organizations to the Social Structure of a City*, unpublished Ph.D. thesis, Sterling Memorial Library, Yale University, 1951.

[19] For a statement of methodological procedures and some findings of a study of marriage practices in New Haven, see August B. Hollingshead, "Cultural Factors in the Selection of Marriage Mates," *American Sociological Review*, Vol. 15 (October, 1950), pp. 619–27, and Hollingshead, "Age Relationships and Marriage," *American Sociological Review*, Vol. 16 (August, 1951), pp. 492–99.

[20] This index was developed by Hollingshead and was used, under his direction, to classify social status of the households in this study. The methodology is described briefly in Chap. 2.

[21] Hollingshead, "Trends in Social Stratification: A Case Study," *op. cit.*, p. 686.

[22] *Idem.*

Looking at the broad perspective, one might say that the "melting pot" has not worked in New Haven in the way in which some earlier students of American society expected. The "Americanization" of the Irish and Italian and German and Polish immigrant, or of his children and grandchildren, has not in this city produced a homogeneous, undifferentiated population which could be readily absorbed into the Yankee culture at whatever level each individual's gifts and energies might place him. The Yankee culture has indeed provided the basic external structure for this community—its legal and political system, its educational system, to a large extent its basic economic structure, and even its language and dress (with modifications). But what emerges from all this study is the discovery, not entirely new, that these externals are not determinants, but simply conditions, of the way in which people associate with one another in the more intimate and value-impregnated associations of marriage and family, religion and the church, social groups and friendships, and above all loyalties and commitments. It is conceivable that, had the Yankees welcomed each new group as friends and equals, these divisions would have disappeared into one all-inclusive American culture. As a matter of fact, however, the Yankees did not, and the divisions between the ethnic groups hardened into fixed patterns of association. The natural cohesiveness of the Italian immigrant group, for example, survives the disappearance of language, dress and customs of the old country; it survives the adjustment to entirely new kinds of work, housing, education and government. And if the Italian culture in New Haven is a far cry from that of Italy, it is still a distinct and recognizable subculture in New Haven and one that in the long run may even be more influential than the Yankee subculture which is presumably dominant.

An unspoken assumption of many individualistic interpretations of the American dream, particularly those stated by Yankees, has been that the natural road to success for the member of the ethnic minority was, in effect, for him to become a Yankee—in speech, value systems, behavior, associations, education, job orientation and all other traits. For those who have come from certain countries, Great Britain in particular, this road has been open and easy. For many others, however, particularly those from southeastern Europe and Africa, this road has for all practical purposes been closed. The strength of these subcultures of ethnic and religious origin, then, is also the testimony of these groups that they are establishing their place and power in American society through other means than that of individually winning an entree into the Yankee group. They are relying, rather, on the inherent strength of the group itself, strength of numbers and strength of organization. They have demonstrated this strength in New Haven by acquiring social, economic and political power. A careful analysis of the economic life of New Haven would unquestionably demonstrate that consumer services, at least, are geared largely to the taste of other subcultures than the Yankee. Indeed, as this study will subsequently document, television itself has established itself in New Haven in response largely to the demands of non-Yankee groups.

To the student of class structure, the most significant conclusion perhaps is that while the mobility of individuals within the class structure seems to be less rather than more likely than a generation ago, the classes themselves are shifting in their relative power, prestige and ability to control social change to their own interests. There is some evidence that the son of a factory worker has less opportunity (or at least is less likely) to become a college professor or a business proprietor than members of his father's generation, but on the other hand the factory worker is in a much better position relative to the professional or business man than he was a generation ago. He controls more of the nation's income, he has more political and economic power, he is organized to enforce his demands, his tastes are catered to by the nation's largest producers of consumer goods. It is still true that the material benefits of membership in the Yankee-dominated upper business and professional classes are substantially above those of any other class level, but the gulf between the classes in material goods has narrowed considerably, and—what may be more important—the ego satisfactions that come with social, economic and political recognition have approached a much greater parity among social classes than was true a few decades ago.

As far as the present study is concerned, it seems to the writers that this analysis drives home the point that mass communication in a field as value-loaded as religion is a tremendously complex and many-sided affair in which the position of a listener in the social structure has as much to do with his reaction to a broadcast religious program as does the content of the program itself. This point will be developed further, but in relation to this chapter we may simply ask the questions: What effect would the identification of a speaker on a television program as "Congregational" have upon a New Haven listener? What associations would leap into the listener's mind? Would they be favorable or unfavorable? Would they not depend very largely on whether this listener was Irish, Italian, Yankee, Negro or Jewish in background; whether he was in the "upper," "middle" or "lower" classes; whether Congregationalists were, for him, an "in-group" or an "out-group"? In other words, would not everything that was said or done on a religious program be colored very largely by the cultural and class context from which the audience sees the program, quite apart from the program's specifically religious content and the intent behind its message?

The reseachers believe that such bias exists and for this reason have placed a great deal of emphasis on the identification of members of the audience by their position in the social class and religious structure of metropolitan New Haven. This short résumé of New Haven social and cultural history is given to provide the necessary background on the socioreligious structure to illuminate data in the chapters that follow.

Bibliography

ATWATER, EDWARD E. The History of the City of New Haven (New York: W. W. Munsell & Co., 1887).

GILBERT, CASS AND OLMSTED, FREDERICK L. New Haven, Report of The Civic Improvement Commission (New Haven: Tuttle, Morehouse & Taylor, 1910).

HOLLINGSHEAD, AUGUST B. "Trends in Social Stratification: A Case Study," American Sociological Review, Vol. 17 (December, 1952), pp. 679-86.

KOENIG, SAMUEL. Immigrant Settlements in Connecticut (Hartford: Connecticut Department of Education, 1938), p. 15.

MITCHELL, M. H. History of New Haven County (Chicago: Pioneer Historical Publishing Co., 1930).

OSTERWEIS, ROLLIN G. Three Centuries of New Haven, 1638-1938 (New Haven: Yale University Press, 1953).

U.S. Census Reports.

WARNER, ROBERT AUSTIN. New Haven Negroes, A Social History (New Haven: Yale University Press, 1940).

CHAPTER 2

The People of Metropolitan
New Haven

The purpose of this chapter is to give an accurate picture of the social matrix within which, in metropolitan New Haven, the processes of mass communication take place. The function of radio and television is to gain the attention of the people in this matrix, or significant groups of them, for whatever purpose the broadcaster has in mind. We have traced in the preceding chapter the developing history of the cultural and ethnic groups that constitute this urban community. In this chapter we shall report contemporary statistics about them which will help to delineate major groups and will also provide some statistical base lines against which to examine the characteristics of television and radio audiences.

The analysis of the metropolitan New Haven population is based upon a 5 per cent random sample of households in the community. The sample was drawn originally by August B. Hollingshead, professor of sociology in Yale University, assisted by Jerome K. Myers.[1] It was compiled from the New Haven *City Directory*, which covers the metropolitan area (City of New Haven, Hamden, East Haven, West Haven and North Haven). There are 3,559 households in the sample. (Metropolitan New Haven— approximately 71,180 households.) Both telephone and nontelephone homes are included, in proportion to their incidence in the population.

Each household drawn in the sample was interviewed and the following data obtained: age, occupation, education, religious background and church affiliation (if any) of the head of the household and spouse (if any); number in the family; age and sex of children; age, sex and relationship of adults living in the household in addition to the household head and spouse; income of the head of the household; home ownership; radio and television set ownership; a record of regular television viewing and radio listening by

[1] See *Acknowledgments*, p. vii f.

adults in the household; a similar viewing-listening record for minor children; a listing of newspapers and magazines read in the household.

The Five Social Classes and Religion

In previous studies of the metropolitan New Haven population, using this sample, Hollingshead had developed a definition of "social classes" or "social levels" within the population, and had established the fact that these categories reflected actual and significant differences in the characteristics and behavior of the social groups thus distinguished. It was hypothesized early in this survey that this pattern of analysis of families by social class would be significant for understanding patterns of viewing and listening, and through much of the remainder of this report it will be seen that most characteristics studied have been analyzed both by religion and by social class.

The concept of social class is now well established as a useful analytical tool in the study of communities and population groups. It is also a contro-versial concept and one that can be dangerous or emotionally provocative if not properly understood. The sociologist's concept of class is not the Marxian concept, for example, which assumes an inevitable conflict of inter-est among economically determined groups; nor on the other hand is it the historic Continental concept of hereditary classes which occupy ordained positions in a hierarchy of status and function. Rather it is for the sociologist a kind of terminological shorthand or composite index he uses to express an observed fact about American communities. Sociologists have demonstrated that when individuals or families are arranged on hierarchical scales accord-ing to such indices as income, education, occupation, type and location of residence, and other objective criteria, their position on one scale will tend to have a high correlation with their position on the other scales. Further it has been noted that these positions have a tendency to cluster in discernible groupings (which are in effect the nuclei of what are here called "classes"), and that on closer observation these groupings reflect patterns of association, behavior, consumption, taste and other less readily measurable social charac-teristics. When these hierarchical clusterings are statistically established for any given community, a surprisingly large number of behavior patterns can be "explained," or significantly correlated, by analysis within the class frame-work.

The social class, in other words, is not an accidental clustering nor is it a statistical manipulation of the sociologist; it is a basic form of contemporary social grouping in a community. It is also true of American communities, and this condition has already been indicated concerning New Haven, that there is a division of social groups according to their ethnic and religious origin, and that the horizontal stratification by class occurs within the framework of vertical stratification by race, national origin and religion, as described in Chapter 1. In this study, then, both of these dimensions seemed to be essential in the identification of persons, households and audiences; and throughout the remainder of this report it will be seen that two variables have been considered basic in all statistical analysis of households: (1) index of social class position, and (2) religious affiliation or background. The latter, for this study, was the most important index of position within a community vertically stratified by race, national origin and religion.

The method of analysis will be clarified by seeing in Hollingshead's own words his description of the class structure of the community, the procedure for establishing social class identification and the major characteristics of the five classes he established by this method:

The [New Haven metropolitan] community's social structure is differentiated vertically along racial, ethnic, and religious lines; each of these vertical cleavages, in turn, is differentiated horizontally by a series of strata or classes. Around the socio-biological axis of race two social worlds have evolved: A Negro world and a white world. The white world is divided by ethnic origin and religion into Catholic, Protestant, and Jewish contingents. Within these divisions there are numerous ethnic groups. The Irish hold aloof from the Italians, and the Italians move in different circles from the Poles. The Jews maintain a religious and social life separate from the gentiles. The horizontal strata that transect each of these vertical divisions are based upon the social values that are attached to occupation, education, place of residence in the community, and associations.

The vertically differentiating factors of race, religion and ethnic origin, when combined with the horizontally differentiating ones of occupation, education, place of residence and so on, produce a social structure that is highly compartmentalized. The integrating factors in this complex are twofold. First, each stratum of each vertical division is similar in its cultural characteristics to the corresponding stratum in the other divisions. Second, the cultural pattern for each stratum or class was set by the "Old Yankee" core group. This core group provided the master cultural mold that has shaped the status system of each sub-group in the community. In short, the social structure of the New Haven community is a parallel class structure within the limits of race, ethnic origin, and religion.

This fact enabled us to stratify the community, for our purposes, with an *Index of Social Position*. This *Index* utilizes three scaled factors to determine an individual's class position within the community's stratificational system: ecological area of residence, occupation, and education. Ecological area of residence is measured by a six point scale; occupation and education are each measured by a seven point scale. To obtain a social class score on an individual we must therefore know his address, his occupation, and the number of years of school he has completed. Each of these factors is given a scale score, and the scale score is multiplied by a factor weight determined by a standard regression equation. The factor weights are as follows: Ecological area of residence, 5; occupation, 8; and education, 6. The three factor scores are summed, and the resultant score is taken as an index of this individual's position in the community's social class system.

This *Index* enabled us to delineate five main social class strata within the horizontal dimension of the social structure. These principal strata or classes may be characterized as follows:

Class I. This stratum is composed of wealthy families whose wealth is often inherited and whose heads are leaders in the community's business and professional pursuits. Its members live in those areas of the community generally regarded as "the best"; the adults are college graduates, usually from famous private institutions, and almost all gentile families are listed in the New Haven *Social Directory*, but few Jewish families are listed. In brief, these people occupy positions of high social prestige.

Class II. Adults in this stratum are almost all college graduates; the males occupy high managerial positions, many are engaged in the lesser ranking professions. These families are well-to-do, but there is no substantial inherited or acquired wealth. Its members live in the "better" residential areas; about one-half of these families belong to lesser ranking private clubs, but only 5 per cent of Class II families are listed in the New Haven *Social Directory*.

Class III. This stratum includes the vast majority of small proprietors, white-collar office and sales workers, and a considerable number of skilled manual workers. Adults are predominately high school graduates, but a considerable percentage have attended business schools and small colleges for a year or two. They live in "good" residential areas; less than 5 per cent belong to private clubs, but they are not included in the *Social Directory*. Their social life tends to be concentrated in the family, the church, and the lodge.

Class IV. This stratum consists predominately of semi-skilled factory workers. Its adult members have finished the elementary grades, but the older people have not completed high school. However, adults under thirty-five have generally graduated from high school. Its members comprise almost one-half of the community; and their residences are scattered over wide areas. Social life is centered in the family, the neighborhood, the labor union and public places.

Class V. Occupationally, class V adults are overwhelmingly semi-skilled factory hands and unskilled laborers. Educationally most adults have not completed the elementary grades. The families are concentrated in the "tenement" and "cold-water flat" areas of New Haven. Only a small minority belong to organized community institutions. Their social life takes place in the family flat, on the street, or in neighborhood social agencies.[2]

[2] August B. Hollingshead and Frederick C. Redlich, "Social Stratification and Psychiatric Disorders," *American Sociological Review*, Vol. 18 (April, 1952), pp. 165 f.

In view of the objectives of this study, we need to belabor the obvious by pointing out that neither social class nor religion, as used in subsequent statistical tables, is to any slightest degree a qualitative measure of social value or religious value. Social class does not measure social worth, and religious identification is a measure neither of intensity of religious feeling nor of strength of adherence to a religious institution. Both types of identification are large categorical bins into which households are sorted statistically, and to say that a man is Roman Catholic is not to say that he is a "good" Catholic, or to say he is in social class I does not mean that this research has rated him among the most useful and significant citizens of the New Haven community. The social class index *tends* to reflect economic position, partly inherited and partly achieved; the religious identification *tends* to reflect cultural and ethnic heritage.

TABLE 1. Distribution of New Haven households by social class

Social Class	Households in Sample	
	Number	*Per Cent*
I	119	3.3
II	328	9.2
III	760	21.4
IV	1,723	48.4
V	629	17.7
Total	3,559	100.0

We point this out because there is an inevitable tendency to equate religious groupings with the purposes, policies and practices of the institutions identified with them. The institutions of religion are a part of any cultural complex, but are by no means identical with the totality of it, and may even at certain points be at odds with the main tendencies of their cultural milieu. In somewhat similar fashion, the "upper" classes of a particular community, while in a position to exert considerable influence on the standards and behavior patterns of that community, are not to be interpreted as representing either the "best" aspects of community life or the most significant and influential trends in a culture.

We have dwelt at some length on these points because this study will be discussing value systems and "constructive character patterns" and similar qualitative matters in later sections; and these patterns and systems will be related to the value systems of Protestantism. We are simply saying here that while the stratification of the community by social class and religion is inextricably entangled with Protestant and other religious value systems, the indices of stratification do not measure people *against* these value systems, nor do they indicate the degree of acceptance by any individual of any value or set of values.

The application of Hollingshead's formula for identifying social class position distributed the sample as shown in Table 1.

The same households, when identified by religion, were distributed as shown in Table 2.

TABLE 2. Distribution of New Haven households by religion

Religion	Households in Sample	
	Number	Per Cent
Roman Catholic	1,879	52.8
Protestant [a]	1,032	29.0
Jewish	328	9.2
Mixed [b]	264	7.4
Other and none	56	1.6
Total	3,559	100.0

[a] In all tables, "Protestant" includes Eastern Orthodox families and persons.

[b] Households in which there is a mixed marriage: Protestant-Roman Catholic, Protestant-Jewish or Roman Catholic-Jewish.

The historical analysis of New Haven (Chapter 1) made it readily apparent that religious identification and social class identification were by no means independent of each other. Table 3 shows the high degree of interrelationship between social class and religion.

The relationship between religious affiliation and social class is significant (p. <.001). Although Roman Catholic households outnumber Protestant nearly two to one in the population, Protestant households outnumber Roman Catholics two to one in social classes I and II. Roman Catholicism and Protestantism are in precisely inverse relationship to the class structure, with classes becoming progressively more Protestant as we move from the lower end of the scale to the upper, and becoming more Roman Catholic as we move from the upper end of the class scale to the lower. Protestants dominate the top two social classes, and Roman Catholics dominate the two lower classes.

Even so, because of the large size of social class IV, there are actually more Protestant households in this class than in any other, and more than half of all Protestant households are in social classes IV and V. The bias of Protestantism toward the upper classes, then, must not be exaggerated; only one in five Protestant households is in the upper two social classes.

It is possible, of course, that regardless of the actual *location* of Protestant families on these social scales, their *orientation* may be toward values and standards that are characteristically upper or middle class.[3] This statistical analysis cannot test a hypothesis of this nature, but orientation will be dealt with later in the report.

TABLE 3. Distribution of households in sample by social class and religion

A. *Number of Households*

| Religion | Social Class | | | | | |
	I	II	III	IV	V	Total
Roman Catholic	28	85	325	1,001	440	1,879
Protestant	70	138	264	434	126	1,032
Jewish	16	72	99	118	23	328
Mixed	2	19	61	150	32	264
Other and none	3	14	11	20	8	56
Total households	119	328	760	1,723	629	3,559

B. *Percentage by Social Class*

	I	II	III	IV	V	Total
Roman Catholic	1.5	4.5	17.3	53.3	23.4	100.0
Protestant	6.8	13.4	25.6	42.1	12.2	100.0
Jewish	4.9	21.9	30.2	36.0	7.0	100.0
Mixed	0.8	7.2	23.1	56.8	12.1	100.0
Other and none	2.6	31.6	15.8	34.2	15.8	100.0
Total households	3.3	9.2	21.4	48.4	17.7	100.0

C. *Percentage by Religion*

	I	II	III	IV	V	Total
Roman Catholic	23.5	25.9	42.8	58.1	70.0	52.8
Protestant	58.8	42.1	34.7	25.2	20.0	29.0
Jewish	13.5	21.9	13.0	6.8	3.7	9.2
Mixed	1.7	5.8	8.0	8.7	5.1	7.4
Other and none	2.5	4.3	1.4	1.2	1.3	1.6
Total households	100.0	100.0	100.0	100.0	100.0	100.0

Jewish households, on balance, are more weighted toward the upper two classes than Protestant (Jewish 26.8 per cent, Protestant 20.2 per cent in social classes I and II); but this condition is due to the considerable Jewish

[3] In criticizing children's television programs, class IV Protestant parents were closer to the views of Protestant parents in classes I, II and III than they were to opinions of Roman Catholic or Jewish parents in their own class. See Everett C. Parker and David W. Barry, "Parents, Children and Television," *Information Service*, Vol. XXXIII, No. 17 (April 24, 1954), p. 5.

concentration in social class II rather than social class I. Jewish representation in social classes IV and V is relatively smaller than that of any other group. Even among Jewish households, however, the largest single group (36 per cent) is in social class IV, the "working class" category.

Mixed marriages seem to be predominantly a phenomenon of class IV, with nearly three out of five mixed households being of this social class.

FIGURE 1. Religious composition of the metropolitan New Haven
population by social class

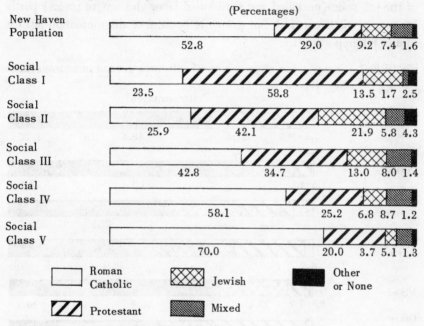

Further evidence of the association of particular religious groups with particular social levels is provided by a breakdown of the various Protestant denominations by social class. Table 4 shows the percentage distribution by social class and denomination of male heads of households who attend Protestant churches in New Haven.

Table 4 shows that within New Haven Protestantism there is a considerable difference among denominations as to the position their members occupy in the social structure. The Congregationalists particularly, and the Episcopalians secondarily, represent the religious organization of the British-American people who founded the city and built up its industrial, commercial and educational establishments. Over one-fourth of the Congregational household heads and nearly one-fifth of the Episcopal are found in social classes I and II. Methodists and Lutherans, on the other hand, represent later migrations. Lutherans were German immigrants. Today they mostly hold skilled and semiskilled jobs in industry or are small businessmen. Methodists tend to be migrants from other sections of Protestant middle class America, more of whom gravitate toward the white-collar jobs than is true with the Lutherans. The high proportion of Baptists found in social class V reflects the large number of Negroes who are Baptist and the position of the Negro in the social structure. The Negro is at the lower end of the job scale (unskilled and semiskilled labor and service trades) partly because of his late arrival, but primarily because of discrimination against him in job opportunities.

FIGURE 2. Social class composition of religious groups in metropolitan New Haven

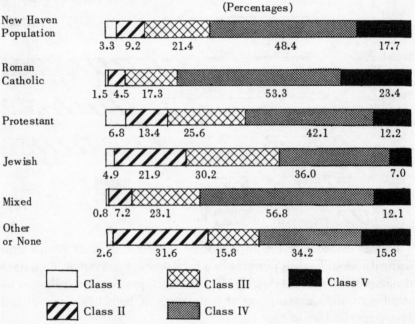

(Percentages)

New Haven Population: 3.3 9.2 21.4 48.4 17.7

Roman Catholic: 1.5 4.5 17.3 53.3 23.4

Protestant: 6.8 13.4 25.6 42.1 12.2

Jewish: 4.9 21.9 30.2 36.0 7.0

Mixed: 0.8 7.2 23.1 56.8 12.1

Other or None: 2.6 31.6 15.8 34.2 15.8

Class I   Class III   Class V
Class II   Class IV

The group of "other" denominations is a miscellaneous category including Presbyterian, Quaker, Greek Orthodox, three Negro Methodist churches (A.M.E. and A.M.E. Zion), and an interdenominational mission, all affiliated with the National Council of Churches through their denominations. It also includes the groups identified sociologically as "sects" (Pentecostal, Holiness, Fundamentalist and "cults" (Christian Scientist, Latter-day Saints), as well as established denominations which are not members of the National Council of Churches (Unitarian, Universalist, Salvation Army, Nazarene). The Negro churches in this category seem to account for the relatively high percentage of family heads in social class V.

Geographical Distribution

The geographical distribution of households in the 5 per cent sample was spotted on New Haven maps according to social class and the religion of the head of the household. Each household in the sample also was spotted against the class of housing in which the family lives. (Classes of housing range from 1 [highest] to 6 [lowest.])

TABLE 4. Percentage distribution by social class of male heads of households attending Protestant churches in metropolitan New Haven, by denomination

| Denomination | | Social Class | | | | | |
		I	II	III	IV	V	Total
Congregational	(N. 270)	9.6	15.9	32.2	38.5	3.7	100.0
Episcopal	(N. 186)	3.8	15.6	25.3	50.5	4.8	100.0
Baptist	(N. 86)	2.3	3.5	5.8	48.8	39.5	100.0
Methodist	(N. 81)	1.2	9.9	34.6	44.4	9.9	100.0
Lutheran	(N. 64)	4.7	7.8	18.8	60.9	7.8	100.0
Other Protestant denominations	(N. 80)	3.8	7.5	16.3	41.2	31.2	100.0
Total	(N. 767)	5.5	12.2	26.1	44.5	11.7	100.0

Since place of residence is one of the three components used to determine social class, the upper class households are, for the most part, located in the more desirable housing areas (housing classes 1 and 2), in both the city and the suburbs.

We have already stated (Chapter 1) that the suburbs have been growing in the last three decades. Among New Haven Protestants the movement to the suburbs of upper class and middle class families has corresponded to population trends in other American cities; and today while the New Haven city proper is only 29 per cent Protestant, the suburbs are 43 per cent Protestant. In fact Protestants have a higher proportional representation in the suburbs than do Roman Catholics in all of the first four social classes.[4] There are few social class V families in the suburbs.

There are substantial numbers of class III and class IV Protestants in the city proper, but the major single concentration of Protestants is among

[4] The Protestant movement to the suburbs should be considered in the light of the concentration of Protestant churches in the inner-city. (Chapter 3.)

Negro families (mostly class IV and class V) in the Dixwell Avenue area of the inner-city.

The city proper is the domicile of most Roman Catholic households of all social classes. The highest suburban concentrations of Roman Catholics occur in East Haven, West Haven and the western portions of Hamden.[5] The majority of these families live in class 3, 4 and 5 housing. Most of the suburban Roman Catholic families are in social classes III and IV, although the highest concentration of upper class Roman Catholics in a suburb occurs among class I and class II families in West Haven. In this suburb class I and class II Catholics outnumber class I and class II Protestants in the sample.

It is important to recognize the fact that the prosperous times since World War II and widespread new building in the suburbs have sparked a Catholic exodus from the city.[6] As this report is being prepared, a Roman Catholic parochial school is being built in the fashionable Whitney Avenue section of Hamden, long a stronghold of upper class Protestantism. In this same area, in two blocks of a single street (class 2 housing) which had only Protestant families prior to the War, fourteen new houses have been built since 1946. Three are unoccupied. Two have been purchased by class I Protestant families. Seven of the remaining eight have been bought by class III and class IV Catholic families and the last by a class III mixed (Protestant-Catholic) household. This example is not cited as typical, but as indicative of a trend.

Jewish families in the sample, of all social classes, are for the most part concentrated in the city of New Haven. However, the trend of movement by Jews, in general, is to the western fringes of the city and by upper class Jewish families to the western suburb of Woodbridge (not included in the sample). Some Jews are also moving to the Hamden–North Haven area, where Jewish families have reached a high enough concentration to establish a community center on Whitney Avenue in the heart of Hamden.

No geographical spotting was done for mixed families or those households of no religious background. It is known, however, that mixed households in the sample have a higher concentration in the city of New Haven than in the suburbs.

---

[5] East Haven and West Haven constitute the points of land forming the east and west arms of the harbor, south of the city proper. Hamden is directly north of the city, and North Haven adjoins it to the northeast.

[6] The Roman Catholics are also facing a problem similar to that of the Protestants of inner-city concentration of churches with consequent lack of church facilities for suburban families.

Occupation, Social Class and Religion

One of the important factors in the definition of social class was the occupation of the head of the household. Naturally, therefore, there is a close correlation between occupation and social class. The actual distribution of the population sample by social class and occupation, however, gives perhaps the best illustration of any table in this study of the kinds of families that make up the population we are studying (Table 5).

The largest group by far consists of the families of skilled and semiskilled workers, who together constitute about half the population and are the great bulk of the 48.4 per cent of the families who are classified in social

Table 5. Distribution of male heads of households by social class and rated occupation [a]

Rated Occupation [b]	Social Class											Total Sample	
	I (N. 119)		II (N. 328)		III (N. 760)		IV (N. 1,723)		V (N. 629)		(N. 3,559)	
	No.	Per Cent	No.	Per Cent	No.	Per Cent	No.	Per Cent	No.	Per Cent	No.	Per Cent
Higher executives, professionals, and proprietors	100	84.0	84	25.6	3	0.4					187	5.3
Lesser executives, professionals and proprietors	2	1.7	136	41.5	68	8.9	3	0.2			209	5.9
Small independent business proprietors; semi-professionals			38	11.6	99	13.0	14	0.8			151	4.2
Clerical and sales workers			16	4.9	349	45.9	199	11.5			564	15.8
Skilled laborers					166	21.8	739	42.9	42	6.7	947	26.6
Semi-skilled laborers					9	1.2	601	34.9	262	41.7	872	24.5
Unskilled laborers							43	2.5	246	39.1	289	8.1
Students	5	4.2	17	5.2	6	0.8	3	0.2			31	0.9
Retired	1	0.8	2	0.6	4	0.5	15	0.9	13	2.1	35	1.0

[a] Classifications for "rated occupation" of males as used in this study were developed by A. B. Hollingshead.
[b] Households without male heads or where occupation is unknown, omitted.

class IV. The next largest group are clerical and sales workers, about one-sixth of the total, who make up most of social class III. At the top of the scale are the proprietors and managers of large and medium-sized businesses and the professional men, comprising about one-tenth of the families, who account for almost all families in social classes I and II. At the other end of the scale are unskilled workers, most of whom are in social class V. Scattered through the middle three social classes are small businessmen, semiprofessionals, students and miscellaneous others.

Table 6. Distribution of wives and female heads of households by social class and rated occupation [a]

Rated Occupation [b]	Social Class											Total Sample	
	I (N. 119)		II (N. 328)		III (N. 760)		IV (N. 1,723)		V (N. 629)			(N. 3,559)	
	No.	Per Cent	No.	Per Cent	No.	Per Cent	No.	Per Cent	No.	Per Cent		No.	Per Cent
Housewife	92	77.3	236	72.0	541	71.2	1,259	73.1	439	69.8		2,567	72.1
Higher executives, professionals and proprietors	9	7.6	4	1.2	2	0.3						15	0.4
Lesser executives, professionals and proprietors	4	3.4	52	15.9	35	4.6	18	1.0	1	0.2		110	3.1
Small independent business proprietors; semi-professionals			2	0.6	4	0.5	3	0.2				9	0.3
Clerical and sales workers workers	3	2.5	15	4.6	114	15.0	102	5.9	7	1.1		241	6.8
Skilled laborers					10	1.3	33	1.9	2	0.3		45	1.3
Semiskilled laborers	2	1.7	3	0.9	27	3.6	219	12.7	90	14.3		341	9.6
Unskilled laborers					2	0.3	42	2.4	63	10.0		107	3.0
Students	1	0.8	3	0.9								4	0.1
Retired	1	0.8	1	0.3	6	0.8	3	0.2	6	1.0		17	0.5

[a] Classifications for "rated occupation" of females as used in this study were developed by A. B. Hollingshead.
[b] Households with no female or where occupation of female is unknown, omitted.

While most (72.1 per cent) of the wives or female heads of the households in the sample were housewives, 23.5 per cent were employed at the time of the survey. The largest single group were semiskilled workers and the next largest, clerical and sales workers. These two groups accounted for two-thirds of the working wives and female household heads (Table 6).

The correlation that exists between occupation and religion is much less pronounced than that between occupation and social class (Table 7). It has, however, a high degree of statistical significance (p. <.001).

TABLE 7. Distribution of male heads of households by religious affiliation and rated occupation

Rated Occupation[a]	Religious Affiliation[b]									
	Protestant (N. 1,032)		Roman Catholic (N. 1,879)		Jewish (N. 328)		Mixed (N. 264)		Total Sample (N. 3,559)	
	No.	Per Cent	No.	Per Cent	No.	Per Cent	No.	Per Cent	No.	Per Cent
Higher executives, professionals and proprietors	88	8.5	57	3.0	30	9.1	8	3.0	187	5.3
Lesser executives, professionals and proprietors	85	8.2	53	2.8	46	14.0	15	5.7	209	5.9
Small independent business proprietors; semiprofessionals	44	4.3	54	2.9	40	12.2	11	4.2	151	4.2
Clerical and sales workers	168	16.3	276	14.7	76	23.2	39	14.8	564	15.8
Skilled laborers	226	21.9	550	29.3	71	21.6	92	34.8	949	26.7
Semiskilled laborers	200	19.4	560	29.8	33	10.1	70	26.5	874	24.6
Unskilled laborers	76	7.4	174	9.3	15	4.6	20	7.6	289	8.1
Students	18	1.7	6	0.3	2	0.6	2	0.8	31	1.0
Retired	7	0.7	25	1.3			3	1.1	35	1.0

[a] Households without male heads or where occupation is unknown, omitted.

[b] Other, none and unknown religion omitted.

A comparison between Protestant and Roman Catholic occupations shows the extent to which Protestants hold the better positions in business, industry and the professions and Roman Catholics provide the bulk of the skilled and semiskilled labor. Roman Catholics constitute nearly one-half (48.4 per cent) of all families, but their male family heads account for only 30.0 per cent of the owners and managers of business concerns and industries and the professional and semiprofessional workers in the sample.

Jewish family heads are especially well represented in business and the professions. The first three categories in the table (business and professional) account for 35.3 per cent of all male Jewish family heads, as compared with 21.0 per cent of the Protestants and only 8.7 per cent of the Roman Catholics.

While recognizing the tendency of Protestants to be especially well represented in the "upper" occupational brackets—professionals and businessmen—it is still important to note that 49 out of every 100 Protestant male household heads work with their hands in skilled, semiskilled or unskilled occupations, and that another 16 out of every 100 are clerks, salesmen, bookkeepers or similar white-collar workers. Male Jewish household heads are found to be 36.3 per cent employed in manual occupations and 23.2 per cent in clerical trades.

Income, Social Class and Religion

Statistics on annual income of the head of the household were secured for all but two of the 3,559 families in the sample. Approximately one-third had incomes of from $2,001 to $3,500, and another one-third, from $3,501 to $5,000 per year. One-eighth had incomes under $2,000, and one-fifth $5,000 and over. Only 2.8 per cent had incomes of over $10,000 per year (Table 8).

Table 8. Income of heads of household by social class

	Social Class										Total Sample
	I (N. 119)		II (N. 328)		III (N. 760)		IV (N. 1,723)		V (N. 629)		(N. 3,559)	
Income	No.	Per Cent	No.	Per Cent	No.	Per Cent	No.	Per Cent	No.	Per Cent	No.	Per Cent
$2,000 or less	5	4.2	18	5.5	40	5.3	215	12.5	173	27.5	451	12.7
2,001-3,500	9	7.6	43	13.1	149	19.6	696	40.4	323	51.4	1,220	34.3
3,501-5,000	13	10.9	67	20.4	327	43.0	648	37.6	110	17.5	1,165	32.7
5,001-7,500	29	24.3	103	31.4	175	23.0	144	8.4	19	3.0	470	13.2
7,501-10,000	19	16.0	56	17.1	54	7.1	19	1.1	3	0.5	151	4.2
10,001-15,000	21	17.1	21	6.4	10	1.3					52	1.5
Over $15,000	23	19.3	20	6.4	5	0.7					48	1.3
Unknown							1	0.1	1	0.2	2	0.1

Table 8 shows that income correlates fairly closely, though by no means exactly, with social class position. Over three-fifths (63.8 per cent) of the family heads with incomes of over $7,500 are in social classes I or II, and

35.8 per cent of the families in social classes I and II have incomes over $7,500 (cf. 7.0 per cent for total sample). At the same time, 22.5 per cent of the class I family heads and 39.0 per cent of the class II family heads reported incomes of $5,000 or less. Here is further documentation of the point made earlier, that income, while certainly significant in the function of social class as measured here, is by no means the sole determining factor.

Income also seems to bear a general relation to religious affiliation, as may be seen in Table 9. The chi square test of this relationship shows a high degree of statistical significance ($p < .001$).

TABLE 9. Income of heads of household by religion

				Religion[a]						
			Roman						Total	
	Protestant		Catholic		Jewish		Mixed		Sample	
	(N. 1,032)		(N. 1,879)		(N. 328)		(N. 264)		(N. 3,559)	
		Per		Per		Per		Per		Per
Income	No.	Cent	No.	Cent	No.	Cent	No.	Cent	No.	Cent
$2,000 or less	161	15.6	221	11.8	27	8.2	29	11.0	444	12.7
2,001-3,500	308	29.8	724	38.5	81	24.7	84	31.8	1,217	34.3
3,501-5,000	312	30.2	643	34.2	85	25.9	107	40.5	1,162	32.7
5,001-7,500	149	14.4	200	10.6	77	23.5	34	12.9	470	13.2
7,501-10,000	59	5.7	50	2.7	31	9.5	7	2.7	151	4.2
10,001-15,000	19	1.8	16	0.9	16	4.9	1	0.4	52	1.5
Over $15,000	24	2.3	11	0.6	11	3.4	2	0.8	48	1.3

[a] Other, none and unknown religion omitted.

Table 10. Distribution of male heads of households by social class and education

					Social Class						Total	
	I		II		III		IV		V		Sample	
Highest	(N. 119)		(N. 328)		(N. 760)		(N. 1,723)		(N. 629)		(N. 3,559)	
Grade		Per		Per		Per		Per		Per		Per
Completed [a]	No.	Cent	No.	Cent	No.	Cent	No.	Cent	No.	Cent	No.	Cent
Graduate or Professional School	90	83.3	55	19.2	5	0.7	2	0.1			152	4.9
1-4 years college	18	16.6	194	67.6	194	29.0	42	2.7			448	14.4
High school graduate			35	12.2	385	57.6	407	26.5	13	2.5	840	27.0
7-11 years			3	1.0	79	11.8	939	61.3	226	43.5	1,247	40.0
Under 7 years					5	0.7	143	9.3	280	53.9	428	13.7

[a] Education unknown and inapplicable (female head of household) omitted from table.

Median income for heads of Roman Catholic families is $3,490, heads of mixed families $3,770, heads of Protestant families $3,780, and heads of Jewish families $4,490. The income data, of course, reflect the occupational distribution of religious groups. Of the family heads with incomes over $7,500, 38.2 per cent are Protestant, 22.0 per cent Jewish, and 33.7 per cent Roman Catholic. Of those with incomes over $15,000, 49.0 per cent are Protestant. However, more than half of the incomes for each of the four religious classifications fall between $2,001 and $5,000; and, except for Jews, more than one-tenth of all incomes are below $2,000.

Education, Social Class and Religion

Educational attainment, like occupation, was a factor considered in the determination of social class, and there is, therefore, a close correlation between education and social class. Five-sixths (83.3 per cent) of the male heads of households in social class I had college and graduate school training, as compared with only one-fifth (19.2 per cent) of the male heads of households in social class II and almost none in classes III, IV and V. The median education for male family heads in class V is six grades; class IV, nine grades; class III, twelve grades (high school graduate); class II, college graduate; and class I, graduate or professional school (Table 10).

Table 11. Distribution of wives and female heads of households by
social class and education

Highest Grade Completed [a]	Social Class										Total Sample	
	I (N. 119)		II (N. 328)		III (N. 760)		IV (N. 1,723)		V (N. 629)		(N. 3,559)	
	No.	Per Cent	No.	Per Cent	No.	Per Cent	No.	Per Cent	No.	Per Cent	No.	Per Cent
Graduate or Professional School	22	19.8	17	5.5	5	0.7	3	0.2	2	0.3	49	1.5
1-4 years college	51	45.9	162	52.3	155	21.3	67	4.1	4	0.7	439	13.0
High school graduate	31	27.9	108	34.8	415	56.9	551	33.4	50	8.6	1,155	34.2
7-11 years	6	5.4	22	7.1	145	19.9	873	53.0	301	52.0	1,347	39.9
Under 7 years	1	0.9	1	0.3	9	1.2	154	9.3	222	38.3	387	11.5

[a] Education unknown and inapplicable (no female in household) omitted from table.

Average educational attainment of wives or female heads of households was in general less than that of husbands and male heads in social classes I, II and III, but higher than the men in social classes IV and V. The discrepancy is particularly marked in classes I and II, where the great majority of husbands are college graduates, but a sizable minority of wives are high school graduates or have even less education (Table 11).

Examination of statistics on educational attainment in relation to religion (Table 12) shows again the same tendency for the characteristics of Protestant and Jewish families to be biased toward the characteristics of social classes I, II and III and Roman Catholic families toward social classes IV and V. Over one-fourth (27.8 per cent) of Protestant male household heads, and over one-third (34.9 per cent) of Jewish male household heads

TABLE 12. Distribution of male heads of households by religion and education

Highest Grade Completed[a]	Religion of Family[b]								Total Sample (N. 3,559)	
	Protestant (N. 1,032)		Roman Catholic (N. 1,879)		Jewish (N. 328)		Mixed (N. 264)			
	No.	Per Cent	No.	Per Cent	No.	Per Cent	No.	Per Cent	No.	Per Cent
Graduate or professional school	71	8.3	37	2.2	28	9.3	9	3.6	152	4.9
1-4 years college	168	19.5	161	9.7	77	25.6	34	13.8	447	14.3
High school graduate	253	29.4	420	25.3	82	27.2	70	28.3	840	27.0
7-11 years	306	35.6	749	45.2	60	19.9	118	47.8	1,248	40.1
Under 7 years	62	7.2	290	17.5	54	17.9	16	6.5	428	13.7

[a] Unknown and inapplicable (female head of household) omitted from table.

[b] Other, none and unknown religion omitted.

have had some college education, as compared with only one-ninth (11.9 per cent) of Roman Catholic household heads. At the same time, it should be noted that about two out of five of the Protestant (42.8 per cent) and Jewish (37.8 per cent) male household heads, as well as over three-fifths (62.7 per cent) of the Catholic male household heads have not completed high school. The relationship between religious affiliation and educational attainment is, as the foregoing indicates, statistically significant (p. <.001).

Home Ownership and Religion

Home ownership is usually assumed to be a measure both of family stability and of economic status. In the total sample, 47.3 per cent of the families owned the homes they occupied (Table 13). Significantly above this average were homes in which the male head was Lutheran (64.1 per cent), Congregational (64.1 per cent), Episcopal (58.1 per cent), or a member of a Protestant denomination not constituent to the National Council of Churches (59.1 per cent). Near the average in home ownership were Methodists (46.9 per cent), Roman Catholics (46.7 per cent), Jewish (45.3 per cent), and homes in which the male head did not attend church (45.7 per cent). Significantly below average were Baptist families, many of whom are Negro (30.2 per cent), and households without male heads (42.0 per cent).

TABLE 13. Home ownership by church affiliation of husband and wife

Church attended by Husband or Wife	Households distributed by church attended by Males[a]			Households distributed by church attended by Females[b]		
		Homes owned by occupants			Homes owned by occupants	
	Total Households	No.	Per Cent	Total Households	No.	Per Cent
None	394	180	45.7	298	134	45.0
Roman Catholic	1,664	777	46.7	1,919	900	46.9
Congregational	270	173	64.1	324	192	59.3
Jewish	245	111	45.3	267	116	43.4
Episcopal	186	108	58.1	234	126	53.8
Baptist	86	26	30.2	107	35	32.7
Methodist	81	38	46.9	101	48	47.5
Lutheran	64	41	64.1	84	54	64.3
Other Protestants	79	41	51.8	100	48	48.0
Households without male head	490	206	42.0			
Households without adult females				125	49	39.2
Total	3,559	1,683	47.3	3,559	1,683	47.3

[a] Includes all male heads of households.
[b] Includes wives and female heads of households.

Age and Sex

The metropolitan New Haven population shows a fairly typical age distribution for a contemporary American city, with a large and increasing number of small children, a deficit of young people from 15 to 24 years of age and an increasing number of older persons.

The differences among religious groups were of particular interest for this study (Table 14 and Figures 3–7).

TABLE 14. Percentage distribution of all persons in sample by religious affiliation of family, age and sex

Age in Years	Protestant		Catholic		Jewish		Mixed		Total Sample	
	M	F	M	F	M	F	M	F	M	F
Under 5	3.9	4.8	4.3	4.5	4.7	4.6	5.3	4.9	4.3	4.6
5-15	9.1	8.8	10.4	9.0	7.3	8.2	9.2	12.3	9.7	9.1
16-24	3.5	4.9	4.8	5.8	4.4	3.8	4.3	3.6	4.4	5.3
25-34	6.4	7.2	8.1	9.5	7.6	9.8	9.0	9.3	7.7	8.9
35-54	13.3	15.6	13.5	15.1	14.0	15.1	13.8	13.7	13.7	15.3
55 and over	9.8	12.4	7.1	7.6	10.2	10.0	6.6	7.7	8.2	9.2
Total	46.2	53.8	48.4	51.6	48.3	51.7	48.4	51.6	47.9	52.1

Protestants and Jews had the largest proportion of older people, the percentage 55 years and over being 22.2 for the Protestant population and 20.2 for the Jewish, compared with 14.7 for Catholics and 14.3 for population in mixed families. At the opposite end of the age scale, mixed households had the largest proportion of children under 16 years of age (31.7 per cent),[7] compared with 28.2 per cent for Catholics, 26.6 per cent for Protestants, and 24.8 per cent for Jews.

While the differences are interesting and of borderline significance, it should be pointed out that the Protestant community does not seem to be at a great disadvantage in relation to the Catholic community in regard to number of children, as is so often assumed. It is possible (this was not analyzed) that the "upper class" Protestant denominations, particularly the Congregational, have relatively the smallest child population and the largest elderly population, but Protestantism as a whole is not too far from the community's average in age.

The effect of social class upon age distribution is actually not so pronounced as might be expected. Table 15 shows the distribution when each of the social classes is divided into three age groupings.

[7] Here as in the other tables it must be remembered that mixed households would tend to report more children because by definition such a household involves a marriage, where other households may include only single persons. We may also assume that mixed households would tend to be younger because of the possibility that one partner in time may convert the other to his or her faith and eliminate the household from this "mixed" category.

FIGURE 3. Age and sex distribution of all persons in metropolitan New Haven

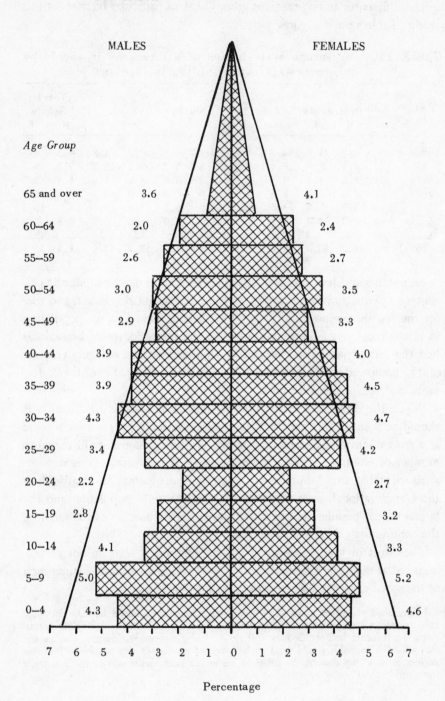

MALES   FEMALES

Age Group

65 and over	3.6	4.1
60–64	2.0	2.4
55–59	2.6	2.7
50–54	3.0	3.5
45–49	2.9	3.3
40–44	3.9	4.0
35–39	3.9	4.5
30–34	4.3	4.7
25–29	3.4	4.2
20–24	2.2	2.7
15–19	2.8	3.2
10–14	4.1	3.3
5–9	5.0	5.2
0–4	4.3	4.6

7 6 5 4 3 2 1 0 1 2 3 4 5 6 7

Percentage

FIGURE 4. Age and sex distribution of persons in Catholic households

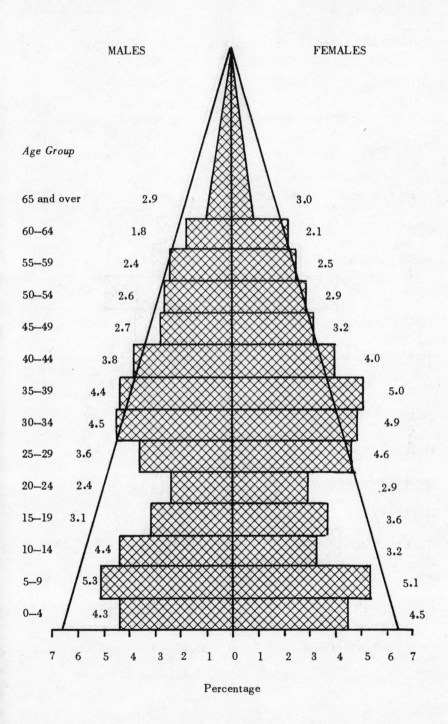

MALES   FEMALES

Age Group

Age Group	Males	Females
65 and over	2.9	3.0
60—64	1.8	2.1
55—59	2.4	2.5
50—54	2.6	2.9
45—49	2.7	3.2
40—44	3.8	4.0
35—39	4.4	5.0
30—34	4.5	4.9
25—29	3.6	4.6
20—24	2.4	2.9
15—19	3.1	3.6
10—14	4.4	3.2
5—9	5.3	5.1
0—4	4.3	4.5

7 6 5 4 3 2 1 0 1 2 3 4 5 6 7

Percentage

FIGURE 5. Age and sex distribution of persons in Protestant households

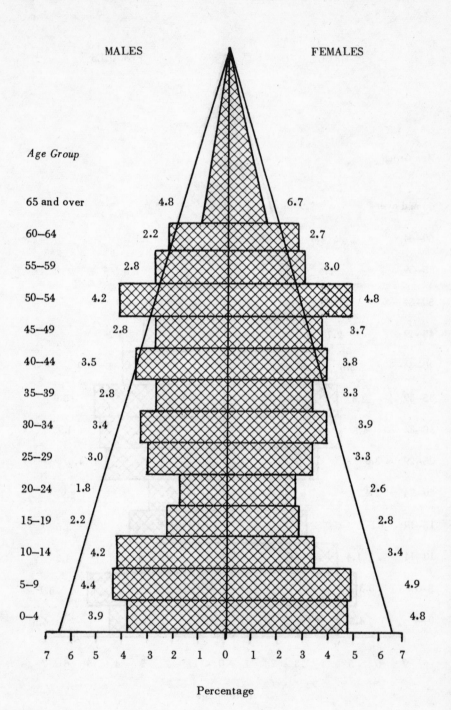

MALES   FEMALES

Age Group		
65 and over	4.8	6.7
60—64	2.2	2.7
55—59	2.8	3.0
50—54	4.2	4.8
45—49	2.8	3.7
40—44	3.5	3.8
35—39	2.8	3.3
30—34	3.4	3.9
25—29	3.0	3.3
20—24	1.8	2.6
15—19	2.2	2.8
10—14	4.2	3.4
5—9	4.4	4.9
0—4	3.9	4.8

7 6 5 4 3 2 1 0 1 2 3 4 5 6 7

Percentage

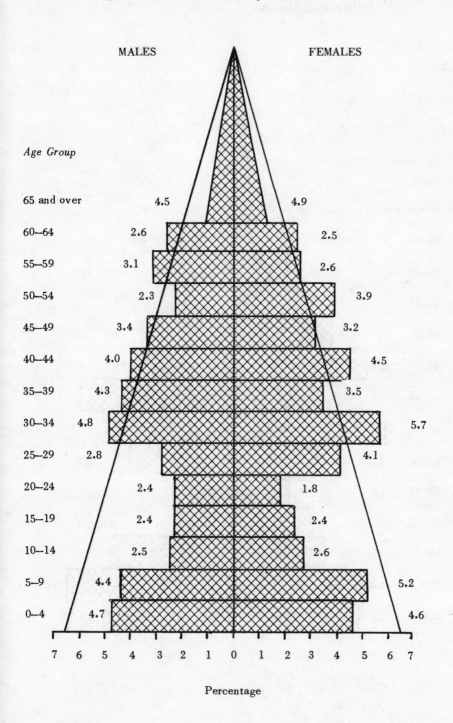

FIGURE 6. Age and sex distribution of persons in Jewish households

MALES   FEMALES

Age Group

Age Group	MALES	FEMALES
65 and over	4.5	4.9
60—64	2.6	2.5
55—59	3.1	2.6
50—54	2.3	3.9
45—49	3.4	3.2
40—44	4.0	4.5
35—39	4.3	3.5
30—34	4.8	5.7
25—29	2.8	4.1
20—24	2.4	1.8
15—19	2.4	2.4
10—14	2.5	2.6
5—9	4.4	5.2
0—4	4.7	4.6

7 6 5 4 3 2 1 0 1 2 3 4 5 6 7

Percentage

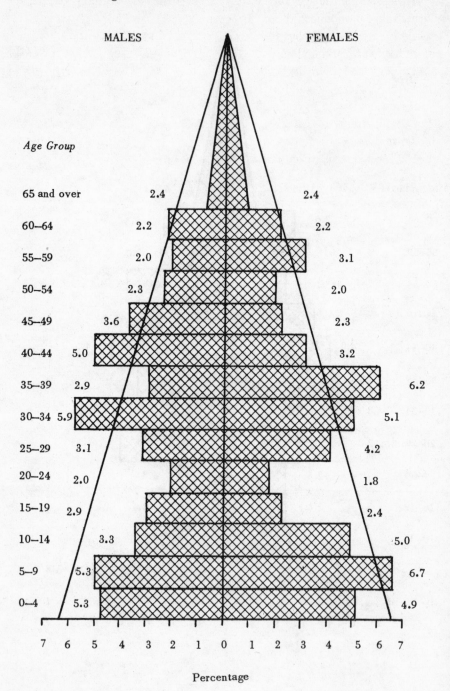

FIGURE 7. Age and sex distribution of persons in households of mixed religious affiliation

If we examine the ages of the male heads of households, however, some rather more pronounced differences among religious groups appear, particularly as between Catholics and Protestants. While only 36.0 per cent of the male heads of Catholic households are 50 years of age and over, nearly half (48.1 per cent) of male heads of Protestant households are in this age bracket. Conversely, while 38.8 per cent of male heads of Catholic households are aged 25 to 39 years, only 27.0 per cent of male heads of Protestant households are in this category. The median age of male heads of Protestant households is 49.0 years; of Catholic households, 43.7 years; of Jewish households, 46.2 years; of mixed households, 42.9 years.

TABLE 15. Age distribution by social class

| Social Class | Percentage of Social Class | | |
	Under 15 years	15 - 24 years	25 years and over
I	21.1	11.5	67.4
II	26.6	7.4	66.0
III	25.4	9.7	64.9
IV	28.1	10.9	61.0
V	23.9	12.4	63.7

When this difference was examined in relation to social class, it was found that the relationship between social class and age of Protestant male heads of household was not significant ($p < .50 > .30$), but for Catholic male heads of households it was significant ($p < .001$). Catholic household heads in social classes I, II and V tend to be over 45 years of age, but in social classes III and IV, the bulk of Catholic male household heads are between 30 and 44 years of age.

The over-all picture of age of household heads by social class is quite interesting. We will summarize the data here only by reference to median age. Male heads of households in the three middle social classes are all about the same median age—43.8 for social class II, 43.4 for social class III, and 43.8 for social class IV. In social class I, however, the median age jumps about five years to 48.6. At the other end of the scale, however, the median age for male household heads is even higher—52.8 years. In social class V, it is evident, we find a concentration of the economic ills that beset the elderly in contemporary urban society. One-fifth of the male household heads in social class V are 65 years and over, and one-third are 60 years and over.

Part of the older group in social class V may have moved downward in the social scale from the position held when younger. In terms of the criteria used for establishing social class, the education of these men would not have changed with age, but they may have been downgraded in occupation or their dwindling income may have required them to move to a less desirable place of residence. This kind of "downward mobility" is often very important in determining social attitudes.

Age of the head of the household would also seem to be an important factor in determining attitudes toward such a new medium as television, and we might predict that the older generations would be less receptive to the new "gadget."

Table 16. Marital status of heads of households by social class

					Social Class					Total	
	I		II		III		IV		V		Sample	
	(N. 119)		(N. 328)		(N. 760)		(N. 1,723)		(N. 629)		(N. 3,559)	
Marital		Per		Per		Per		Per		Per		Per
Status	No.	Cent	No.	Cent	No.	Cent	No.	Cent	No.	Cent	No.	Cent
Male married	92	77.3	267	81.4	633	83.3	1,428	82.9	470	74.7	2,890	81.2
Male widower			6	1.8	5	0.7	36	2.1	23	3.7	70	2.0
Male divorced					1	0.1	2	0.1			3	0.1
Male separated							5	0.3	2	0.3	7	0.2
Male unmarried	7	5.9	7	2.1	15	2.0	18	1.0	7	1.1	54	1.5
Female widowed	13	10.9	21	6.4	71	9.3	176	10.2	97	15.4	378	10.6
Female divorced			1	0.3	3	0.4	14	0.8	7	1.1	25	0.7
Female separated					1	0.1	10	0.6	12	1.9	23	0.6
Female unmarried	7	5.9	26	7.9	31	4.1	33	1.9	11	1.7	108	3.0

Marital Status

Eight out of ten households in metropolitan New Haven are headed by a married male whose wife is alive and living with him. One out of ten households has a widow at its head. Half of the remainder have a single woman or a single man as head of the household, and the remaining few are headed by widowers or by divorced or separated men or women.

Table 16 shows that the "normal" (husband-wife) family situation is found most frequently in social classes III and IV, while other marital situations are found most frequently in the two extreme groups, social classes I and V. Widows, for example, are relatively most frequent in social class V and next most frequent in social class I. Numerically, however, social class IV, with its large population, provides the most actual cases in any given type of family situation.

Unmarried males as heads of households are relatively most frequent in social class I and unmarried females as heads of households in social class II.

In Table 17 we see that mixed and Jewish families are most likely to have the "normal" husband-wife family situation, and Protestant families least likely, although even in the Protestant families three-fourths are headed by a husband-wife combination. One out of seven Protestant households is headed by a widow and one out of seventeen by an unmarried woman. Altogether, 21.3 per cent of all Protestant households have female heads.

TABLE 17. Marital status of heads of households by religious affiliation of families

Marital Status[a]	Religion of the Family[b]									
	Protestant (N. 1,032)		Roman Catholic (N. 1,879)		Jewish (N. 328)		Mixed (N. 264)		Total Sample (N. 3,559)	
	No.	Per Cent	No.	Per Cent	No.	Per Cent	No.	Per Cent	No.	Per Cent
Male married	765	74.1	1,564	83.2	284	86.6	230	87.1	2,890	81.3
Male widower	17	1.6	41	2.2	6	1.8	5	1.9	70	2.0
Male divorced			1	0.1	1	0.3	1	0.4	3	0.1
Male separated	3	0.3	4	0.2					7	0.2
Male unmarried	26	2.5	24	1.3	3	0.9			54	1.5
Female widowed	150	14.5	177	9.4	28	8.5	18	6.8	378	10.6
Female divorced	6	0.6	11	0.6	3	0.9	5	1.9	25	0.7
Female separated	4	0.4	13	0.7			5	1.9	23	0.6
Female unmarried	60	5.8	44	2.3	3	0.9			108	3.0

[a] Unknown omitted.

[b] Other, none and unknown religions omitted.

Table 18. Distribution of households in metropolitan New Haven by type

	No.	Per cent	Households No.	Per cent
Family groups, including husband, wife and minor children			1,970	55.4
Husband, wife and children	1,796	50.4		
Husband, wife, children and grandparents	102	2.9		
Husband, wife, children and close relatives	72	2.0		
Family groups including husband, wife, no minor children			901	25.3
Husband and wife only	742	20.8		
Husband, wife and parents	34	1.0		
Husband, wife and close relatives	54	1.5		
3 or 4 (married) generations	71	2.0		
Broken families with minor children			248	7.0
Widower with children	28	0.8		
Widower with children and close relatives	11	0.3		
Widow with children	128	3.6		
Widow with children and close relatives	38	1.1		
Separated or divorced father with children	3	0.1		
Separated or divorced mother with children	26	0.7		
Grandparents with grandchildren	14	0.4		
Adults living alone			241	6.8
Single male	28	0.8		
Single female	53	1.5		
Widower	22	0.6		
Widow	129	3.6		
Separated or divorced male	2	0.1		
Separated or divorced female	7	0.2		
Other adult households without minor children			199	5.5
Adult male with parents	4	0.1		
Adult female with parents	10	0.3		
Adult male with close relatives	19	0.5		
Adult female with close relatives	53	1.5		
Widow with close relatives	26	0.7		
Unrelated females	11	0.3		
Unrelated males	3	0.1		
Unrelated mixed males and females	5	0.1		
Miscellaneous other combinations	68	1.9		
Total all households			3,559	100.0

Type of Household

Radio listening and television viewing occur primarily in the home. It seemed important, therefore, to discover and describe as accurately as possible the actual kinds of household situations in which this activity takes place. Table 18 gives a detailed picture of metropolitan New Haven households in terms of the persons who compose them and the relationships of family members to one another.

Perhaps the most noteworthy thing in this table is the *variety* of household types that actually exist. The survey identified 28 types, with an additional 68 households that could not be fitted into these classifications.

Table 19. Distribution of types of households by social class

| Types of Households | Social Class | | | | | | | | | | Total all Households | |
| | I (N. 119) | | II (N. 328) | | III (N. 760) | | IV (N. 1,723) | | V (N. 629) | | (N. 3,559) | |
	No.	Per Cent	No.	Per Cent	No.	Per Cent	No.	Per Cent	No.	Per Cent	No.	Per Cent
Husband, wife and minor children	50	42.0	168	51.2	419	55.1	1,030	59.8	303	48.2	1,970	55.4
Husband, wife, no minor children	37	31.1	99	30.2	213	28.0	386	22.4	166	26.4	901	25.3
Broken families with minor children	4	3.4	10	3.0	34	4.5	122	7.1	78	12.4	248	7.0
Adults living alone	15	12.6	19	5.8	54	7.1	106	6.2	47	7.5	241	6.8
Other adult households without minor children	13	10.9	32	9.8	40	5.3	79	4.6	35	5.6	199	5.5

Only half of all households resemble the conventional picture of the contemporary American family with husband, wife and minor children; and only slightly more than half (55.3 per cent) if we add grandparents or other relatives to the picture. One out of five households consists of only husband and wife, or one out of four if we add homes where adult relatives live with such a couple. One household in eight represents a marriage broken by death, divorce or separation, and in more than half of these households there are minor children. One household in fifteen consists of an adult liv-

ing alone—over three-fourths of them being women. Minor children are
found in five households out of eight.

Tables 19 and 20 give this same information in condensed form by social
class and religious affiliation. Families with husband, wife and minor children are relatively most frequent in social class IV and least frequent in
social class I, while the reverse is true where there are no minor children.
Broken families with children are relatively most frequent in social class V.

TABLE 20. Distribution of types of households by religious
           affiliation of family

| | Religious Affiliation[a] | | | | | | | | Total | |
| | Protestant (N. 1,032) | | Roman Catholic (N. 1,879) | | Jewish (N. 328) | | Mixed (N. 264) | | Sample (N. 3,559) | |
Types of Households	No.	Per Cent	No.	Per Cent	No.	Per Cent	No.	Per Cent	No.	Per Cent
Husband, wife and minor children	448	43.4	1,149	61.1	190	57.9	166	62.9	1,970	55.4
Husband, wife and no minor children	306	29.7	413	22.0	89	27.1	65	24.6	901	25.3
Broken families with minor children	67	6.5	143	7.6	22	6.7	12	4.5	248	7.0
Adults living alone	120	11.6	88	4.7	17	5.2	14	5.3	241	6.8
Other adult households without minor children	91	8.8	86	4.6	10	3.0	7	2.7	199	5.6

[a] Unknown, none and other religious affiliation omitted from table.

Examining these households by religious affiliation, we again note the
tendency of Protestant families to exhibit the characteristics of the upper
social classes. The frequency of households with minor children is least for
the Protestants, greatest for Catholic and mixed households. Protestant
households have the highest incidence of entirely adult situations, whether
in family groups, in single-person households or in other adult combina-

tions. This relationship between type of household and religious affiliation is statistically significant (p <.001).

Size of Household

The data on types of households is reflected in the statistics on size of household. New Haven households in the sample varied in size from one to fourteen persons, the median household consisting of 3.71 persons and the average household, 3.36 persons. There is a steady increase in median household size, however, from 3.24 persons in social class I households to 3.36 in social class II, 3.56 in social class III, and 3.86 in social class IV. The median household in social class V is slightly smaller, 3.76 persons.

Protestant households again reflect the characteristics of the upper social classes, and the distribution of Protestant households by size is remarkably similar to that of the households in social class I (see Tables 21 and 22). The median Protestant household had 3.26 persons, as compared with 3.99 for Catholic households, 3.82 for mixed households, and 3.49 for Jewish. Table 22 shows that 44.5 per cent of the Protestant households contain only one or two persons, as compared with 26.3 per cent of the Catholic households.

Table 21. Number in households by social class of families

	Social Class										Total	
	I		II		III		IV		V		Sample	
	(N. 119)		(N. 328)		(N. 760)		(N. 1,723)		(N. 629)		(N. 3,559)	
Number in		Per		Per		Per		Per		Per		Per
Family	No.	Cent	No.	Cent	No.	Cent	No.	Cent	No.	Cent	No.	Cent
1	15	12.6	20	6.1	54	7.1	105	6.1	46	7.3	240	6.7
2	39	32.8	115	35.1	225	29.6	392	22.7	166	26.4	937	26.3
3	25	21.0	81	24.7	181	23.8	426	24.7	135	21.5	848	23.8
4	20	16.8	64	19.5	166	21.8	443	25.7	138	21.9	831	23.8
5	13	10.9	34	10.4	100	13.2	229	13.3	71	11.3	447	12.6
6	6	5.0	10	3.0	16	2.1	78	4.5	43	6.8	153	4.3
7 or more	1	0.8	4	1.2	18	2.4	50	2.9	30	4.8	103	2.9
Median		3.24		3.36		3.56		3.86		3.76		3.71

The chi square test for statistical significance shows that the difference between Catholic and Protestant households in number of persons per household is significant in every social class (social classes I and II—p <.01; social classes III, IV and V—p <.001). It also shows that among Protestant households, social class makes a statistically significant difference as to size of household (p <.001), and that the same is true for Catholic households (p <.001). We may conclude, therefore, that *both* religious affiliation *and* social class are related as causal factors, or functions, or both, to the size of households.

Table 22.　Number in households by religious affiliation of family

	Religious Affiliation										
	Protestant (N. 1,032)		Roman Catholic (N. 1,879)		Jewish (N. 328)		Mixed (N. 264)		Other Religious Groups, None and Unknown (N. 56)		Total all Households (N. 3,559)	
Number in Household	No.	Per Cent	No.	Per Cent	No.	Per Cent	No.	Per Cent	No.	Per Cent	No.	Per Cent
1	120	11.6	86	4.6	17	5.2	14	5.3	2	3.6	239	6.7
2	340	32.9	408	21.7	99	30.2	61	23.1	29	51.8	937	26.3
3	219	21.2	451	24.0	98	29.9	70	26.5	12	21.4	850	23.9
4	192	18.6	484	25.8	82	25.0	64	24.2	8	14.3	830	23.3
5	105	10.2	275	14.6	26	7.9	39	14.8	2	3.6	447	12.6
6	32	3.1	105	5.6	4	1.2	11	4.2	1	1.8	153	4.3
7 or more	24	2.4	70	3.7	2	0.6	5	1.9	2	3.6	103	2.9
Median		3.26		3.99		3.49		3.82		2.90		3.71

CHAPTER 3

The Protestant Churches
of New Haven

The central function of the evangelical churches is communication. The churches exist to communicate a belief—a Gospel—and their entire life presumably is built around the concept of transmitting this belief. The lines of communication are multiple: from God to man, from one generation to the next, from the better educated (in religion) to the less educated, from the more experienced (in religion) to the less experienced, from the in-group to the out-group. The pulpit and the church school class are the two major symbols of this central function.

It is true enough, of course, that the church has other functions—notably worship—that cannot be delimited by the concept of "communication." It is equally true that like other social institutions the church can gradually shift its attention so far from evangelical activity that the mechanisms for communication (preaching, teaching, "testimony," et cetera) become formal and routine, and the life of the church seems to be focused on the preservation of a social group and an institution rather than on the communication of a message and a faith. Still, the Christian community is distinctively an evangelizing, testifying, *communicating* group in its genesis and genius, and it is this function we are concerned with here.

Radio and television when employed by the churches are generally interpreted in terms of their communicating function. The rationale for use of these media is almost invariably that they extend the range of the church's normal work; that they enable the church to talk to and motivate people whom the church and its workers cannot reach more directly. They are, in other words, simply an extension of the normal program of the churches, and in the final analysis they are to perform the function, directly or indirectly, of bringing the Christian message to listeners and leading these

49

listeners into active church participation or tying them more closely to churches to which they are already related.

If this be the case, it is necessary to examine the churches which form the institutional context for New Haven religious broadcasting, and to determine the functional relationship between the physical church in being and the church on the air. What are these churches like, of which religious broadcasting is an extended arm? The report on them, encompassed in this chapter, is based on visits to churches, detailed interviews with pastors and church leaders and examination of church records, supplemented by data concerning religious affiliation and attendance from the 5 per cent sample census of households.

Religious Groups and Church Membership

Chapter 2 (Table 2) shows the distribution of New Haven households by general religious affiliation or background, as revealed by the population sample. With the information in the sample as our basis, we can estimate the distribution of all *individuals* in the metropolitan New Haven population by religious affiliation or background as follows:

Total Population	250,000
Roman Catholic	150,000
Protestant[1]	74,500
Jewish	21,750
Other and none	3,250

These are religious "populations," and not actual membership counts. The organized institutions of religion in no case reach all the people of a given religious tradition. The Protestant churches reported an actual constituency (all participants in church and subsidiary organizations) of 46,713 persons, or 62.7 per cent of the "Protestant population" listed above. The Roman Catholic parishes indicated a baptized membership of 128,995, or 85.7 per cent of the "Roman Catholic population."

Number and Membership of Protestant Churches

There were 102 Protestant churches in metropolitan New Haven[2] at the time of the study. These churches had a resident membership of 37,721; 50.6 per cent of the "potential" of 74,500 and 15.1 per cent of the total population of 250,000. The resident constituency (members plus actively related nonmembers) totaled 18.7 per cent of the population (see Table 23).

---

[1] Includes Eastern Orthodox.
[2] As compared with 31 Roman Catholic parishes and 14 Jewish synagogues.

Fewer than one out of five persons in metropolitan New Haven were actively related to a Protestant church.

If the Protestant population is divided by the number of churches, there was one Protestant church for every 730 persons. Excluding the churches of denominations not related to the National Council of Churches, there was one church to every 950–1,000 available persons.[3]

Size of Churches

The average size of New Haven Protestant churches was 376 members and the median membership was 262. There are no universally accepted standards as to what is the optimum size of a city church. Obviously, the concept of optimum size is related to what is expected of a church in program, budget, staff and the maintenance of personal relationships among the members and their leaders. There is some consensus among city church research specialists that an urban church should have between 500 and 1,000 members to maintain an adequate staff and building, and to assure groups of various age, sex and interest levels of sufficient size to conduct a significant program.

New Haven Protestantism appeared to be in an overly competitive situation. Of the 102 churches, 56, or 54.4 per cent, reported fewer than 300 members. The average church size was brought up to 376 only by the existence of a few large churches. New Haven Protestantism thus finds itself with the average church, and certainly the median church, smaller than those found in other cities that have been studied. There is a consequent limitation upon the effectiveness of program and leadership in an urban situation where there is strong competition for the time and attention of the lay person.[4]

Location of Churches

Roman Catholic churches in general are organized around the concept of the parish—a fixed geographical area which a given church serves regardless of what population groups move into or out of it. Protestant churches, on the other hand, have been more inclined to relate themselves to social groups. As social groups in the city tend to be not only selective but mobile,

[3] Standards currently used by the National Council of Churches suggest that a community is adequately churched where there is one Protestant church per 2,000 to 4,000 available population.

[4] See H. Paul Douglass, "Some Protestant Churches in Urban America," *Information Service*, Federal Council of Churches, Jan. 21, 1950.

the Protestant churches often find themselves in the dilemma of having geographically fixed institutions and mobile constituencies.

In New Haven, as in most other cities, the older and larger Protestant churches tended to locate downtown and on the major thoroughfares; but the constituencies they served and serve have tended to be in the forefront of the movement of population to the suburbs. The homes left behind by these constituents have been occupied by non-Protestant families, by Protestant families of other denominations, and most recently by Negro immigrants. None of these groups comes readily into the older, established churches—for a variety of reasons, including differing cultural patterns and social distance. These churches, therefore, put a great deal of effort into "holding" the families who now live at a considerable distance. Ultimately these families tend to transfer to a neighborhood church (or to become inactive) and these outlying churches grow into stronger institutions, reflecting the strength of Protestantism in their local parishes. In New Haven, however, this process of development of outlying neighborhood Protestant churches has not as yet gone very far. While Protestants (except Negro Protestants) have moved out of the city proper in large numbers, many have kept their memberships (as reflected in size of church membership) in the central churches.

This distribution of church members needs to be discussed in relation to our basic question concerning communication. The program of the Protestant church is based on the assumption, by and large, that it does its work *within* the building. Except for pastoral visits, which are likely to be little more than annual events, and for literature, which is not always read, the constituent comes to the church rather than having the church come to him. The problems created by population mobility, then, are a real threat to the effectiveness of church program. A widely dispersed constituency is not easy to communicate with when the major mechanisms for communication are fixed at one spot in a city. It is not accidental, therefore, that in New Haven, as well as in other cities, the pastors of the "downtown" churches are more likely to be interested in the broadcasting media than are the pastors in outlying, more compact neighborhood parishes.

We may make a note here also, to return to in a later chapter, that in a population characterized by such rapid mobility as the urban American population, the mass media are in a uniquely favorable position to communicate directly with families where the normal contacts with a church have been weakened or severed.

Denominational Composition

Table 23 shows that Protestant strength is concentrated in two denominations, Congregational Christian and Protestant Episcopal.

Table 23. Churches by denomination, membership and average size

Denomination	No. of Churches	Resident Members	Per Cent of Total Membership	Constituents	Per Cent of Total Constituents	Average Church Size
Congregational	24	11,875	31.5	15,157	32.5	495
Episcopal	18	11,114	29.5	13,367	28.6	617
Methodist	11	3,488	9.2	4,284	9.2	318
Lutheran	6	2,922	7.7	3,457	7.4	487
Baptist	9	2,527	6.7	3,153	6.7	209
Other National Council member denominations [a]	7	2,403	6.4	2,716	5.8	343
Other denominations, not National Council members [b]	20	2,797	7.4	3,733	8.0	155
Pentecostal [c]	7	595	1.6	846	1.8	85
Total all churches	102	37,721	100.0	46,713	100.0	376

[a] This grouping, used for convenience in analysis, includes churches whose denominations are members of the National Council of Churches, but which are represented in New Haven by only one or two churches. The seven local churches in this classification are Presbyterian U. S. A., Friends, A. M. E. Zion (2), Greek Orthodox, Russian Orthodox and the Oak Street Parish (Interdenominational).

[b] The twenty churches in this classification, also grouped thus for convenience in analysis, include independent churches and denominations which have not joined the National Council of Churches. Again, only one or two churches are represented in any denominational grouping.

[c] Pentecostal churches include all types. None is affiliated with the National Council of Churches or the New Haven Council of Churches.

It is interesting to compare the reports from the churches with the results of the sample census. We may roughly estimate the "constituency" of the major denominations from information reported in the sample census. Table 24 shows the results for the five leading denominations.

This comparison, while based on somewhat rough estimates, is important. Apparently there are more than 15,000 people in New Haven who consider themselves to be related to these five denominations alone—at least sufficiently so that household heads will so inform an interviewer—and yet they are not on the records of any church of these denominations as members of the church or its subsidiary organizations. The largest group are nominally

Congregationalists, which is to be expected in a region where Congregationalism has for three centuries been predominant in Protestantism. But the second largest group are Baptists, and if these data are accurate, they indicate Baptists are third rather than fifth in nominal strength in the New Haven population.

TABLE 24. Constituency reported by churches compared to constituency found through sample

Denomination	Total Constituency		Excess of Sample over Church Reports
	Reported by Churches	Estimated from Sample	
Congregational	15,157	20,800	5,643
Episcopal	12,367	14,700	2,333
Methodist	4,284	6,380	2,096
Lutheran	3,457	5,180	1,723
Baptist	3,153	6,760	3,607

Racial data were not gathered in the sample, so we can only advance the hypothesis that many of these Baptists would be Negro, among whom nominal Baptist adherence is a cultural pattern stronger than nominal Congregational adherence is among New England whites. But the ratio of "unchurched Baptists" to "churched Baptists" is more than one to one, while the comparable Congregational ratio is only one to three and the Episcopal ratio about one to five. Kenneth D. Miller, executive director of the New York City Mission Society, gives this explanation: "Negroes are supposed to be incurably religious, but the city seems to do a good job of curing them of their religion."

There is wide difference among the denominations as to average size of church, as may be seen from Table 23 and Figure 8. The Congregational Christian, Protestant Episcopal and Lutheran communions show less tendency to have their total membership divided into small units. These denominations come closest to fulfilling the size requirements for successful operation of city churches. It will be recalled from Chapter 1 that the Congregational Christian and Protestant Episcopal are the churches of the older Yankee group, longest established and economically most prosperous. The Lutheran churches, with their German and Scandinavian memberships, represent the later immigrant groups who rank highest socially and economically.

The Congregational Christian and Protestant Episcopal communions, with two out of five churches, together claim three out of every five Protestant constituents (Figure 9). The five leading denominations have 85 per cent of all Protestant constituents. The denominations which are members of the National Council of Churches together account for 91.2 per cent of the Protestant constituency. (In the country as a whole, the National Council denominations represent about two-thirds of Protestantism.) Since these same churches constitute the membership of the New Haven Council of Churches, they form a remarkably strong potential base for co-operative planning and effort in New Haven. This situation is especially important for effective use of television and radio by the churches, as available air time is limited and station managers are usually more receptive to programs representative of all Protestant churches than to those which are denominationally competitive. New Haven has the instrument for such co-operative programming in the Council of Churches. How this opportunity is used in practice is discussed in later chapters.

FIGURE 8. Membership of Protestant churches, by denomination

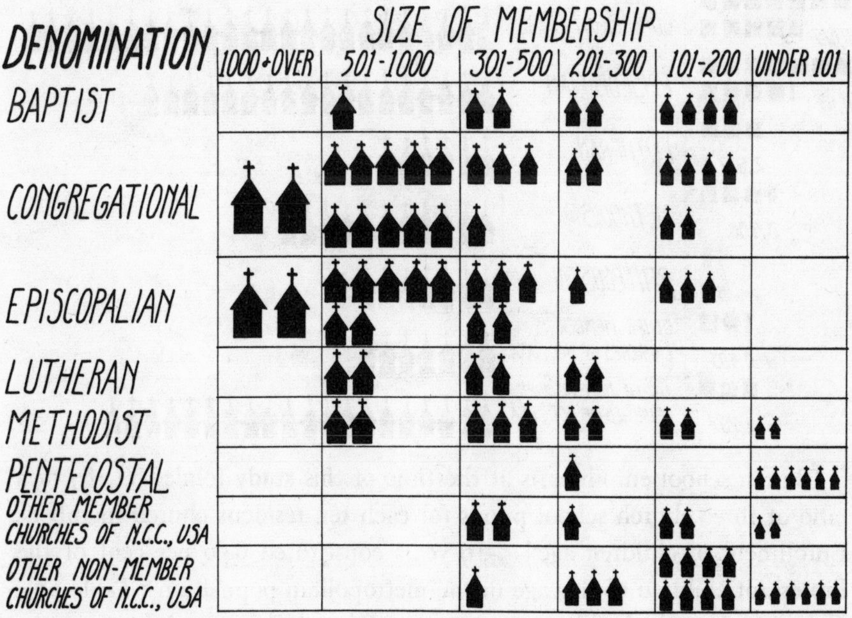

DENOMINATION	SIZE OF MEMBERSHIP					
	1000 + OVER	501-1000	301-500	201-300	101-200	UNDER 101
BAPTIST		⛪	⛪⛪	⛪⛪	⛪⛪⛪⛪	
CONGREGATIONAL	⛪⛪	⛪⛪⛪⛪⛪⛪ ⛪⛪⛪⛪⛪	⛪⛪⛪ ⛪	⛪⛪	⛪⛪⛪⛪ ⛪⛪	
EPISCOPALIAN	⛪⛪	⛪⛪⛪⛪⛪⛪ ⛪⛪	⛪⛪⛪		⛪⛪⛪	
LUTHERAN		⛪⛪	⛪⛪	⛪⛪		
METHODIST		⛪⛪	⛪⛪	⛪⛪	⛪⛪	⛪⛪
PENTECOSTAL				⛪		⛪⛪⛪⛪⛪⛪
OTHER MEMBER CHURCHES OF N.C.C., USA			⛪⛪	⛪	⛪⛪	⛪⛪
OTHER NON-MEMBER CHURCHES OF N.C.C., USA			⛪	⛪⛪⛪	⛪⛪⛪⛪	⛪⛪⛪⛪⛪⛪

Sex of Church Members

The Protestant churches report their resident membership to be 55 per cent women and 45 per cent men. (The population of metropolitan New Haven is 52.1 per cent female, 47.9 per cent male.) Of the major denominations, Methodists and Baptists have the highest percentage of women (61.3 per cent and 62.0 per cent), and Lutherans and Congregationalists the lowest (52.1 per cent and 52.8 per cent).

The Church Schools

All of the New Haven churches consider their church schools to be the major educational arm of their ministry. Ninety-nine of the 102 churches conduct Sunday church schools, while the remaining three unite in a common school.[5] There is no released time religious education in New Haven; but it is common practice for two or more churches to unite in conducting a summer vacation church school, usually of two weeks' duration.

FIGURE 9. Distribution of churches and members, by denomination

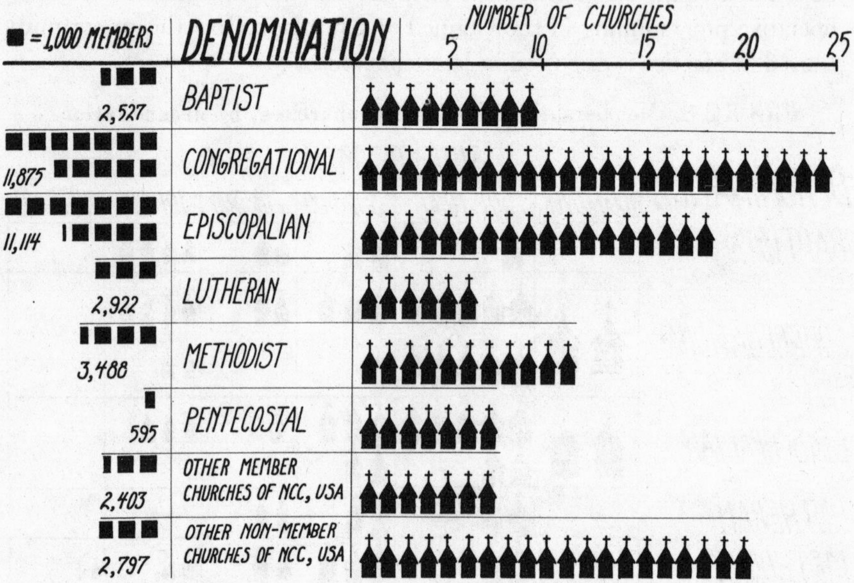

Church school enrollments at the time of this study totaled 11,187 or a ratio of three church school pupils for each ten resident church members. Enrollment of children aged 5–19 years constituted 64.0 per cent of the Protestant children of this age in the metropolitan population (Table 25). This ratio compared with 51.9 per cent of Roman Catholic children receiving religious instruction through their churches.

[5] The program of the church school in New Haven and its effectiveness will not be discussed in this text. However, the Communications Research Project conducted two major studies in the New Haven church schools, dealing with use of motion pictures and other audio-visuals, teacher training, teaching methods, effectiveness of curriculum and rates of student learning. See Everett Parker, J. J. Stein, Paul Vieth and Edith Welker, *Film Use in the Church* (New York: National Council of Churches, 1955).

Church schools in New Haven are not large. Only two of the 100 schools had enrollments over 300, and only nine more had enrollments of between 200 and 300. Attendance is as important as enrollment in evaluating church schools. Attendance of junior department children (fourth, fifth and sixth grades) averaged 10.43 out of 13 Sundays in the last quarter of 1952; and 9.4 out of 13 Sundays in the first quarter of 1953 in 15 schools studied in detail.

TABLE 25. Age groupings of church school children and Protestant children in the population

| Age Group | Protestant Children in Population a | Church School Enrollment | | |
		Per Cent of this Age Group Enrolled in Church School	No.	Per Cent of Total Church School Enrollment
Total 0–19 years	18,980	54.1	10,280	91.8
Under 5 years	5,380	29.3	1,576	14.1
5–14 years	11,120	67.6	7,516	67.2
15–19 years	2,480	47.9	1,188	10.5
20 years and over			907	8.2

a Based on 5 per cent sample.

Church schools are largely an enterprise for children, secondarily for young people, only incidentally for adults. The primary and junior age groups appear to be well covered by the type of religious education offered in the church school. This situation is especially true for the Congregational Christian and Protestant Episcopal denominations which have the bulk of church-school enrollments (55.7 per cent [Table 26]).

The failure to hold young people in the church schools, as indicated in Table 26, is all the more striking in view of the enrollment of children. Young people's groups are conducted in most of the churches, and apparently have tended to replace the church school for the 15–19 year olds.

RECRUITMENT OF CHURCH SCHOOL PUPILS

The churches depend upon the church school as a source for adult members, since one of the aims of the educational program is to train the child for active adult participation in the church. If the New Haven church schools were the only source from which to recruit new church members (which of course they are not), then the churches, to maintain existing membership levels, would need to be educating 27.4 children aged 5–14 years for every 100 members on the church rolls.[6] Actually the Protestant churches in New Haven have only 19.9 children in this age group for every 100 members (Table 27).

TABLE 26.   Percentage distribution of church school pupils by denomination and age

| Denomination | No. of Pupils | Per Cent of Total Church School Enrollment | Percentage Distribution of Pupils by Age | | | |
			0-4	5-14	15-19	20 and over
Congregational Christian	3,620	32.4	16.0	74.0	8.0	2.0
Protestant Episcopal	2,652	23.7	12.7	72.3	11.5	3.5
Baptist	1,025	9.2	11.5	49.5	11.0	28.0
Methodist	1,021	9.1	14.6	63.4	9.7	12.3
Lutheran	713	6.4	14.3	74.7	5.3	5.7
Other National Council member denominations	378	3.4	10.5	72.0	9.5	8.0
Other denominations not National Council members	1,348	12.0	13.4	56.0	19.4	11.2
Pentecostal	430	3.8	11.2	47.2	12.3	29.3
Total	11,187	100.0	14.1	67.2	10.5	8.2

The denominations not constituent to the National Council of Churches are evidently reaching a noticeably larger proportion of children relative to their adult membership than are National Council denominations.

The majority of the Protestant churches have no consistent, working plan for recruiting new pupils for the church school. Neither has a city-wide strategy been developed to bring religious education to the more than 7,000 children of Protestant background aged 5–14 years who are not enrolled in church schools.

Television in Christian Education

For two years, the Project staff produced weekly experimental television programs for direct Christian education of children and to put churches in touch with children who were not registered in church school. The pro-

[6] Based on the theoretically normal age distribution of a stable population group.

grams were conducted by Edith F. Welker. They were aimed at fourth, fifth
and sixth graders. Subject matter was drawn from standard church school
curricula. Successive series of programs dealt with home missions, foreign
missions, Advent and the meaning of Christmas, Lent and the meaning of
Easter, God and Nature. They bore titles such as "Adventures in Africa"
and "Adventures at Christmas."

TABLE 27. Church school enrollments and ratios to membership

Denomination	Church School Pupils	Ratio to 100 Church Members	Ratio of Pupils Aged 5-14 Years to 100 Church Members
Replacement ratio			27.4
Congregational Christian	3,620	30.4	22.5
Protestant Episcopal	2,652	23.8	17.2
Baptist	1,025	40.5	20.0
Methodist	1,021	29.2	18.5
Lutheran	713	24.3	18.2
Other National Council member denominations	378	15.4	11.3
Other denominations, not National Council members	1,348	48.1	27.1
Pentecostal	430	72.2	34.1
Total all denominations	11,187	31.5	19.9

Each program consisted of three parts: direct teaching of subject matter,
demonstrations by the leader and children of how to make and do things,
worship. Motion pictures, still photographs, drawings, diagrams, models, exhibits and demonstrations were used regularly for visual interest. Textbooks
were sold to viewers. Children in the audience participated in projects, such
as visits to places studied (a migrant camp, a children's hospital, a store-
front church and parish); making drawings and other art works and writing
essays for presentation on the air; collecting clothes for migrant children
and filling "friend kits" to send to children in Africa.

Audience response to these programs, as indicated in textbook sale and
participation in projects, was excellent. It is certain that more than 3,000
children regularly watched the series, which was broadcast over Station

WNHC-TV, New Haven. The names of more than 1,000 children without church school affiliation were sent to local churches in the station's viewing area; but we have no indication that any of the churches called in these homes for purposes of recruitment.

Church Budgets

Seventy-two of the 102 churches prepared budget analyses for the study, and 20 others reported their total budgets. The remaining churches do not operate on a budget.

Expenses of the 72 churches for a year totaled $1,118,789 (Table 28).

TABLE 28. Distribution of budget expenditures, 72 reporting churches

Expense Item	Total Expenditures	Per Cent of Budget
Salaries	416,530	37.2
Program	153,102	13.7
Building construction and repair	172,327	15.4
Building maintenance	212,573	19.0
Benevolences	164,257	14.7
Total expenditures	$1,118,789	100.0

Figure 10 shows the share of the total funds available which went to each denomination and how the churches of each communion used their budgeted funds. In the aggregate, one dollar out of seven went to benevolences, and one out of three to building and maintenance. The remaining half (50.8 per cent) of the money went to maintain the program of the church, and of this money three dollars out of every four went into salaries. Thus one dollar in eight is available for general program expense other than salaries. Figure 10 shows that the major denominations paralleled one another rather closely in their proportionate spending. Here is indication of a generally accepted pattern for the allocation of local church funds. None of the churches budgeted for use of radio and television either alone or through a contribution for that purpose to the New Haven Council of Churches. Only a handful of churches provided a small allowance for purchase or rental of motion pictures and other audio-visual materials.

There was great variation among the 92 total budgets reported. Twenty-three churches had budgets of over $20,000, while 17 had budgets of under $5,000. The typical budget was between $10,000 and $15,000, but 43 churches (47 per cent) had budgets under $10,000.

FIGURE 10. Share of total church budgets and percentage distribution of expenses, by denomination

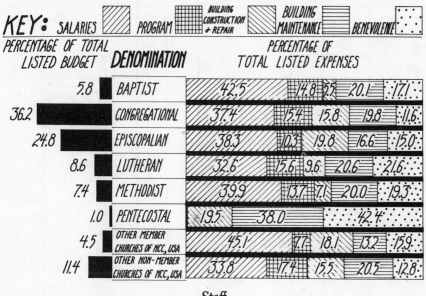

Staff

Size of staff was directly related to size of budget. Of the 102 churches, 58 were one-man institutions; that is, 58 churches had the full-time services of only one professional person. Six churches had only a part-time pastor. Only 24 churches had two or more full-time professional staff members, or their equivalent in part-time staff. In most of the churches, there was little possibility of having specialized staff for specialized duties; the minister had to be a jack-of-all-trades (Figure 11).

The total full-time professional staff in the 102 churches numbered 154, or one staff person to 304 constituents. There were 383 other part-time, paid staff persons, of whom 185 were paid choir members. If we eliminate the singers, the part-time staff gave an amount of time equivalent to 41 additional full-time staff persons. Full-time and part-time staff added together gave the equivalent of one staff person for 240 constituents.

This situation imposes a heavy work load on the paid staff, if the constituency expects personal services from the paid personnel. Interviews with lay people show that many expect such service. Moreover, the lay members tend to look to the professional staff to furnish personal leadership for a majority of the organizations and services of the church. They also expect

FIGURE 11. Distribution of metropolitan New Haven churches according to number of paid program persons on staff

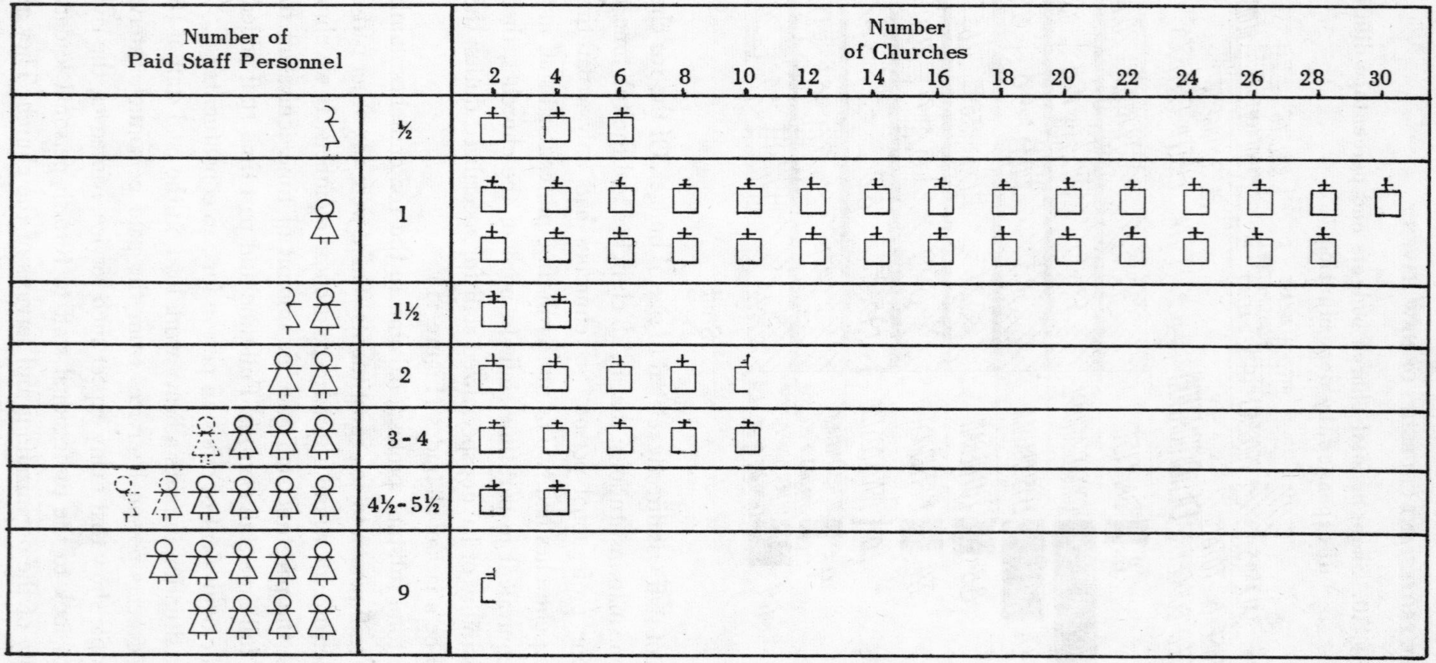

Number of Churches

Number of Paid Staff Personnel	2	4	6	8	10	12	14	16	18	20	22	24	26	28	30
½															
1															
1½															
2															
3 - 4															
4½ - 5½															
9															

the professionals to be experts in such fields as church administration, business management, curriculum for education, counseling, television and radio, and procurement and use of audio-visuals. Cultivation of new members, as will be shown later, also falls squarely upon the shoulders of the ministers.

TABLE 29.   Employed professional staff in metropolitan New Haven churches by type of job and amount of time

Job Category	Full Time	Number of Staff Persons Half Time or More	Less than Half Time	Total
Pastors	100	9	17	126
Assistant or associate pastors	7	4	11	22
Directors of religious education	5	3	8	16
Organists, choir directors, directors of music	6	7	80	93
Church visitors	6		3	9
Secretaries	18	7	22	47
Youth group advisors	6	3	17	26
Paid choir members			185	185
Miscellaneous	6	1	6	13
Total	154	34	349	537

The proportional distribution of salary paid to professional staff within the denominations is indicated in Figure 12.

Program and Attendance

REGULAR CHURCH ACTIVITIES

In the average month, according to the churches, there was a total attendance at all regularly scheduled church activities of 137,263. (This is a gross figure, as are all attendance records quoted. It does not mean unduplicated attendance by 137,263 persons. For example, a member who attended worship services four times in a month, church school four times, and choir practice four times was counted twelve times in monthly attendance figures. Duplication of individuals was the rule, rather than the exception, since most members attended more than one function at the church in a typical month.) One-half of the total attendance (50.4 per cent) was at worship service, one-fifth (19.9 per cent) at church school, one-eighth (12.1 per cent) at children's and young people's groups and the remainder mostly at women's and mixed adult groups (Figure 13).

A clearer picture of program activities may be had from studying weekly attendance figures. On the average Sunday, 17,649 persons worship in the Protestant churches of metropolitan New Haven. Two of every nine "Protestants," or one of every fourteen residents of metropolitan New Haven attend the service of divine worship in the Protestant churches.

FIGURE 12. Denominational salary payments in proportion to total professional staff

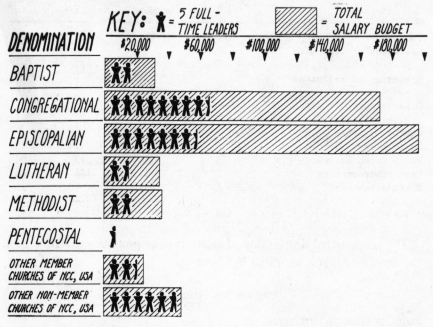

From the point of view of communication, we underline the fact that the Protestant pulpit speaks weekly to only one in fourteen of the people of New Haven.

The church schools drew about half as many persons as did worship services. On the average Sunday, 8,244 people, mostly children, attended.

Speaking again from the standpoint of communication, it must be emphasized that each week only one person in ten of the Protestant population, or one person in 31 in metropolitan New Haven, receives religious instruction in the church schools. The majority of the New Haven church schools are closed during the summer months from mid-June to mid-September.

All other regularly scheduled church activities combined had an average weekly attendance of 8,424 persons, just about equal to that of the church schools.

The grand total of average weekly attendance at all regularly scheduled activities, therefore, was 34,317. Even if this attendance represented separate individuals, they would total less than one-half of the Protestant population, or about one-seventh of the metropolitan New Haven population. Actually, of course, duplication makes the number of individuals who participated much lower.

SIZE AND COMPOSITION OF GROUPS

The church schools comprised 900 individual classes, the typical size being eleven to twelve pupils. There were 743 other church groups and organizations meeting regularly on a weekly, bi-weekly or monthly basis with an average attendance of seventeen persons.

FIGURE 13. Percentage distribution of monthly attendance at church functions

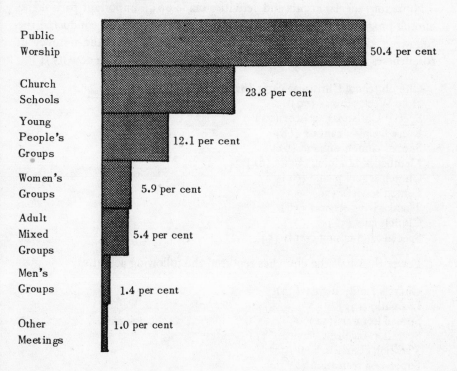

Public Worship — 50.4 per cent

Church Schools — 23.8 per cent

Young People's Groups — 12.1 per cent

Women's Groups — 5.9 per cent

Adult Mixed Groups — 5.4 per cent

Men's Groups — 1.4 per cent

Other Meetings — 1.0 per cent

Aside from the worship services, *the organized church life of Protestant New Haven is built around small groups rather than mass activities.* In the average month, there are 2,007 meetings of such groups in addition to church school class sessions. Table 30 lists the small-group organizations most often found, together with frequency of meetings. Only groups that meet on an interest basis are included; thus official boards, trustees and other official bodies are omitted.

TABLE 30. Average size and meeting frequency of regularly scheduled church interest groups

Type of Group	Total Number	Meetings Per Month	Average Attendance
Women's organizations	267	411	20
Children and young people	257	968	14
Mixed adult (mostly choirs)	140	413	19
Men's organizations	52	116	14
Miscellaneous	27	99	27

SPECIAL EVENTS

Numerous special events and activities made up an important part of the church program. More than half the churches reported they conducted the following kinds of activities in the church year studied (the number in parentheses indicates the number of churches reporting each activity):

Church school Christmas party (82)
Holy Week services (79)
Special Christmas services (71)
Every member canvass (68)
Special church dinners (62)
Membership training classes (61)
Church school picnic (61)
Lenten services (59)
Thanksgiving services (58)
Church fairs (56)
Special fund-raising events (54)

Fewer than half the churches reported the following activities:

Church family nights (35)
Dramatics (32)
Special lecturers (32)
Special evangelistic services (31)
Vacation church school (30)
Supervised recreation (27)

Forums or public meetings on contemporary issues (22)
Special mission study classes (14)
Miscellaneous activities (Holy Day services, rummage sales, dances, recitals, prayer groups, group trips) (52)

No accurate records were available of attendance at these special affairs.

Sources of New Membership

The churches exist to "proclaim a Gospel." Almost the only available measures of their effectiveness in performing this function are the statistics on accessions or losses of members.

There are three sources of local church membership. The first source is individuals who, moving to a new community, bring their letters of membership from their former churches and join churches near their new homes. The second source is children from the local congregation who reach the age when they may be confirmed into adult church membership. The third source is persons, with or without religious training, who may be persuaded to join a local church. It is to these latter persons, the "strangers," that the "evangelistic" program of the church is directed, and these people are peculiarly the concern of agencies interested in the religious use of the mass media of communication.

We have already noted that were the church schools the only source of adult church members, the New Haven Protestant churches would need to be training 10,200 children aged 5–14 years as potential new members to maintain their present membership enrollment. Actually there are fewer than three-fourths of this number in the church schools—a "shortage" of 2,700. The children necessary to make up this shortage are available to the churches in New Haven families of Protestant background who have no local church affiliation. Evidently a problem exists in effective communication between the churches and these children and their families.

The churches are also training adult recruits and baptizing them, confirming them and receiving them into full membership. They are all processes by which "new" members are brought into the church, as distinct from people who have been church members elsewhere and are received as members in New Haven churches by letters of transfer. The studies of H. C. Webber[7] have examined the matter of the ratio of "new" members

[7] H. C. Webber, *Evangelism, A Graphic Survey*. Webber studied the membership records of the major denominations over a period of fifty to one hundred years. He concluded that the average church in the United States should be receiving 5.6 "new" members each year for each 100 old members, if it were to maintain its membership and keep pace with the country's population growth.

received each year through baptism, confirmation and confession of faith to old members already on the roll, which Webber terms the "evangelistic index." He proposes after studying denominational records over several decades that the "norm" for the evangelistic index should be 5.6 new members each year per 100 old members. Few Protestant churches of New Haven measured up to this recruitment standard in the year studied.

Table 31 Recruitment of "new" members, by denominations

Denomination	New Members Received by Baptism, Confirmation, or Profession of Faith [a]	Evangelistic Index
Congregational Christian	391	2.7
Protestant Episcopal	450	3.8
Methodist	88	2.2
Lutheran	83	2.7
Baptist	78	2.7
Other National Council member denominations	20	1.2
Other denominations, not National Council members	378	19.6
Pentecostal	65	10.6
Total all denominations	1,553	3.9

[a] Of the 1,553 new members received, 363, or 23 per cent, were reported to be former Roman Catholics.

When one considers the number of unchurched persons in metropolitan New Haven, this record of recruitment of "new" church members is not impressive. The member denominations of the National Council show up poorly in relation to the nonmember denominations as regards their evangelistic activity. None of the major denominations came up to the recommended evangelistic index of 5.6. Of the denominations having three or more churches in metropolitan New Haven, only the Pentecostals exceeded the recommended ratio.

Rather than relying upon the church school and adult envangelism as methods of recruiting new members, the Protestant churches seem to have depended for their growth on processes of seeking out newcomers to town, or to their particular communities, and persuading them to transfer their church membership letters to a local church. Of 92 churches reporting on their methods of reaching strangers, 67 have systems for indentifying visitors to church services and inviting them into active participation. Twenty-five churches indicated they had done door-to-door canvassing in the past year.

The churches recognize their obligation to reach out to unchurched persons. Seventy-seven churches reported a total of 2,055 calls per month on nonmembers. The ministers made 71 per cent of these calls. Not all calls were on unchurched families; some calls were made on newcomers seeking local church affiliation. Of the leading denominations, Lutheran churches averaged 41 calls per month on nonmembers, Baptist 29, Protestant Episcopal 24, Congregational Christian 22 and Methodist 19.

It is not likely that with the limited professional staff available to the New Haven churches and the lack of tradition for vigorous lay evangelism the near future will see an increase in personal calling aimed at persuading unchurched families and people to come to church. Here is a point at which television and radio could be of service to the churches in performance of their regular function, by enabling representatives of the Church to speak directly to people with whom they would not normally come into contact.

CHAPTER 4

The "Unchurched"

Chapter 3 constituted a summary of the reports the *churches* of New Haven made about themselves. This chapter endeavors to summarize statistically what the *people* of New Haven said about their relationship to the churches, and particularly who the people were who claimed no church relationship.

We do not deal here with attitudes and opinions, which come in a later section, but with the statistical patterns that emerged from the answers to the question, "What church do you attend?" asked in the sample census. The concern here, as in preceding chapters, is to establish statistical base lines against which to interpret subsequent data on radio and television audiences.

The category here called "church attendance" or "church-relatedness" was developed to designate a relationship to a local church. In interviewing families in the sample, canvassers asked the question, "What church do you attend?" If the respondent was able to name a specific New Haven church, he was counted as attending that church. If his answer was vague —"Protestant," "the church on Whitney Avenue," etc.—or if the church he named was not in the New Haven area, or if he said he did not attend church, he was placed in a nonattending category. This information was secured for the husband (or male head of household) and wife (or female head of household) in each case. The answers, it is obvious, do not refer to frequency of attendance nor even to recent attendance. As nearly as can be determined from the replies, the question meant this to most respondents: "If you ever go to church, or if you should go to church, what church would you go to?" Respondents who had already identified themselves by religious tradition (Protestant, Roman Catholic, Jewish) were now identifying themselves in relation to a specific New Haven church.

Conversely, people who said "none," or did not specify a local church, appeared to be those who felt no such local identification.

This kind of question, which assumed a church relationship as normative (as compared, for example, with this question: "Do you attend church?"), influences the respondent to give a positive answer, and the result inevitably is a set of answers biased in favor of church-relatedness. This bias was considered to be desirable from the standpoint of this study, because the basic data sought here concerned self-identification in religious terms.

At the same time, the data which follow must not be confused with empirical findings on physical attendance at church, nor even with "constituency" as the churches themselves define it. If responses to this question were to be taken as trustworthy data on church affiliation, then 89 per cent of the New Haven population, or about 222,500 persons, "attend" church. It has already been pointed out (Chapter 3) that Protestant and Catholic churches together *claim* only 175,708 constituents, with at most 15,000 to 18,000 Jews in any kind of constituent relationship to synagogues and temples. It is scarcely conceivable that there are over 30,000 persons in New Haven who "attend" churches of whom the churches themselves have no record. It is conceivable, however, that there are that many who through past association, history, family relationships, or other more or less vague connection have in their own minds identified themselves with certain institutions of religion, or will do so for whatever obscure satisfactions or self-conceptions are involved in the curiously complex process of answering an interviewer's simple question: "What church do you attend?"

Whatever this question measured, therefore, we must consider it to be more in the nature of attitudes than of behavior, and we shall give it the name of "church-relatedness" in the analysis of these data.

Individual Patterns of Church-Relatedness

In the total sample, 12.8 per cent of all male household heads and 8.7 per cent of all wives or female household heads were, by this definition, not "church-related" (Table 32).

TABLE 32. Percentage distribution by religious affiliation of male heads of households and wives or female heads of households not related to local churches

Religious Group	Male Heads of Households	Wives or Female Heads of Households
Protestant	18.8	12.7
Roman Catholic	6.0	3.5
Jewish	18.2	17.6
Other or none	79.3	55.6
Total	12.8	8.7

Table 32 shows that Roman Catholics, particularly Roman Catholic women, reported much more church-relatedness than did either Protestants or Jews. Jewish and Protestant households had the lowest percentage of church-relatedness of the three groups among men, and Jewish households among women, with Protestants close behind.

Table 33 shows that church-relatedness seems to be significantly related to social class.

Table 33. Percentage of nonchurch-related men and women, by social class and religion

A. *Male Heads of Households Related to No Church As a Percentage of Male Heads of Households in Each Group*

Religious Affiliation [a]	Social Class					
	I (N. 100)	II (N. 280)	III (N. 664)	IV (N. 1,505)	V (N. 521)	Total (N. 3,070)
Protestant (N. 1,081)	25.0	22.9	14.3	19.3	19.6	18.8
Roman Catholic (N. 1,882)	15.4	6.3	4.1	6.3	5.9	6.0
Jewish (N. 330)	37.5	16.9	12.9	20.2	22.2	18.2
Other-None [b] (N.31)	b	b	b	b	b	79.3
Total (N. 3,324)	26.0	19.6	10.5	12.2	11.5	12.8

[a] Unknown omitted.
[b] Too few cases for significant computation.

B. *Wives and Female Heads of Households Related to No Church As a Percentage of All Wives and Female Heads of Households in Each Group*

Religious Affiliation [a]	Social Class					
	I (N. 110)	II (N. 313)	III (N. 737)	IV (N. 1,671)	V (N. 602)	Total (N. 3,433)
Protestant (N. 1,083)	23.5	15.7	10.9	11.5	12.1	12.7
Roman Catholic (N. 1,970)	8.3	6.6	2.6	3.5	3.3	3.5
Jewish (N. 330)	37.5	17.4	17.6	15.7	13.6	17.6
Other-None (N. 27)	b	b	b	b	b	55.6
Total (N. 3,433)	23.6	16.3	8.5	7.2	5.8	8.7

[a] Unknown omitted.
[b] Too few cases for significant computation.

However, when we test these data for statistical significance, using the chi square test, we find that the relationship between church-relatedness and social class varies among the major religious groups. For Protestant male household heads and Protestant wives or female household heads, the relationship is significant ($p. < .05 > .02$). For Catholic, Jewish, and mixed groups, male and female, however, the relationship is nonsignificant at the .05 level. In all major religious groups, social class I has the poorest "attendance" record, and social class III has the best record in every category except Jewish women. This finding supports a thesis that is expressed frequently—that churchgoing is a conventional behavior pattern and that the "middle class" (i.e., white collar, medium income) families tend to be conventional in behavior.

Other factors than social class and religion, however, proved to be significantly correlated with "church-relatedness." One of the clearest relationships is between church "attendance" and the number of persons in the household, which in turn, of course, generally reflects the presence or absence of children. Table 34 shows a clear correlation between size of household and church-relatedness.

TABLE 34. Church-relatedness of male household heads and of wives and female household heads, by number in household

No. of Persons in Household	No. of Households	Per Cent of Male Heads Related to No Church	Per Cent of Wives or Female Heads Related to No Church
1	239	39.7	13.5
2	937	16.0	12.1
3	850	13.4	8.5
4	830	9.8	6.8
5	447	9.6	4.8
6 or more	256	9.6	6.0
Total	3,559	12.8	8.7

Men who live alone, without wives, children or relatives, had by far the poorest record of church-relatedness; while fathers with two or more children at home seem to have had the best record among the men. The same pattern holds true for the women, except that more women than men were church-related in every type of household, particularly as far as women living alone are concerned.

Other factors assumed to be importantly linked to church-relatedness were education, occupation and age. Table 35 shows a striking correlation between educational level and nonchurch-relatedness for both men and women. Only a little over one-tenth of the total population reported no church relationship, but for college graduates the proportion without church relationship was one-fifth, and for those with graduate or professional training, it was one-third. Advanced education did not seem to be conducive to church-relatedness in New Haven.

TABLE 35. Education and church-relatedness of males and
          females

Highest Grade Completed by Husband and Wife[a]	Male Heads of Households			Wives or Female Heads of Households		
	Total No.	Related to No Church		Total No.	Related to No Church	
		No.	Per Cent		No.	Per Cent
Graduate school	142	39	27.5	48	21	43.8
College graduate	223	32	14.3	200	30	15.0
1-3 years college	203	20	9.9	238	21	8.8
High school graduate	798	83	10.4	1,139	93	8.2
10-11 years	310	32	10.3	346	19	5.5
7-9 years	843	116	13.8	984	81	8.2
Under 7 years	375	36	9.6	380	20	5.3
Education unknown	175	36	20.6	96	13	13.5
Total	3,069	394	12.8	3,434	298	8.7

[a] Or single male or female household head.

Occupational groupings follow the same pattern as education. Men in the higher business executive and professional occupations—which are usually associated with higher education—were least likely to be related to a local church (21.8 per cent nonrelated for higher executives and professionals, 18.7 per cent for lesser executives and professionals), and their wives had similar though slightly more frequent patterns of relationship (18.3 and 16.5 per cent nonrelated respectively). Only students had a higher ratio of nonrelationship (30.0 per cent). All other occupational groups were considerably higher in church relationships.

Age did not prove to be so important a factor in church relationship, except in showing that the youngest and oldest household heads reported somewhat less church relationship than those aged 40–60 years (Table 36). Other studies have shown that the middle years are the ones of greatest participation in community institutions and organizations such as churches.

Finally, it seemed likely that the *type of household* might have some bearing upon the church relationship of the heads of the households. Analysis of church-relatedness by type of household supported this hypothesis.

TABLE 36. Male heads of households and wives or female heads of households by age and church relationship

| Age of Husband or Wife[a] | Total No. | Male Heads of Households | | Wives or Female Heads of Households | | |
| | | Related to No Church | | Total No. | Related to No Church | |
		No.	Per Cent		No.	Per Cent
20-24	48	8	16.7	105	14	13.3
25-29	251	31	12.4	368	39	10.6
30-34	398	50	12.6	455	35	7.7
35-39	403	53	13.2	463	36	7.8
40-44	398	41	10.3	402	24	6.0
45-49	311	28	9.0	354	31	8.8
50-54	317	38	12.0	358	22	6.1
55-59	287	33	11.5	280	20	7.1
60-64	219	32	14.6	233	18	7.7
65-Over	350	52	14.9	362	51·	14.1
Unknown	85	26	30.6	50	8	16.0
Total cases	3,067	392	12.8	3,430	298	8.7

[a] Under 20 omitted.

The influence of the family situation upon church-relatedness is quite clear, especially in the case of the men. A stable marriage and the presence of minor children seem to be important factors that encourage identification with a church.

TABLE 37. Percentages of male heads of households and of wives or female heads of households not related to a local church, by type of household

| Type of Household | Per Cent Not Related to Church | |
	Male Heads	Wives or Female Heads
Households including husband, wife and minor children	9.9	6.5
Households including husband, wife and no minor children	14.5	12.2
Broken families with minor children	27.6	8.5
Adults living alone	39.0	13.5
Other adult combinations	26.7	9.7
Total	12.8	8.7

Family Patterns of Church-Relatedness

These findings led us to look into *family patterns* of church relationships as well as *individual patterns*. An analysis was made of the combined church relationship of husband and wife in each household. Table 38 shows the results, by social class of household.

TABLE 38.   Patterns of church-relatedness of husbands and
            wives, by social class of husband, in percentages

Pattern of Attendance	Households by Social Class (Per Cent)					
	I	II	III	IV	V	Total for Sample
Neither attends church	23.1	14.0	7.8	7.2	6.2	8.3
Both attend same church	57.2	62.7	68.9	69.7	64.5	67.6
Wife attends, husband does not	1.7	2.4	3.4	4.5	5.8	4.2
Husband attends, wife does not		1.5	1.1	1.0	1.0	1.0
Attend different churches, same faith	0.9	1.2	2.4	0.7	2.1	1.4
One attends Protestant, other Roman Catholic	0.9	1.8	3.2	2.7	0.8	2.3
One attends Jewish, other Christian				0.2		0.1
Widows, widowers, single, separated, divorced	16.2	16.4	13.2	14.0	19.6	15.1
Total	100.0	100.0	100.0	100.0	100.0	100.0

Two out of three households include a husband and wife who attend the same church. This pattern is most typical in social class IV, and least typical in social class I, although even in social class I it is characteristic in 57 per cent of the households. Households where neither husband nor wife attends church are most frequent in social class I, where they represent nearly one out of four households, and least frequent in social class V. Households where the wife attends and the husband does not, however, show the reverse pattern. They are least frequent in social class I and most frequent in social class V. Families where husbands and wives are related to different churches constitute only 3.7 per cent of all households.

Implications

The churches are vitally concerned to see that every person in every household is effectively related to an institution of religion. Most New Haven households seemed at least to consider themselves related to some such institution, even if the relationship in many cases was tenuous and infrequent. There is a hard core of nonchurch-related adults, however, and this section of the report has attempted to identify them according to a number of characteristics.

Table 39. Estimate of the total number of male heads of households and wives or female heads of households in metropolitan New Haven who do not attend church

	Male Heads of Households	Wives or Female Heads of Households
Total of Nonattending Persons	7,880	5,960
By Religious Background		
Protestant	3,600	2,760
Roman Catholic	2,080	1,380
Jewish	1,100	1,160
Other-None	1,100	620
By Education		
Graduate school	780	420
College graduate	640	600
1-3 years college	400	420
High school graduate	1,660	1,860
7-11 years	2,960	2,000
Under 7 years	720	400
Education unknown	720	260
By Occupation of Head of Household		
Higher executive—professional	760	640
Lesser executive—professional	720	680
Small independent business	360	340
Clerical	900	720
Skilled laborer	2,020	1,400
Semiskilled laborer	1,700	1,020
Unskilled laborer	720	540
Student	180	120
Retired	100	40
No occupation or unknown	420	460

This sample is, by various tests, an accurate cross section of the 71,180 households in metropolitan New Haven. It may be interesting, therefore, to try to summarize this section by projecting the data here presented to give an estimate of the total nonchurch-related population in New Haven. There are, we may estimate, 61,400 households that contain a husband or male head, and 68,680 households that contain a wife or female head. How many of these husbands and wives (or male heads and female heads) are so completely without church attachment that they could not identify themselves with any metropolitan New Haven church? Table 39 enumerates them by several pertinent characteristics.

This secularized group constitutes the hard core of persons who are opposed, or at least indifferent, to the work of the churches in the community. Yet the majority of them, interviewed in the sample census, reported a religious background. At one time most had some relation to a religious institution—however tenuous—but this relationship has been lost. Since they reject the church, it is logical to assume they will not be voluntarily drawn to worship services or other program activities held in the churches and synagogues. If they are to be reached, it must be by some form of personal contact which carries the church to them. This contact may take the form of a personal call by a clergyman or a layman, but it does not appear from this study that the churches of New Haven will increase their evangelistic work of this type in the foreseeable future.

It is clear that this nonchurch-related group has special significance to those persons who deal with religion on radio and television. We shall see later (Chapter 11, Table 81) that about one in eleven of the audience for religious programs is drawn from this group—or just about the group's proportionate number in the population. But these people are not only statistically significant in this study. They are also, more than any other, the persons to whom the churches have access only through such impersonal and anonymous media as television and radio. If we are correct in assuming they are the households which have rejected the conventional programs of the church and have failed to respond to the explicit and implicit invitations to worship—if they are in truth the "unconvinced" and the "unconverted"—then they would seem to be a particularly important segment of the potential audience for religious broadcasting.

PART II

The Religious Broadcasters, Their Views and Actions

CHAPTER 5

What the Protestant Clergy Think About Television and Radio

This study is focused on the relationship of religion to mass communication. Clergymen are the professional persons in our society who are entrusted above all other groups with communicating religion and extending the influence of religious institutions among all people and groups. Obviously, it is important to know how ministers view the mass communication media, and in what ways they consider them useful. This is not the same thing as saying that ministers are experts in the use of these media for religious purposes, any more than it would be accurate to say that the professional educator is the expert who is most competent to develop a program of educational television. However, we must look to the professional educator to state the philosophy and aims of education, as well as the institutional framework within which an educational television program might be developed. The minister holds a similar position in religious broadcasting. It is fundamental to a study of religious television and radio that we have some understanding of the clergyman's philosophy as to what the church is undertaking to do in society, so that a discussion of religious broadcasting can develop in relationship to the minister's understanding of the function of religion. Therefore, this chapter deals with the attitudes of the ministers toward radio and television in general and, specifically, in relationship to their use in behalf of the churches.

The ministers of the 102 New Haven Protestant churches were interviewed to determine their attitudes toward current policies and practices in religious broadcasting. Their likes and dislikes were recorded, together with their opinions of the effects of religious programs on the members of their congregations. Later the ministers and their families were interviewed in the same manner as the households in the 5 per cent population sample, to find out what kind of viewing and listening they do in their own homes and what their wives and children see on television and listen to on the radio.

The ministers as a group have had more opportunity to participate in radio broadcasting, both in planning and performance, than any other professional group in New Haven. All ministers who serve churches affiliated with the New Haven Council of Churches are offered the opportunity to broadcast from time to time. A smaller group of twelve to fifteen men carries major responsibility for planning and production of Council programs.

Program Preferences in Television and Radio

In their general preferences in television and radio programs, the ministers and their families seem to make decisions and derive satisfactions from the media in much the same manner as other New Haveners of their general social and cultural background. Preferences and attitudes of the ministers themselves with respect to religious programs are something else. Frequently judgment is passed not on the excellence of a program from the performance standpoint nor on its accomplishments with a given audience, but upon whether or not the clergyman who is commenting agrees with the religious broadcaster.

Ninety-one of the ministers interviewed expressed opinions on radio and television. Television was still a new thing to the ministers in 1952. Only six of them had appeared on a television program, though the great majority had radio broadcasting experience. In television set ownership ministers fell well below the average for both the general population and Protestant households. Only 42 of the 91 ministers had television sets (46.2 per cent), as compared with 76.2 per cent of the metropolitan New Haven households and 62.8 per cent of the Protestant households. All except two ministers did have radio sets (Table 40).

TABLE 40. Radio and television set ownership by Protestant ministers compared to Protestant families and all New Haven households

	Protestant Ministers		Per Cent of Protestant Families	Per Cent of New Haven Families
	No.	Per Cent		
Own television sets	42	46.2	62.8	76.2
Own radio sets only	47	51.6	36.4	23.0
Own neither radio nor television	2	2.2	0.8	0.8

The ministers generally reported they have little time for looking at television and listening to the radio. However, only one man stated he neither listened nor viewed, while 14 reported both viewing and listening, 28 view television only and 48 confine themselves to radio listening. The study of family habits of regular listening and viewing showed that ministers and their families differ hardly at all from the general population in their use of television, but do differ significantly in their use of radio. Here is the frequency of use by each group of *program types*.

Television

Protestant Ministers' Families	All Families
1. Drama (all types)	1. Drama (all types)
2. Sports	2. Sports
3. Quiz	3. Variety
4. Variety	4. Quiz
5. News	5. News
6. Religion	6. Religion
7. Music	7. Music
8. Other types	8. Other types

Radio

1. Music	1. Sports
2. News	2. Drama (all types)
3. Religion	3. News
4. Sports	4. Music
5. Drama (all types)	5. Religion
6. Quiz	6. Quiz
7. Variety	7. Variety
8. Other types (including news commentators)	8. News commentators
	9. Other types

It is interesting to note that both ministers' families and the general population rank religious programs sixth in preference among program types on television. On the radio, where there are more religious programs available and where some programs have been on the air for more than a quarter of a century, families of ministers rank religion third in preference and the general population ranks it fifth. There are two other places at which there is a discrepancy of more than one degree in ranking between the two groups. On radio, the general population ranks drama of all types second and the ministers' families rank it fifth in preference. Music and sports are exactly reversed in the two rank groups. The general public ranks sports first, music fourth; ministers' families, music first, sports fourth. It is also important to note that if the listening done by the general public to news commentators is added to the listening to news bulletins to form a general "news" category, news replaces drama (all types) as the second most used program type. A similar linking of news bulletins and news commentators heard by the ministers' families will not change the position of news as the second ranking program type. The conclusion may be drawn that the ministers and their families use radio for direct news bulletins more and for opinion forming less than do the members of the general public who listen to news on the radio.[1]

Preference in television *programs* is also almost identical between the ministerial households and the metropolitan New Haven population (Table 41). Of the first fifteen programs viewed regularly by each group, eleven are included in both lists. The ministers and their families named two religious programs among their first fifteen in preference, Bishop Fulton Sheen and This Is the Life, while the general population named only Sheen among religious programs.

Radio *program* preference is markedly different between the families of ministers and the general population of New Haven. The ministers' families named five serious music programs among the first fifteen to which they listened regularly, while the general list contains only two such programs. Ministers' families preferred four religious programs among the first fifteen —The Lutheran Hour, Evensong, Old Fashioned Revival Hour and National Radio Pulpit—to two religious programs—The Catholic Hour and The Greatest Story Ever Told—chosen by the general population. No daytime serials appear in the ministerial list, while the general public chose My True Story as the fourteenth ranking program.

SOCIAL, CULTURAL AND THEOLOGICAL IDENTIFICATION OF THE MINISTERS

Most of the 91 ministers with opinions on broadcasting are in the upper social class groups. Fifty-five are in social class I, 27 in social class II, eight in social class III, none in social class IV and only one in social class V. Eighty of them had graduate education in a seminary or divinity school. Six are lay leaders of such groups as the Friends (Quakers), Latter-day Saints, Christian Scientists and Pentecostals. Five others act as full-time ordained ministers but have had no theological education.

The ministers rated themselves on their theological viewpoints. They were given the choice of the following positions:

[1] This conclusion is not vitiated by the fact that ministers' families list three news commentators (Lowell Thomas is not a commentator), and the general public only two among their fifteen most popular radio programs (Table 41).

It is interesting to note that the commentators who are most popular among ministers' families (Gabriel Heatter, Fulton Lewis, Jr.) are generally considered to be spokesmen for special interest groups of an ultraconservative nature. The general audience lists Lewis as their most popular commentator, but they also rate among the first fifteen programs the commentary of Edward R. Murrow, who has received acclaim (such as the Peabody Award) for his unbiased interpretation of the news.

Orthodox	Modern
Conservative	Catholic
Middle-of-the-road	Fundamentalist
Liberal	Other

Table 41. Order of program preference, families of Protestant ministers and general population of metropolitan New Haven

Ministers' Families	All Families

Television

Ministers' Families	All Families
1. John Cameron Swazey	1. John Cameron Swazey
2. Studio One	2. I Love Lucy
3. Voice of Firestone	3. Studio One
4. Arthur Godfrey	4. Philco Playhouse
5. Strike It Rich	5. Milton Berle
6. I Love Lucy	6. Fulton J. Sheen
7. Toast of the Town	7. Arthur Godfrey
8. Fulton J. Sheen	8. Strike It Rich
9. Your Show of Shows	9. Voice of Firestone
10. This Is the Life	10. Groucho Marx
11. Philco Playhouse	11. Suspense
12. Fred Waring	12. Your Show of Shows
13. Kate Smith Hour	13. Toast of the Town
14. Lux Video Theatre	14. Colgate Comedy Hour
15. Mama	15. Lux Video Theatre

Radio

Ministers' Families	All Families
1. Metropolitan Opera	1. The Catholic Hour
2. NBC Symphony	2. Arthur Godfrey
3. Longine Symphonette	3. Strike It Rich
4. New York Philharmonic Symphony	4. Groucho Marx
5. WELI Morning News	5. Telephone Hour
6. Twenty Questions	6. Voice of Firestone
7. Lowell Thomas	7. Greatest Story Ever Told
8. The Lutheran Hour	8. Jack Benny
9. Telephone Hour	9. Twenty Questions
10. Evensong	10. Lux Radio Theatre
11. Railroad Hour	11. Break the Bank
12. Jack Benny	12. Railroad Hour
13. National Radio Pulpit	13. Lowell Thomas / Fulton Lewis, Jr. } Tie
14. Old Fashioned Revival Hour	14. My True Story
15. Gabriel Heatter / Fulton Lewis, Jr. } Tie	15. Edward R. Murrow

The majority placed themselves somewhere in the following scale: Orthodox —Conservative—Middle-of-the-road—Modern—Liberal. Middle-of-the-road was most often linked with one or more of the other terms. Fifty-eight ministers so classified themselves. Ten other ministers called themselves Conservative; five, Fundamentalist; five, Catholic; and four considered

Table 42. Last religious program seen or heard by Protestant ministers

Program	Sponsor	Mentions
Television		
Greatest Story Ever Told	Goodyear Tire & Rubber Co.	8
Bishop Fulton J. Sheen	Admiral Corporation	6
Billy Graham	Independent	4
Frontiers of Faith	National Broadcasting Co. (Interfaith)	3
Youth on the March	Independent fundamentalist	2
New Haven Council of Churches Lenten Series	New Haven Council of Churches	2
New Haven Council of Churches Christmas Program	New Haven Council of Churches	2
Special Christmas Services		2

Programs mentioned once: Helen Kenyon Program (New Haven Council of Churches), Old Fashioned Revival Hour (Independent fundamentalist), Lamp Unto My Feet (Columbia Broadcasting System—Interfaith), This Week in Religion (DuMont—Interfaith), This is the Life (Missouri Synod Lutheran), Bible Puppets (National Council of Churches—New Haven Council of Churches). Unknown 5.

Program	Sponsor	Mentions
Radio		
Evensong	New Haven Council of Churches	11
A Mighty Fortress	New Haven Council of Churches	6
Billy Graham	Independent	6
Religion at the News Desk	New Haven Council of Churches	5
National Radio Pulpit	National Council of Churches	4
Old Fashioned Revival Hour	Independent fundamentalist	4
New Haven Council of Churches Lenten Series	New Haven Council of Churches	3
Greatest Story Ever Told	Goodyear Tire & Rubber Co.	2
The Catholic Hour	National Council of Catholic Men	2
The Eternal Light	Jewish Theological Seminary of North America	2
The Lutheran Hour	Missouri Synod Lutheran	2
Revival Hour	Independent	2

Programs mentioned once: The Art of Living (National Council of Churches), National Vespers (National Council of Churches), Church of the Air (Columbia Broadcasting System — Interfaith), Salt Lake City Tabernacle Choir (Latter-day Saints [Mormon]), Faith in Our Time (WOR), William Ward Ayer (Independent fundamentalist), Youth on the March (Independent fundamentalist), Upper Room (Methodist Church), Stations of the Cross (Roman Catholic), Baptist Negro Hour, Calvary Baptist Church (Independent fundamentalist), Music for Worship, Danbury Baptist Church (Independent), Pillar of Fire (Pillar of Fire Church). Unknown 5.

themselves to be independent of any of the positions suggested (Unitarian, Mormon, etc.). Nine ministers classified their theological position as "Pentecostal."

PERSONAL LISTENING AND VIEWING HABITS FOR RELIGIOUS PROGRAMS

The ministers were asked what religious programs they had listened to on radio and seen on television most recently. (Question: "What was the last religious program you listened to on radio [saw on television]? When?") Only 18 of the 91 had heard or seen a religious program in the five weeks preceding their interview; but most of them could remember the last religious program they had heard. Fourteen television and 27 radio programs were identified as the most recent programs seen or heard.

On television, the ministers who watched may have been keeping an eye on the religious programs that were most interesting to the general public, The Greatest Story Ever Told and Fulton Sheen. Billy Graham and Frontiers of Faith ranked next in the ministers' most recent viewing. The rest of their viewing was scattered.

On radio, programs sponsored by the New Haven Council of Churches constituted over one-third of all those mentioned as being last heard; and the four series presented by the Council were all included among the first seven programs mentioned most frequently. On the other hand, men who reported listening last to national programs (such as National Radio Pulpit) had tuned in more recently than had those who mentioned local broadcasts. Local programs often bore a date a month or more prior to the interview, while national programs usually had been heard the week preceding the interview.

The clergymen tended to be selective in their hearing and viewing of religious programs. They tuned in to specific programs they had decided in advance to hear or see.

Attitudes Toward Religious Broadcasting

The 91 minister respondents generally favored the use of television and radio as media of communication for the churches. They made more statements in favor of specific programs than against. When asked if religious broadcasting affects church attendance, 26 replied in the affirmative. Eight of the 26 felt religious broadcasting hinders church attendance, and were opposed to use of television and radio by the churches. Fifty-one ministers thought broadcasting did not affect attendance in their churches, but favored it as a means of church recruitment. The rest had no opinion on effects on church attendance.

Some ministers view radio and television as solidifying denominational ties. The Mormon leader explained, "Our people listen to the [CBS] Church of the Air, also to Music and the Spoken Word [Salt Lake City Tabernacle Choir] quite regularly. The latter is a personal church relationship, giving contact with the church authorities."

The Pillar of Fire is another sect, with one church in New Haven, which apparently relies on radio for some contact with the parent group. The Pillar of Fire owns local stations in New Jersey and Denver. The New Haven minister reported regular listening to the New Jersey outlet.

The New Haven congregation of the Lutheran Church, Missouri Synod, considers both the Lutheran Hour on radio and the television dramas, This Is the Life, to be programs that present the national denominational viewpoint. The local church purchases billboards and other advertising to publicize these programs.

The Seventh-day Adventists also sponsor national broadcasts, The Voice of Prophecy on radio and Faith for Today on television. The single New Haven minister feels these programs provide a strong bond with the national fellowship as well as an effective missionary arm for the local congregation. In addition to the national programs, the local church also uses radio. "Ninety per cent of my own people listen to my broadcast. A similar number listen to the Voice of Prophecy," said the local minister. "Our local church board discusses the type of program and financing of the program aired locally. Value? Strengthening faith. Also pride of sponsorship," he concluded.

Prestige value is an important factor in the attitudes of the smaller religious groups toward radio and television. A Christian Scientist layman discussing the news analyses of Erwin Canham said, "He gives 'tone.' People hear him and our other fine radio programs and know we have something to offer." Pentecostal ministers reported that evangelistic programs on the radio carry more weight with the unconverted than do the same evangelistic messages delivered in person.

There is some tendency to regard religious programs in the same light as other radio and television shows. A Congregational minister said, "My people comment frequently on religious programs. The Greatest Story Ever Told seems most effective with all age groups. Its value, of course, is entertainment, same as any other good program."

Other ministers feel that religious programs help in Christian education and Christian nurture. Following are pertinent comments:

The chief values of religious programs are enjoyment and appreciation. On Religion at the News Desk, for instance, information is conveyed, argument is engendered. People derive conviction from the show; its Christian position is appreciated. [Congregational]

There is discussion (by my people) on points raised (in religious programs). Even programs like Fuller's stimulate thinking. [Methodist]

They develop interest which cannot be satisfied short of corporate worship experience. [Congregational]

The listeners are glad to be reminded of what they believe, and have latent convictions made more articulate. Useful programs are those that touch the imagination, as to the output of religion as well as the input—what you can give as well as what you can get. One Great Hour of Sharing is an example. [Congregational]

Only a few ministers showed serious skepticism about religious programming, but these tended to be among the more able and experienced broadcasters, such as the Congregational minister who said, "When I broadcast, or any of the other ministers, there is a lack of confidence that this fifteen minutes will reach anyone; and I know, even then, that it goes only to church members."

The responses to this study give evidence that for most New Haven clergymen, the mass media are only on the periphery of their conception of their ministry.

There is little concern over a strategy for effective use of these media. Most of the men have given little thought to radio and television; they take their turn on the air when it comes around as a sort of chore to be done in behalf of the ecumenical work through the Council of Churches. Few of the ministers of the churches affiliated with the Council seemed to feel that Protestantism has any prestige at stake when they broadcast. Generally, they were not opposed to the various Protestant plans to use television and radio to reach unchurched families and individuals; rather they had not given this matter much thought as it related to their own work.

Radio and television, if considered at all, were looked upon as specific tools, auxiliary to the ministry, but useful for minor tasks—comforting shut-ins, preaching sermonettes at off-hours, telling Bible stories to children. For example, in counseling with parishioners the pastors often discuss stewardship of time; but none indicated he had studied or commented on constructive utilization of the mass media, although they constitute a major element in the leisure-time activity of church members.

The ministers were asked: "Do your constituents discuss religious radio and television programs with you? Other radio and television shows? What values, if any, do they seem to get out of listening?"

The five ministers who replied that they had discussed radio and television at all with parishioners said that the topic had come up casually and in three contexts: shut-ins mention their favorite programs when the minister calls; the parishioners comment when the minister himself appears on the air; occasionally there is discussion of some controversial issue that has been treated by radio or television.

Ministers articulated the value they thought people received from religious programs in such terms as "enhancing spiritual outlook," "supporting general religious attitudes," "maintaining general interest in religion," "articulation of latent convictions" and similar phrases.

When considering the possible audience for religious broadcasting, the clergymen seemed to visualize two groups: Protestant churchgoers and all-the-rest. (Possibly three groups: my parishioners, parishioners of other Protestant ministers and all-the-rest.) Most ministers interviewed seemed to have accepted uncritically the assumption that there is a single mass audience. They showed little conception of the plurality of audiences, or of the need to do something different on the air from what is done in the church service if they wish to reach through the broadcasting medium people who have rejected the church or drifted away from it.

There was general agreement among clergymen on the audience that listens most readily to their programs—the shut-ins. The ministers were asked: "Do you think religious programs reach people who do not go to church?" The interviewers purposely did not define the phrase "people who do not go to church," in order to discover how ministers understood it in relation to people who listen to religious broadcasts. Of 72 affirmative replies to this question, 62 referred to shut-ins as the nonchurch attenders reached by the broadcasts.

This assumption that religious broadcasting is primarily for the "ready-made" audience—the people the minister knows in advance are going to listen to him and agree with what he says—is obviously a self-limiting concept. In our religiously pluralistic society any such group is a minority and a message directed to it will ignore the needs of the majority in the potential audience. If the mind of the broadcaster visualizes only the initiated as listening when he speaks, they, indeed, will be all who are there; for the others will tune out, their needs unmet.

This problem was further complicated in New Haven by the rotation system whereby different clergymen successively appeared on the two local religious broadcasts, A Mighty Fortress and Evensong. Since each program is individually developed, and since many weeks elapse between one appearance of a given clergyman and his reappearance, there is no possibility of the cumulative effect of a single powerful personality nor, even, the cumulative impact of a series planned to develop a consistent theme with changing personnel.

Evaluation of Specific Religious Programs

Each minister was asked to name three or more religious radio and television programs he thought were effective and three or more programs he thought were not effective, and in each case to explain the "why" for his judgment, outlining both strengths and weaknesses of the programs.

BASES FOR APPROVAL AND CRITICISM

Content was the dominating factor upon which ministers based their judgments of religious programs. Excellence of broadcasting technique was secondary; and there was a third, minor, factor which might be termed the personality communicated by a speaker. The judgment seemed on the whole to be based on the ministers' personal reactions to the programs rather than on any serious effort to understand and evaluate the reactions of lay audiences.

When the New Haven minister criticized a broadcast as to content his judgment was most frequently based on the theological position of the broadcaster. (Personal theological disagreement was frequently equated with a judgment that the program was not effective.) Other forms of content such as subject discussed, illustrations, information communicated, music, et cetera, were also cited. While content was cited twice as often as technique in criticizing radio programs, men who thought the programs of the New Haven Council of Churches effective tended to comment on content, while those who thought them ineffective usually mentioned defective technique.

Television technique obviously interested the ministers, probably because it was new to them. Specific comments on television techniques outnumbered comments on content five to three.

PROGRAMS DISCUSSED[2]

The 91 ministers named 25 radio and 12 television programs which they considered to be effective. In addition one man lumped all programs pro-

[2] These programs are described in Chap. 6.

Table 43. Religious programs judged effective and ineffective by New Haven Protestant clergymen

Program	Number Judging Effective	Number Judging Ineffective	Total Mentions
Television[a]			
Bishop Fulton J. Sheen	7	3	10
Greatest Story Ever Told	7		7
Special Holiday Programs	6	1	7
Frontiers of Faith	4	1	5
Billy Graham	2	3	5
Youth on the March	3	1	4
Old Fashioned Revival Hour	1	1	2
WPIX TV Chapel	2		2
Morning Chapel, WABD		2	2

Programs mentioned once and judged to be effective: Faith for Today, Lamp Unto My Feet, Bible Puppets

Program	Number Judging Effective	Number Judging Ineffective	Total Mentions
Radio			
Religion at the News Desk	26	2	28
Greatest Story Ever Told	14	2	16
National Radio Pulpit	12	2	14
Old Fashioned Revival Hour	10	12	22
Billy Graham	6	5	11
The Catholic Hour	8	3	11
The Lutheran Hour	8		8
A Mighty Fortress	3	5	8
Evensong	6	1	7
Voice of Prophecy	3	3	6
National Vespers	5		5
Art of Living		5	5
The Eternal Light	5		5
Calvary Baptist	2	2	4
Salt Lake City Tabernacle Choir	4		4
Rosary Hour		4	4
Message of Israel	3		3
Hartford Evangelical Hour	3		3
CBS Church of the Air	2	1	3
Trinity Church Choir	2		2
Word of Life Hour		2	2
Light and Life Hour	2		2
This I Believe[b]	2		2

Programs mentioned once and judged to be effective: William Ward Ayer, Youth on the March, In Fullness of Time, One Great Hour of Sharing, Ave Maria Hour.

Programs mentioned once and judged to be ineffective: Baptist Negro Hour, New Haven Council of Churches Lenten Series, Christian Science.

[a] Many ministers were unable to comment on two programs in which they professed interest, What's Your Trouble? with Dr. and Mrs. Norman Vincent Peale and This is the Life. Both programs were aired in New Haven on Sunday morning when the ministers were in church.

[b] Some ministers consider This I Believe a religious program. Few people in the general audience who reported hearing it felt it was religious. It is not so considered in this study.

duced by the New Haven Council of Churches together and labeled them effective. They thought 17 radio and 12 television programs were ineffective. Nine men thought all "pentecostal," "evangelical" and "Gospel type" programs were ineffective, and four people so judged the New Haven Council programs, as a group (see Table 43).

Since so many of the judgments of effectiveness are subjective, it is well to note the total mentions of each program. The programs mentioned most frequently seem to be ones which were most in the consciousness of the ministers; but they are not necessarily ones to which the men listen regularly. They are the programs which are controversial or which have achieved some degree of public reputation that is apparent to the ministers. For example, 26 ministers listed Religion at the News Desk as effective and two thought it ineffectual, yet only six listened to it regularly. This program is a commentary on the news by Yale Divinity School students and is sponsored by the New Haven Council of Churches. It has been attacked by some laymen as being too liberal and for reflecting the views of the Democratic party. It became necessary for the Council and WELI, the originating station, to take a stand in favor of continuing this program despite opposition. The Old Fashioned Revival Hour with ten effective and twelve ineffective mentions is fundamentalist in outlook and splits ministers on theological lines. Norman Vincent Peale (Art of Living), mentioned five times as ineffective, is disapproved of by some ministers because of his psychological treatment of problems of religious living. Yet all who criticized him felt he had a large audience. The Greatest Story Ever Told with sixteen mentions in radio and seven in television had been widely publicized among ministers, and they were also apparently aware it had widespread acceptance among laymen. Similarly Fulton J. Sheen, who had the most mentions in television (ten) was receiving major publicity when this study was made.

Let us examine three programs that rank high in mentions, evoked sharp disagreement as to effectiveness: The Old Fashioned Revival Hour, Billy Graham and A Mighty Fortress. The first two offer examples of how judgment on effectiveness was colored by theological outlook. All of the commentators, except one, who judged the Fuller program to be effective listed themselves as conservative, fundamentalist or pentecostal in theology. The exception was a middle-of-the-road Methodist who said, "Fuller's theology and music appeal to ordinary people." This was the only judgment based upon relation of the program to the audience it is designed to reach. The opposition to Fuller came, again with one exception, from men in the mainstream theological groupings. The exception, a pentecostal, said, "For one who doesn't know, it is fun; but for one who has lived under a living apostle, it is very ersatz."

The ministers also split on theological lines in evaluating Billy Graham (both the radio and television presentations). Pentecostals and conservative-fundamentalists thought Graham effective. The judgment of ineffective again came from the more established denominations, plus the Mormon and Universalist ministers. Three middle-of-the-road ministers after judging Graham ineffective on the basis of personal theological position, modified their comments to concede Graham *is* effective with *his* audience. One said:

[He is effective because of his] affirmativeness and dogmatism. People want people who are sure, not ones who give two sides to a question.

While judgment of Fuller and Graham was made on the basis of content, a different standard was noted for programs produced by the New Haven Council of Churches. A Mighty Fortress was a Sunday morning, prechurch broadcast[3] on which the ministers who are members of the Council rotate as speakers. All of the men who mentioned this program were in the mainstream theological positions and all were members of the Council. Critical judgment of the *production* dominated the listings of ineffectiveness:

It is simply a church service taken over without being adapted to the medium of radio. Is a concession to the minister.

[It] attempts to transfer a sermon and worship service bodily from sanctuary to microphone. Fails.

Favorable judgments were mixed.

Local interest. You know the man on it yourself. [Personality]

Well-integrated music and speaking. Message well prepared. [Production technique]

Puts one in a worshipful mood. [Personal response]

INDIVIDUAL PROGRAM EVALUATION

With the foregoing bases for judgment in mind, let us see how the clergymen evaluated certain of the programs which are most in their minds. The judgments of the clergymen should be evaluated in the light of the manifest purposes of the broadcasters (Chapter 6) and the audience actually attracted (Chapter 11).

---

[3] The program has been discontinued.

Radio Programs

Religion at the News Desk was discussed most frequently, mainly by men who described themselves as orthodox or modern-liberal in theological position. One "fundamentalist," one "pentecostal" and one Unitarian approved it; but generally it was men in the mainstream theological positions who were aware of the program and thought it to be effective.

Thought Program Effective

[It is] a serious attempt to approach current social and political problems on a basis of explicit Christian convictions. [Congregational]

Deals with contemporary events, injecting what Christianity has to say. Objective, not sentimental. [Lutheran]

Makes faith relevant to secular life. Head and shoulders above most services. [Congregational]

Effective for limited audience. No general appeal. [A Student Pastor]

Well done, intelligent. The news analysis is not mature. [They] lack mature Christian judgment at times. [Methodist]

Thought Program Ineffective

Too high-brow in language and thought for us. Too academic for average church member or nonchurch member. Not popular in presentation, language or situational appeal. People will probably listen to other newscasts. Good in theory, but I doubt the communication value or appeal to more than a score of people outside Yale Divinity School and other student circulation. [Interdenominational Mission]

The Greatest Story Ever Told (radio and television) crosses theological lines. The ministers thought it is popular with laymen and that it is effective in content and format.

Thought Program Effective

Dramatically satisfying. [Congregational]

Dramatic. A little overdone. Takes some liberties with the Bible. [Episcopal]

The atmosphere is solemn, very impressive. Depiction of the Master on television was weak. [Lutheran]

[It is] Biblically accurate, artistically good, technically good . . . . The teaching wasn't complete. [Methodist]

Simple, yet effective, presentation of Biblical occurrence. [Mormon]

Drama effective, but not done in the light of best Biblical scholarship. [Methodist]

Technical excellence. [Congregational]

Communicates Bible truths to average man. [International Mission]

Has horse sense, three dimensional, projects characters in authentic setting so as to make them acceptable and interesting. [Episcopalian]

Brings religion into my family life. [Episcopal]

Touches annoy me. [Congregational][4]

Thought Program Ineffective

Sentimental. [Congregational]

A little saccharin, too pious. [Lutheran]

National Radio Pulpit (Dr. Ralph Sockman, speaker) was evaluated only by men in the mainstream theological positions, especially liberals, with the exception of a Pentecostal minister who said simply that he likes Sockman very much and thinks he is effective.

Thought Program Effective

The content is well suited [to the audience]. It is satisfying over a period of time. [Congregational]

The illustrative material is good. [Congregational]

Great themes are presented with intelligence and simplicity. [Methodist]

His personality is appealing. [Congregational]

[He] uses picturesque language, unexpected forms of thought. He deals with real life problems; reaches people as persons. [Methodist]

[He] preaches the Gospel, doesn't use it in the name of politics. [It is the] Gospel, not lectures. [Episcopal]

Think Program Ineffective

The sermon is too long for the radio medium. People listen in paragraphs. [Congregational]

He did meet a worship need; but the program is heavily dominated by personality. [Lutheran]

National Vespers (Dr. John Sutherland Bonnell, speaker) was mentioned by the same group that commented on Sockman. No one thought the program ineffective.

High quality of leadership. . . . High level of preaching. [Methodist]

[He is] fascinating. Has his feet on the ground. [Baptist]

Art of Living (Dr. Norman Vincent Peale, speaker), was the only program on which this study was able to gather conclusive evidence[5] that the broadcasts motivate nonchurchgoers to seek a church relationship. No minister judged this program to be effective. Five men in the mainstream theologically stated the program is ineffective, and berated it in the process.

---

[4] This man thought The Greatest Story Ever Told is effective as a program type, and that it and The Eternal Light have the best potential for communicating religion of any programs regularly on the air. He felt drama is the most effective form for religious broadcasts, and lamented the fact that The Greatest Story Ever Told is not a better program, more concerned with the great truths of the New Testament.

[5] See the depth interview analyses for Peale listeners and viewers, Chap. 15.

[He] limits Christianity to personal problems. [He is] highly repetitive, tells stories poorly, is superficial, egotistical. [Methodist]

Columbia Church of the Air interests the ministers, although they cannot listen regularly, because it is broadcast at a time when most of them are in church. But any minister may find an opportunity to broadcast by being recommended to the Columbia Broadcasting System by his denominational radio director. Two ministers of local churches thus have the opportunity to broadcast nationally each week on the two segments of the Church of the Air. All of the ministers knew the Church of the Air, and men of varying theological positions knew of members of their own communions who had opportunity to broadcast. Most of the ministers felt they had not heard enough programs to evaluate the series accurately; but three men stated they listened regularly and commented on content and performance.

Thought Program Effective
Followed familiar order of worship. Good sermon. Voice too ecclesiastical and annoying. [Congregational]

Good opportunity to hear doctrines and attitudes of various churches. Good way to get information. [Mormon]

Thought Program Ineffective
Too general. Tries to please everyone. There is too much emphasis on the preacher. [Episcopalian]

Evensong is generally thought effective by ministers of churches that are members of the New Haven Council, yet this study indicates that no more than 200 New Haven families listen to it regularly.

Thought Program Effective
It makes a place in our broadcasting schedule for people who want a Christian message on Sunday evening. [Episcopal]

The format and design visualize people at the time and place. It uses "living room words." [Congregational]

It is good because most programs are scraped clean of the ordinary homiletic pattern. [Congregational]

Thought Program Ineffective
It is not designed for people out of the church or on the fringe. There is too little preparation. [Episcopal]

Television
Bishop Fulton J. Sheen was discussed by men of all theological viewpoints. Several reported they had gone to homes of parishioners or otherwise made a special effort to see him on television.

Thought Program Effective
The content and presentation held me *in spite of opposition to the viewpoint.* [Congregational]

For people with Roman Catholic presuppositions he is effective to give a sense of importance and to strengthen beliefs. He is irritating to Protestants. [Congregational]

I follow him very closely. He is an effective speaker. The program is aimed at intelligent people. [Greek Orthodox]

Well planned. He judges the psychology of the audience, is specific. [AME Zion]

Direct discussion of profound thoughts. [Methodist]

The information of the speaker, his fluency, wealth of illustrative material, solidness of the message, his dress all make it effective. [Lutheran]

The informal manner of speaking, terminology at the listeners' level, his personality are effective. [Congregational]

Thought Program Ineffective

He seems to have an axe to grind. I disagree. [Congregational]

Hypocritical. That is not what Catholics stand for or believe. [Episcopal]

He pretends a reasonable approach, but is actually dogmatic. The dress, the jokes, the references to authority are all calculated to throw you off guard so you will accept his line without thinking. [Congregational]

Frontiers of Faith was evaluated only by men in the middle-of-the-road theological positions.

Thought Program Effective

Presents Protestant worship at its best. [Congregational]

Has good variety in presentation. [Congregational]

Thought Program Ineffective

It is unreal in its setting. Very boring to look at. [Congregational]

Evaluation of the Influence of Programs

Do ministers think they are being helped or hindered in their work by religious radio and television? Actually, the ministers, on the whole, did not seem to regard television and radio as a primary form of communication to the people of New Haven, or as part of the general social context of the people whom they serve, and by which these people are influenced. Recruitment is a pressing concern, yet only ten ministers thought radio reached unchurched people. Seven of the ten viewed religious radio as a substitute for churchgoing. Comments included: "It's a choice of Sockman over church," "People listen to them who are too lazy to come to church," "They use it [radio] as an alibi for not doing their duty."

Some men thought religious broadcasting might help attendance in two different ways:

1. It convinces them of their need to attend.

It develops an interest which cannot be satisfied short of corporate worship attendance.

2. Broadcasting creates an atmosphere favorable to church attendance.

It turns their thoughts to God.

Two men had direct evidence that the present broadcasts reach unchurched people (not shut-ins), both experiences being based on Religion at the News Desk. "Religion at the News Desk reaches nonchurched people and influences them. I've talked to them," is the substance of their report as voiced by one of them.

The ministers were more hopeful of positive results from television as a means of recruiting members. Thirty-six said unchurched people, other than shut-ins, are reached by religious television, but the reasoning is typified by the following:

People don't turn TV off.

They turn sets on and leave them. It's a novelty.

They have the set on and unless they are antagonistic, I think they would listen.

VALUE OF PROGRAMS TO PARISHIONERS

Those ministers who had experienced some reaction from their parishioners about religious programs were asked to delineate the values they thought their constituents received from religious broadcasting. Four out of five of the benefits suggested dealt in terms of the status quo; that is, religious broadcasting helps people to keep on being just what they are. The minority 20 per cent postulated some advancement in knowledge, critical judgment and religious experience from contact with the broadcasts.

Twenty-six replies dealt with personal development:

Enhances spiritual outlook.

Articulates latent convictions.

Supports general religious attitudes.

Maintains general interest in religion.

Gives inspiration.

Fourteen others stated: "It gives comfort to shut-ins." Three replies dealt with the concept of prestige of the church:

It gives a sense of prestige and identity in feeling a part of the church as it puts on a good religious program.

Five men believed the chief results are immediate entertainment and enjoyment without any lasting effects.

In the minority were eleven comments which reported that religious programs are instructing and informing parishioners; and three others which stated that the programs stimulate thinking about other religious viewpoints than that of the listener.

Improvement of Programs

The study wished to find whether the ministers were satisfied with the status quo in national religious broadcasting and programs aired locally in New Haven, and their opinion was sought on constructive changes and improvements. The question was asked: "What specific suggestions would you make for improving the use of radio and television by churches and religious agencies?" Two-thirds (64) of the 91 respondents made suggestions for improvement. The rest either were satisfied with things as they are, or, if dissatisfied, did not have suggestion for improvement. Some men who responded had only one suggestion, others offered five, six or more.

· The number of responses is not as important as the categories into which they fall. One out of four of the suggestions called for trained personnel to conduct the programs. Interestingly enough, only one man, one of the most able and busy ministers in the community, interpreted this to mean more training for himself and his fellow clergymen. He contended they should take the responsibility and give the necessary time for effective use of the mass media, and offered his own time in addition to the heavy schedule of co-operative work he already carried. This man also joined with five others in urging more planning and rehearsal for programs produced locally.

Thirty-eight suggestions dealt with matters of quality, content and format of programs. Twelve stressed matters of quality:

> Improve music.
> Permit more originality of expression.
> Improve voice production.

Six suggestions were for more dramatic programs and five for more musical series. Five men wanted more services broadcast from churches, while two would have eliminated church services entirely. One man wanted to cut down on national religious programs and substitute locally sponsored shows.

Only one person suggested the creation of religious education programs, and he was interested in adults. While this study and others show that children and young people are very much influenced by, and certainly have made extensive use of, television,[7] not a single minister had anything to say about the potentialities of either radio or television for such things as education of children or young people.

Suggestions about content (one out of five) were mostly to correct faults in current programs. The present programs were characterized as "too intellectual," "cold," "dreary," "high-toned." "More relevance to the listener," "Better theology," "Preaching of the gospel" were urged. One man in speaking of the program of the national and local councils of churches said:

We need to learn something from the methods and warmth of sects already on the air. Every program should have a message and preach salvation through Christ.

Eighteen men were concerned with matters of broadcast policy and the choice of performers. They urged co-ordination between the various programs and the persons who broadcast, and selection of broadcasters on the basis of ability. There was general agreement that the radio-television committee of the New Haven Council of Churches should be strengthened and should give close supervision to the various broadcasts. A wider variety in program planning and production and more lay participation in broadcasting were other concerns of this group; and they wanted clear-cut policies developed that can be transmitted to the broadcasting industry.

The need for promotion and publicity for radio and television programs and for studies of audience response concerned one out of ten of the ministers.

Suggestions for the use of the mass media for recruitment came from only one in twenty of the ministers, although the desire to use radio and television in this way was apparent in the majority of the 91 clergymen. The recruitment suggestions were the least specific of any that called for program changes:

Do more than interest people, move them to take part in the corporate fel-fellowship.

Urge church attendance.

Show what you can give as well as what you can get; provide channels that will lead into the church.

[7] See Everett Parker and David Barry, "Parents, Children and Television," Ibid.

One thoughtful minister summed up the need for four kinds of improvements:

We need more money allocated to broadcasting; more co-ordinated planning between all churches; more professional aid, which in turn will bring out more voluntary aid; and more house-to-house surveys to find out who listens to us.

An Evaluation of Local Religious Broadcasting in New Haven

The typical New Haven minister as revealed by these interviews has two personalities where radio and television are concerned. As a listener or viewer, he is much like other folks. He likes a variety of programs. He enjoys sports, drama, variety, music and the other types of entertainment. He gets news from radio or television. In radio he is somewhat more selective in his program choices than the general public, inclining to serious music and other cultural programs; but in television he and his family watch about as other people do, and seem to like it. The minister knows that even in his own family there are program type preferences and program preferences, and that such tastes extend into the general audience.

But in his personality of religious broadcaster, the average minister thinks in different terms. There he sees only one audience—the kind of an audience he preaches to on Sunday morning, the "churched" people; so his "message" is aimed at them, and the rest are left to find another program or tune out. "Message" is used advisedly, rather than program, since the average minister conceives of the religious program in terms of a clergyman making a speech, just as he would in church, with, perhaps, some music added for trimming. Again, by this program device, he limits his audience to those persons who are loyal to the church and used to the form of communication employed in the church.

This is not to say that the New Haven ministers are deliberately avoiding good radio and television technique, although there is apparent resistance to change in some of the programs that have been standard for years. But the average minister has not had adequate training as a radio broadcaster—and now the television camera is staring him in the face.

The New Haven Council of Churches has been in the forefront among councils that have sought to use radio effectively. In 1947 it began appointing Yale Divinity School students as part-time directors of radio. Two students each year now act in this capacity, making the equivalent of one full-time director for radio and television. Since 1948 the Council has received eleven awards for excellence of its radio programs from the annual

Religious Radio Workshop. In 1952 both Religion at the News Desk and a series of documentaries produced by the Council won awards from Ohio State University's Institute for Education by Radio and Television.

In spite of this good record in initiative, it is doubtful if the co-operative religious broadcasting in New Haven has made a major impression on the community or greatly benefited the churches in their program. The ministers' general lack of training in the use of the mass media, their ignorance of the audience potential and their failure to plan continuously in terms of the needs and interests of the community are major blocks to effective local religious broadcasting. Of the three radio programs regularly presented by the Council, this study showed only Religion at the News Desk (Saturdays, 7:00 P.M.) had any substantial audience. It ranked eighth among religious radio programs and had an indicated regular audience of about 600 families. No audience beyond forty or fifty families was found for A Mighty Fortress (Sundays, 8:30–9:00 A.M.), the weekly program on which ministers rotated as speakers. Evensong (Sundays, 10:30–11:00 P.M.), a program of music with prayers and readings, as already indicated, reached about 200 families.

The Council began regular television programming over WNHC-TV in the summer of 1952. The series of experimental religious education programs for children, called Adventures in Religion, has already been described. A series of weekly programs for adults, One Foundation (Thursdays, 12:00 noon–12:15 P.M.), has failed to garner a measurable audience. It is significant to note that Adventures has had the exclusive services of a paid director and has featured a single personality, Edith F. Welker, associate executive secretary of the Connecticut Council of Churches. One Foundation, on the other hand, has been conducted by a committee of ministers working in their spare time, has not had an integrated theme and has not had continuity of format or performers.

Observation of the experience of the New Haven Council of Churches in television production leads to the conclusion that local councils cannot work in television in the same casual way many of them have done radio programming in the past. Television production is too complicated to be handled by part-time committees of ministers who, at best, can devote only the fringes of their time to broadcasting activities. Nor can successful television programs be developed under the rotation system, where each minister takes his turn broadcasting, often without benefit of adequate rehearsal or an integrated plan to link program to program. The New Haven Council has found that its successful television program—Adventures—

has required: (1) careful planning in terms of theme, format and content; (2) content carefully tailored for a selected audience, and *that audience only*; (3) a performer, schooled in television broadcasting, who has appeared on the air and also spent approximately half her time in program planning; (4) a paid, semiprofessional director; (5) adequate funds to cover costs for personnel and materials (approximately $50 per week); (6) at least four hours' rehearsal for each fifteen minutes of air time. This procedure is minimal for a successful series of programs. Many councils of churches will find this kind of program service difficult to achieve. Indeed, in view of the past performance in radio, it is questionable whether the average council will be able to furnish its community with an adequate religious television program service from within its own resources. It may need to depend upon outside sources, such as the National Council of Churches, for most of its program material.

In New Haven, the apparent lack of influence of some of the local religious programs concerns the ministers who make broadcasting policy. The executive secretary of the New Haven Council helped organize a statewide television committee, of which he was chairman, to broaden the resources available for programming over WNHC-TV.

The chairman of the New Haven Council's radio-television committee feels that "radio and television do something entirely different from any other church activity." He is concerned that in New Haven the Council of Churches shall have "the funds to do a good job, to make religious programs not only equal to but better than other kinds."

Another clergyman opposes the practice of broadcasting church services or of imitating them—the studio "service in miniature" like A Mighty Fortress. He said:

Religious broadcasting needs to be church-centered; dramatizing the mainstream where the Christian life flows, which has served through generations. Current religious broadcasts are highly individualized—meditative, not communal, not churched. This does not mean they should televise or broadcast church services, which is not the same thing. The problem is to assert the centrality of the church while dramatizing the meaning faith gives to each individual's life.

Still another minister summed up his critique of religious broadcasting with this analysis of the local situation:

. . . Determine the constituency to be served . . . [it should be] a goal of not less than all. . . . Recognize many levels of culture . . . emotional, intellectual. Ideally every program should contain elements for all levels. If the message is intellectual, songs should appeal to emotion. . . . A great many have revulsion for one element or another. Then you lose a listener. . . . There is merit in separate types of programs; but we must avoid alienating segments by giving the impression that a particular program is the sole expression of religion.

Whom are we trying to reach? Are we reaching the ones who most need a radio ministry? Something needs to be solved in all of our communications work: "Is a program effective because it meets certain predetermined cultural standards or because it reaches the people in their need?"

Enlightened leadership will help, but it will not guarantee a successful future for religious broadcasting in New Haven. The available evidence indicates that the ministers seem destined to carry the major burden of broadcasting for adults, even in television. Actually, there is no indication they would have it any other way. It may be concluded, therefore, that all the ministers—not only those on the broadcasting committee—need to be radio — and television "wise." It seems axiomatic to point out that, lacking professional leadership, the New Haven ministers can help themselves through whatever training they can get in national and local religious broadcasting institutes. Training, planning in terms of the audience and limitation of programs to a number—however small—that can be produced creatively and— efficiently seem essential to future successful use of television and radio.

CHAPTER 6

Content Analysis of Selected Religious Programs

Religious agencies are interested in the mass media of communication because they have something to communicate—a message with a specific content to be transmitted to large numbers of people. The content is a body of ideas and attitudes which the churches and overhead church organizations hope to present with sufficient force to win—at least—respectful attention and—at best—acceptance.

The research staff studied scores of religious broadcasts. They discovered that the great bulk of these programs deal directly with religion as such. The time available to religious groups is used, in one form or another, mostly to present basic religious beliefs and their implications for living. It is much less often used for what may be considered auxiliary purposes, such as promoting the institutions of religion (e.g., programs designed to entice people to church or to raise money for churches),[1] or presenting current news in the religious world, or espousing secular causes the churches endorse or secular policies that might benefit the churches, or any of numerous other purposes for which the churches might find television and radio useful. When the churches—of whatever faith—go on the air, it is to talk about religion.

The analysis of effects, then, can be begun by examining the content of the messages—the ideas and attitudes—that are broadcast in the name of religion. The effects of a program depend upon the content in relation to the needs of an audience. If a program is to be successful, the content must be suited to the purpose of the program, its context and its intended audience. If the purpose is to change opinion or to motivate action, the content must be adapted to these ends. Whatever the audience for which the program is intended, content must be adapted to the tastes of that audience,

[1] There are, of course, many religious programs—radio and television—on purchased broadcast time which raise money to pay for the program itself, and some sustaining programs raise money—but not over the air—to defray expenses of production and supervision.

106

or the effects will be seriously limited or even quite different from those intended.

Content alone is, of course, only one of a complex of factors that determine an audience or its reactions. The verbal content is inextricably bound up with such things as music, format, style, appearance and ability of the performer, the availability of the program to the audience and of the audience to the program and other factors to be discussed later. But the verbal content is presumably central to this complex even if, on occasion, the message may be obscured by the manner of presentation.

Information from Religious Broadcasters

The research staff felt that, before beginning this analysis, it was essential to know something about the purpose and policies of the programs analyzed. Accordingly, a questionnaire was designed and sent to the sponsoring body and principal speaker on each national religious program (network, recorded and filmed) and each local series originated in New Haven. They were asked to define: (1) the audience they were trying to reach (sex, age, education, vocation, economic and social status, church relationship, marital status, et cetera; (2) methods used to relate program content to the experience and beliefs of this audience; (3) the objectives they wished to achieve with the audience; (4) the central theme of the broadcasts; (5) problems which they considered to be of vital importance for treatment over the air.

Opinions were sought on the following questions: (1) Do you feel religious broadcasts should deal with controversial subjects; i.e., race relations, international affairs, economic affairs, conflict between ideologies such as capitalism versus communism, relations between religious faiths, et cetera? (2) How do you evaluate in importance the various parts of your program —talk, music, liturgy, et cetera, in influencing listeners? What is the function of each part? (3) What do you consider to be evidence of the success of your program?

Certain facts were requested: (1) Do you attempt to relate your program series to the beliefs and activities of a particular church or churches? If you do, how is this relationship accomplished? (2) How long has the program been on the air? (Of speakers: How long have you been the broadcaster?)

The programs were monitored and recorded so format and content could be studied. In many cases scripts, recordings and kinescopes were furnished by the sponsors for detailed analysis.

Thirty programs responded to the questionnaire—a great majority of the religious broadcasters who have been on the air for a number of years. Bishop Sheen was the most conspicuous nonrespondent among the national religious series. The replies are treated in detail because (1) they show the variety of religious fare available to the New Haven resident; (2) they reveal clearly the objectives of the religious broadcasters; (3) knowledge of the broadcasters' conscious intentions concerning target audience, purpose, content and the like makes the content analysis of selected programs more meaningful; (4) analysis of the returns afforded a means of surveying more programs than could be given individual, intensive analysis. Here, then, is the over-all view of the aims and practices of the religious broadcasters.

Format

Table 44 shows that the two most common formats are talks and programs that include blocks of material presented in dramatic form. Both formats are equally used and between them they account for two-thirds of the programs.

Table 44. The format of religious programs

	Nondenom- inational	N.C.C.[a]	Other Protestant	Roman Catholic	Jewish	Total
Drama	2	4	1	2	1	10.
Talk	1	2	7			10
Miniature church service	1	4	1	1		7
News commentary			1			1
Interview	1					1
Variety	1					1
Total	6	10	10	3	1	30

[a] National Council of the Churches of Christ.

Most of the programs that use drama carry a summary message after the dramatic episode, either in the form of a "clincher" talk or of a discussion. Seven of the ten talk programs consisted of a combination of devotional music with a talk or sermon. In several cases the musical portion of the program was longer than the talk. It is interesting to note that seven of the ten talk programs were produced by Protestant groups not connected with the National Council of Churches. The third most commonly used format was the miniature church service, employed in seven of the thirty programs. The largest concentration of church services was found in National Council programs, where four used this format. The three other formats in use had only one program each.

Conception of the "Target Audience"

The definitions of the "target audience" by the broadcasters are particularly significant, since they indicate there is a general lack of denominational —or interdenominational—policy as to what audiences should be the objectives of religious programs. No one, it is true, said that the target audience was "people who agree with our point of view." Only one program *intended* primarily to communicate to people wedded to its persuasion. All are trying to reach outsiders. Seventeen programs, indeed, specified all-inclusive audiences: "everyone," "all unchurched," "all adults," "all families." The conclusion is evident that most religious programs are conceived of as means whereby a religious in-group can make some contact with the multitude outside the fold. We shall see subsequently (Chapters 10 and 11) that for most of these programs, especially those with smaller audiences, achieve-

Table 45. The target audiences of religious broadcasters

	Nondenominational	N.C.C.[a]	Other Protestant	Roman Catholic	Jewish	Total
Everyone	1	1	5	1	1	9
All unchurched		1	2			3
All adults		1		1		2
All families	1			1		2
Adults, unchurched but sympathetic to religion	2					2
Older women with some relation to a church	1					1
Upper middle class of middle age or older		1				1
Businessmen, 20-60 years of age		2				2
Middle and upper class adults			1			1
Middle class adults of middle age or older			1			1
Middle class, unchurched teens through middle age		1	1			2
Teenagers, unchurched	1					1
Children, 9-14		1				1
Children, 7-11		1				1

[a] National Council of the Churches of Christ.

Table 46. The purposes of religious programs

	Nondenominational	N. C. C.[a]	Other Protestant	Roman Catholic	Jewish
"Persuade to better lives"	1				
"Induce...more favorable attitudes toward religion"	1				
"To view church as broader than local church"	1				
A substitue or supplement for church	1				
Teach the value of Christian character... Beatitudes...Golden Rule	1				
To make Bible readers	1				
To proselytize		1	5	3	
Teach individual self-understanding and adjustment in light of God's word			1		
Familiarize with Bible		1			
Teach Christ as rational policy for personal and social salvation		1			
Commit minds and hearts to Christ		1			
Teach Christ as design for personal living		1			
Teach religion is practical way to success, wealth, happiness		2			
Teach to live Christian ethic		1			
Attach to church as vital organization for meeting personal and social problems		1			
Teach Christian attitudes and behavior on today's crucial issues			1		
Teach religious behavior through enjoyable experience of it			1		
Make good Christians via Bible			1		
Affirm dignity of all human beings before God					1
Not stated		1	1		

[a] National Council of the Churches of Christ.

ment of this purpose is a highly optimistic assumption. The audience actually is composed almost wholly of the faithful, rather than of potential converts. One is forced to the decision that few of the broadcasters have any clear picture of the audiences which their programs actually reach.

Table 45 summarizes the broadcasters' reports of their target audiences.

The targets cluster significantly. They have been arranged in a generally descending order of universality and age; in other words, those at the top of the table tend to be most undifferentiated and older, those at the bottom, most differentiated and younger. It is significant that the first four target groups (everyone, all unchurched, all adults, all families) are the objective of over half of the programs. It is not surprising that all three of the Roman Catholic programs fall into these most undifferentiated classes; as subsequent analysis of such programs will show that their content is expected to reach children through channels of parental and priestly authority. Similarly, it is not surprising that fewer than half of the National Council programs have these most general targets, nor that almost as many of the National Council programs (three) are aimed at children and youth as are directed at the most general audience. It is also important that seven out of ten of the target audiences for "other Protestant" programs are concentrated in the first four groups.

The Avowed Purposes of Religious Broadcasters

Our perceptions of the explicit statements of purpose of the various religious programs are summarized in Table 46.

Two comments can fairly be made on this extended list of purposes. The first is that it is noteworthy that frank intent to recruit converts characterized all three Roman Catholic programs and half of those produced by "other Protestant" groups, but only one of the programs of the National Council of Churches, This Is the Life, a series distributed by the National Council but produced by and representing the views of the Lutheran Missouri Synod which is not a member of the Council. Complementary to the first observation is the conclusion that programs that do not overtly proselytize have a wide diversity of professed aims. These "themes" and "purposes" presumably provide the policy base for the selection of content. They are stated in broad terms of the value of religious knowledge and belief to the personal lives of the audience members. These are programs intended to "help," to "assist," to "bring peace to the heart," to "provide comfort, devotion and inspiration," to "save the lost," to "sharpen the conscience of the community," to "help develop a design for living."

One cannot quarrel with the nobility of purpose expressed in these aims. If the programs live up to their avowed objectives, they will be of great help to their listeners. It must be granted, also, that it is not easy to state fairly a complicated purpose in a single generalization. But when the aims are viewed together with the sweeping designations of target audiences, one suspects that the religious broadcasters are expecting to accomplish too much with too large and heterogeneous an audience. The looseness of the purposes of many of the programs betrays lack of thoughtful program policy formulation. More modest aims with smaller and more carefully defined target audiences might produce more measurable results.

Should Religious Programs Deal with Controversial Subjects?

Still another dimension of the perspective of the producers of religious programs is their attitude toward admitting to such programs the reality of controversy. Table 47 summarizes the answers to the question: "Do you feel religious broadcasts should deal with controversial subjects . . . ?" The replies have been grouped into the absolutes of "yes" and "no" and the middle grounders who will admit "a little" controversy.

Table 47. Policy of religious broadcasters on admission of controversial issues

	Nondenominational	N.C.C.	Other Protestant	Roman Catholic	Jewish	Total
Television programs						
"Yes"		1				1
"No"		3				3
"A little"	3		1			4
Radio programs						
"Yes"		3	1	3	1	8
"No"	3	2	8			13
"A little"		1				1
Total						
"Yes"		4	1	3	1	9
"No"	3	5	8			16
"A little"	3	1	1			5
Total	6	10	10	3	1	30

Half of all these programs reject completely all treatment of controversial issues. Striking differences exist as between the denominational groups, however. All of the Roman Catholic programs and the single Jewish program (The Eternal Light) do deal with such issues. At the other extreme, almost all of the "other Protestant" programs avoid them, while none of the nondenominational programs deals with them without major limitations. Four of the latter are sponsored by networks, one by a commercial advertiser and the last by the American Bible Society. The National Council programs are split; half of them avoid controversial issues and half deal with them wholly or partially.

Summary of Religious Programming, Based on Broadcasters' Avowed Policy, Themes, Purposes and Practices

The way programs are handled (purpose, target audience, format, empathy devices, et cetera) would be expected to reflect the point of view of the producing agencies. Analysis of the questionnaire answers justified this expectation. The avowed thematic content and the methods of treatment are consistent with the policies and practices of the sponsors. Thus the Roman Catholic programs unhesitatingly proclaim their intent: to bring unbelievers into a proper relationship with that church. To serve this purpose, these programs aim at broad audiences, using a multilayered program content. They range widely in specific content, from dramatic presentations of lives of their Saints, to sermons, to current human problems treated dramatically. And when they deal with present-day human problems, they take advantage of the interests of various social classes in the society in one or another aspect of controversial issues, such as labor relations and communism. While the material presented has wide scope in terms of potential audience appeal, it is consistently the same in thematic treatment. This treatment has two characteristics. It involves the consistent application of sharp dichotomies: the world and all men in it are good or bad. Man's relation to his fellow men and his spiritual relationships are sharply marked with the qualities of extreme virtue or extreme evil. The second characteristic links with the first: the individual is called upon to submit to the authority of the church. In making this submission, the person is required to change both his attitudes toward himself and toward his fellow men. It is in man's relation to his obligations to his fellow men that the Roman Catholic programs give sharp directives (within the bipolarized semantic framework previously described) in their treatment of controversial issues.

The lone Jewish program, according to its producers, matches the Roman Catholic programs in the emphasis it gives to the importance of dealing openly with today's social problems. Here, however, the resemblance stops. For the policy of The Eternal Light does not envisage men as puppets, either of God or of the Devil. The semantic framework of this program sees men as complex mixtures of motives and as being endowed with both personal autonomy and dignity. Indeed, the purpose of the program was stated to be: "to affirm the dignity of all human beings." The Jewish program does not aggressively seek conversion to its faith.

Generalization concerning the remaining 26 programs is difficult. One (that of the American Bible Society) had a special purpose, namely, the promotion of the use of the Bible, and may be left out of account in this analysis. The remaining programs may be grouped in three classes, employing the dimensions used in the discussion of Roman Catholic and Jewish programs.

One of these classes we may call, for lack of a better name, the "fundamentalist" Protestant programs. These programs all explicitly emphasize their purpose to make converts to the church. None of them countenances the treatment of controversial issues in their content. While all of them operate within the traditional Protestant framework of individual responsibility to God, their thematic treatment policy employs a sharpness in bipolarizing human beings which is close to the semantic position of the Roman Catholics. In this group we would place: The Old Fashioned Revival Hour (Fuller), The Back to God Hour (Christian Reformed Church), The Baptist Hour, Showers of Blessing (Nazarene), The Voice of Prophecy (Seventh-day Adventist), and The Healing Ministry of Christian Science.

A second group of Protestant programs is distinguishable from the fundamentalist group on several counts. The programs in this group, in thematic treatment, appear to avoid the semantic device of sharp bipolarizing. They appear to treat individuals as endowed with inalienable dignity and with the potential for growing in the process of working out their own problems. Moreover, the problem content in this group of programs emphasizes mankind's responsibility for the social problems which today are controversial issues. None of them aggressively seeks converts to its faith. In this group we place: This Is the Life, All Aboard for Adventure, Bible Puppets, Let There Be Light, Religion at the News Desk, and National Radio Pulpit.

The third group of programs includes both nondenominational and Protestant programs None of them actively promotes conversion to any particular faith. All of them avoid the treatment of controversial issues if it is possible to do so. And all of them give religious experience primarily an intrapersonal reference rather than one of concern for fellow men. Because some of them appear to practice bipolarization much more than do others, no statement of this dimension is possible for the group as a whole. In this group we would place: Frontiers of Faith, Lamp Unto My Feet, Look Up and Live, What's Your Trouble?, Dumont Television Chapel, The Columbia Church of the Air, Faith for Today (Seventh-day Adventists), National Vespers, Art of Living, Evensong, Salt Lake Tabernacle Choir and The Greatest Story Ever Told.

Content Analysis of Specific Programs

Examination of the formal statements of purpose and intended audience for the religious programs was preparatory to the analysis of the program content designed to implement the purposes with the target audiences. The need for selection was obvious, in view of the wealth of available material. An intelligent basis for selection was not so obvious. The staff listened to or viewed several broadcasts of all religious programs aired in New Haven to become acquainted with the different formats and points of view and the varying methods of communicating religious concepts. After considerable deliberation, it was decided that for analysis of program content, the selection of programs should be made basically in terms of the major Christian traditions that are represented on the air. Broadly speaking, they seemed to fall into three groups: Roman Catholic, "fundamentalist" Protestant, and "co-operative" Protestant, the last-named meaning the characteristically middle-of-the-road position of programs sponsored by the major national agencies of interchurch co-operation and their local counterparts.

While these designations are so broad that the broadcasters to whom they are applied would consider them of little value for identification of theological positions, they are categories that our interviews indicated appear to have some meaning to much of the radio and television audience. The differences between one "fundamentalist" preacher and another, or one National Council preacher and another, basic as they may be to the clergy involved, tend to be viewed as marginal differentiation by the larger part of the lay audience.

At any rate, selection was made of programs that could represent these major viewpoints. Life Is Worth Living was selected as the television program and The Catholic Hour as the radio program to represent the Roman Catholic viewpoint on the air. These programs were so far ahead of any other Roman Catholic presentations in size of audience that no other choice was possible. National Radio Pulpit was chosen because it was the leading Protestant program in size of audience, and is also the oldest network radio program and the oldest program presented under interdenominational auspices. The Old Fashioned Revival Hour has been on the radio over twenty years and was selected as representing conservative, evangelistic, "fundamentalist" religion on the air.

The popularized psychological-religious approach to religious problems of Dr. Norman Vincent Peale in What's Your Trouble? (television) and the Art of Living (radio) seemed a fruitful field for research into effects; therefore these programs were chosen for content analysis. In addition, This Is the Life was selected for analysis because of the dramatic form in which its problem-oriented religious message is cast. Thus, in all, the research staff chose for detailed content analysis seven programs, of which three were on television and four were on radio. All are national programs.

Methodology of the Analysis

The first approach to content analysis was made by inviting experts from several disciplines (theology, psychology, education, et cetera) to listen to and analyze the content of selected programs, each from the standpoint of his respective field of knowledge. Results of this effort were too spotty to be used, except as background material for the research staff. One of these analyses, however, was particularly interesting and is reproduced in its entirety in Appendix A. Its interest and value lie particularly in the fact that it was prepared by a theologian, Professor Julian Hartt of Yale University Divinity School, a professional student of the field of knowledge with which the programs deal.

The research concern was centered in a concept of values. After considerable experimentation with various content analysis techniques, the research staff concluded that the different kinds of programs required varying methods of analysis. In dramatic programs, for instance, the interpretation of content by the director and the cast is invariably as important as the material the writer has put into the script. Stereotyping in characterization (type casting) and superficial interpretation of thought and emotion by the actors can make deep and abiding truths appear trite and unimportant. Conversely, realistic characterization and skillful interpretation can turn a thin piece of writing into an exciting experience for the audience.

The process of communication is quite different when the format is a speech than when it is a drama. The written content of the drama is perceived by the audience as it is interpreted through the action of the characters. The sympathies of the audience must be engaged by the qualities of the protagonist, those of the antagonist or the relationship between them. Unless the performance of one or both of these actors offers some facets of character which are congruent with the feelings and tension-states of the listener-viewer, his attention will shift elsewhere and he is effectively out of the communication field of the broadcaster. It is easy to assume that the portrayal of the drama must assume the same stereotypes that are held by audience members in order to engage their sympathetic attention. While in a sense this assumption is probably true, the danger is always present that an oversimplified formula for dramatic presentation will, through stereotypical casting, acting and direction, lose the essential qualities of Christian love and the Christian imperative. The assumption may too easily be conveyed to the audience that in real life people are either entirely good or entirely bad. It is part and parcel of the common assumption that things are as they seem, that there are only two sides to any question—an assumption we have termed excessive bipolarization.

The speechmaker has a different and perhaps quite as complicated a problem in attempting to reach his target audience. His appearance (if the program be on television), his voice, his personality, his pace, his gestures all qualify the reception his words alone might receive. The viewer or listener who tunes in a speaker for the first time may be expected to make a largely unconscious evaluation of all of these factors in an instant, when he gauges whether his interest in the program is sufficient to warrant giving attention to it further. This gauging process essentially involves the matching of elements in the feelings and tension-state of the audience member with elements in the speaker which allay or increase the tension-state. The winning of new listeners or viewers by the speechmaker on the religious program thus depends on whether he has (1) correctly forecast the needs of potential listener-viewers who (2) are likely to be tuned to the station he is broadcasting through (3) at the time his speech begins. The evidence presented in Chapter 11 suggests that for many preachers who talk over radio and television the audience is rather static: e.g., few new listener-viewers come to it, and its body consists of a relatively small number of loyal believers. For such an audience, what the speaker says is consciously the center of their attention and the speaker should judge what he can say to them with an eye on this backlog of listening-viewing loyalty on their part.

Proof of the extent of such listener-viewer loyalty was obtained in the depth interviews reported on in Part IV where the question was often asked of regular users of religious programs, "How would you feel if someone other than Dr. X said what he says in his program?" The answer summed up for such users to "it wouldn't be the same; it's not what he says, but how he says it that we like." Superficially, it appeared that fondness for the speaker and general agreement with his viewpoint led the listener-viewer to accept, almost uncritically, what he had to say. As we have suggested earlier, this finding probably means that when the relation of loyalty was being established, the audience member tested out the tension-reducing consequences of using the program and found them rewarding. He simultaneously obtained reinforcements for the attitudes which were congruent as between himself and the speaker. Conversely, we found that dislike of the speaker and suspicion of his affiliation or his doctrinal or social views were associated with nonuse of the program.[2]

We must bear in mind one other caution in dealing with the content of a communication made from person to person. We can describe, dissect, judge the written content of a communication; but we cannot by such process of analysis forecast its effects, nor can we wholly comprehend its meaning for any given member of the audience. In any audio-visual communication, the total content is a construct of the script (thought and language) plus the performance (voice and action). One cannot be divorced from the other in assessing meaning. This situation poses a dilemma for the analyst. On the one hand he can be scientific about counting words and phrases, identifying ideas and their relationship to each other, evaluating diction, even assessing style. On the other he is faced with a judgment that is wholly subjective. How does one assess the content implications of as simple a statement as: "It is the responsibility of the parent to train the child in religious and moral values," when it is made by a bishop of the Roman Catholic Church, standing in the full panoply of his robes before a statue of the Virgin Mary? How evaluate the influence on content of his magnetic eye as the camera zooms in for a full-face close-up; his smile; the joke he cracks; his unqualified statement that the authority he cites *is the authority*?

This enormously intricate communication process makes it necessary to evaluate content of radio and television programs within the whole context of the productions as they are broadcast to the audience. This process was followed in the current study. No program was analyzed on the basis of script alone. Each radio program analyzed was recorded on tape and heard by the research staff. Television programs were seen on the air or on film.

In the end, the research staff decided that the most simple framework of

[2] These findings paralleled those of other studies on the role of the communicator in audience acceptance of the communication. See Carl I. Hovland, A. A. Lumsdaine and F. D. Sheffield, *Experiments on Mass Communication* (Princeton: Princeton University Press, 1949) and Herbert C. Kelman and Carl I. Hovland, " 'Reinstatement' of the Communicator in Delayed Measurement of Opinion Change," *The Journal of Abnormal and Social Psychology*, Vol. 48, No. 3, July, 1953.

analysis was actually the most meaningful for comprehending the value-content of the communications that were received by the radio listeners and television viewers. Dramas have been analyzed on the basis of idea content in relation to stereotyping in casting and performance. The general analytical pattern used to analyze speeches is a simple dichotomy of value-loaded words and concepts into two groups: the concepts presented as *good* (*i.e.*, desirable) and the concepts presented as *bad* (*i.e.*, undesirable) by the broadcasters. The method was adopted because it permits comparison between speakers in concrete terms. However, the word-count method employed has one defect which will be apparent to anyone who has followed the preceding analysis. It fails to measure the *degree* though it does measure the amount of bipolarization in the programs. Thus, Bishop Sheen employs his "bad" and "good" words in sharp contrast to each other and with the implication that each is mutually exclusive of the other. Per contra, Dr. Sockman, whose text is remarkably free of such extreme bipolarization, is measured by the same yardstick as is Sheen, e.g., the number of bipolar words. In short, the method adopted has the failing of not measuring the semantic distance between the concepts, but rather, tacitly assuming that all antonymic words are the same semantic distance from each other, regardless of the context in which they are employed. In part this defect is offset by the fact that the significant words are themselves reproduced in the analysis and their meanings suggest (if they do not measure) the degree of bipolarization practiced.

Sermons by Bishop Fulton Sheen

Bishop Sheen's sermons were easily the most complex, subtle and multi-layered in meaning of those studied by the research staff in the course of the Project. Their intricacy was due partly to the agility of the Bishop's mind, the fertility of his imagination and the scope of his vocabulary; and partly, the research staff decided, to the fact he seemed to have in mind a many-faceted audience and was using the same symbols to say different things to different groups at different levels of meaning. Sheen, of all the religious broadcasters, seemed most consciously to be trying to attract and hold a cross-section audience that would represent society as a whole. He appears to have succeeded in attracting an audience that in its basic sociological characteristics is broadly representative of the New Haven population (Chapter 11). Some concept of the psychological types within these broad sociological groups may be seen from the description of his followers presented in Part IV.

THE CATHOLIC HOUR SERMONS

The Catholic Hour is a thirty-minute program, presented each Sunday afternoon over the National Broadcasting Company radio network under the auspices of the National Council of Catholic Men. The program is semi-liturgical in form, consisting of organ and choral music, prayers and an eighteen- to twenty-minute sermon by a priest. For some fifteen years prior to 1953, Sheen annually delivered one or more series of addresses on The Catholic Hour. He was, in fact, the principal speaker on the program, and it was through his Catholic Hour broadcasts that he built up a large share of his national reputation.

Sheen gave up his association with The Catholic Hour when the success of his television program became assured. His last series of sermons on The Catholic Hour was broadcast from January through April, 1952, just as this study was getting under way. Five sermons from this series were chosen for analysis, covering the period January 13–February 10, 1952.

We found that words and concepts with "unfavorable" associations outnumbered words with "favorable"[3] associations by two to one (224 to 107). The 224 "unfavorable" words or concepts were used 528 times; the 107 "favorable" ones were used 479 times.

Over one-third of all the "favorable" or "desirable" uses were represented by four concepts: "God" (Father), "Christ" (Blessed Lord, Son of God), "soul," and "Body of Christ," which accounted for 173 of the 479 "favorable" or "desirable" value-loaded words used. This usage hints at what the researchers actually found; that the Bishop in his description of the evil forces in man's existence roams widely across the landscape, referring to a large number and variety of "bad" or sinister forces in the experience of the audience, but in his treatment of "good," he focuses his attention on a much more narrow range of experience, centering around the Roman Catholic Church and its doctrines.

This conclusion is best explained with an example. Sheen's sermon on The Catholic Hour for January 13, 1952, was entitled "Temptations." In this talk, as in many other sermons, he emphasized bipolar concepts (God versus Satan, good versus evil) and the necessity of making a choice. The language was literary and poetic, and the style was emotional; concepts were introduced, left, and returned to impressionistically and at a rapid tempo; none was developed at great length.

What was the net effect of this message upon the audience? One may

_____

[3] "Favorable" meaning that the speaker spoke of them with approval or respect; "unfavorable" meaning that they were used in a context of disapproval.

safely assume that, whether or not the listener was agile enough mentally to follow the Bishop's argument, at the very minimum he was left with a series of basic impressions. Clearly he must have understood—given minimum intelligence and receptivity—that Sheen was describing a situation of conflict between "good" forces and "bad" forces. The minimum content communicated, therefore, must have been this conflict between the forces of good, identified with God and Jesus Christ, and the forces of evil, explicitly identified in this sermon with Satan.

The Bishop proceeded to identify a series of concepts, words and ideas with each of these major foci of the sermon—the "good" focus and the "bad" focus. These associations may be diagrammed in blocks of terms related to one another, with each block also related to the "good" focus of God-Christ-Heaven or the "bad" focus, Satan-Devils-Hell. (See diagrams, pages 122 and 123.)

It should be made clear just what is meant by "association." "Universities" are associated with Satan, not because Sheen said they are instruments of the devil, but because the only reference to them was to the effect that Satan has his "stooges in the universities." As there was nothing in the sermon to balance this comment—no suggestion, for example, that Christ may also have his emissaries in the universities—the net effect of this particular sermon was presumably to leave the impression that universities are suspect because they house agents of Satan.

Similarly, references to social reform, when it is concerned with agitation for housing, or security, or labor unions, or the improvement of man's material condition upon this earth, were presented in a negative fashion and with the clear implication that such agitation is a device of communism. Superficially, this conclusion was balanced by a brief passage declaring Christ's interest in social justice, but the concrete references for "social justice" in the sermon were (1) starvation in India, (2) slave labor camps in Siberia and (3) the deprivations and sufferings of missionaries. There was nothing to relieve the implication that social or political action in this country directed toward better housing, higher wages or social security is anything other than the exploitation of men's selfish desires by sinister left-wing groups interested in power.

Following are brief digests of four of the sermons studied, summarizing their content.

The Beatitudes

The Sermon on the Mount is inseparable from the Mount of Calvary. The soft Christian virtues are directly opposed to the watchwords of the world—security, revenge, laughter, popularity, getting-even, sex, armed

Words and Concepts with Favorable Association

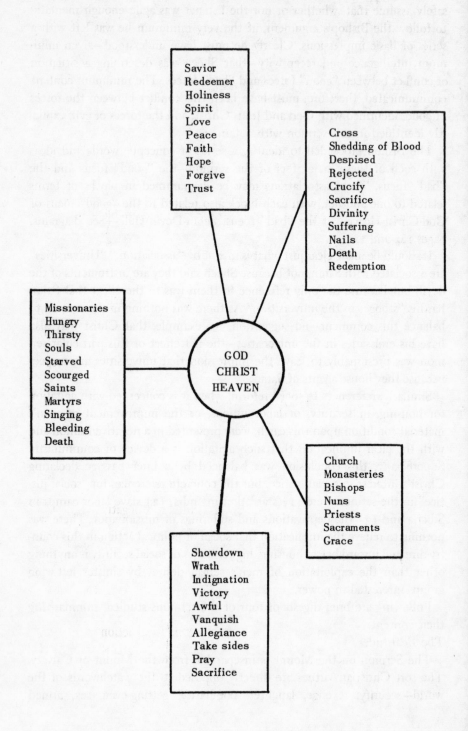

Savior
Redeemer
Holiness
Spirit
Love
Peace
Faith
Hope
Forgive
Trust

Cross
Shedding of Blood
Despised
Rejected
Crucify
Sacrifice
Divinity
Suffering
Nails
Death
Redemption

Missionaries
Hungry
Thirsty
Souls
Starved
Scourged
Saints
Martyrs
Singing
Bleeding
Death

GOD
CHRIST
HEAVEN

Church
Monasteries
Bishops
Nuns
Priests
Sacraments
Grace

Showdown
Wrath
Indignation
Victory
Awful
Vanquish
Allegiance
Take sides
Pray
Sacrifice

Words and Concepts with Unfavorable Associations

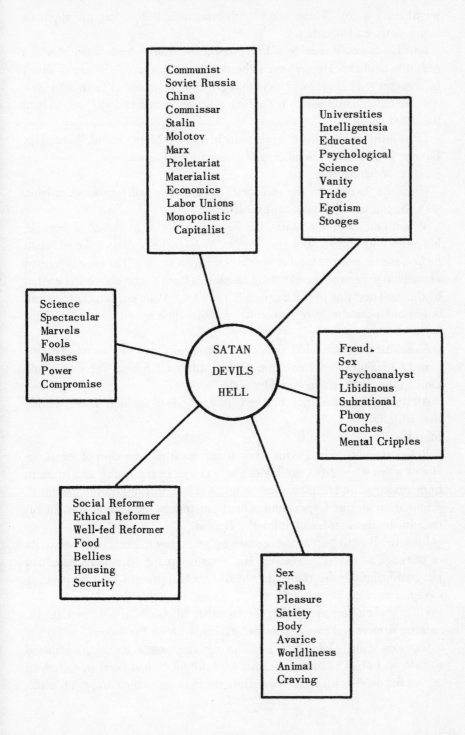

might and comfort. These watchwords bring mental disorders, unhappiness, hopes, fears, and anxieties.

Our Lord, who is outside of time, speaks the Beatitudes to a world which commits adultery. He says even the desire is sin. He tells a world which believes sin is due to environment and glands that sin comes from man himself. He tells a world which believes in revenge, hatred and violence to turn the other cheek.

Let Christ come into a world which follows Marx, Freud, Nietzsche, Dewey James, Sartre, Schiller, and he is crucified again.

Feeding of Multitudes

Until people come to the real life of faith, they usually associate religion with the full life of plenty on this earth.

When Our Lord announces the Eucharist, not as a symbol of himself, but as his body, blood, soul and divinity, he loses the masses or the common people, the elite or the intellectuals and spiritual leaders. The masses wanted a bread-king who would make them satisfied. The intellectuals were alienated by the hard doctrine of the Eucharist. They say, "Why not forget this bread of life and make it a figure of speech?" wanting their agnostic reason without faith.

Judas, carnal-minded like the masses, betrayed Our Lord, convinced that Christ's religion offered no hope for his ambitions. Simon Peter answered Christ, "Lord, to whom should we go?"

All through the centuries it is the Christ, who lives again in the Eucharist, that irritates.

John the Baptist

Religion ceases to be Divine when it reduces itself to a kind of social service or when it identifies itself with physical well-being, health and freedom from anxiety. The bread-king idea is rejected by Our Lord on the Mount of Temptation and at Capernaum. Our Lord rejects the second idea in his reaction to the murder of John the Baptist.

John the Baptist prepared his death by preaching the text of the sanctity of marriage as He who preached the Sermon on the Mount prepared for His crucifixion. Unlike the leaders of the world, John was bent on pleasing God not man, so he resolved to talk against divorce.

Herod, when he had nothing else to satiate his guests at his banquet (for nothing is more sickening than the organized joy of the jaded), called for a sensuous dance. Herodias, a conniving, degenerate mother, whispered to Salome, out of whom all decency and simplicity had been uprooted, to ask for the head of John the Baptist. At the bidding of the child of an adulteress, Herod had murdered the forerunner of Christ, the "greatest man ever born of woman."

Herod sought to see Our Lord "because he hoped to witness some miracle of his." Our Lord refused to speak to Herod. Herod who silenced the Voice in the Wilderness will not hear the Word.

Our Lord could have saved the life of John if he so willed. On the contrary, he thundered out, "There is no need to fear those who kill the body." Martyrdom is not the destruction of either body or soul, but the well-being of both.

This is an age of head-losing—in martyrdom, as with John, or to wine, pleasure, hate, bigotry, communism, anti-God, as with Herod.

Woman at the Well

Our blessed Lord in speaking with the Samaritan woman at the well taught that all human suppliances for the cravings of body and soul have one defect—they do not satisfy forever. When he compared the natural waters of the world with the supernatural water which he gives, he did not condemn or forbid earthly streams. Rather, as water never rises above its level, so earthly joys can rise no higher than the earth. Christ's living water flowing from the infinite, elevates to the infinite.

There are only two classes of people in the world—those who have found God and those who are looking for Him. The great sinners are closer to God than the proud intellectuals. The man who thinks he knows will rarely find the Truth; the man who knows he is a miserable, unhappy sinner is closer to peace and joy and salvation than he knows.

LIFE IS WORTH LIVING

The Sheen television series is aired Thursday nights under the sponsorship of a manufacturer of electrical appliances. Each program has a complement of commercial announcements.

The setting is akin to a library. A statue of the Virgin Mary is prominent in the center background. To the left of the viewer, and off camera except when in use, is a blackboard which the speaker uses from time to time. After use, this board is wiped clean by a property man, off camera. Sheen has created a character out of this property man who never appears on camera, and jokes about the "angel" who cares for the blackboard, a regular feature of the talks.

Sheen is introduced by a musical theme at the beginning of each program. He strides with vigorous purpose to the center of the set, dressed in his bishop's robes, and faces the studio audience, which also puts him full-face to the television cameras. The program from then on consists of a speech; and the Bishop employs the technique of a public speaker—or perhaps of an exceptionally dynamic classroom lecturer. He relies upon camera movement and closeups to give the television audience a sense of intimate contact with him. The speaking style, however, is that of person to group, not person to person. He is a dynamic, compelling speaker who is able to employ a kaleidoscopic range of vocal variety, facial expression and gesture. However, the research staff concluded that he talks with implicit authoritarian condescension to the studio and home audiences. At the end of the program he bows deeply in response to the applause of the studio audience.

Publicity for Life Is Worth Living has billed the program as nonsectarian in content. Actually, the Bishop's television broadcasts, on analysis, turn out to be very similar in content to his radio talks except at one point: explicit references to the authority, stucture, and doctrine of the Roman Catholic Church are greatly toned down or are made implicit.

Following are brief summaries of two television sermons on Life Is Worth Living:

March 2, 1954

The point of the parable of the Good Samaritan is not "Who is my neighbor?"—the object of charity, but "Have you the neighborly spirit?" "Are you a worthy subject of charity?"

The creators of social problems, the robbers of today, are not only the communists who steal land and possessions but also those who steal from the young the image of God that is within them—educators who tell them they have no will, intellect, soul; that they are just beasts, animals.

Social problems are ignored by the communists who believe a person of and by himself is without any value, and by a minority of social workers who, influenced by communist philosophy, believe there are only social problems, not personal problems. Rather, society can only be remade by remaking persons. Long investigations, financed by foundation grants, are not helping people directly. Our Lord fed the multitudes and in feeding found their number.

March 9, 1954

The level of civilization depends on the level of its womanhood. Women who do not fail are of three kinds:

1. Women who go out into the social, political and economic order and use their opportunities to demonstrate the specifically feminine qualities of sympathy, kindness, tenderness, equity, mercy, neatness, gentleness, heal-

"Desirable" Words and Concepts Associated with Three Kinds of
Successful Women in March 9, 1954, Sheen Telecast

Professional Women

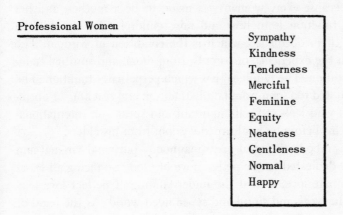

Sympathy
Kindness
Tenderness
Merciful
Feminine
Equity
Neatness
Gentleness
Normal
Happy

Mothers

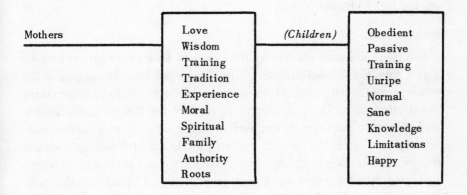

Love	*(Children)*	Obedient
Wisdom		Passive
Training		Training
Tradition		Unripe
Experience		Normal
Moral		Sane
Spiritual		Knowledge
Family		Limitations
Authority		Happy
Roots		

Nuns

Ideals	Heaven
Dedicated	Hand of God
Consecrated	Perfect
Virginal	Service
Love of God	Sanctified
Sacrifice	Grace
Pure	Beautiful
Divine	Passionless passion
Flame	Wild tranquility

ing. These women are normal and happy. *Illustration:* The women who work for the National Catholic Welfare Conference.

2. Mothers, because every woman was made to be a mother, and her most important function is to bear and raise children. Raising children means teaching them obedience, which is the condition of wisdom. The child learns from the experience of parents, from moral and spiritual training and from tradition. The family is that which perpetuates tradition. The child who is uprooted too soon from family tradition and teaching of obedience is the child who feels too self-important and speaks on international and social problems before he has learned wisdom from his elders.

3. Nuns, who embody the ideal of womanhood—pure and virginal and consecrated lives dedicated to the perfect love of God, sacrificing all lesser loves to this ultimate love, so that the understanding of perfect love may be kept before the weak and sinful and sex-minded world. As the hand of man plucks a rose and destroys its life in the garden for the higher uses of man, so the hand of God plucks a young woman from her human life to use her for His higher purposes.

CONCLUSIONS

Several conclusions concerning the policy of Sheen's broadcasts may be drawn from the word-association analysis employed here. Inspection of the words presented with favorable associations discloses that they fall into three broad categories: (1) words identifying parts of the Roman Catholic hierarchy, doctrine and organization, such as Savior, Church, monasteries, bishops, nuns, et cetera; (2) words signifying a relation of dependence on authority, such as allegiance, hope, trust, take sides, pray, et cetera; (3) words signifying extreme punishment, such as shedding of blood, crucify, nails, death, suffering, bleeding, scourged, starved, martyrs, et cetera. Psychologically, the pattern is unquestioning acceptance of authoritative direction which will lead to peace, redemption and holiness.

A parallel examination of the words presented with unfavorable associations shows three principal themes around which such words play variations. One theme is that of science—intellectualism—psychology. Universities and the intelligentsia are one variant on this theme. Psychology and psychoanalysts are another. Such concepts are linked with words like egotism, fools, stooges, vanity, phony, mental cripple, couches and libidinous. A second major theme is that of social reform which at one semantic level is linked with derogatory references to bellies, security, well-fed reformers; and at another level, with communist, Soviet Russia, China, commissar, Stalin,

Molotov, Marx, labor unions, materialists. The third major theme is sex —flesh, pleasure, satiety, body, avarice, worldliness, animal, craving. Observation of the Bishop's television programs indicates that this theme is frequently interwoven with those of science (when the Kinsey reports are made to represent science) and the evil aspects which the Bishop finds in psychology. Notable in all of the Sheen programs is the facility with which references to these three themes are touched upon forcefully and aggressively on different levels. Thus, on one program the attack on science was pitched at the intellectuals, the attack on social reform was on the communism level, and the attack on sex was in terms of a brief treatment of Epicurean philosophy. On another program, the science theme might be explicitly concerned with some of Freud's concepts, the social reform theme with material addressed to the asserted futility of seeking security through labor unions and social legislation and the sex issue may be treated scornfully in terms of Kinsey. The program strategy appears to be one of building a consistent message, with consistent themes deployed on levels designed to engage the interests of widely different groups in the population, ranging from intellectuals to the most intolerant of people.

The world which the Bishop describes to his listeners, then, emerges in fairly clear form as one in which a man should look with suspicion on a good deal of his social environment—universities, social workers, foundations, research, social reformers, labor unions, psychiatrists, the "intelligentsia"—as forces which, if not evil in themselves, are quite likely to be possessed of evil demons associated with the names of Marx, Freud and Dewey. Within that environment only one institution, the Roman Catholic Church, is clearly without taint and worthy of full confidence. It is the mediator which relates man to God.

The *normative belief and behavior* sought of the audience is obedience to authority and through established authority to omnipotent God. The individual is expected to reject knowledge or principles that do not come through established authority. There is to be conformity of belief and behavior, which connotes an antilibertarian, antirational, antiliberal, antiintellectual, antinatural attitude as normative. Everyone has an ordained position. There are no shadings of "good" and "bad" either within the pattern of authority or outside of it.

How far from the norm is the audience conceived to be? The audience members are far from the norm to the extent that they have indulged themselves in intellectual and political freedom and have explored other paths of belief and behavior than the "right" way—the way laid down by authority.

"Good" is equated with obedience, "evil" with diversity of thought and action.

It is implicit in the assumptions underlying the Bishop's position that anyone who stands at any distance from the "right" formula for living is virtually as "bad" as the evil forces to which he is thereby exposed. Here is the semantic trap which awaits those who are engaged by sharp bipolarized evaluations. It is parallel to the logic by which a McCarthy assumes that any critic of his perforce must be a "communist"—for obviously a noncommunist would support him.

What techniques are used to institute change? Scorn, ridicule and contempt are heaped on "wrong" beliefs and behavior. Inducements to conform are couched in strong emotional symbols (mother, sex, blood, etc.), and there are threats of awful consequences for those who stray. There is accepted Christian doctrine, especially in the radio sermons. There is also the appeal of humor and of personal winsomeness. Finally, there is the attractive offer of affiliation with a strong person, representative of a strong group which can nourish and protect its members.

What road maps does he give for guidance toward the desired behavior? Himself! Beyond that—by implication in the television broadcasts—the listener can put his trust in the Roman Catholic Church and related authorities. The way is to be found through uniform training and application of the training as directed by the mediator.

Sheen recommends no *auxiliary aids* to assist the individual.

Sermons by Dr. Ralph W. Sockman

National Radio Pulpit, on which Dr. Sockman, pastor of the Park Avenue Christ Church, Methodist, in New York City, has been the featured speaker since 1936, is a thirty-minute program broadcast Sundays over the National Broadcasting Company radio network under the auspices of the National Council of Churches. Its format is a Protestant church service in miniature —call to worship and invocation, hymns and anthems, Scripture reading, sermon and prayer. Music is by a quaretette accompanied by an organ. The sermon is eighteen to twenty minutes long and is usually a condensation of the sermon Sockman preached in Christ Church the previous Sunday. It may be presumed, therefore, to have been aimed primarily at a Park Avenue congregation consisting of New Yorkers heavily interspersed with out-of-town visitors. Sockman himself has stated he is seeking to serve a well-educated, upper middle class audience, and the statistical analysis of his New Haven audience (Chapter 11) plus the analysis of the depth interviews

(Part IV) indicate he does reach people of that type, plus other important segments of the population.

Sockman employs a cultured, quiet style of speech that may be attention-deflecting because of stereotypical tone, pace and diction. He may be typified as intellectual rather than evangelistic in his technique of speaking. He is at all times the gentleman, the expositor, the logical explainer, rather than the declaimer or special pleader.

What kind of world does Sockman live in, as he reveals it to his listeners? An analysis of six sermons (January 6–February 17, 1952) shows it to be a predominantly optimistic world, in which favorable references outnumber unfavorable references by more than three to one. If we count the words in these sermons that are "value-loaded" and make a simple dichotomy between those that connote positive ("favorable" or "desirable") references on the one hand and those that connote negative ("unfavorable" or "undesirable") references on the other hand, we find that "favorable" words or concepts were used 966 times, while "unfavorable" words or concepts were used 297 times—a very different ratio from Sheen's.

Nearly half (451) of Sockman's favorable words or concepts deal with the nature of the Christian life. These ideas can be subdivided into three broad groups, as in the following illustrations:

Personal Moral Life	Social Relationships	Religious Life
Goodness	Friend	Spiritual
Love	Fellow man (Fellowship)	Faith—belief
Moral	Mankind—world	Repentance
Courage	Brotherhood	Silence
Character	Race	Cross
Strength	Reconciliation	Heart
Righteousness	Kindness	Confession
Patience	Freedom	
Confidence	Home and family	
Conscience	Peace	
	Neighbors	

Next in frequency come theological words and concepts relating to God (Father, Son and Holy Spirit); the Kingdom of God, the eternal and the divine. They totaled one-third of all favorable references (340), with Christ (Guide, Master) first in frequency, God (Father) second, God as law and principle and order third, and the Holy Spirit, the Kingdom of Heaven and similar concepts much less frequent.

A third group of references, totaling 102, dealt with the specific nature and rewards of the Christian religion, and included such concepts as the church, revealed truth, forgiveness and redemption, help, hope, light, victory and grace. A fourth group of favorable references, totaling 96, were to Scripture and Scriptural characters.

Finally, came a group of favorable references which, while relatively small in number (73), were significant because they dealt with those aspects of present-day life which Sockman presented in a favorable light as contributing to constructive Christian living: education and scholarship, art, history, medicine, psychiatry and similar concepts which he related to "wisdom" and "creativity."

The "unfavorable" concepts and words are few compared with the "favorable" references in Sockman's sermons. They can be summed up in the following list of illustrations:

Sin and Death (116)	Sinful Man (98)	The World (83)
Sin	Fears	Worldly
Death	False (Falsehoods)	Times
Wrong—evil	Immoral	Business—dollars—
Suffering	Foolish	money
Darkness	Bad	War
Pain	Self-centered—	Conditions
Hurt	sufficient	Crowd
Past	Troubled	Corrupt
Bury	Hate	Politics
	Bitterness	Government
	Bodies	Problems

If we diagram the world of Sockman in terms of words and concepts that center around the forces of good, or positive values, and words and concepts that center around the forces of evil, or negative values, we create a schematic picture as indicated in the diagrams on pages 134 and 135.

The picture that emerges from this kind of word analysis is of a world in which the forces of good center in constructive character traits developed by the individual in his personal religious life through his direct relationships with God the Father and Christ the Master and Guide. Educational and religious institutions and Scriptures support this process of developing constructive character traits, and their principal mode of expression is through right (brotherly, loving) relations among men. Against these good traits are posed the forces of evil: sin, death, suffering, which in man produce fears and frustrations and ignorance, and in the world produce a materialistic money-centered culture, war, the "crowd" mentality and corruption in business and politics.

Sockman's world has little or none of the demonology of Sheen's. He does not evoke a picture of a world in which demonic powers have captured the universities, the psychiatrists, the sciences, the labor unions, the "intelligentsia," as does the Bishop. Sockman's attitude toward evil is one of sorrow rather than of fear or anger; he sees it usually as the diversion of the individual's life energies from Christian goals to ignoble ends. Sockman, on the whole, impresses upon the listener the fact he has no one but himself to blame for his failures. Moreover, the listener is assured that it is not abnormal for a man to find himself a complex mixture of drives and attitudes, some of which are admirable and others deplorable. Sockman does not use the semantic trap of sharp bipolarization.

Despite the preoccupation of Sockman's sermons with the individual, his social orientation is clearly that which has been known as the "social gospel." He places his influence on the side of those social developments which are generally classified as "liberal": i.e., the right of labor to organize, the participation of the United States in the United Nations, the extension of the benefits of education to larger groups, the end of racial discrimination. But the avenue to social change is clearly for him the reformation of individuals. In the sermons analyzed, he is not a "social reformer" nor an advocate of specific social action, although in other sermons he has made such advocacy.

Following are digests of six Sockman sermons which may clarify his basic themes.

Faith for These Times

Our faith is victorious because it helps us overcome fears of our time, i.e., economic insecurity, moral collapse, lost liberties, hostile forces. Christian courage is not born of desperation but of dependence on God.

Deepest faith in God rises out of the hardest experiences. Disbelief is most often found in the quarters of the shallow and comfortable.

Christian faith gives us forbearance and appreciation of others.

Brotherly love must be rooted in God's love to keep growing.

Company We Keep

A Christian, like Christ, must expose himself to risk in redeeming the company he seeks to help. To fulfill this difficult task, a Christian must preserve a *distinctive goodness*. We must be more than respectable, and carry our virtues with easy grace. We must cultivate a *spiritual fellowship*, cells of Christian comradeship. We must develop a *seasoning* and *redemptive quality*. The Christian must enter politics, civic and social movements.

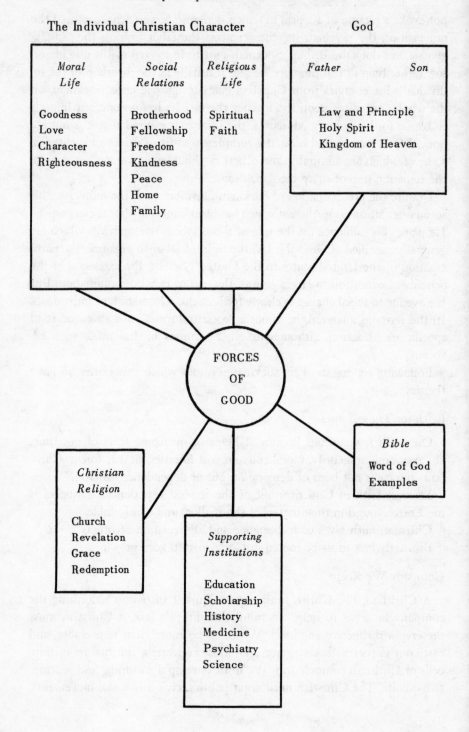

Conceptual pattern of Sockman sermons

The Individual Christian Character   God

Moral Life	*Social Relations*	*Religious Life*	*Father* *Son*
Goodness	Brotherhood	Spiritual	Law and Principle
Love	Fellowship	Faith	Holy Spirit
Character	Freedom		Kingdom of Heaven
Righteousness	Kindness		
	Peace		
	Home		
	Family		

FORCES
OF
GOOD

Bible

Word of God

Examples

Christian Religion

Church
Revelation
Grace
Redemption

Supporting Institutions

Education
Scholarship
History
Medicine
Psychiatry
Science

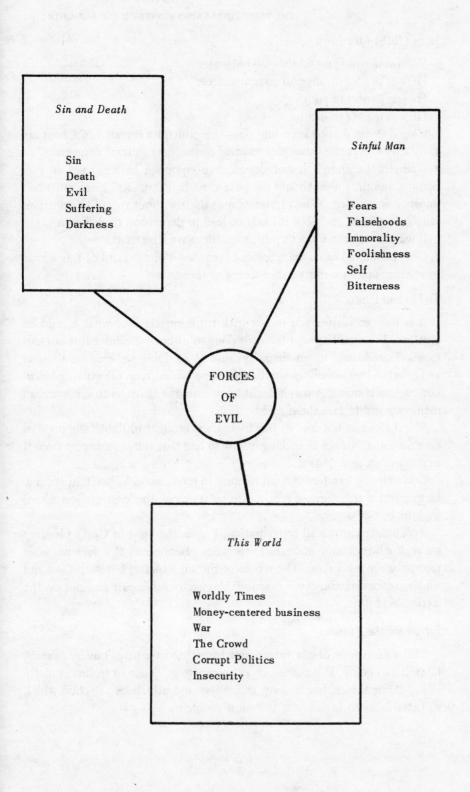

Jesus Christ Our Lord

We are not judging Christ—he judges us.

He was master of physical circumstances.

He was master of pain.

He was master of death.

Closed doors do not keep him out—the principles revealed in Christ are as inescapable as the principles revealed in the stars in their courses.

Granted the church is not designed or equipped to be expert in economics, and the pulpit should not pose as such, it must still speak out when injustice is revealed. When business runs itself without regard to principles taught by Christ, its greed is likely to lead to depression or deflation.

If we play false to Christ's principles, life plays false to us.

Christ is more than a masterpiece of manhood—he is Lord of Life whose ruling principles we must either accept or reject.

To Do and Undo

It is folly to torture our minds with futile regrets over what cannot be changed. We should forget the evils done to us but we cannot toss our sins cavalierly aside and forget them; because by so doing we keep on sinning, and also the bad memories we thought were buried keep on working below our conscious mind. A psychologist or psychiatrist helps us to discover bad memories and to face them calmly.

Moral sin does not lose its bad look when brought to light. The hope of cure for moral sin lies in making it look so bad that the sinner turns from it in abhorrence and disgust.

God helps us to advance from remorse to repentance. When Christ came he quickened the spirit of repentance by revealing the kind of God whom we hurt by our sins.

Repentance must lead to reparation. But in the light of God's blessings we realize we cannot make full reparation. Because of this fact we need reconciliation with God. The record of the sin remains; but with God and sinner reconciled, the eye is taken off the irretrievable past and put on the retrievable future.

Fitted for the Future

Christ assures us of the future, not by giving us a map, but by offering himself as a guide. We cannot expect concrete guidance in technical methods of doing things, but he gave us motives and principles of action which will enable us to handle our technical problems.

God not only gave us Christ as a guide, and the Holy Spirit to keep him a *living presence;* Christ is also an *unfolding revelation.*

The Lift of a Large Outlook

There is an arresting association between God and mountains. Our greatest artists often paint a hint of mountains in a picture portraying the Holy Family. Both Bethlehem where Our Lord was born and Nazareth where he grew up were hill towns.

In the Old Testament we learn that Abraham took his son, Isaac, to a mountaintop to be sacrificed; and Moses received the Ten Commandments on Mount Sinai. The Hebrews came to think of their most sacred places as being in the mountains.

What accounts for the kinship between the thought of God and mountains? Silence and an air of mystery are characteristic of both. Both suggest security and majesty.

As the psalmist wrote, "I will lift up mine eyes unto the hills, . . . whence cometh my help." From the low state of moral law that I see in myself and around me, I need to lift up my eyes unto the hill of Sinai, where I see the moral law in its grandeur. The second mountain to which I lift my eyes is the Hill of Grace, where Christ taught his disciples, saying, "Blessed are the poor in spirit." And I will lift my eyes to a third hill which has become known to Christians as the Mount of Transfiguration, where the closest of Jesus' disciples caught a new comprehension of their mission. And the fourth hill, the hill of Calvary, gives direction for the whole range of God's hills.

CONCLUSIONS

The *normative belief and behavior* which Sockman seeks of the audience is the acceptance and exercise of personal and social responsibility, within the framework of a liberal Christian ethic in which love and brotherhood are dominant themes. Behavior is based on the ethic taught by Jesus, and the Christian life is justified by the victory of Christ over death. Sockman's faith is reasonable. He indicates he expects it to be held and action to result from it, even at personal cost.

How far from the norm is the audience conceived to be? Sockman aims his message at upper middle class Protestants. He is talking to "mature" persons of fairly high educational standards. They are evidently conceived to be fairly close to the norm he is enunciating. He is evidently speaking to an audience already oriented to this norm, and presumably with experience and education in this kind of belief and behavior. If they are not practicing according to their beliefs, it is because they are backsliders rather than heathens.

What techniques are used to institute change? Sockman lays down no step-by-step course of action for the convinced Christian to follow. Rather, he introduces the listener to Christ and leaves the Holy Spirit to guide him further. There is dignified exhortation (gentle and genteel), but Sockman does not attempt to manipulate people. He assumes rational behavior on the part of his listeners, and that they will make free and responsible decisions. He presents a philosophical position and leaves the application to the individual.

What road maps are given for guidance toward the desired behavior? His own sermonic interpretation of the Christian Gospel is foremost. Copies of the sermons are offered free to persons who want to study them. His sermonic message is so well developed that there is a tendency for some listeners to make it a surrogate for church participation (see Part IV).

The church, at least by implication, is offered as an *auxiliary aid* to achieve the belief and behavior Sockman advocates. It is not, however, in the forefront of most of his sermons.

Sermons by Dr. Charles E. Fuller

Those who are familiar with "revival preaching" in American Protestantism can recognize immediately the content and format of the Old Fashioned Revival Hour; those who have not been exposed to revival sermons and the Protestant culture which nourished them may find the language and symbols somewhat difficult to grasp. The language is that of personal salvation through acceptance of Jesus Christ as Lord and Savior. Salvation is from sin, death, darkness and worldliness to forgiveness and the eternal life of the spirit with Christ.

The program itself is really an "Hour." It is sixty minutes long and includes lively gospel songs, Scripture reading, the reading of testimonial letters from listeners and indirect appeals for funds. The high point of each program, of course, is the twenty- to twenty-two-minute sermon by Dr. Fuller, followed by his vigorous altar call directed at his live audience.

The Old Fashioned Revival Hour is not a sustaining program. Broadcast time is purchased from stations by the Fuller organization, presumably using funds supplied by listeners. The programs originate in the Long Beach, California, municipal auditorium before an audience which Fuller treats as he would a church congregation.

Fuller's sermons for the four weeks January 20–February 10, 1952, were studied in detail. A word count showed the frequency of positive ("favorable") concepts outnumbering the frequency of negative ("unfavorable") concepts nearly three to one, 1,091 to 372. Fuller's concepts and terminology fall into a readily identifiable pattern revolving around the theme of acceptance of Christ as personal Savior. The research staff concluded that all of Fuller's sermons are so closely tied to the one theme that their basic content could be most quickly grasped from a summary "sermon" written in his style and cadence, and employing the "favorable" and "unfavorable" words and phrases abstracted in the word count. The summary which follows uses only Fuller's words. It has "favorable" words and phrases in large type and "unfavorable" ones in italics, with the numbers after each word or phrase showing the number of times each was used in the four sermons analyzed.

Take your BIBLES[7] and turn to (BIBLE REFERENCES).[74] I want to give you the SCRIPTURES,[13] not what I think, but what GOD'S[106] WORD[26] says. The GOSPEL[8] tells us that through the BLOOD[9] of the LORD JESUS CHRIST,[99] the ONE[34] FOUNDATION,[22] we are SAVED[20] from *darkness*[16] and SPIRITUAL[27] *death*.[21] Is that clear? At the very moment of CONVERSION,[5] we are BORN AGAIN[16] through the GIFT[34] of GRACE,[32] our *sins*[40] are FORGIVEN.[9] Let's get it straight—if you BELIEVE[28] on him in your HEARTS[13] as your PERSONAL SAVIOR,[8] you will be found WORTHY[13] of the BAPTISM[17] of the HOLY SPIRIT.[17] You are REDEEMED[4] by FAITH[16] to ETERNAL[16] LIFE.[23] In the *natural*[7] state without CHRIST,[99] all *men*[5] are members of *Satan's*[14] kingdom of the *world*,[12] SPIRITUALLY[27] *dead*,[21] *unconverted*,[3] *unregenerated*,[5] *unclean*,[5] *unprofitable*,[4] *blind*,[7] *bitter*,[7] *confused*,[4] *cut off*[3] from GOD.[106] Through his LOVE[12] we are no longer *alienated*[15] by the *lusts*[4] and *vanity*[3] of the *flesh*,[6] but are CALLED[18] out to WALK[32] in the GLORY[9] of the LIGHT.[13] Listen carefully. My chief concern is that you are a TRULY[13] BORN-AGAIN[16] BELIEVER[28]—a MEMBER[14] of GOD'S[106] TRUE[13] SCRIPTURAL[13] CHURCH,[36] the ONE[34] BODY OF CHRIST.[27] You who are *outside*[2] the BODY OF CHRIST,[27] BELIEVE[28] in GOD[106] today and then begin to act like a CHRISTIAN.[12] Measure up to the high CALLING[18] and in PRAYER[6] and HOPE,[6] DILIGENTLY[5] seek UNITY[10] and PEACE[8] in the FELLOWSHIP[10] of CHRIST.[99] We must WALK[32] WORTHILY,[13] not *stand still*,[1] in all FORBEARANCE,[5] GENTLENESS,[5] HUMILITY,[6] and LOWLINESS,[8] LONG SUFFERING[9] and SUBMISSIVE,[7] in the face of *trial*.[7]

After each sermon, Fuller made an altar call which can be summarized as follows:

Who will be the first to raise his hand and say, "I need Christ as my Personal Savior; Brother Fuller, pray for me?" God bless you, sailor boy. God bless you. In the balcony on my right . . . I'm pressed a little for time . . . God bless you . . . Continue in prayer . . .

Following are general summaries of three Fuller sermons.

Ephesians 4:1–3

Practical Christianity is based on doctrinal Christianity and doctrinal Christianity upon historical Christianity. Historical Christianity is based on certain well-defined established facts as follows: Incarnation of God's beloved son, the Lord Jesus; the Lord's sinless life among sinful fallen humanity; the Lord's death and resurrection, his Ascension and his personal, visible return from glory in the future.

We must measure up to the high calling and act according to it. We must walk worthily, not stand still, in all lowliness and humanity, meekness, submission and gentleness. He illustrates by a woman confined to her wheel chair with polio and a family in which the two boys were taken in one day by an epidemic that the trials of life can produce bitterness, or sweetness in character. We must have forbearance; be slow to anger; work diligently to keep unity of the spirit in the bond of peace.

You who are outside of the body of Christ, believe in God today and then begin to act like a Christian.

Feed My Sheep

Today the church is divided into many religious groups. A young convert must decide which is the true scriptural group. All in the world, unless born again, are members of Satan's kingdom. Through preaching of the gospel of grace those who really believe receive the gift of eternal life and become members of the body of Christ, the one true scriptural church. Every citizen of the heavenly kingdom should become affiliated with those who are like-minded no matter what their name. Not all members of all local assemblies are members of God's true scriptural church. But all true members of the scriptural church, the body of Christ, should be members of some local assembly where Christ is held forth as head.

There is only *one* body in Christ. God has set every member in the body *as it pleases him.*

At the moment of your conversion the Holy Spirit grafts you to the wounded body of Christ. This is the work of grace in your heart, the baptism of the Holy Spirit. Since faith without works is dead, then go and be baptized after you have been saved. Baptism (by water) will never save you alone. My chief concern is that you are a truly born-again believer—a member of God's one true scriptural church, the one body of Christ.

Alienated from God

All of us have sinned—the church still lives in an evil world. Pause to consider the true picture of our hearts, since all are sinners, outside of Christ. After you see your sinful condition may the Holy Spirit lead you gently to the blood of Jesus Christ.

1. Alienated from the life of God, shut out from fellowship of God, you belong to Satan who is your master.

2. We are in mental darkness, spiritually blinded. We cannot see the Kingdom of God unless we are born again.

3. We are in a state of moral degeneracy. Unless you repent, you will become insensible to all feeling; you will have no control over lust, the flesh.

4. We experience physical depravity. "Except ye repent ye shall likewise perish."

It's a dark picture but it's God's picture. If you sin willfully after receiving the knowledge of truth, there is no hope. If you dare trample the blood of Christ any more under your feet, God have mercy on your soul. You may fool men but you can't fool God. If there is the slightest yearning to be saved come now. Who will indicate, "I need Christ as my personal Savior?"

CONCLUSIONS

The world which Fuller depicts is an evil one in which men are sinners and are, literally, in danger of eternal punishment. But this danger can be quickly and, presumably, easily swept aside by the voluntary act of accepting Christ as Savior and being "born again." God is present at all times and man can take advantage of His availability by accepting Christ. God is related to individuals—atomistically. He is evidently not related to society, for Fuller does not preach a redeemed society. Instead, he urges people to flee society spiritually by accepting Christ; thereby by implication condoning evil society.

Fuller's standard of normative belief and behavior is acceptance of Christ as personal Savior; acceptance of status in this life and preparation for reward in afterlife; avoidance of sinful pleasures and practice of pietistic morality. His formula for a belief and behavior pattern equates conventional personal morality with good, conventional personal immorality—"sinful pleasures"—with evil. It is a polarized conception of living encased in extremely narrow intellectual boundaries. While the texts for Fuller's sermons come most frequently from the New Testament, his ethical preachment is that of the Ten Commandments. He puts no emphasis on the responsibility of the individual to make ethical decisions, which is explicit in Jesus' teaching, "Love God. . . . Love your neighbor." The Christian doctrine of forgiveness is interpreted in one dimension only—that of being forgiven. The concomitant responsibility to forgive and to live in love and charity with one's neighbor was not stressed, or indeed mentioned at all in the sermons analyzed.

How far from the norm is the audience conceived to be? Although Fuller claims he is addressing "everybody" in his sermons, his program actually is beamed at lower middle class Protestants of limited education, rural or small town either now or in background, to whom conventional revival language and style are familiar (see Chapter 11). The audience is addressed in the sermon as if it were composed of sinners being exhorted to accept Christ; but implicit in the presentation—program format, speech style, the coded language, the specialized music, the appeals for funds—is the assumption of an audience of the initiated. There is only a sprinkling of sinners. Most Fuller listeners are already "saved."

What techniques are used to initiate change? Each program seeks to arouse a conviction of sin based upon guilt feelings about past or present conduct.

What road maps does he give for guidance toward the desired behavior? Actually, Fuller offers no guidance, because salvation is immediate and not a process. Therefore, no road maps are needed. Fuller does recommend Bible reading and prayer, but without clear explanation of their place in Christian living.

Fuller recommends no *auxiliary aids* to assist the individual. He does not urge church attendance, but he does mention the church as the community in which the "saved" should live their "born-anew lives."

The Programs of Dr. Norman Vincent Peale

Dr. Peale conducts two weekly programs, The Art of Living on radio and What's Your Trouble? on television. The programs are similar in basic content, but they will be discussed separately, because of differences in technique of presentation.

Peale does not preach sermons on the air. He is not expounding doctrine. His talks on the radio and his discussions with Mrs. Peale on television are person-centered and problem-centered. Peale uses a psychological approach to personal problems, offering his audience techniques for their solution. The value structure of his talks is fairly simple to describe. He starts from a generalized Christian framework, indicates desirable goals for the individual ("happiness" or "peace of mind"), outlines some of the blocks to achieving these goals ("defects," "worries") and then describes methods ("prayer," "Bible reading," "faith") whereby these blocks can be overcome and the goals achieved.

Peale's treatment of his themes is simple and repetitive, amply sprinkled with concrete illustrations. It urges nondirective self-therapy as a cure for anxiety. It is also polarized. He offers listeners the possibility of change from "bad" personal relationships and psychological moods to "good" ones through use of his techniques. His talks, like the sermons of the other two Protestant ministers we analyzed, have much more positive content than negative content. His approach is inherently optimistic; you can achieve salvation if you come to terms with yourself and let God speak to you.

THE ART OF LIVING

This is a fifteen-minute talk aired over the National Broadcasting Company radio network Sunday mornings. Peale is introduced by an announcer. There is no music. Inspirational booklets by Peale are offered free to listeners.

Four of Peale's Art of Living talks were studied in detail (January 20–February 17, 1952). The count of words and ideas showed "favorable" or "desirable" concepts were used 1,103 times, while "undesirable" concepts were used only 329 times. The listing of words and concepts used most frequently in these four talks gives the flavor of their content. (See next page.)

Peale's talks move easily from the language of "lay" psychology to the terminology of the Christian life, with values borrowed rather indiscriminately from each field and mixed together without evaluation. His general approach and methods may be seen from the digests of his talks which follow.

Simple Secret of Peace of Mind

What this generation wants about as much as anything is peace of mind. People today are crowding the churches and buying religious literature because they want peace of mind.

You can get rid of the attitudes and habits that destroy inner peace by tremendous spiritual experience. But you can also get rid of them by starting to practice the attitude of peace of mind and by casting out all thoughts that disturb the serenity of the inner life.

Such great minds as Masefield, Epictetus, Seneca, Marcus Aurelius, Emerson, Calvin Coolidge and St. Theresa practiced serenity and tranquility by filling their minds with serene, peaceful, quiet thoughts. To gain peace of mind you must also get near to God, let Christ come into your life.

List of Peale Words

Favorable			Unfavorable
The Content of the Christian Religion	Methods of Achievement	Desirable Goals and Traits	Undesirable Traits and Blocks to the Christian Life
Jesus Christ, Lord 34	Pray(er) 35	Happy(iness) 71	Defects 20
God 19	Minds 19	Peace of Mind 23	Unhappiness 11
Bible—Scriptures 11	Faith-	Wonderful 20	Wrong 11
Churches 6	Belief 18	Simplicity 19	Problems 9
Religion 5	Art (of) 16	Great 16	Troubles(d) 8
Preachers 2	Practical 13	Spirit(ual) 12	Worries 8
	Charge 13	Good 11	Difficulties 7
	Love 12	Beautiful 8	Old 5
	Power 11	Clean 7	Devil 5
	Healed 9	Confident(ly) 7	Confused 4
	Listen 9	Peace 7	Failure 4
	Methods, techniques 9	Inner peace 6	Sin(ful) 4
	Overcome 8	Wise(dom) 6	Weak 4
	Read 7	Satisfactions 5	Hate 3
	Correct 6	Tranquility 5	Misery 3
	Study 5	Marvelous 5	Nervous 3
	Secret 5	Perfect(ly) 5	Distressed 3
	Solve 5		Dejected 3
	Forget 5		High-strung 3

Your Self-Defects Can Be Corrected

There is an infinite perfectibility about human nature. If you get firmly fixed in your mind the dynamic of change and will apply faith to your mental attitude, whatever your defect is, it can be corrected. Many of us have defects of the emotions or of the personality. Another type of defect is a moral defect. This, too, can be corrected. It is a fact that there is no change that cannot take place in a human being, none whatsoever, provided that individual wants to change and provided he will believe.

A Wonderful Life

One of the most amazing facts of this present generation is the number of people who are learning to make their lives more wonderful. As one man who writes me says, "Oh, what wonderful goodness God has laid up for those who trust Him." Everyone should ask himself, "Am I going to be a victim all my life of these weaknesses and defects that I now have?" I believe that if a person wants it he can have a marvelous new life. There are just two simple little things that can help bring that to pass: put your faith in God and Jesus Christ and live a day at a time. The secret of living a day at a time is to dedicate each day to God. If you've done a stupid thing in the past, derive what insight you can from it, and forget it and go ahead.

Most unhappiness in life comes from what we are within. There are people who have not been released from the weaknesses and imperfections within themselves; people who have committed sins, have never had them forgiven and who do not have the moral strength to overcome them. The most superlative genius in the art of changing people is Jesus Christ.

How To Be a Happy Person

Abraham Lincoln told us that he had decided that most people were just about as happy as they made up their minds to be. I realize this sounds very simple but the structure of the universe is based on certain very simple principles, and one of the simplest is that our happiness or lack of happiness is determined by what goes on in our minds; and it is also a fact that we can control what goes on in our minds.

The over-all way to accomplish happiness is to get the spirit of Jesus Christ in your heart. Let him fill your mind and heart and your heart will almost burst with joy.

The thing that will assure you of being a happy person is to get simple. Christ says that the way to live in this world is to become as a little child. The great simplicities of life produce happiness. We find happiness in the home, country, love, in our families and friends, in goodness and in God.

WHAT'S YOUR TROUBLE?

This is a fifteen-minute program on motion picture film, distributed weekly by the Broadcasting and Film Commission of the National Council of Churches to individual television stations. The stations broadcast the program at their convenience on sustaining time, usually under the auspices of the local council of churches. The program format is that of a conversation or discussion between Dr. and Mrs. Peale. The background is a library or living-room-type set in which the participants are seated at right angles to each other. There is little physical movement on the part of the Peales. Sometimes one of them enters at the beginning of the program or rises to get a book or paper. The rest of the time they remain seated while the camera cuts back and forth from close-up to two-shot.

This simple format puts the whole burden of the program on the two participants and what they say. Peale on television appears as a rather familiar, homey sort of person who might really be talking things over with his wife in the living room. He opens each program with a cordial, "Hello there, how are you?" to the viewer which includes him in the conversation. During the program there are numerous statements and questions directed to the viewer, aimed to keep alive the fiction of a three-way talk. Peale is bluff and hearty; he smiles frequently. His speech is plain and familiar, and he avoids studied gestures. He is also self-assured and positive, a literal "success" symbol for the viewer. Mrs. Peale is attractive and vivacious. She can score telling points in the conversation, when she is given freedom to do so. More often, she is cast as a foil for the development of his views.

The research staff concluded that, on the whole, the Peales give the appearance of an intelligent professional couple in the process of talking out problems of daily living, but with emphasis on a success that appears to be easy of achievement. There is also present, by implication at least, the example of the Protestant minister and his wife working at problems as a team, each contributing a unique experience and judgment to the discussion. The presence of Mrs. Peale places her husband in a family situation that may jibe with the family experience of the audience members.

The content of *what is said* deals directly with personal problems and how to solve them, and closely parallels the content of the radio talks. Digests of two programs will suffice as an example.

Are You Bored?

Mrs. Peale expressed surprise that anyone could be bored with life and stated that she had never in her life been bored for one single moment. She laughingly assured her husband that there is never a dull moment living with him.

Peale offered a technique for overcoming boredom: (1) stop thinking about yourself; (2) get active in something besides yourself; (3) have a spiritual experience with God. Mrs. Peale described the church service as "the creation of an atmosphere in which a spiritual miracle can take place." Peale closed the conversation by reading from the Bible, "I am come that you may have life and have it abundantly."

Illustrations were used to show how to overcome boredom. (1) A man who wanted a two-week vacation because he was bored was described to show that it takes more energy to be bored than to be happy. (2) A couple attended night clubs every night of the week seeking the "glamorous" life, but never finding satisfaction. They were persuaded to become active in Peale's church and in political precinct work in the city. (3) A former drunkard and heavy debtor wrote Peale that it was "nothing short of a miracle" that in six years he had found happiness and peace of mind by doing a "day-to-day job on myself."

Are You Happy?

Peale stated that happiness is the most discussed subject in history. "You must realize that you have the power within to be happy," he said, "that you can overcome any difficulty, that you can lick it. . . . You must practice inner quietness to be happy."

He prescribed a technique to secure inner peace: Three times a day for two weeks, (1) sit down and ask forgiveness for sins, and accept forgiveness, (2) forgive everyone you are mad at, (3) read the Bible for fifteen minutes each day, and sit and think of God's healing balm sinking into your mind and personality.

Mrs. Peale added that the best way to be happy is to scatter happiness around you. Peale closed the conversation by reading from the Bible, "Who so trusteth in the Lord, happy is he."

The following illustrations were used to describe how happiness works for people: (1) A man remained self-confident and cheerful through prayer and faith, although he was out of work for six weeks. (2) A newspaper advertisement was read which advised persons looking for a job to relax and believe that "God is guiding me to the right job. You will be surprised at the results." (3) A "happiness salesman" was described, a man who has on the back of his business card the advice, "Live simply, expect little, give much, keep the heart free from hate and the mind free from wrong. Try for one week."

The programs stressed success in solving the problems of boredom and unhappiness by simple means. Peale was prone to use superlatives in describing the people who succeeded in overcoming unhappiness and boredom: "He is the happiest person I know." "He's been happy ever since." "He is the happiest man I ever saw." "I never saw such an active couple." "He overcame all his defeats." "Most dynamic couple in that town."

In these two television programs and generally in his broadcasting, Peale stresses the compatibility between his practical religion and medicine. He frequently mentions physicians who consult him for spiritual guidance for themselves or their patients. He also plays up the importance of doctors in helping people solve psychological problems. "Doctors and ministers are close together. If you are sick, see your doctor *and* your minister. The mind and body go together."

CONCLUSIONS

Interpersonal relationships dominate the *normative belief and behavior* which Peale seeks from his radio and television audiences. He wants them to learn to get along with other persons without anxiety or frustration. A belief in God and faith in His willingness and power to help the individual are implicit in all of Peale's teaching. God is pictured as a benign, omnipresent person who is there to help you overcome evil, if you will call upon Him. Man's maladjustment, rather than his sin, is emphasized. Man's goodness is revealed in the achievement of happiness and peace of mind, in getting along with people, in realizing his potentialities, and in being successful in the eyes of his peers. Evil is pictured as unhappiness, anxiety, frustration, boredom, breaches in personal relations. There is no need to adopt a theological position, nor to take a stand on social problems. Man achieves success by adjusting to society, not through attempts to change or transcend it.

How far from the norm is the audience conceived to be? Distance from the norm is measured in the degree the person is suffering from anxiety, frustration, failure and emptiness.

What techniques are used to institute change? Peale requires people to face and admit personal problems. He insists that everybody has such problems. Once they are felt and the tensions involved are understood, he offers various "simple" methods for the finding of inner peace and relief from anxiety: (1) Prayer and Bible reading, doing acts of kindness to others to bring a person to the realization that he has power within himself to meet any difficulty. (2) Use of score sheets, reading reminders and memoranda as the basis for daily practice of his techniques for relaxation and reflection. (3) "Refueling" the spiritual life by setting aside regular periods each day for complete relaxation and meditation. The mind must be drained of frustrations and hatred, and the "healing balm of the love of God" allowed to soak into the personality. Inherent in all of these processes is a direct relationship with God and acceptance of His forgiveness, both necessary for the finding of peace of mind and a successful life.

What road maps does he give for guidance toward the desired behavior? Peale has four major guides for behavior: prayer, Bible reading, his own booklets which are offered as premiums on the programs, and the illustrations he gives on the air and in his writings of people who have successfully solved their problems.

As *auxiliary aids* Peale suggests the local minister, church attendance and membership, a physician if necessary. Peale strongly advocates the minister and the church as resources for spiritual guidance.

Peale's programs must be differentiated in content from those of all of the other speakers we have analyzed, because of their concentration on the "inner" or "psychological" life as the scene of battle between constructive and destructive forces. Both Sockman and Fuller preach individualistic sermons, but both of them see the individual in much more objective terms than Peale, whose gospel is subjective. Sheen is preoccupied with the forces of social evil, and Sockman and Fuller recognize them as factors influencing human behavior and choice; but for Peale the forces of evil are internalized as defects, frustrations, failures and troubles. Naturally, Peale resolves them in this area also, as changes in attitude, outlook, faith and personal behavior.

In the dimension of social judgment, especially, Peale and Sheen represent extremes. Sheen paints a vivid picture of a society in which "good" and "evil" are at war; Peale's picture of the social world is obscure and undefined. The listener presumably emerges from Peale's sermons with a clear picture of his own responsibility for his personal happiness and adjustment, but with no clarification of the Christian's role in society.

Peale's theory of personal adjustment is applicable to persons of all classes and creeds. But Peale self-limits his audience. He imposes the limits by the illustrations he uses and the kind of "success" he posits. He deals with living within the standards and at the level of the middle and upper class business and professional groups. All of the illustrations cited from What's Your Trouble? were of this type. Peale seldom discusses problems or paints a success picture in terms of factory workers. His treatment—but not his theory —eliminates farmers, laborers, and industrial and craft workers from experience-centered interest in the content.

This Is the Life Dramas

This series of thirty-minute dramatic programs is produced by the Lutheran Church, Missouri Synod, and distributed by the Broadcasting and Film Commission of the National Council of Churches. The programs are filmed in Hollywood and released to television stations for broadcasting at their convenience on sustaining time.

This Is the Life is situation drama that deals with familiar, universal and recognizable human problems in the context of a believable family and community situation. The greatest weakness of the programs, as drama, is their lack of suspense in relation to denouement, since the audience cannot help but know that a solution of each problem will be found within the context of Christian doctrine. Nevertheless, some suspense is maintained over the *method* of solving the problem, and the solution is usually both believable and realistic.

The plots are laid in a community that might be either small town or suburban. They revolve around a stock middle class American family, the Fishers. Grampa Henry Fisher is about 65, unemployed, whimsical, ingratiating. He is a cracker-barrel philosopher whose stock in trade is Christian platitudes. Technically, he is a narrator who introduces the plot and bridges scenes. Grandpa lives with his son Carl and Carl's family in a modest, single-family house, furnished in prosaic Grand Rapids style. Carl, about 42–44 years old, is an attractive, strong character who owns a drugstore. His wife, about 40, is cast as a believably efficient housewife and loving wife and mother. There are also a teenage son and daughter and Freddy, 11, "a typical American boy." The community is peopled with other citizens, including a town gossip, newspaper reporter and a minister.

Plot use of the Fishers is flexible. Sometimes one of them is the protagonist, infrequently the antagonist. In other programs they play supporting roles. But they are the nucleus around which all of the programs revolve. The impact of the programs can be best understood from a description of the action in one episode, coupled with an evaluation of the characterization and the interpretation of the script by the cast.

Jonathan and Sara

This program opens with Grampa Fisher sitting, full face to camera, looking at a photograph album. He points out an empty spot where a picture has been torn out, and explains that a picture of Jonathan was there. He shows a picture of Sara, Jonathan's wife and Mrs. Fisher's sister. Sara is dead, he explains. Then, in flashback, the story of Sara and Jonathan is told.

Sara and Jonathan are young, attractive and in love. Jonathan is a rolling stone, ambitious for success and wealth. He proposes to Sara, promising her money and the biggest house in town. She asks only for "the little things," and that he be happy.

Jonathan promises to settle down. He buys a gasoline filling station. They are married, move into a small house. She tends the house, plants flowers. The good life for her is finding happiness in simple things. But Jonathan is restless and unhappy, disgusted with his work. When she urges him to go to a church supper, he refuses. He bursts out, "I can't get clean any more. I hate the sight and smell of it!" (The grease on his hands.) Here is the first clue that Joanthan feels guilt over his selfishness—guilt which alienates him from the love and forgiveness of God. Sara, sensing his distress, asks what he really wants to do. His answer, "Do people ever do what they really want to do?" implies his lack of responsibility toward Sara and his failure in obedience to the will of God, subsequently demonstrated in his decision to satisfy his selfish desires for wealth, adventure and freedom. He deserts Sara, asking her in a note to "forget there ever was a person named Jonathan."

Jonathan disappears. Sara dies of some vague, undefined illness, presumably complicated by a broken heart. Some years later, Jonathan returns seeking Sara. On finding that she has died, he is filled with remorse.

When Jonathan returns, Mr. and Mrs. Fisher refuse to welcome him. Grampa suggests that Jonathan may be truly sorry for his errors and urges that the family accept him. Freddie, reciting the Beatitudes that he learned in Sunday school, cannot understand why everyone hates Jonathan. He asks Jonathan to explain, and gets the answer, "They have a right to, because I did an awful thing." "But I do bad things and people don't hate me," Freddie assures him; "if you are sorry and believe in Jesus, that's all there is to it." Jonathan tells Freddie that it is not that simple.

Still seeking an answer to his question, Freddie asks his mother, "Since Jonathan is sorry and hates himself for what he did, aren't people supposed to forgive him? In Sunday school they say, whether hard or easy, you must forgive people." She does not answer him. Grandpa assures him. "That's what the Bible says, only sometimes. . . ."

The Word of God is presented as a simple truth understood by a child from his Sunday school lesson, embarrassing to an adult mind that has learned deeper hates and resentments from wider experiences. However, the parents ultimately see their hardness of heart through the direct medium of the church service and the sermon by their minister. The pastor, understanding the situation, preaches directly to their need:

Because God sent his Son to die for our sins we stand today, pardoned, justified and forgiven. We pray, forgive us our trespasses because God's Son has paid all our debts. Unless we promise to forgive those who trespass against us, we are actually praying, "God, don't forgive me for I have no intention of forgiving my fellow man." . . . Judge not that ye be not judged . . . Let each ask, am I as merciful to others as I expect others to be to me? . . .

Jonathan, who did not attend the service, asks the minister in his study, "How could I come to church after what I've done?" The pastor tells him that the Savior's forgiveness was meant for people like him. "He who comes to me, I shall in no wise cast out." Each of us as a sinner is required to repent of his sins and to accept God's healing power of forgiveness and His love.

The Fishers, now conscious of their own need of God's forgiveness, in turn forgive Jonathan and ask him home for dinner. Jonathan, through a new understanding of the meaning of Jesus' death, is able to accept their forgiveness.

At the end of the drama an announcer, speaking over a picture of an open Bible, explains that the story is addressed to all people, the inference being that all stand in need of the saving grace of God's forgiveness. "There are thousands of Jonathans in the world today, afraid to live, to look at God, to die." A free booklet is offered to listeners with the promise it will "help you to get right and stay right with God."

This program has a clear-cut theme which is explicit throughout the script and is not clouded by the introduction of subthemes and complications in plot structure. This theme is, of course, the Christian doctrine of forgiveness. The members of the Fisher family and Jonathan, the wayward brother-in-law, are portrayed as children of God, basically good, but also humanly unkind, unmerciful, resentful and selfish—standing in need of the forgiveness of God. The relationship between a perfect God and His erring children is a dynamic one. Men are not made whole and perfect at a single moment of insight into His love for them. God's redeeming action, continuous and sure, reaches out in new ways to the Fisher family in their human relationships and daily decisions.

The Fishers are law-abiding citizens and regular churchgoers. Their family ties are strong, and Jonathan's desertion of Sara is for them an unforgivable act, especially since they feel Sara's death, at least in part, was the result of a broken heart. They are unmerciful and unkind toward Jonathan until, through the church, they face their own need of forgiveness.

Though Jonathan's sin is great, he is made to feel his importance as a child of God and is finally able to accept for himself God's redeeming grace. He is truly sorry and repentant, and although his desire to change his ways is clear, the plot in no way indicates that he will not transgress again.

Grampa, the kind gentle narrator, and Freddie, his grandchild, follow the typical good-bad characterization of the other members of the Fisher family in a less explicit way, because of their roles in this particular episode. Grampa, perhaps wiser from his greater experience, and Freddie, perhaps naïve because of his youth, do not find it hard to forgive Jonathan. Both are instrumental, though in a less important way than the church, in the eventual acceptance of Jonathan by the other members of their family.

CONCLUSIONS

In applying certain standardized evaluation instruments, the research staff came to the conclusion that This Is the Life has two major content weaknesses. The first is the stereotyping of characters. No character in these programs is a *person* in his own right. Each one represents a type and reacts always in the type pattern, i.e., Grampa—whimsical, kindly, lovable, wise, never obstinate, confused or irascible; Carl—good, strong, upright, never selfish, scheming, harassed, undecided, afraid; Mrs. Fisher—kindly (even when she "hates" Jonathan), affectionate, orderly, happy, never shrewish, disorganized, tired, discouraged; the minister—kindly, firm, authoritative, never hesitant, doubtful, indecisive. The characters are, therefore, one-dimensional; they do not have the rounded personalities of true human beings with both strengths and weaknesses, lovable traits and unpleasant ones. The actors who portray these characters are themselves type cast. They do not play roles; they merely read lines. The techniques used by both writer and director of This Is the Life are those of the daytime serial on radio and television. They require a minimum of creative effort and expense to make a point, but they sacrifice the believability and warm, human complexity that bring dramatic characters to life in the minds and emotions of the audience.

The second major content fault in the scripts is the contrived nature of some of the situations. We have already stated that the solutions of the problems are realistic within the basic doctrinal orientation of the programs. The same thing cannot always be said of plot events leading up to the solution. In Jonathan and Sara, for example, both the events leading up to Jonathan's desertion and Sara's death are mere devices to set up the problem the writer wanted to treat, Jonathan's return and rejection. The death, in particular, lacks dramatic validity, since the character of Sara, as portrayed, is that of a woman of faith and strength, who tries to convey her convictions to Jonathan. She does not appear to be a person who would pine away and die. Furthermore, the audience is not prepared for her death by dramatic action. The narrator merely announces her death—a writing *faux pas* unbelievably elementary in character.

The sponsors of This Is the Life list as their audience nonchurchgoing Americans of all ages. The analysis of audience for this program (Chapter 11) shows it does reach a fair cross section of the New Haven population, but Table 81 also shows *it does not reach people who are not church affili-*

ated. Interestingly enough, 67 per cent of the audience for This Is the Life consists of Roman Catholic families. The content and the dramatic format are attractive to lower middle class family groups.

The *normative belief and behavior* sought of the audience is that of Christian orthodoxy, conceived in Lutheran terms and presented in contemporary American dimensions. Man is to approximate the behavior of Jesus, the Christ—doing the right thing, no matter what the consequences, understanding and helping others. He is to recognize himself as a sinner, but to know, also, that sinful man is saved by the grace of God through the ransom paid by his Son. Justification is by faith. Man reveals his faith by living according to the tenets of conduct laid down in the New Testament, and their interpretation by church and pastor.

How far from the norm is the audience conceived to be? A logical inference of the theological position of the sponsors of This Is the Life is that no one is nearer the norm than anyone else, except by the grace of God. But the program is addressed to all people, of whatever state of grace, on the theory that Christ died that *all* men might experience the forgiveness and love of God.

The concept we have used of semantic bipolarization has a double application here. On the one hand it is used as a dramatic device—character is thinned out into stereotypes of the good and the bad. This polarization is in part a matter of incompetence in dramatic writing and can be criticized on the level of technique. But at a deeper level, there is the bipolarization implicit in most orthodox Christian doctrine, and particularly Lutheran doctrine, as between the sinner and the redeemed man. Here there is a parallel with both Sheen and Fuller in the basic premise that the distance between the "saved" and the "unsaved" is so great that the relative moral stature of one sinner as against another is unimportant.

There is an important difference between the Lutheran program and the Sheen and Fuller programs, however. On This Is the Life the sinner is never reviled, as on Sheen's programs, nor consigned to eternal torment, as in Fuller's formula; but he is rather the object of an imaginative and loving campaign to win him for Christ. The sinner is never shamed, nor ridiculed, nor frightened into the fold. The "out-group" is never depersonalized or dehumanized so that it can be verbally punished and made the scapegoat for all human problems. Thus within a doctrinal formula of extreme bipolarization, the distance between the two groups is minimized by charging the "redeemed" group with a ministry of reconciliation and redemption to the "sinful" group, a ministry that will always be aided by the grace of God.

What techniques are used to initiate change? The chief technique used is the presentation of workable solutions for problems that most families face. Secondarily, the authority of the Lutheran church backing the solution may help to gain acceptance and action. As in the Sheen programs, there is also the offer of affiliation with a strong group that can both protect and guide the individual.

What road maps are given for guidance toward the desired behavior? Several specific guides are provided: a consistent representation of successful family living; a believable representation of the role of the church and its pastor in the family and in the community; a convincing representation of the Bible as the Word of God; supporting free literature to lead viewers into *Lutheran* church membership. The denominational emphasis, however, does not appear in the program except in identification of the sponsor; it appears rather in the follow-up literature.

The *auxiliary aids* offered by the program are essential to finding the desirable way of life—active participation in the church and counseling by the pastor. The importance of the dedicated layman is also apparent from the characterizations in the programs.

PART III

The Television-Radio Audience in Metropolitan New Haven

CHAPTER 7

The Concepts of Media and Audiences

The terms "mass media" and "mass communication" occasionally conjure up the picture of an entire population glued to its television sets, responding like robots to the carefully contrived stimuli of astute writers and directors. This specter of George Orwell's 1984 seems to be only a specter, and audiences upon investigation turn out to be composed of familiarly heterogeneous human beings, differentiated not only by age, sex, religion, income and similar criteria, but also by a great variety of responses to identical stimuli.

Insofar as the term "mass" connotes, therefore, a *sameness* or *homogeneity* as one characteristic of modern communication, it must be applied to the medium rather than to the audience reached by the content. The same picture, the same sounds, the same voice and smile do appear at the same moment in thousands of living rooms; they project their message impersonally and simultaneously to millions of people; and this event is the new and unprecedented fact in the history of communication. Its effects upon the character of the American people are yet to be assessed adequately. But the people themselves are far from uniform units of personality or taste or position. They choose in the first place to listen or not to listen; and even when two or more choose to listen to the same program, the variation in what they actually see and hear, or how they interpret what they see and hear, is sometimes quite unexpected.

It must further be pointed out that at the time of this study the most popular program in New Haven—a news program—reached regularly only one-half of all families. Most programs reached a much smaller proportion of the people. Thus, even if we were to use the term "mass audience," we would need to remember that for any given program this audience is almost *never* even a simple majority of a population, and for most programs it is a relatively small minority.

The statistical analysis of audiences, therefore, typically reduces itself to the problem of describing the minority of a population group who constitute an audience, comparing it with the total population, and trying to discover in this process what characteristics the audience has that differentiate it from the rest of the population. If these characteristics delineate a fairly distinct group (e.g., housewives), the researcher may go on to hypothesize some relationship between the format and content of the program on the one hand and the needs and tastes of the audience on the other, in terms of the known characteristics of the particular audience.

This process is essentially the procedure we have followed in evaluating audience groupings. Later chapters describe a different approach to the analysis of audiences: namely, "depth" studies of individuals and families who had been identified as members or nonmembers of audiences. The advantage of the latter approach is that it can get closer to a valid answer to the question of why people listen to or view particular programs. The advantage of the approach described at this point is that it gives statistically valid answers to the question: How many families of what different subgroups in the population constitute the audience for various programs?

CHAPTER 8

Television and Radio
Set Ownership

A prime essential in the defining of a radio or television audience, of course, is that its members shall have receiving sets available for their use. Each family in the 5 per cent sample of New Haven population, therefore, was questioned to determine what radio and television sets they had *in the home*. Table 48 summarizes this information.

Table 48. Television and radio set ownership

	Number	Per Cent
Total Sample	3,559	100.0
Families with radio and television sets	2,587	72.7
Families with radio sets only	819	23.0
Families with television sets only	126	3.5
Families with neither radio nor television sets	27	0.8
Total Families with Radio Sets	3,406	95.7
Total Families with Television Sets	2,713	76.2

Social Class and Set Ownership

Social class proved to be a significant factor in relation to ownership of radio and television sets, as may be seen in Table 49 (p <.001).

It might be assumed that higher social class, which is associated with higher income, would be closely correlated with ownership of television sets. The reverse was true. Only one-half (50.5 per cent) of the class I families owned television sets. The percentage of television ownership increased steadily through social classes II and III to social class IV, in which four out of five families (80.7 per cent) owned television sets. The percentage of ownership in social class V was somewhat less (75.8 per cent), possibly because incomes in this group are quite low, but even here the percentage of set owners was half again as high as in social class I.

Figures for families with radio sets, but without television sets, show the reverse pattern. Nearly half (49.5 per cent) of the social class I families had radio without television; over one-third (36.0 per cent) of the social class II families; nearly one-fourth (23.7 per cent) of the social class III families; and fewer than one-fifth (18.3 per cent) of social class IV families. Social class V was about equal to social class III in percentage owning radio sets without television sets (22.6 per cent). What these figures indicate is that *in New Haven* and *at the time of the sampling* television set ownership was especially characteristic of the large "working-class" population designated in this study as social class IV. This group, representing 48.4 per cent of the households, owned 51.3 per cent of all television sets. Households in social classes I and II, representing 12.5 per cent of all households, owned only 9.8 per cent of all television sets. On the other hand, these latter households (I and II), constituted 21.6 per cent of all households with radio sets only, while households in social class IV accounted for only 39.2 per cent of these "radio-only" homes.

TABLE 49. Television and radio set ownership by social class

Social Class	Own Television		Own Radio Only		Own No Radio or Television		Total	
	No.	Per Cent	No.	Per Cent	No.	Per Cent	No.	Per Cent
I	60	50.5	59	49.5			119	100.0
II	209	63.7	118	36.0	1	0.3	328	100.0
III	576	75.9	183	23.7	1	0.1	760	100.0
IV	1,392	80.7	317	18.3	14	0.8	1,723	100.0
V	476	75.8	142	22.6	11	1.7	629	100.0
Total	2,713	76.2	819	23.0	27	0.8	3,559	100.0

Religion and Set Ownership

Religious affiliation was analyzed next to discover whether it was significantly related to ownership of television sets. Significance was found in the case of Protestants (Table 50).

Among the Roman Catholic, Jewish and mixed families, approximately four out of five owned television sets. Among Protestant families, however, only three out of five owned television sets. The obverse, of course, is also true: Protestants constituted a larger segment of the audience for radio only. Protestant families, representing 29.0 per cent of all families, accounted for 46.2 per cent of the families who had radio sets but did not have television sets.

Table 50. Television and radio set ownership by religious affiliation

Religion of Family	Own Television		Own Radio Only		Own No Radio or Television		Total	
	No.	Per Cent	No.	Per Cent	No.	Per Cent	No.	Per Cent
Roman Catholic	1,563	83.2	304	16.2	12	0.6	1,879	100.0
Protestant	644	62.4	378	36.6	10	1.0	1,032	100.0
Jewish	259	82.2	54	17.2	2	0.6	315	100.0
Mixed	210	79.5	51	19.3	3	1.2	264	100.0
Other or none	37	53.6	32	46.4			69	100.0
Total	2,713	76.2	819	23.0	27	0.8	3,559	100.0

A further indication of the relationship of religion to set ownership is shown in Table 51, in which percentages of homes without television sets are shown for families according to the denominational affiliation of the male head of the household.

TABLE 51. Distribution of households without television sets by church affiliation of male head

Church Affiliation of Male Head	Total Households	Households without Television Sets	
		No.	Per Cent
None	394	126	31.9
Roman Catholic	1,664	222	13.3
Jewish	245	34	13.9
Congregational	270	83	30.8
Protestant Episcopal	186	53	28.5
Baptist	86	21	24.5
Methodist	81	24	29.6
Lutheran	64	18	28.2
Other Protestant denominations	79	28	35.4
Total all households	3,559	846	23.8

Table 51 illustrates again the marked difference between Catholics and Jews on the one hand and Protestants on the other in regard to ownership of television sets. The difference holds true for all Protestant denominations, regardless of the general theological position or socioeconomic position of any particular denominational group, and we may, therefore, hypothesize it is related to traditions and standards inherent in the "Protestant culture."

Households without male heads (i.e., households headed by single, widowed, divorced or separated women) which were 13.8 per cent of all households, accounted for 28.0 per cent of the homes without television sets. It is very likely here that limited income is a key factor in explaining the high proportion of homes without television. (This assumption was confirmed in interviews with single women of limited income, especially older ones.)

Religion, Social Class, and Set Ownership

TELEVISION

It has already been pointed out (Chapter 2) that there is a definite correlation between religious affiliation and social class. As both factors would appear to influence television set ownership, the question naturally arises, which seems to be more significant? Table 52 analyzes the relationship of social class to set ownership *within* the major religious groups.

TABLE 52. Percentages of families owning television sets, by social class and religious affiliation

Religious Affiliation	Social Class				
	I	II	III	IV	V
Roman Catholic	81.5	75.3	80.8	85.3	80.6
Protestant	33.8	50.7	65.9	69.7	60.7
Jewish	82.4	78.6	87.1	78.3	62.5
Mixed	50.0	66.7	81.1	88.0	90.5

This table indicates first of all that Protestant set ownership was substantially less than Roman Caholic, Jewish or mixed family set ownership in *all* social classes. Second, it indicates that the correlation between social class and set ownership was most pronounced among—and largely to be accounted for by—the set ownership pattern of Protestant and mixed families.[1] Whatever factor was responsible for this correlation, it appears to have been at work among Protestant and mixed families, and not to have affected Catholic and Jewish families to a degree that was at all comparable. Indeed, the Jewish pattern was, if anything, contrary to the Protestant pattern.

Lacking any more definitive data, we may again surmise that something in the nature of a "Protestant culture," vague as it might be, influenced Protestant families in New Haven against the purchase of television sets and thus made the Protestant proportion of the general television audience smaller than the proportion of Protestants in the total population. Religion, in other words, seemed to be related more definitely than social class[2] to differentials in set ownership; or, to be more precise, there appeared to be

[1] In the majority of mixed families, one of the mates is Protestant in background.

[2] The reader should be reminded again that "social class" is a composite index derived from rated occupation, education and place of residence.

(1) a lower correlation between Protestant affiliation and television set ownership, and (2) among Protestant and mixed families only, inverse correlation between social class level and television set ownership.

The actual percentage distribution of all households in the sample with television sets is given in Table 53.

TABLE 53. Percentage distribution of households with television sets, by social class and religion

Religion of Household	Social Class					
	I	II	III	IV	V	Total
Roman Catholic	0.8	2.4	9.7	31.8	13.3	58.0
Protestant	0.8	2.7	6.6	11.7	3.0	24.8
Jewish	0.5	2.0	3.2	3.5	0.5	9.8
Mixed		0.4	1.6	4.0	0.7	6.8
Other and none		0.2	0.2	0.2		0.6
Total	2.1	7.7	21.3	51.3	17.6	100.0

RADIO

Inasmuch as radio sets are owned by over 95 per cent of the households, the households with radio sets only and without television sets are distributed in a pattern approximately the reverse of those homes with television sets. Protestant households are much more prominent in this group, and Catholic and Jewish households much less so (Table 54)

TABLE 54. Comparative percentages of households with radio sets, *but without television sets*, in each religious group and social class

Religion of Household	Per Cent with Radio Only Social Class				
	I	II	III	IV	V
Roman Catholic	18.5	24.7	18.9	14.1	17.8
Protestant	66.2	48.6	34.1	29.2	37.0
Jewish	17.6	21.4	12.9	20.8	33.3
Mixed	50.0	33.3	18.9	12.0	9.5

The actual percentage distribution of households with radio sets only is shown in Table 55.

FUNCTION OF TELEVISON VERSUS RADIO

Figure 14 provides a graphic illustration of the relationships between religious background and television and radio set ownership. It is obvious that, although New Haven is primarily a television market, radio is an im-

FIGURE 14. Set ownership by religion and social class

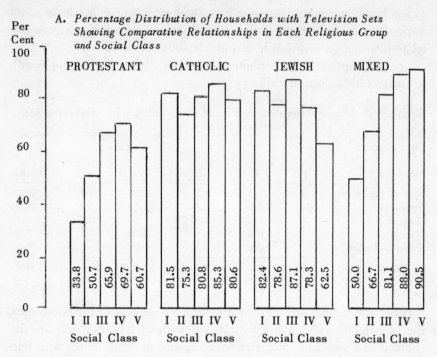

A. *Percentage Distribution of Households with Television Sets Showing Comparative Relationships in Each Religious Group and Social Class*

Per Cent

PROTESTANT   CATHOLIC   JEWISH   MIXED

PROTESTANT: I 33.8, II 50.7, III 65.9, IV 69.7, V 60.7
CATHOLIC: I 81.5, II 75.3, III 80.8, IV 85.3, V 80.6
JEWISH: I 82.4, II 78.6, III 87.1, IV 78.3, V 62.5
MIXED: I 50.0, II 66.7, III 81.1, IV 88.0, V 90.5

I II III IV V Social Class

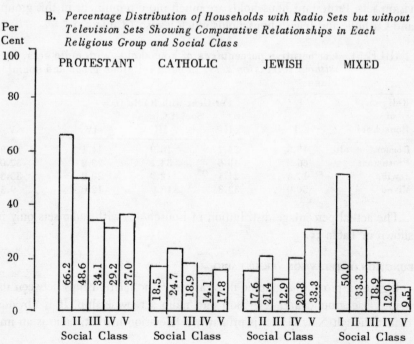

B. *Percentage Distribution of Households with Radio Sets but without Television Sets Showing Comparative Relationships in Each Religious Group and Social Class*

Per Cent

PROTESTANT   CATHOLIC   JEWISH   MIXED

PROTESTANT: I 66.2, II 48.6, III 34.1, IV 29.2, V 37.0
CATHOLIC: I 18.5, II 24.7, III 18.9, IV 14.1, V 17.8
JEWISH: I 17.6, II 21.4, III 12.9, IV 20.8, V 33.3
MIXED: I 50.0, II 33.3, III 18.9, IV 12.0, V 9.5

I II III IV V Social Class

portant medium for reaching Protestant families. Similarly, television clearly is the stronger of the two media for reaching the bulk of Roman Catholic, Jewish and mixed families.

Here again, however, we must take care not to fall into the trap of making a "mass audience" judgment. There are important deviations within the over-all picture of audiences to be reached by the two media. For example, the study, "Parents, Children, and Television,"[3] shows that New Haven children of all ages watch television regularly, somewhere, even if they do not have sets in their homes. Children averaged thirteen hours of regular television viewing per week (plus an undetermined amount of random viewing) as against a maximum of two hours of regular radio listening, for those children who listen to radio at all. Any program beamed at children will find the great majority of its potential audience oriented to television.

Table 55. Percentage distribution of all households with radio sets, *but without television sets*, by social class and religion

Religion of Household	Social Class					
	I	II	III	IV	V	Total
Roman Catholic	0.6	2.6	7.6	17.5	9.8	38.1
Protestant	5.5	8.6	11.3	16.3	6.1	47.8
Jewish	0.4	1.8	1.6	3.1	1.0	7.8
Mixed	0.1	0.7	1.2	1.8	0.2	4.2
Other and None	0.4	0.9	0.4	0.5		2.1
Total	7.0	14.6	22.1	39.2	17.1	100.0

Another major factor that helps to determine audience through set ownership is the incidence of television set ownership in homes where there are minor children. The presence of minor children in a home in families of all social class and religious backgrounds seemed to exert an almost irresistible pressure for the family to own a television set. Table 56 shows that television set ownership by families with children is greater than ownership by households in general in all groupings.

Since these studies show that radio is less often used in television homes, any program beamed at parents—the largest, the most active and vigorous group in the population, and the most important consumers—will most easily find an audience if it is on television.

Conversely, radio evidently has a function in audience areas where television holds the dominating position. One important example is the Catho-

3 *Op. cit.*, p. 3.

lic Hour, which ranked first in popularity in radio listening. Obviously, a radio program which appears to meet their interests and needs can attract an audience of adult Roman Catholics. The Greatest Story Ever Told enjoys a similar advantage. It draws family groups of all faiths as listeners, even in television homes.

Table 56. Percentage of television set ownership in households with minor children compared to total social class and religious groups

	Percentage of Set Ownership in Total Group	Percentage of Set Ownership in Homes with Minor Children
Social Class		
I and II	60.2	76.7
III	75.9	89.0
IV	80.7	90.3
V	75.8	92.1
Religion		
Roman Catholic	83.2	93.5
Protestant	62.4	77.9
Jewish	82.2	85.8
Mixed	79.5	90.4

CHAPTER 9

Television and Radio Programs: Availability and Audience

We have described the *potential audience* for broadcasting in terms of the *distribution* of television and radio sets in metropolitan New Haven, and the *kinds of households* in which the equipment was found. The next important questions are: What kind of program fare was offered to this potential audience by the broadcasters? What portions of the potential audience actually watched or listened to these programs?

This chapter will report on the amount and kinds of programs available to the New Haven audience at the time of this study, and second on the number and kinds of households that constituted the *actual* audiences for these programs.

The Major Program Types

All programs seen or heard in New Haven were classified by type.[1] The types, with examples, are listed in Table 57.

The analyses that follow are based on reported listening or viewing within the foregoing program types. This method of analysis is used not merely because of the tremendous number of individual programs reported, but also because it is assumed that these types represent to some degree continuing tastes, whereas individual programs may fluctuate considerably in popularity. (A number of programs, indeed, have changed a good deal in popularity since the time this sample was taken.)

[1] The typology is based upon the typology of television programs developed by Dallas W. Smythe for the National Association of Educational Broadcasters monitoring studies. Percentage availability of types in New Haven is reported in Table 58.

Table 57. Program types and examples

Program Type	Examples	
	Television	*Radio*
Entertainment		
Sports	Boxing, Baseball	Baseball, Football
Variety	Your Show of Shows, Toast of the Town	Arthur Godfrey, Jack Benny
Quiz	Strike It Rich, Groucho Marx	Break the Bank, Queen for a Day
Personalities	Person to Person, We the People	The Fitzgeralds, Tex and Jinx
Music	Voice of Firestone, Your Hit Parade	Telephone Hour, Railroad Hour
General drama	Studio One, Philco Playhouse	Lux Radio Theatre, Theatre Guild
Comedy drama	I Love Lucy, Our Miss Brooks	Ozzie and Harriet, Life with Luigi
Crime drama	Dragnet, Suspense	Martin Kane, Mr. and Mrs. North
Domestic drama	Mama, Search for Tomorrow	My True Story, Our Gal Sunday
Western drama (adult)	The Cisco Kid, The Lone Ranger	The Lone Ranger, Gene Autry
Information		
News reports	John Cameron Swazey, Sunday News Special	John Cameron Swazey, NBC Roundup
News commentators	Walter Winchell, John Daly	Edward R. Murrow, Fulton Lewis, Jr.
Domestic information and variety	Nancy's Kitchen, Kate Smith	Mary Margaret McBride, Betty Crocker
Orientation		
Public issues and events	American Forum, Meet the Press	America's Town Meeting, Meet the Press
Religion	What's Your Trouble? Life Is Worth Living	Greatest Story Ever Told National Radio Pulpit

Availability of Television Programs

New Haven has one television station, WNHC-TV (Channel 8),[2] which lays down a clear signal throughout the metropolitan area, even when only an indoor antenna is used. With an outdoor antenna, most families in New Haven are able to receive the New York City stations, as well as WNHC. Thus, New Haven viewers had as wide a selection of programs available to them as did viewers anywhere outside the New York metropolitan area.

Since WNHC is the only television station in the New Haven market, it can choose its program fare from all four of the national networks. The station does, in fact, draw most of its programs from the networks and other sources outside its own studio. In a typical week studied in 1953 WNHC originated 16.5 per cent of the quarter hours the station was on the air, 83.5 per cent of the quarter hours of programming being drawn from outside New Haven. As a single station market, however, WNHC is able to choose the top-rated shows from the various networks, which makes for a strong schedule of national programs, especially in the evening on weekdays and afternoon and evening on Sundays. Most WNHC programs originate with NBC or CBS.

MONITOR STUDY OF WNHC-TV

Programs broadcast over WNHC-TV were systematically monitored during the week of May 15–21, 1952, by the staff of the Communications Research Project. This analysis followed the pattern of monitoring studies developed by Dallas W. Smythe in his studies of television program content in New York and Los Angeles, conducted for the National Association of Educational Broadcasters. The data on New Haven television, separately published,[3] can thus be compared with Smythe's data on New York television programming in the same season (January 4–10, 1952). Comparisons with New York television programming are given below, not only because most New York stations can be received in New Haven and are, therefore, optional choices for the New Haven viewer; but, also, because New York as headquarters of the television networks sets national standards for programming.

[2] WNHC occupied Channel 6 during the time data for this study were gathered. Early in 1954 the Federal Communications Commission moved WNHC to Channel 8 The relocation of WNHC blocked out New York Channels 7 and 9 for New Haven viewers and opened Channel 5. However, the move did not affect the procurement and analysis of data for this study.

[3] Dallas W. Smythe, New Haven Television, May 15–21, 1952 (Urbana: National Association of Educational Broadcasters, 1953).

During the week studied, WNHC was on the air 117 hours and twelve minutes. It provided 31 per cent more program time than the average of the New York stations, and 7 per cent more than the total time on the air of WCBS-TV, the New York station with the longest daily broadcast schedule in 1952. Most of New Haven's extra hours on the air resulted from early sign-on in the morning.

Entertainment-type programs dominated the broadcast fare available to New Haven viewers. They constituted 73 per cent of New Haven program

Table 58. Percentage distribution of types of programs, New Haven and New York, 1952

Type	New Haven	New York
Entertainment		
All Drama	28.3	42.4
Drama, adult	24.3	35.7
Drama, children	4.0	6.7
All Variety	19.2	10.9
General adult variety	15.1	6.2
Domestic variety	1.1	2.3
Teenage variety		0.1
Children's variety	3.0	2.3
All Quiz, Stunts and Contests	10.1	7.0
Adult quiz, stunts and contests	10.1	6.3
Children's Quiz, Stunts and Contests		0.7
All Sports	10.6	7.2
Spectator sports	10.1	6.8
Participant sports and recreation	0.5	0.4
All Music	4.1	4.2
Personalities	1.1	2.3
Fine arts		0.1
Other children's programs		0.1
Total	73.4	74.2
Information		
News (News reports, special events, features)	13.3	7.1
Domestic information	4.4	7.5
General information (science, travel, etc.)	2.2	2.9
Weather	0.4	0.4
Information and instruction (children)	0.5	0.9
Total	20.8	18.8
Orientation		
Public issues	1.4	1.9
Public events		1.4
Public institutional programs	3.4	1.6
Religion	0.8	1.0
Personal relations	0.2	1.0
Preschool entertainment		0.1
Total	5.8	7.0

time, 74 per cent of New York time. Information-type programs were 21 per cent of total time in New Haven, 19 per cent in New York. Orientation-type programs accounted for the remainder, 6 per cent of the time in New Haven, 7 per cent in New York (Table 58).

Drama constituted the largest single type of programming in both New Haven and New York. But drama programs were about one-third less frequent in New Haven, which devoted 28 per cent of total time to them, than they were in New York, where they took up 42 per cent of total broadcast time. Variety shows were second in bulk ranking in both cities, but here the proportions were reversed. WNHC devoted 19 per cent of broadcast time to variety, proportionately almost twice as much as the 11 per cent averaged by New York stations.

The New Haven station also telecast relatively more sports and quiz, stunt and contest shows than did the New York stations. Sports (baseball, boxing, wrestling) accounted for 10.6 per cent of air time in New Haven as compared with 7 per cent in New York. Approximately the same proportion was maintained for quiz, stunt and contest shows; 10 per cent in New Haven, 7 per cent in New York. The time devoted to musical programs (4 per cent) was virtually identical in the two cities. Other types of entertainment programs accounted for 1 per cent of broadcast time in New Haven and 2.5 per cent in New York.

Information-type programming centered mostly in news telecasts. WNHC devoted 13 per cent of its time on the air to general news programs, as compared to 7 per cent in New York. However, proportionately fewer direct news reports were available in New Haven than in New York. WNHC used 4 per cent of its broadcast time for this purpose, as compared with 5.9 per cent of time in New York. In the broadcasting of news features and special events, New Haven had forty times the proportion found in New York, 8.5 per cent of total time as compared with 0.2 per cent. This large quantity of special events and features resulted from the Monday-Friday broadcast in New Haven of the entire two hours of the Dave Garroway program, Today.

Domestic information shows accounted for more than half of the remaining information-type programs in both cities (4.4 per cent in New Haven, 7.5 per cent in New York). These programs dealt with cooking; shopping and merchandise; personal care; arts, crafts and hobbies and other domestic interests. General informational programs accounted for only 2.2 per cent of the time in New Haven and 2.9 per cent in New York. In both cities 0.4 per cent of total time was devoted to weather reports.

Public institutional programs (civil defense, conservation, tuberculosis prevention and treatment, charity promotions, et cetera) made up the bulk of the orientation-type programming in New Haven, 3.4 per cent of total program time, compared to 1.6 per cent in New York. Public issues were treated 1.4 per cent of the time in New Haven and 1.9 per cent in New York.

Religion fared least well among the major orientation-type programs. In New York 1 per cent of total time was given to religion. WNHC devoted 59 minutes to religion out of its weekly schedule of 117 hours and twelve minutes on the air, or 0.8 per cent of the total for the week. However, within a year after the monitoring study WNHC, working in co-operation with local and national religious organizations, had increased its religious programming two and one-half times, to 160 minutes per week. The schedule included programs representatives of Protestant, Roman Catholic and Jewish viewpoints, and in each case included both programs originated nationally and live programs originated locally.

WNHC did not provide any programs in two orientation classifications, public events and pre-school entertainment. New York stations devoted 1.4 per cent and 0.1 per cent of their time respectively to these two types. Later, when Ding Dong School was originated by the National Broadcasting Company, WHNC scheduled it.

COMPOSITION OF ENTERTAINMENT PROGRAMS

Since entertainment programs bulked so large in the program schedules both in New Haven and in New York, an analysis of the subclasses under this classification is needed for a meaningful understanding of the program fare offered to New Haven viewers. Table 59 shows the breakdown of types under the subclass of drama.

Crime drama stood first in both New Haven and New York, but there was only about half the emphasis on this type of program on WNHC as compared to the New York stations. General drama ranked second in both cities, with New Haven offering slightly more than half as much of such programming as the average of the New York stations. Domestic drama ranked third in New Haven, accounting for 5.3 per cent of program time (New York, 4.0 per cent), and comedy drama was fourth, with 4.1 per cent of total time, about the same as in New York.

Western drama provides a unique program situation. In New York westerns aimed at adults actually ranked third among drama types with 4.2 per cent of total time. In New Haven they were much less important as program fare (0.4 per cent). Later, it will be seen that the New Haven adult audience had little interest in this type of program.

Variety programs aimed at mixed adult audiences were two and one-half times as numerous in New Haven as in New York, providing 15.1 per cent of all WNHC broadcast time (6.2 per cent in New York). The proportions of domestic variety programs were almost exactly reversed, with New Haven carrying half as many programs (1.1 per cent) as New York (2.3 per cent).

All of the quiz, stunts and contest programs on WNHC were directed to the general adult audience. There was relatively more time given to such programs in New Haven (10.0 per cent) than in New York (6.3 per cent).

The structure of music programs was virtually the same in New Haven and New York. Popular music dominated the 4 per cent of total time devoted to music in both cities. There was no serious music broadcast in New Haven and virtually none in New York. New Haven had a small amount of light music, New York none.

TABLE 59. Percentage of television program time devoted to drama programs, New Haven and New York, 1952

Classification	New Haven	New York
Adult Drama	24.3	35.8
Crime	8.5	14.9
General (romance, classics, action, musical)	6.0	9.6
Domestic	5.3	4.0
Comedy	4.1	3.1
Western	0.4	4.2
Children's Drama[4]	4.0	6.7
Western	3.2	4.1
Adventure and historical	0.6	0.7
Children's action	0.2	0.2
Comedy		1.2
Crime		0.2
Fairy tales		0.1
Classics		

ADVERTISING

An important adjunct to actual programming was the amount of advertising to which New Haven viewers were exposed during the week of the monitoring study. A random viewer tuning in WNHC during the week would have had close to one chance in four of striking an advertisement.

[4] Children's programs are not analyzed and discussed here. For a complete study of children's television programs in New Haven, made by the Communications Research Project, see "Parents, Children and Television," op. cit.

Total advertising in New Haven occupied 24.3 per cent of program time (28 hours, 30 minutes) as against 18 per cent in New York. WNHC's advertising time was 20 per cent greater than the total for WNBT, the New York station which carried the greatest amount of advertising, and was only 2 per cent lower than WABD, the New York station with the highest saturation of advertising and the smallest total amount of time on the air. Advertising on WNHC was divided between 13 per cent of time given to primary advertising and 11 per cent to secondary advertising.[5] New York stations averaged 8 per cent of total time in primary advertising and 10 per cent in secondary advertising.

No attempt has been made in this study to evaluate the impact of television commercial advertising on the members of the audience.

Availability of Radio Programs

No effort was made to monitor in detail any of the radio stations heard in New Haven. Programs of all of the national radio networks are readily available to New Haven listeners from stations in New York, New Haven, Hartford and other nearby cities. Even on FM, New Haven listeners can receive signals from the New York stations. No single radio station could be chosen for study, as was done with WNHC-TV, in the knowledge that it constituted a major program source for the majority of New Haven listeners.

The Actual Audience for Radio and Television Programs

ASSUMPTIONS

Two decisions were made that conditioned the kind of data gathered in the study and reported here.

1. It was decided that the interest of this study was in regular listening and viewing habits, not incidental, occasional or random viewing. We assumed that in studying effects, particularly of religious programs, consistency of use would be as important as consistency of participation is assumed to be in evaluating church affilation; it is an index of loyalty, of involvement, of exposure. The data here are therefore not comparable to most commercial audience surveys; they rely more on "recall" than do methods which sample

---

[5] Primary advertising is defined as "commercial announcements which interrupt the flow of program material," and secondary advertising is "commercial material which either accompanies program material, or in fact constitutes the material of the program." Product packages, brand names or slogans used as backdrops or reference to product cr sponsor within the program format are all secondary advertisements. A commercial "pitch" carried on through the whole program segment, as in the Charles Antell "Programs," is an example of an entire program that is secondary advertising.

an audience while a program is being broadcast or shortly thereafter. In this study, the data gathered tend to eliminate the random or "accidental" viewers. On the other hand, the method used here has a certain predictive value in that it tends to identify the programs a family will intentionally tune in at their scheduled times. It further tends to identify the programs remembered favorably and those with which a family identifies its media use, both of which may be considered in some sense indices of program influence or impact.

2. It was decided that *households* rather than individuals would be the unit for analysis of listening and viewing habits. The assumptions involved here were less theoretical than practical: it seemed an impossible task to disentangle the viewing habits of individuals in a household of four or five persons where there was one television set. On the theoretical side, however, it did seem that the *household* (or the *family*, which is most frequently the equivalent of the household) would be the unit of central concern in analysis of effects. The stimulus of a television show plays not merely on individuals, but on individuals-within-a-family-framework; and subsequent interview data show that frequently effects become apparent in terms of roles and interpersonal relationships, if they are to be understood at all. Finally, individual program preference is not a good measure even of exposure to programs, as exposure is usually the result of a compromise among family tastes, combined, in the case of children, with highly varying degrees of parental supervision and exercise of parental authority.

The data which follow, therefore, refer to *regular* listening and viewing habits of *households* in the *sample*, based on the report of a senior member of the household to an interviewer.

INDIVIDUAL PROGRAM POPULARITY

The most popular programs do amass large audiences, and the findings of this study reveal such audiences in New Haven. For the reader who is interested, the most popular television and radio programs in New Haven at the time of the study are listed in Tables 60 and 61. Individual programs, however, were not used as the units for subsequent analysis.

The names of these programs are familiar ones in popularity ratings; New Haven seems to have no mass tastes that differ drastically from other cities. We have cautioned the reader against comparing these data with those from commercial audience surveys, but it is interesting to note that they conform quite closely to some audience surveys that were taken at about the same time by commercial audience analysts for the local stations and national agencies.

The regular audience for the most popular individual radio program was markedly smaller than that of the fifteenth ranking television show. The spread in size of audience among the leading radio programs was also con-

Table 60. Most popular television programs in New Haven

Name of Program	No. of Households in Sample that View	Per Cent of of Total Sample (N. 3,559)	Confidence Interval[a]	Estimated Total Households Estimated	Plus or Minus[a]	Per Cent of Television Set Owning House- holds Which Regularly View
John Cameron Swazey	1,866	52.4	1.64	37,320	1,168	68.8
I Love Lucy	1,206	33.9	1.55	24,120	1,107	44.4
Studio One	1,081	30.4	1.51	21,620	1,076	39.8
Philco Playhouse	972	27.3	1.46	19,440	1,042	35.8
Milton Berle	844	23.7	1.40	16,880	995	31.1
Bishop Fulton J. Sheen	832	23.4	1.39	16,640	990	30.7
Arthur Godfrey [b]	809	22.7	1.38	16,180	980	29.8
Strike It Rich	793	22.3	1.37	15,860	973	29.2
Voice of Firestone	584	16.4	1.22	11,680	866	21.5
Groucho Marx	515	14.5	1.16	10,300	823	19.0
Suspense	482	13.5	1.12	9,640	800	17.8
Your Show of Shows	435	12.2	1.08	8,700	766	16.0
Toast of the Town	418	11.7	1.06	8,360	753	15.4
Comedy Hour	401	11.3	1.04	8,020	739	14.8
Lux Video Theatre	377	10.6	1.01	7,540	720	13.9

[a] To the reader not familiar with this kind of analysis, some explanation needs to be given. The figures in the third column in Tables 60 and 61, under the heading "Confidence Interval," represent percentages of the total sample. What they mean is that the researcher can be confident that nineteen times out of twenty (95 per cent) another sample taken of the same population at the same time by the same method would have yielded results within this many percentage points of the figure in column two. For example, we can be 95 per cent confident that a comparable sample taken at the same time would have found not less than 22.01 per cent (23.4 per cent minus 1.39 per cent) and not more than 24.79 per cent (23.4 per cent plus 1.39 per cent) of all households to be regular viewers of Sheen. Thus, assuming our sample to have been accurately representative of the total population, we can reasonably project the figures in column four as the *total* audience (the sample multiplied by twenty), allowing for the margin of error in column five. This margin becomes relatively larger when the number of listeners reported is smaller. See Appendix C.

It should be pointed out that the reliability of these figures is considerably higher than the results reported in a typical commercial audience survey of a town this size, which according to usual practice would be based on a sample of about 500 homes.

[b] In obtaining data from viewers, it was impossible to distinguish between the various Godfrey programs.

siderably less than the television audience spread. However, the radio audience was still a substantial one. We may notice, also that five of the leading radio programs had their counterparts in the television list: Godfrey, Strike It Rich, Voice of Firestone, Lux Theatre, Sheen.

THE USE OF PROGRAM TYPES FOR ANALYSIS

Program types, rather than individual programs, were used as the basis for statistical analysis. This practice was a result of considerable discussion and thought, which we will outline here briefly.

The standard measure for the importance of a program is its "popularity" rating, or the size of its audience. In approaching the study of effect of programs, the unwary researcher, and more particularly the policy-makers in the mass media, can easily fall into the trap of equating popularity with effectiveness. Actually the popularity index seems to be of dubious value in measuring effects, or even in measuring taste and interests. Popularity is a composite of many factors, of which "popular demand" is only one, and sometimes perhaps not even a major one.

Table 61. Most popular radio programs in New Haven

Name of Program	No. of Listeners in Sample	Per Cent of Total Sample (N. 3,559)	Confidence Interval [a]	Estimated Total Households		Network
				Estimated	Plus or Minus [a]	
The Catholic Hour	287	8.06	0.89	5,740	637	NBC
Arthur Godfrey	259	7.30	0.85	5,180	608	CBS
Strike It Rich	181	5.08	0.72	3,620	514	CBS
Groucho Marx	158	4.44	0.68	3,160	482	NBC
The Telephone Hour	136	3.82	0.63	2,720	448	NBC
Voice of Firestone	129	3.62	0.61	2,580	437	NBC
The Greatest Story Ever Told	128	3.60	0.61	2,560	435	ABC
Jack Benny	121	3.40	0.60	2,420	424	CBS
Twenty Questions	120	3.37	0.59	2,400	422	MBS
Lux Radio Theatre	119	3.34	0.59	2,380	420	CBS
Break the Bank	111	3.12	0.57	2,220	407	ABC
The Railroad Hour	93	2.61	0.52	1,860	373	NBC
Lowell Thomas	92	2.59	0.52	1,840	371	CBS
Fulton Lewis, Jr.	92	2.59	0.52	1,840	371	MBS
My True Story	76	2.14	0.47	1,520	338	ABC
Edward R. Murrow	68	1.91	0.45	1,360	320	CBS

[a] See footnote Table 60, and Appendix C for explanation.

The most obvious factor other than demand influencing program popularity is the relationship of program availability to audience availability. It is evident that a second-rate television show can garner a larger child audience in the early evening hours or a larger adult audience in the later evening hours than can a much superior show at midday. No show yet produced has been able to develop a substantial audience early Sunday morning. The time a program is available obviously has much to do with size of audience.

Even at favorable hours, popularity is conditioned by choices available.

If at six o'clock all channels carry a children's program, or at nine o'clock all carry crime programs—which is not infrequently the case—the margin of choice of the audience is extremely narrow, and more basic tastes or interests have little influence upon choice among programs. Rather, they influence choice as between television and other resources for leisure time use.

These decisions—what shall be presented and when it shall be shown—are largely matters of administrative decision among sponsors, networks and stations. The tastes of the audience influence these decisions only indirectly, as they are filtered through audience surveys to the administrators, and even then they must be evaluated against such factors as the sponsor's ideas, the interest of the advertising agency, the cost of time and talent, and a multitude of other factors.

Most religious programs—most of those studied here, at any rate—are in the category of "public service" broadcasts. Most commercially sponsored programs, the financial lifeblood of radio and television, are, as the first part of this chapter shows, "entertainment" programs. Their purpose is to provide "least common denominator" program material that will attract as large an audience as possible, so this audience can be exposed to the advertising message. It is a prevailing assumption in radio-television circles that public service programs have narrowly selected—therefore, small—audiences, while entertainment programs have broadly selected—therefore, large—audiences. Public service programs are relegated to class B or class C time on this assumption, while entertainment programs, even when they are not sponsored, go into the much more valuable class A time.

There is much evidence that this assumption is the natural rationalization of an industry that wishes to market its most valuable asset—class A time—profitably. The documentation is not only in such special events as the Kefauver and the McCarthy-Army hearings, but also in religious programs such as Bishop Sheen's and The Greatest Story Ever Told. The latter two, because they deal with religion, would normally be expected by the industry to draw small audiences; but, thanks to commercial sponsorship, they occupy class A time, and are able to show they can compete with entertainment shows on an equal footing and draw very respectable audiences.

There were other reasons as well why the audiences for program types rather than individual programs are analyzed here. Individual programs were, of course, too numerous for very detailed analysis. Further, the selection of an individual program often reflects other factors than taste or interest—the appeal of a particular star, for example, or the fact that the program is talked about by neighbors. Further, the dominance of WNHC-TV in the New

Haven market automatically gives shows carried by the station an advantage in audience availability.

In search of some statistical measure that would reflect deeper and more lasting audience response, therefore, the research team decided to deal with programs as types. The groupings decribed at the opening of this chapter are the categories used for the statistical analysis which follows. While this procedure by no means eliminated the bias introduced by all the factors just mentioned, particularly program availability, it did tend to modify it in the direction of giving somewhat more weight to the factor of audience taste. We were seeking from these data some indication of audience interest in a particular kind of material: namely, religious programming. We assumed, to give a parallel, that it would be a great oversimplification to say that the outstanding popularity of I Love Lucy meant an overwhelming audience interest in comedy drama as such; the interest might only reflect the time the program occupied, the personalities of the stars, the publicity given the program, and the lack of an attractive option on another channel. The interest in comedy drama as a type of program would be better reflected by statistics of audience use of all such programs during the week, and similarly with religion, news, serious drama, music and the like.

Sports viewing is a good illustration of the thesis that individual program popularity is not consistently parallel with general usage of program types. Table 62 shows the popularity index of four leading types of sports programs.

Table 62. Per cent of households viewing sports programs in New Haven

	No. of Households in Sample that View	Per Cent of Total Sample (N. 3,559)	Confidence Interval [a]	Estimated Total Households Estimated	Plus or Minus [a]	Per Cent of Television Set Owning Households Which Regularly View
Baseball	1,581	44.42	1.63	31,620	1,162	58.3
Boxing	1,482	41.64	1.62	29,640	1,153	54.6
Football	1,029	28.91	1.49	20,580	1,060	37.9
Wrestling	674	18.94	1.29	13,480	916	24.8

[a] See footnote, Table 60 and Appendix C for explanation.

Baseball and boxing have a larger bulk audience than do fourteen of the fifteen most popular television programs; and football, the third ranking sport, has a larger audience than any but the first three programs in popularity rank.

In querying families on their regular viewing habits, it was impossible to distinguish between sports programs per se. The viewers themselves do not distinguish between boxing bouts seen on the Cavalcade of Sports, the Blue Ribbon Bouts, or some other program. Boxing is boxing. The only distinction is between good and bad fights. The same thing is true of baseball and football except that in baseball, fans "follow" specific teams, and thus watch the channels that carry those teams. No distinction is made by individual program. However, while the individual program is not identifiable, Table 63 shows that sports as a program type are watched more than any other type of television program, when programs are analyzed according to how many families watch two or more programs of a type.

Television Viewing by Program Types

Table 63 summarizes by program types the regular viewing habits of the households in the sample. Seven out of eight families with television sets watched at least one news program regularly. More than four out of five watched some sports program regularly, and nearly as many watched a variety show. Three out of four watched a quiz show. "General drama" (the "playhouses," "theaters," et cetera) was seen by nearly two-thirds. Sixth in popularity came religious programs (57.2 per cent), with a larger audience by a fair margin than the 50 per cent of all television households who watched comedy drama. The other categories dropped off rather sharply: music and crime drama with fewer than two-fifths of the television households, domestic drama with less than one-fourth; then domestic variety with only one in eighteen, and public issues (educational) programs and western drama each with about one household in twenty-five.[6]

A reasonable inference from these comparisons would seem to be that the television industry was offering relatively a good deal more crime drama than the audience in New Haven wants, and relatively a good deal less religion than is desired. The percentage of time devoted to religion was not only the least among the ten categories listed, but was also less than several categories not included in the table because of lack of audience, such as western drama (see Tables 57 and 59). Here is evidence—telling, if not wholly conclusive—that religion on television in New Haven operates under the serious handicap of insufficient allocation of program time. We may add,

[6] Table 63 reports adult viewing habits only. If children's viewing were included the rating of western drama would increase considerably. Children spend more than one-third of their television viewing looking at westerns.

Table 63. Number of households [a] regularly viewing adult television programs, by program types and number of programs regularly viewed

Program Type	No. of Households by No. of Programs Regularly Viewed									Total Households Viewing at least One Program[a]		Total Households Viewing Two or More Programs[a]		Total Prog. Viewed
	Viewed No Prog.	One Prog.	Two	Three	Four	Five	Six	Seven to Nine	No. not specified	No.	Per Cent	No.	Per Cent	
News	351	1,383	597	105	12				266	2,363	87.1	714	26.3	3,206
Sports	489	534	607	486	371	90	27	8	102	2,225	82.0	1,589	58.6	5,462
Variety	574	744	626	318	148	53	19	11	221	2,140	78.9	1,175	43.3	4,224
Quiz	631	771	580	295	86	36	8	2	305	2,083	76.8	1,007	37.1	3,707
General drama	957	668	658	291	78	14	9	2	37	1,757	64.7	1,052	38.8	3,344
Religion	1,177	1,319	198	31	3	1				1,552	57.2	233	8.6	1,825
Comedy drama	1,354	965	316	39	5				35	1,360	50.1	360	13.3	1,769
Music	1,661	635	166	22	6	2		1	221	1,053	38.8	197	7.3	1,297
Crime drama	1,740	461	264	88	30	4	3		124	974	35.9	389	14.3	1,535
Domestic drama	2,065	396	160	36	5	2	1		49	649	23.9	204	7.5	909
Domestic variety	2,564	133	13						4	150	5.5	13	0.5	163
Public issues	2,599	94	17	4						115	4.2	21	0.8	140
Western drama	2,609	36	6	2	1				60	105	3.9	9	0.3	118

[a] Of 2,713 households with television sets.

from observation of schedules, that it operates under the equally serious
handicap of poor broadcast time for the securing of audiences.

The statement of this apparent fact does not, of course, place responsibility for it. Many things are involved in getting programs on the air—ideas,
money, talent, producing skills, availability of stations and of time, network
and station management's concept of its public responsibility, et cetera.
Here, we can simply say there seems to be a serious discrepancy between
what the audience indicates to be its interest in religious television and the
amount and variety of program material to satisfy this interest.[7]

Table 64. Audience preference for program types compared to availability
of types

Rank in Terms of Audience Preference			Rank in Terms of Percentage of Broadcast Time			
			New Haven		New York [a]	
Television Programs Regularly Viewed by Sample	Rank	Program Type	Rank	Per Cent of Tele- cast Time	Rank	Per Cent of Tele- cast time
5462	1	Sports	3	10.6	3	7.2
4224	2	Adult variety	1	15.1	6	6.2
3707	3	Quiz	4	10.1	5	6.3
3344	4	General drama	6	6.0	2	9.6
3206	5	News	2	13.3	4	7.1
1825	6	Religion	10	0.8	10	1.0
1769	7	Comedy drama	8.5	4.1	9	3.1
1535	8	Crime drama	5	8.5	1	14.9
1297	9	Music	8.5	4.1	7	4.2
909	10	Domestic drama	7	5.3	8	4.0

[a] Average of all stations.

Another way to examine the audience for program types is to see how
many households watch two or more programs in any given type. This
method presumably identifies somewhat more closely the households which
like a type of program well enough to seek out more than one program in
this category. When this criterion was used, there were significant changes in
the order of preference. News programs dropped from first place to fifth,
with the first four places in popularity going to sports,[8] variety, general drama,
and quiz shows, in that order. Religious programs dropped from sixth to
eighth place in popularity, with crime drama moving up to sixth and comedy

[7] See also "Parents, Children and Television," op. cit., p. 6, on this point.
[8] Sports programs tend to be seasonal, shifting from summer baseball to autumn football and winter basketball, but with boxing a year-round attraction. Thus the category of
"sports programs" gets more frequent mention in this tabulation than year-round programs.

drama to seventh. Evidently news programs and religious programs tended to be "one-program" categories; only one person in three who saw a news show sought another one to watch; and only one person in six who saw a religious program sought out another one. In contrast, half or more of the regular viewers of sports, variety, quiz, and general drama shows regularly saw more than one show of this type every week.

The 2,713 television set-owning households in the sample reported a total of 27,699 programs regularly watched on television, an average of 10.2 regular programs per television household. Nearly half (48.4 per cent) of these shows were of three types: sports, variety, and quiz. Nearly one-fourth more (23.7 per cent) were in the two next most popular categories: general drama and news. Religion accounted for 6.5 per cent of the programs and comedy drama about the same. The remaining six categories combined (crime drama, music, domestic drama, domestic variety, public issues, and western dramas) totaled only 15.0 per cent of all programs reported.

Religion, Social Class and Program Preference

We were particularly interested to find out what kinds of households exhibited a preference for what kinds of programs. Audiences for the different program types were therefore analyzed according to the two major variables used throughout this study: religious affiliation and social class. Tables 65 and 66 summarize these analyses and the fourteen tables in Appendix B give a more detailed breakdown of the audiences by religion and social class for each program type.

Table 65. Percentage of television set-owning families viewing specified program types by religious affiliation

Program Type	Catholic	Protestant	Jewish	Mixed	Total
News	87.6	86.3	86.4	86.4	87.1
Sports	82.9	80.1	79.7	83.2	82.0
Variety	79.3	78.3	75.1	82.1	78.9
Quiz	76.3	80.6	72.2	75.1	76.8
General drama	65.6	60.6	69.9	64.3	64.7
Religion	62.6	52.3	32.3	56.8	57.2
Comedy drama	51.3	49.5	43.6	50.2	50.1
Music	39.5	36.0	37.9	41.6	38.8
Crime drama	36.4	37.8	23.6	42.1	35.9
Domestic drama	24.0	24.0	22.9	31.3	23.9
Domestic variety	4.4	7.9	7.9	7.0	5.5
Public issues	3.8	4.5	5.6	6.4	4.2
Western drama					3.9

Briefly, these analyses revealed no clear, general pattern of association between program preferences and either social class or religious affiliation. A summary of the findings follows; based on the statistical data in Appendix B.

1. PROGRAM TYPES ASSOCIATED PRIMARILY WITH SOCIAL CLASS

a. News program viewing was slightly higher in social classes II, III, IV, lower in I and V. This difference was especially pronounced in Protestant and Jewish households.

Table 66. Percentage of television set-owning families viewing specified program types, by social class

Program Type	I	II	III	IV	V	Total
News	80.0	88.2	89.8	87.9	82.0	87.1
Sports	71.6	80.3	84.1	82.3	79.9	82.0
Variety	65.0	72.0	81.0	79.1	80.1	78.9
Quiz	73.3	72.5	80.1	77.0	74.9	76.8
General drama	65.0	66.1	73.1	63.2	58.1	64.7
Religion	53.3	51.4	55.0	58.4	56.4	57.2
Comedy drama	50.0	48.5	51.3	49.1	51.8	50.1
Music	36.6	38.7	39.3	38.9	37.4	38.8
Crime drama	18.3	23.5	37.1	37.4	37.4	35.9
Domestic drama	15.0	18.6	21.6	26.2	26.1	23.9
Domestic variety	5.0	3.9	5.2	5.9	6.9	5.5
Public issues	11.6	5.3	6.7	3.8	1.8	4.2
Western drama						3.9

b. Sports program viewing was higher in social classes II, III and IV, especially III. Again this type of viewing was especially pronounced in Protestant and Jewish households.

c. Variety program viewing was highest in social classes III, IV and V especially in Catholic and mixed households; but differences between groups were not significant, except in the case of class I households.

d. General drama viewing was highest in social classes II and III, especially III. There was least viewing of these programs in Protestant and class V households.

e. Domestic drama viewing was highest in social classes IV and V, especially class IV Protestant and class V mixed households. It was also high in class III Catholic households. Mixed households (III–V) viewed proportionately more domestic drama than did others.

f. Public issues program viewing generally followed social class rather consistently, being highest in the higher social classes (exceptions: class V mixed; class II Jewish).

2. PROGRAM TYPES ASSOCIATED WITH RELIGIOUS AFFILIATION

a. *Music* program viewing was distributed with remarkable evenness Catholic viewing highest; then mixed, Protestant and Jewish, in that order. (This condition reflected the dominant position of the Sheen program.)

b. *Domestic variety* program viewing reflected religious affiliation, with Catholic households (except class II) and mixed households (except class V) lower than Protestant or Jewish households.

3. PROGRAM TYPES ASSOCIATED WITH BOTH SOCIAL CLASS AND RELIGION

a. *Crime drama* program viewing followed social class, with classes I and II low; III and IV high. However, Jewish families at all social levels were notably lower than other religious groups.

4. PROGAM TYPES ASSOCIATED WITH NEITHER SOCIAL CLASS NOR RELIGION

a. *Music* program viewing was distributed with remarkable evenness through all social classes in all religious groups.

b. *Comedy drama* also had an even distribution except for Jewish households.

c. *Quiz* program viewing showed an even distribution through most social classes in all religious groups.

Where social class made a difference in viewing habits, it seemed to affect Protestant and Jewish households more than Catholic or mixed households. There was a tendency for the television set to be used more frequently in Catholic and mixed households than in Protestant and Jewish households, and in class III and IV households than in class I, II or V households.

These were minor tendencies and should not be exaggerated. What is perhaps more remarkable is the similarity of taste among all the subgroups examined. Whatever the social class and whatever the religious group, the percentage who regularly viewed any given program type was surprisingly uniform.[9] This uniformity might, of course, have resulted more largely from program availability than from personal taste. The order of the program popularity followed rather closely the distribution of programs by frequency at a time when adults might have been presumed to be watching television.[10] At the same time, the evening television schedules of WNHC-

[9] See results of the "viewing pattern" analysis, pp. 188–195.
[10] See Table 60 for the fifteen most popular programs.

TV, plus the New York stations, permitted more flexibility of choice than these data would indicate was actually exercised by religious and class groups, as groups. Individually, of course, families could and did vary widely from the frequency patterns described.

"Saturation Viewers"

In a small group of 51 households (1.4 per cent of the sample), the television set was turned on in the morning to Channel 6 and left on all day until the family went to bed at night. These were the "saturation" viewers, those whose tastes were presumably indiscriminate, or at least sufficiently unexacting so that they accepted all television fare presented to them. Or, alternately, these were the compulsive viewers, or escapists, or whatever may be the appropriate psychological terminology for persons for whom continuous stimulation is a necessity. Or, finally—and most probably—these were the people with no resources other than television to occupy their leisure time.

What were the sociological characteristics of these 51 households? Interestingly, they were distinguished only by their age and the absence of minors. The household head was 55 years of age, or older, in 43.2 per cent of these families, as compared with only 25.1 per cent of the sample as a whole. Only 45.1 per cent had minor children, as compared with 62.4 per cent of the sample as a whole. Otherwise, their characteristics generally resembled those of the population. They included a somwhat larger than average proportion of Roman Catholics, skilled and semiskilled laborers and family heads who had not finished high school; but in general they reflected the composition of the sample, except for their age and the absence of minor children.

Patterns of Television Viewing

Most studies of audiences for the different types of mass communications media have dealt with usage either of particular programs or specific types of programs (such as daytime serials on radio), or the relative appeal of one medium as against another (i.e., radio versus television). In studying radio listening, for example, researchers have frequently sought to determine what specific programs appeal to women in general, or what is the psychological orientation of women who are attracted to a particular program.

This concentration on a single program or program type is satisfactory for most analysis purposes, where the objective is to ascertain for an advertiser the kinds of people who listen to his program and those who are attracted to the programs of his competitors. The present research was interested, however, in something beyond the attraction or lack of attraction of single programs or groups of programs. The concern has been with the ascertainable effect of television on the individual viewer and on the family group of which he or she is a part. Therefore, reaction to a single program or program type is subordinate to the total viewing behavior of the audience—that is, to the combination of programs which comprises the whole field of impact of television.

One problem of the research, therefore, was to determine whether there are recognizable classifications of television viewing that can be described and evaluated in a frame of reference similar to that used for developing the social class status of the households in the 5 per cent sample. That is, are there clusters of individual households which are tied together in a pattern of television usage based upon the types of programs viewed, the thematic content, mode of presentation or some other factor or factors? The concept to be tested was essentially that which is involved in the examination of the varying contents of consumers' market baskets. One finds that the owner of a Cadillac automobile is likely to buy steak, hors d'oeuvres and stuffed olives, while the owner of a Chevrolet confines himself to the purchase of more staple items such as hamburger, canned tomatoes and coffee in paper bags. The first set of purchases falls into a "luxury" pattern, the second into a "necessity" pattern. In both of these situations—the study of food consumption and the study of consumption in mass communications —the object is to organize data on a large number of individual practices into a much smaller number of patterns of behavior.

The Communications Research Project went to the Bureau of Applied Research of Columbia University with this problem of pattern analysis. Hanan Selvin and Arnold G. Simmel were assigned by the Bureau to make a latent structure analysis of the data on regular television viewing by the households in the 5 per cent sample of metropolitan New Haven. The aim of the analysis was to construct patterns of television viewing that would condense the viewing behavior of the New Haven television audience into a small number of patterns. The description of this effort, which follows, is drawn from the report prepared by Selvin.

BASIS OF THE "PATTERN" RESEARCH

The possibility of applying a latent structure analysis to the New Haven data was suggested by two earlier studies of radio listening. Neither one is exactly comparable to the present study, but there is enough similarity that a pattern analysis seemed warranted. In a preliminary study[11] W. S. Robinson analyzed the program preferences of college students, using a set of categories similar to those employed in the present study. Three factors or patterns of programs were found, although Robinson's interpretations of these factors are not clear, perhaps because the students were asked for their preferences and not for their actual listening behavior. A later study by W. A. Gibson,[12] using data gathered the National Association of Radio and Television Broadcasters, found six factors in *evening* radio listening. Both these studies started with data roughly comparable to the New Haven material, and both found distinguishing patterns of radio listening. It seemed reasonable, therefore, to expect that patterns of television viewing would be found in the New Haven sample.

PROCEDURES AND RESULTS

The basic data for this analysis were the frequencies with which the adult members of each sample household, *taken as a unit*, viewed each of the following types of programs, singly and in combination:

Types of programs

1. News
2. Sports
3. Variety
4. Religion
5. Comedy drama
6. General drama
7. Domestic drama
8. Crime drama
9. Quiz
10. Musical
11. Domestic science and variety
12. Public issues, education, and information
13. Western drama
14. Personalities[13]

For simplicity, differences in the amount of viewing within each program type were ignored; each family owning a television set was classified as a "viewer" of a program type if it regularly watched one or more programs of that type. An exception was made for news broadcasts where, because of the large number of programs offered every day, viewing two programs regularly was required for a household to be considered a viewer of news.

The next step in identifying patterns of viewing was to see the extent to

11 W. S. Robinson, "Preliminary Report on Factors in Radio Listening," *Journal of Applied Psychology*, Vol. 24, 1940, pp. 831–37.

12 W. A. Gibson, "Applications of the Mathematics of Multiple-Factor Analysis to Problems of Latent Structure Analysis," Unpublished MS, 1950.

13 "Personalities" was dropped at an early stage because these programs had so few viewers, only 66 households.

which viewing of each type of program was related to viewing of every other type. This compilation is shown numerically in Table 67.[14] Table 67 is of crucial importance in the search for patterns of television viewing. If patterns exist, they must be visible as significant relationships in this table.

The most striking fact about Table 67 is the small size of most of the correlations. Fully a third of the 78 correlations are not significantly different from zero (at the .05 level).[15] Even more important there is no systematic patterning among the remaining correlations. It is not easy to see this lack of pattern in a table of phi-coefficients since, as explained above, the size of the phi-coefficients is not a good indicator of the degree of relationship. The lack of significant patterning emerges clearly in the successive procedures of factor analysis, but the following analysis based on Table 68 demonstrates the lack of relationship much more simply. Each entry in Table 68 is a "conditional probability"—the probability that, if a household views program type A, it will also view program type B. For example, the entry of 0.84 in the first row and second column of Table 68 is the proportion (per cent) of all households viewing news programs that also view sports programs. In the fourfold table of types A and B, this is the ratio:

$$\frac{a}{a+c}$$

[14] The figures in Table 67 are "phi-coefficients." For dichotomous ("yes-no") variables, these are the same as the ordinary product-moment correlation coefficients customarily employed for continuous variables. They are calculated by means of the following formula:

$$\phi = \sqrt{\frac{P_{ij} - P_i P_j}{P_i P_j (1 - P_i)(1 - P_j)}}$$

where P_{ij} is the proportion of households viewing both program types i and j
P_i is the proportion of households viewing program type i
P_j is the proportion of households viewing program type j

Phi differs from r, the product-moment correlation coefficient for continuous variables in its range of variation. While r may take on any value from -1 to $+1$, the range of phi depends on the relative sizes of p_i and p_j. Phi can attain the values $+1$ or -1 only when $p_i = p_j$. When $p_i = p_j$ the maximum positive value of phi is less than $+1$, and the maximum negative value is less than -1. This makes it somewhat difficult to compare different phi-coefficients, since the same numerical values may represent different degrees of association, depending on the relative sizes of p_i and p_j. While certain other measures of association do range between -1 and $+1$, the advantage of phi is that statistical tests are available to test whether it differs significantly from zero. This is not true for other known coefficients that would be satisfactory for the New Haven data.

[15] That is, with samples of 2,800 one would expect phi-coefficients as large as 0.03 to occur by chance about 95 per cent of the time when the true population correlation is zero.

Table 67. Correlations between program types (Phi-coefficients)

	Sports	Variety	Religion	Comedy Drama	Quiz	Other Drama	Musical	Domestic Drama	Crime Drama	Domestic Science and Variety	Public Issues, Education and Information	Western Drama
News	.15	.26	.14	.12	.11	.14	.09	.09	.09	.04	.02	.00
Sports		.43	.13	.07	.09	.12	.06	.04	.08	.05	.02	.02
Variety			.17	.01	.17	.18	.06	.13	.16	.09	.06	.01
Religion				.01	.07	.07	.07	.04	.05	.04	.06	.01
Comedy drama					.09	.19	.14	.15	.09	.01	.00	.05
Quiz						.09	.05	.08	.10	.06	.04	.02
Other drama							.05	.07	.07	.01	.04	.03
Musical								.02	.01	.01	.01	.04
Domestic drama									.07	.07	.02	.02
Crime drama										.01	.02	.15
Domestic science and variety											.05	.02
Public issues, education and information												.02
Western drama												

View Type i

		Yes	No	
View Type j	Yes	a	b	a + b
	No	c	d	c + d
		a + c	b + d	N

These probabilities are, in a rough sense, measures of the information about the viewing of each program type that is added by knowledge of the viewing of each other type. For clarification, let us consider in detail the relationships between viewing of religion and the viewing of the other twelve program types.

The summary of percentages of households viewing each program type (bottom of Table 68) shows the proportion of all households viewing religion regularly was 57 per cent. Now, of those households that watched news programs, the proportion also viewing religious programs was only slightly different, 59 per cent. And of those viewing sports the proportion also viewing religious programs was 60 per cent. In fact, with the exception of the three program types at the bottom of the table,[16] these conditional probabilities are all very close together, averaging 60 per cent as shown in the last line of the table.

The probability that religious programs will be viewed is almost unaffected by the probability of viewing any other program type. The same conclusion holds for the other types; in no case does the viewing of any one type make much difference in the viewing of any other. Each type of program has its own level of attractiveness to the households in the sample, and this attractiveness has little to do with the other programs viewed by the household. In other words, there are no significant patterns of viewing tied together by similar subject matter or similar presentation; the likelihood of a particular household viewing a pair of programs is almost exactly what would be predicted from the likelihood of viewing each program by itself.

INTERPRETATION OF RESULTS

The negative finding, that no meaningful set of patterns existed in the viewing of the various television program types, was not what had been ex-

[16] The entries for domestic science and variety; public issues, education and information; and western drama show more variation than the rest of the table. This variation results from statistical instability, rather than real differences in the relationships among these three types and the other ten, since so few households viewed these three types.

TABLE 68. Conditional probabilities (Proportion of households viewing one type of program who also view other types)

i \ j	News	Sports	Variety	Religion	Comedy Drama	Quiz	Other Drama	Musical	Domestic Drama	Crime Drama	Domestic Science Drama and Variety	Public Issues, Education and Information	Western Drama
News		.84	.82	.59	.52	.50	.43	.40	.25	.20	.07	.04	.04
Sports	.90		.85	.60	.52	.51	.43	.40	.25	.20	.07	.04	.04
Variety	.90	.88		.60	.50	.52	.43	.40	.26	.21	.07	.05	.04
Religion	.91	.86	.83		.50	.52	.43	.42	.25	.21	.07	.05	.04
Comedy drama	.91	.84	.78	.57		.53	.50	.45	.30	.22	.07	.04	.05
Quiz	.90	.86	.84	.60	.55		.45	.41	.27	.23	.08	.05	.04
Other drama	.93	.88	.85	.61	.62	.55		.41	.27	.22	.06	.05	.04
Musical	.91	.85	.81	.61	.59	.52	.43		.25	.18	.07	.04	.05
Domestic drama	.93	.85	.86	.60	.64	.56	.46	.41		.24	.10	.05	.10
Crime drama	.94	.88	.89	.62	.59	.59	.47	.37	.30		.07	.05	.10
Domestic science and variety	.93	.90	.90	.64	.52	.61	.38	.40	.35	.21		.08	.06
Public issues, education and information	.83	.85	.87	.71	.50	.59	.50	.40	.26	.24	.12		.06
Western drama	.88	.85	.80	.57	.65	.54	.47	.47	.62	.49	.10	.01	
Proportion viewing each program type P(j)	.87	.82	.79	.57	.50	.49	.40	.39	.24	.19	.07	.04	.04
Average of each column[a] P(j/i)	.91	.86	.85	.60	.56	.53	.45	.41	.27	.20	.07	.05	.09

[a] The last three rows are excluded (see text).

pected. It does not, of course, negate common-sense reasoning and the experience of certain radio-listening studies that there is individual program preference, as between different people. Viewing preferences and behavior do vary among individuals within the limits of program availability. However, the lack of relationship between the various program types revealed in the present data is not inconsistent with individual program preferment. It reveals primarily the heterogeneous character of television viewing. People are more likely to look at any program that comes along, just for the sake of viewing television, than they are to listen to whatever happens to be available on radio. More important, since most television viewing is done in the evening, the lack of pattern among program types probably reveals a willingness within the family to compromise individual preferences in favor of a family consensus. This tendency is illustrated by one family where the mother stated, "When the children come out of school until the time they go to bed they listen to what they want to listen to, and when they go to bed we listen to what we want."

The lack of viewing patterns is enormously important to program sponsors. It appears that—again within the limits of current availability in relation to audience—a particular program type will be viewed in the average television family in New Haven about in proportion to its relative importance in the schedules of the television stations.

Further research is needed into the relationship between the viewing behavior of individuals and the viewing behavior of households, and into correlations between the sexes in the viewing of adult programs. It may also be that programs found in several of the types used in the present study have a peculiar emotional appeal that makes them attractive to a certain type of personality.[17] The present program categories may thus obscure relationships between individual programs that would indicate new categories based on different descriptive assumptions. The problem of "patterning" is complex and should be pursued through further study of adequate population samples.

Radio Listening

In radio listening as in television viewing, regular use of program type was assumed to be more important in judging impact than was popularity of individual programs. Again, sports provide an example. Table 69 shows that each

[17] In some of the families studied there appeared to be a relationship between (1) opinions held and the group pattern of family living and (2) affinity for a combination of programs including boxing and Groucho Marx (on television or radio) and an "authoritative" news commentator such as Fulton Lewis, Jr. or Gabriel Heatter.

of the three most popular types of sports broadcasts outdistances the most popular individual radio program—baseball two and one-half times to one, boxing almost two to one, and football one and one-half to one. Table 70 shows that on a "fan" basis, i.e., when two or more programs of a type are heard regularly, sports outrank all other program types.

TABLE 69. Ranking of sports broadcasts among New Haven radio
           listeners

Sport	Per Cent of New Haven Households Listening Regularly
Baseball	21.1
Boxing	14.2
Football	12.4
Basketball	3.5

Radio Listening by Program Types

While there were 25 per cent more households with radio sets than with television sets in metropolitan New Haven at the time of the survey, the households in the sample reported 160 per cent more regular television viewing than radio listening, by number of programs. The 3,406 households with radio sets reported listening regularly to 10,652 radio programs, an average of 3.2 per radio household (cf. average of 10.2 television programs per television household).

The distribution of these radio programs by program type is given in Table 70. As with television, news programs led the list in the proportion of households (one-third) that heard at least one news broadcast regularly. Three out of ten households listened to at least one sports broadcast, and nearly the same number to at least one religious broadcast, making religion the third most popular program type.

Slightly under one-fourth of the families heard quiz shows and music programs. One-fifth heard variety programs. The seventh most popular category, news commentators (11.9 per cent), is one which did not appear in any significant numbers in the television listing. Domestic dramas ("soap operas") and crime dramas each reached about one-tenth of the radio-owning households. All other program types had less coverage.

Again, as in television, the rank order changes if we look at the households that listened regularly to two or more programs of a given type. News broadcasts drop from first to fifth place, and religion from third to fourth. Both tended to be "one-program" types, as in television.

TABLE 70. Number of households[a] regularly listening to adult radio programs, by program types and number of programs regularly heard

Program Type	Heard No Prog.	One Prog.	Two	Three	Four	Five	Six	Seven to Nine	No. not specified	Total Households Listening to at Least One Program No.	Per Cent[a]	Total Households Listening to Two or more Programs No.	Per Cent[a]	Total Prog. Heard
News	2,239	674	148	28	3				314	1,167	34.3	179	5.3	1,380
Sports	2,391	365	290	177	99	15	2	1	66	1,015	29.8	584	17.1	2,033
Religion	2,419	802	143	27	12	2	1			987	29.0	185	5.4	1,233
Quiz	2,569	399	193	57	14	1	2		171	837	24.6	267	7.8	1,200
Music	2,592	423	136	75	33	9	1	2	135	814	23.9	256	7.5	1,252
Variety	2,745	400	107	37	7	3	1	1	105	661	19.4	156	4.6	886
Commentators	2,999	242	113	28	11	3	1	1	8	407	11.9	157	4.6	632
Domestic drama	3,083	121	66	36	25	7	5	4	59	323	9.5	143	4.2	614
Crime drama	3,084	131	86	29	7	2	1	3	63	322	9.5	128	3.8	522
General drama	3,155	173	54	6	2	1			15	251	7.4	63	1.8	327
Comedy drama	3,200	141	40	11	4				10	206	6.0	55	1.6	280
Domestic Variety	3,316	72	13	2	1				2	90	2.6	16	0.5	110
Personalities	3,336	62	8							70	2.1	8	0.2	78
Western	3,351	32	7	1					15	55	1.6	8	0.2	64
Public issues	3,367	35	2						2	39	1.1	2	0.1	41

[a] Of 3,406 households with radios.

It is interesting to compare the rank order of regular viewing of program types on television with that of regular listening on radio (Table 71.)

Dramatic and variety programs seem to have relatively greatest appeal on television, while music and religion do better on the radio. Popularity of news commentators seems to be confined largely to radio.

Table 71. Rank order of popularity of program types on television and radio

Television Households		Radio Households	
One or More Programs Viewed	Two or More Programs Viewed	One or More Programs Heard	Two or More Programs Heard
News	Sports	News	Sports
Sports	Variety	Sports	Quiz
Variety	General Drama	Religion	Music
Quiz	Quiz	Quiz	Religion
General drama	News	Music	News
Religion	Crime drama	Variety	Commentators
Comedy drama	Comedy drama	Commentators	Variety
Music	Religion	Domestic drama	Domestic drama
Crime drama	Domestic drama	Crime drama	Crime drama
Domestic drama	Music	General drama	General drama
Domestic variety	Public issues	Comedy drama	Comedy drama
Public issues	Domestic variety	Domestic variety	Domestic variety
Western drama	Western drama	Personalities	Personalities
		Western drama	Western drama
		Public issues	Public issues

It is also interesting to note the difference in proportion of the different types of drama heard regularly on radio as compared with the same types on television:

Per Cent of Total Drama Mentions

	Radio	*Television*
Domestic drama	34.0	11.8
Crime drama	28.9	20.0
General drama	18.1	43.6
Comedy drama	15.5	23.0
Western drama	3.5	1.6

Serious (i.e., general) drama fares better on television. Radio at the time of this study was still the stronghold of the daytime serial.

Radio music programs heard regularly were of the following types:

Serious music—52.8 per cent
Popular music—29.4 per cent
Light classics—17.8 per cent

This was, of course, adult listening. Teenage listening leans much more heavily to popular music. However, it is noteworthy that serious music received such a high rating in view of the overwhelming predominance of popular music on all of the AM stations most easily heard by New Haveners. The New Haven AM stations provide only a few isolated programs of serious music. Their turntables grind out Tin Pan Alley tunes from sign on to sign off. As of this writing, the four major network outlets in New York (WABC, WCBS, WRCA, WOR) broadcast a single fifteen-minute program of serious music (WRCA, Mondays, 7:15 P.M.) in their entire weekday schedule, Monday through Friday, 7:00 A.M. to 8:00 P.M. The popularity ranking of radio programs (Table 61) indicates that New Haven listeners have sought out the few serious music programs available to them. There are three serious music programs—and no popular music shows among the first fifteen in rank. Households with FM radio sets reported a substantial amount of listening to serious music over WBIB,[18] New Haven, which carried the WOXR network programs. AM households located in those parts of the metropolitan area where WQXR, New York, can be heard reported regular listening to it.

It may well be, though, that the ranking of serious music in first place among musical programs is more a function of identification than of the amount of listening involved. It may be assumed that serious music "fans," because they have relatively few programs available, tune in purposefully, and can, therefore, identify the programs they hear. Popular music is so prevalent that anyone who wants to hear it can find it being played at any hour of the day or night. Furthermore, popular music programs are hard to identify, since this music is not programmed in titled segments (like dramatic, quiz or variety shows), but is usually recorded "filler" used between spot announcements.

Of the total 10,652 radio programs reported as regularly heard, one-fifth were sports programs and one-eighth were news. Music, religion and quiz programs each represented one-ninth of all mentioned. Variety programs totaled one-eighth. The remaining nine program types totaled only one-fourth of all programs mentioned.

Television Summary

The important findings in this chapter concerning television viewing may be quickly summarized as follows:

1. Entertainment-type programs dominated New Haven and New York

[18] WBIB has been closed down.

television, utilizing three-fourths of available time. Information-type programs ran second, with one-fifth of the time, and orientation-type programs had the remaining time.

2. Drama dominated the entertainment-type programs, with crime drama leading and general, domestic, comedy and western drama following in that order.

3. Religious programming represented only 1 per cent of the available time in New York and even less in New Haven.

4. In spite of the shortage of religious programs available, three out of five (57 per cent) of the households with television sets watched at least one religious program regularly; and religious programs as a type were sixth in popularity among the thirteen categories used here. The five most popular program types were: news, sports, variety, quiz and general drama.

5. Viewing habits in the use of program types were fairly uniform throughout most social class and religious groups.

6. There is no discernible pattern of relationship among program types in the viewing habits of the sample households. The probability that a family will watch religious television, for example, is almost unaffected by the fact that it watches or fails to watch any other given program type or combination of types.

CHAPTER 10

The Audience for Religious Broadcasting

The audience for religious programs on radio and television totaled 2,128 households, or 59.8 per cent of the 3,559 households in the sample. The distribution of these 2,128 households by listening and viewing is shown in the following chart:

FIGURE 15. Regular audience for religion

(Per Cent of all Households)

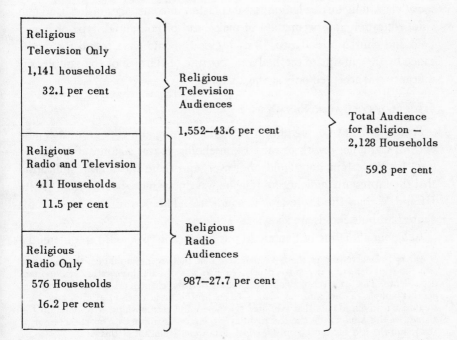

Religious
Television Only

1,141 households

32.1 per cent

Religious
Radio and Television

411 Households

11.5 per cent

Religious
Radio Only

576 Households

16.2 per cent

Religious
Television
Audiences

1,552—43.6 per cent

Religious
Radio
Audiences

987—27.7 per cent

Total Audience
for Religion —
2,128 Households

59.8 per cent

The Audience for Religion Compared to the Nonaudience for Religion

Three out of five households indicated they were a part of the regular audience for one or more religious programs. In the next chapter, we shall examine the specific programs they watched or heard. In this chapter, however, we should like to look carefully at this group of 2,128 households to see whether they were in any way a distinct segment of the population. What were the characteristics of the "audience for religion" that distinguished it from the "nonaudience for religion?"

TABLE 72. Social class composition, by percentage, of Protestant households in audience and nonaudience

Social Class	Audience	Nonaudience
I	4.9	9.4
II	12.8	14.2
III	26.8	23.8
IV	41.4	43.0
V	14.1	9.6
Total	100.0	100.0

To answer this question, a series of analyses was made of the "audience for religion" comparing it with the "nonaudience" by a number of criteria: social class, religious affiliation, set ownership, income, ages of husband and wife, education and occupation of male head of household, type of household and church attendance. In each case the data were tested for significance by the chi-square method and, because of the size of the sample, significance was accepted only at the .01 level.[1]

RESULTS OF COMPARISON ANALYSIS

Social class was not significant in distinguishing audience from nonaudience in Catholic, Jewish or mixed households. It was significant at the .02 level for Protestant households, however, and there was a clear indication that the Protestant audience for religion was drawn more heavily from classes III and V than the Protestant nonaudience. The percentages by class for *Protestant* households are shown in Table 72.

Religious affiliation of household was significant ($p < .001$) in differentia-

[1] It is a characteristic of the chi-square test that the larger the sample, the more sensitive it is in detecting dependence between two sets of data, even rather unimportant dependence. The .01 level of significance means that the chances are 99 out of 100 that another sample of the same population taken by the same method at the same time would have produced data that exhibited the same set of relationships. It is more usual in a study of this kind to use the less rigorous .05 level of significance (95 chances out of 100), and the text indicates points at which data were significant at this level.

ting audience from nonaudience. Table 73 shows the percentage distribution by religious affiliation.

The difference between faith groups is largely due to one program, that of Bishop Sheen, which heavily weights the religious audience statistics.

TABLE 73. Percentage distribution by religion of families in audience and nonaudience

Religious Affiliation	Audience	Nonaudience
Roman Catholic	57.1	48.5
Protestant	28.3	31.0
Jewish	7.2	12.7
Mixed	7.4	7.8
Total	100.0	100.0

Set ownership also was significant in distinguishing the religious audience from the nonaudience. Television set owners were 79.7 per cent of the religious audience and only 65.7 per cent of the nonaudience. Households with radio sets only were 20.3 per cent of the audience and 24.7 per cent of the nonaudience. Households with neither radio nor television were 9.8 per cent of the nonaudience.

Income seemed to have some significance[2] in distinguishing audience from nonaudience. Families with incomes above $5,000 constituted 17.3 per cent of the audience, but 24.1 per cent of the nonaudience. However, variations from the normal population distribution in both income and set ownership can be attributed largely to differences between religious groups. Protestant households have higher incomes and fewer television sets, and are more frequently in the nonaudience than are households of the other faith groups.

Church attendance might be assumed to have some significance in determining the audience for religion. Analysis showed attendance to be significant only in the cases of Catholic and Protestant wives or female heads of households. Households where the wife did not attend church constituted a larger proportion of the nonaudience in both cases than did those where the wife was a churchgoer. The same thing was true to a lesser degree of Jewish and mixed households (significant at .02 and .05 levels respectively). The pattern of church attendance of husband and wife together, however, made no difference in listening and viewing habits for religious programs: whether both attended the same church or different churches, or only one attended, or neither attended, did not seem to affect listening and viewing.

Education of the male head of the household was significant only in Jew-

[2] The "measure of dependence" here was very low. See Appendix C for explanation of "measure of dependence."

ish households, where the pattern was curious. High school and college education seemed to be associated with nonlistening, but graduate education was associated with membership in the religious audience. In the other religious groups there was no significant difference between audience and nonaudience by educational level.

Age of the wife or female head of household made a definite, but not too important,[3] difference, with households where the wife or female head was between 45 and 64 years of age contributing a larger share to the audience than did those in other age brackets. A breakdown of households by age of male head and his religious affiliation showed the age of the male head to be significant in Jewish households (more Jewish men in the audience were aged 30–45 years), but not significant in Catholic, Protestant or mixed households.

Occupation of the male head of household was not significant at the .01 level, although it was significant at the .05 level. There was a small tendency for the clerical and skilled and semiskilled labor occupations to contribute the larger share of the audience, and for business and professional households to contribute the larger share of the nonaudience.

Type of household was not significant in determining the audience.

SIMILARITY AND DIFFERENCES BETWEEN THE AUDIENCE AND THE NONAUDIENCE

Table 74 gives the composite picture, by religious affiliation and social class, of the percentages of various population groups which are found in the audience for religion.

It is clear that there are a number of differences between the audience for religion and the nonaudience. Most obvious is the difference between Protestants and Jews on the one hand and Catholic and mixed families on the

TABLE 74. Percentage of social class and religious groups included in audience for religion

Religious Affiliation	Social Class					Total
	I	II	III	IV	V	
Roman Catholic	53.5	64.7	68.3	63.4	61.1	63.6
Protestant	41.4	55.0	60.6	56.9	66.6	57.7
Jewish	56.2	37.5	45.4	47.4	56.5	45.7
Mixed	a	61.9	52.4	62.0	56.2	59.3
Total	47.4	54.1	61.2	60.5	61.8	59.8

a Only two cases in sample—both in audience.

[3] Measure of dependence only .0032.

other. Among Protestant households, as already indicated, there is a tendency for higher social class to be associated with a minimum of religious listening and viewing. Among Jewish households the social class pattern is similar and even more marked, except for class I Jewish households, where this tendency is sharply reversed. Jews do less religious listening and view-

TABLE 75. Religious affiliation, by percentage, of television and radio audiences for religion

Religious Affiliation of Households[a]	Per Cent of Television and Radio Audiences for Religion	
	Television	Radio
Roman Catholic	63.6	45.0
Protestant	21.8	36.9
Jewish	5.5	9.9
Mixed	7.7	6.4

[a] Religion other, none, or unknown, omitted.

ing than do members of any other religious group.[4] Catholic and mixed households, on the other hand, follow a fairly consistent pattern of close to 60 per cent viewing and listening households at all social levels.

These differences, however, must not be permitted to obscure the basic similarity among all groups in the table. While the religious audience ranges from 38 per cent of class II Jews to 68 per cent of class III Catholics, it is a substantial proportion of every group. In sixteen out of the twenty cells (socioreligious groups) in Table 74, more than half of the households are a part of the audience for religion.

Insofar as these data can be said to measure the taste for religious programs, therefore, it is important to note that this taste has a marked universality. Whether we divide our sample by social class, religious affiliation, church attendance, occupation, age of adults, education, income or type of household, we find an audience for religious radio and television representing, in the great majority of cases, over half of any given group.

Once we start subdividing the audience for religion we begin to get more

4 This situation may be attributable not to lack of interest in religious broadcasting on the part of Jews, but to the fact there are so few Jewish programs on the air in comparison to Protestant and Roman Catholic programs. There are no Jewish programs aired regularly in New Haven under local auspices, although rabbis of synagogues affiliated with the New Haven Council of Churches take their turns under the rotation system in force on some Council programs. Nationally, at the time of the study, the Jews had no television program of their own, although they shared time with Protestants and Roman Catholics on a proportional basis on Lamp Unto My Feet (CBS), Frontiers of Faith (NBC) and DuMont's religious news roundup. On radio, The Eternal Light (NBC) and Message of Israel (ABC) are weekly Jewish programs, and rabbis are allocated a proportion of the time on the CBS Church of the Air.

noticeable differences. The substantial difference between Roman Catholic and Protestant television ownership, for example, was reflected in the distribution of the *television* audience for religion as compared with the *radio* audience for religion (Table 75).

A similar situation is reflected in the social class distribution (Table 76).

TABLE 76. Social Class, by percentage, of television and radio audiences for religion

Social Class of Households	Per Cent of Television and Radio Audiences for Religion	
	Television	Radio
I	2.2	3.4
II	7.0	9.4
III	20.8	22.6
IV	52.3	47.0
V	17.7	17.5

Within the Protestant audience for religion, the distribution of households by denominational affiliation followed closely their distribution in the total population. There were, however, some small differences by denomination between the radio audience and the television audience for religious programs (Table 77).

Table 77. Percentage distribution by denomination [a] of households in the Protestant audience for religious radio and television programs, compared with total Protestant households

Denomination	Protestant Households in Audience for Religious Radio and Television			All Protestant Households
	Television	Radio	Total Audience	
Congregational	34.0	31.9	33.2	35.2
Episcopal	25.7	22.7	24.5	24.3
Baptist	13.9	13.1	13.1	11.2
Methodist	9.7	13.9	10.9	10.6
Lutheran	7.3	7.2	7.8	8.4
Other	9.4	11.2	10.5	10.3
Total	100.0	100.0	100.0	100.0

[a] Denomination of Male Head of Household

Differences became more marked when we analyzed the audience for individual programs. It is there that personal background and taste became apparent. Chapter 11 is a report of the program-audience analysis.

CHAPTER 11

The Audiences for Specific Religious Programs

Protestant and Roman Catholic Program Audiences

The audience for programs identified[1] with the Roman Catholic faith exceeded the audience for Protestant programs by a margin considerably larger in percentage than Roman Catholics outnumber Protestants in the population on a percentage basis. Accordingly, an analysis was made of five leading Roman Catholic programs and eleven leading Protestant programs[2] to establish the characteristics of the audiences for each group.

Table 78. Audiences for five Roman Catholic and eleven Protestant radio and television programs, by religious affiliation of households in audience

Religious Affiliation of Households in Audience	Households Listening to or Viewing These Programs					
	5 Catholic Programs		11 Protestant Programs		Total Households	
	No.	Per Cent	No.	Per Cent	No.	Per Cent
Roman Catholic	775	75.9	76	29.7	851	66.7
Protestant	139	13.6	145	56.6	284	22.2
Jewish	22	2.2	13	5.1	35	2.7
Mixed	85	8.3	22	8.6	107	8.4
Total	1,021	100.0	256	100.0	1,277	100.0

[1] While the religious identification of most programs was clear, some presented difficulties. Bishop Fulton J. Sheen, for example, is now commercially sponsored on television and nominally nonsectarian. Content analysis, however, showed the program to be clearly Roman Catholic and audience interviews showed it is generally viewed as such.
[2] *Roman Catholic:* Fulton Sheen, Catholic Hour, What One Person Can Do, Rosary Hour, Sacred Heart Hour.
Protestant: What's Your Trouble?, This Is the Life, Bible Puppets, The Lutheran Hour, Art of Living, National Radio Pulpit, National Vespers, Old Fashioned Revival Hour, Hour of Decision, Religion at the News Desk, Evensong.

The five Catholic programs came regularly into 1,021 different households and the eleven Protestant programs into 256 different households, or only one-fourth as many. The Catholic programs had an audience that was 76 per cent Catholic, while the Protestant programs had an audience that was 57 per cent Protestant. Or, putting it the other way, the audience for Catholic programs was only 14 per cent Protestant, while the audience for Protestant programs was 30 per cent Catholic.

On the face of it, this would indicate that the formulae used on Protestant programs have been twice as successful as those on Catholic programs in reaching an audience of a different faith from the sponsor. In relative terms, this was true. In absolute terms, it was not. The relatively larger audience for Catholic programs meant that in absolute numbers almost as many Protestant families (139) were seeing or hearing Catholic programs regularly as were seeing or hearing Protestant programs (145).

The actual coverage of these programs is seen even more clearly if we ex-

Table 79. Audience for five leading Roman Catholic programs and eleven leading Protestant programs as a percentage of all households, by religion and social class

A. Percentage of All Households by Religion

| Religion of Household | Total Households | Households in Audience | | | |
| | | 5 Catholic Programs | | 11 Protestant Programs | |
		No.	Per Cent	No.	Per Cent
Roman Catholic	1,879	775	41.2	76	4.1
Protestant	1,032	139	13.5	145	14.1
Jewish	315	22	7.0	13	4.1
Mixed	264	85	32.2	22	8.3
Total	3,559	1,021	28.7	256	7.2

B. Percentage of All Households by Social Class

| Social Class of Household | Total Households | Households in Audience | | | |
| | | 5 Catholic Programs | | 11 Protestant Programs | |
		No.	Per Cent	No.	Per Cent
I	119	22	18.4	13	10.9
II	328	75	22.9	24	7.3
III	760	232	30.5	57	7.5
IV	1,723	518	30.1	116	6.7
V	629	174	27.7	46	7.3
Total	3,559	1,021	28.7	256	7.2

amine it as a percentage of all households in the sample by religion and social class (Table 79.)

Only among Protestant households, the table shows, do the Protestant programs have an audience comparable in size to the Catholic programs. In no social class do the eleven Protestant programs reach a regular audience as large as the audience for the five Catholic programs, and only in social class I is it even half as large.

Size of Audience for Individual Programs

Table 80 gives the size of the audience for the seven leading religious television programs and the ten leading religious radio programs in New Haven at the time of the survey, according to the information secured in the sample. The table also gives confidence intervals for these statistics on audience

Table 80. Size of regular audience for seven leading religious television programs and ten leading religious radio programs

| | Number of Households in Regular Audience | | | | |
| | No. of Viewers (or Listeners) | Per Cent of Total Sample (N. 3,559) | Confidence Interval [a] | Estimated Total Households | |
Name of Program				Estimated	Plus or Minus [a]
Television					
Life is Worth Living	832	23.4	1.39	16,640	990
Greatest Story Ever Told	268	7.5	0.87	5,360	620
What's Your Trouble?	53	1.5	0.40	1,060	285
Christopher Hour	50	1.4	0.39	1,000	280
Frontiers of Faith	39	1.1	0.34	780	240
This Is the Life	30	0.8	0.30	600	215
Lamp Unto My Feet	24	0.7	0.27	480	190
Radio					
Catholic Hour	287	8.1	0.89	5,740	637
Greatest Story Ever Told	128	3.6	0.61	2,560	435
Eternal Light	61	1.7	0.43	1,220	305
National Radio Pulpit	58	1.6	0.42	1,160	300
Rosary Hour	44	1.2	0.36	880	255
Old Fashioned Revival Hour	42	1.2	0.35	840	250
Billy Graham	37	1.0	0.33	740	235
Religion at the News Desk	29	0.8	0.30	580	215
CBS. Church of the Air	26	0.7	0.28	520	200
Art of Living	21	0.6	0.25	420	180

[a] See footnote 3 and Appendix C for explanation

size and an estimate of the total number of households in metropolitan New Haven that listened regularly to each program.[3] (Also see Figure 16.)

FIGURE 16. Audiences for selected religious programs: percentage of total New Haven households

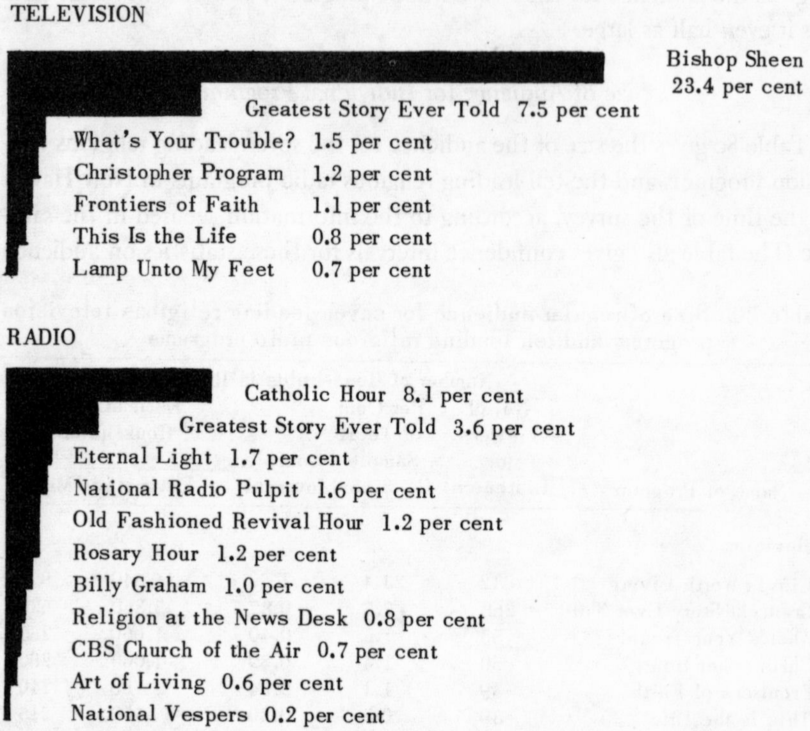

TELEVISION

Bishop Sheen 23.4 per cent

Greatest Story Ever Told   7.5 per cent

What's Your Trouble?   1.5 per cent

Christopher Program   1.2 per cent

Frontiers of Faith   1.1 per cent

This Is the Life   0.8 per cent

Lamp Unto My Feet   0.7 per cent

RADIO

Catholic Hour   8.1 per cent

Greatest Story Ever Told   3.6 per cent

Eternal Light   1.7 per cent

National Radio Pulpit   1.6 per cent

Old Fashioned Revival Hour   1.2 per cent

Rosary Hour   1.2 per cent

Billy Graham   1.0 per cent

Religion at the News Desk   0.8 per cent

CBS Church of the Air   0.7 per cent

Art of Living   0.6 per cent

National Vespers   0.2 per cent

[3] To the reader not familiar with this kind of analysis, some explanation needs to be given. The figures in the third column in Table 80, under the heading "confidence interval," represent percentages of the total sample. What they mean is that the researcher can be confident that nineteen times out of twenty (95 per cent) another sample taken of the same population at the same time by the same method would have yielded results within this many percentage points of the figure in column two. For example, we can be 95 per cent confident that a comparable sample taken at the same time would have found not less than 22.01 per cent (23.4 per cent minus 1.39 per cent) and not more than 24.79 per cent (23.4 per cent plus 1.39 per cent) of all households to be regular viewers of Life Is Worth Living. Thus, assuming our sample to have been accurately representative of the total population, we can reasonably project the figures in column four as the *total audience* (the sample multiplied by twenty), allowing for the margin of error in column five. This margin becomes relatively larger when the number of listeners reported is smaller. See Appendix C.

The reliability of these figures is considerably higher than the results reported in a typical commercial audience survey of a town this size, which according to usual practice would be based on a sample of about 500 homes.

The domination of religious television by Sheen's program was the most obvious fact revealed by these data. His audience was larger by far than that of the next six religious television programs combined, and was also larger than all ten religious radio programs combined. Remembering the data on the churches in Chapter 3, we may note that if an average of as many as two persons per household was watching Sheen, his total weekly audience would have been nearly twice the average weekly attendance (17,649) at Sunday morning worship in all Protestant and Orthodox churches in metropolitan New Haven.

The Catholic Hour did not fare quite so well as Sheen's television program, but it was still the most popular religious radio program, with a larger audience than the three next most popular programs combined.

The Greatest Story Ever Told occupied second position on both radio and television. This program and Sheen seem to have been in a class by themselves so far as popularity is concerned. The remaining programs all had fairly small audiences, as radio and television audiences go, although each audience would constitute a very large congregation if brought together in a church building.

Audience for Specific Programs

Audience analyses were made for ten selected programs to try to establish the characteristics of the households that viewed or listened. The programs were chosen to be representative of the different kinds of religious emphases available at the time of the survey. From the religious television programs available, the following were selected for analysis:

> Life Is Worth Living (Bishop Fulton J. Sheen)
> Greatest Story Ever Told (Nonsectarian)
> What's Your Trouble? (Dr. and Mrs. Norman Vincent Peale)
> Frontiers of Faith (Interfaith)
> This Is the Life (Missouri Synod Lutheran dramatic series)

The audiences for the following radio programs were analyzed:

> The Catholic Hour (Various speakers)
> National Radio Pulpit (Dr. Ralph Sockman)
> Old Fashioned Revival Hour (Dr. Charles E. Fuller)
> Hour of Decision (Rev. Billy Graham)
> The Art of Living (Dr. Norman Vincent Peale)

Selected data on the audiences for each program appear in Tables 81 and 82 and Figures 17–22. The tabular relationship between class and religion of audience members is shown in tables in Appendix D. It was previously indicated that the audience for religious radio and television was spread widely across the entire spectrum of religious affiliation and social class. To a degree this distribution is also true for individual programs, but on the whole their audiences are much more well-defined and the appeal of certain programs seems to be much stronger in certain groups than in others. One can almost draw a profile of the typical audience for each program. We shall describe these ten audiences briefly.

Table 81. Percentage distribution by religion of households in the audience for ten selected religious television and radio programs

| Name of Program | Religion of Household | | | | |
	Roman Catholic	Protestant	Jewish	Mixed	Other and None
Television					
Life Is Worth Living (Sheen)	75.5[a]	13.4	2.2	7.9	1.0
The Greatest Story Ever Told	49.3	36.9	3.4	9.7	0.7
What's Your Trouble? (Dr. and Mrs. Peale)	35.9	47.2	9.4	7.5	
Frontiers of Faith	33.3	38.4	15.3	10.4	2.6
This Is the Life	66.8	16.7	6.6	6.6	3.3
Radio					
The Catholic Hour	71.8	14.6	3.1	9.5	1.0
National Radio Pulpit (Sockman)	10.3	77.7	1.7	8.6	1.7
Old Fashioned Revival Hour (Fuller)	14.3	78.6	4.8	2.3	
Hour of Decision (Graham)	8.1	78.4	2.7	8.1	2.7
Art of Living (Peale)	18.9	66.7	4.8		9.6
Total Sample	52.8	29.0	9.2	1.4	1.6

[a] Percentages italicized when they are five percentage points or more *above* the figures for the households in the population sample.

1. *Life Is Worth Living* not only has the biggest audience (largely Roman Catholic in composition), but among the ten programs analyzed has the audience most nearly representative of the total population. It draws a slightly larger proportion of adults in the 30–44 year age group, apparently couples with minor children, than are found in the general population, and correspondingly fewer adults living alone.

2. *The Greatest Story Ever Told* definitely appeals to families with minor children, particularly among skilled, semiskilled and clerical workers who have not gone beyond high school. It finds half of its audience among Ro-

man Catholics, but also has wide appeal among Protestants. The separate analysis of church relatedness showed 7 per cent of the audience drawn from families with no church affiliation. The audience for the radio version of The Greatest Story Ever Told is similar in composition to that for the television segment, hence is not analyzed separately here.

3. *What's Your Trouble?* seems to be particularly appealing for clerical workers under 45 years of age, with some college or business school training and without minor children. Although its audience is half Protestant, on a percentage basis it has a broad appeal for Catholics and even greater attraction for Jews.

Table 82. Percentage distribution by social class of households in the audience for ten selected religious television and radio programs

Name of Program	Social Class of Household				
	I	II	III	IV	V
Television					
Life Is Worth Living (Sheen)	2.2	7.8	22.5	51.8	15.7
The Greatest Story Ever Told	1.5	8.2	23.5	48.9	17.9
What's Your Trouble? (Dr. and Mrs. Peale)	1.9	9.4	24.5	45.3	18.9
Frontiers of Faith	*10.3*[a]	2.6	25.6	43.6	17.9
This Is the Life	3.3	3.3	20.7	*56.7*	16.7
Radio					
The Catholic Hour	2.1	8.0	23.7	47.7	18.5
National Radio Pulpit (Sockman)	*10.3*	*19.0*	17.2	48.3	5.2
Old Fashioned Revival Hour (Fuller)		2.4	16.7	38.1	*42.8*
Hour of Decision (Graham)		2.7	18.9	51.4	*27.0*
Art of Living (Peale)		*23.8*	*38.1*	23.8	14.3
Total Sample	3.3	9.2	21.4	48.4	17.7

[a] Percentages italicized when they are five percentage points or more *above* the figures for the households in the population sample.

4. *Frontiers of Faith* has a fairly even age distribution except for a large proportion of older women, some married but without children and some living with other adults. It also draws broken families with minor children. Educational level is high—college and graduate school—and clerical workers represent a good proportion of the audience.

5. *This Is the Life* resembles *The Greatest Story Ever Told* in its appeal to couples with minor children, and in the general educational level of the audience (high school graduate). Occupational spread is even. On a percentage basis, this program has a greater appeal for Roman Catholics and Jews than does any other Protestant program.

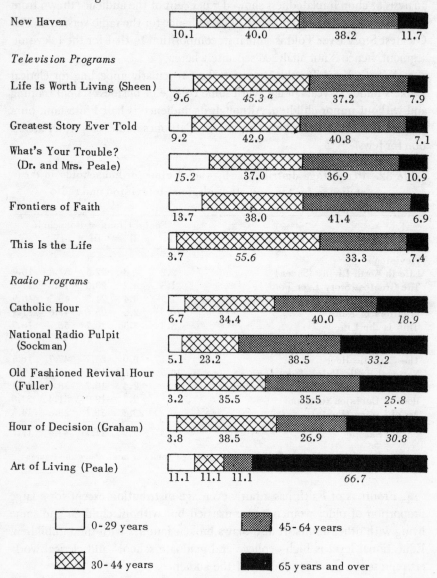

FIGURE 17. Religious television and radio program audiences: percentage distribution of male heads of households by age

New Haven
10.1   40.0   38.2   11.7

Television Programs

Life Is Worth Living (Sheen)
9.6   45.3 [a]   37.2   7.9

Greatest Story Ever Told
9.2   42.9   40.8   7.1

What's Your Trouble?
(Dr. and Mrs. Peale)
15.2   37.0   36.9   10.9

Frontiers of Faith
13.7   38.0   41.4   6.9

This Is the Life
3.7   55.6   33.3   7.4

Radio Programs

Catholic Hour
6.7   34.4   40.0   *18.9*

National Radio Pulpit
(Sockman)
5.1   23.2   38.5   *33.2*

Old Fashioned Revival Hour
(Fuller)
3.2   35.5   35.5   *25.8*

Hour of Decision (Graham)
3.8   38.5   26.9   *30.8*

Art of Living (Peale)
11.1   11.1   11.1   *66.7*

☐ 0-29 years   ▨ 45-64 years

▨ 30-44 years   ■ 65 years and over

[a] Percentages italicized when they are five percentage points or more *above* the figures for the total New Haven population.

FIGURE 18. Religious television and radio program audiences: percentage distribution of wives and female heads of households by age

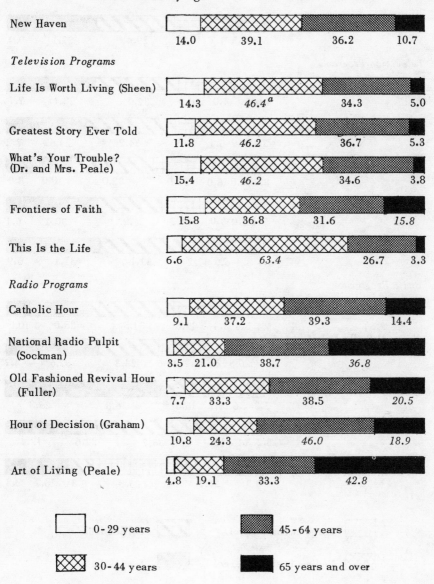

New Haven
14.0   39.1   36.2   10.7

Television Programs

Life Is Worth Living (Sheen)
14.3   46.4[a]   34.3   5.0

Greatest Story Ever Told
11.8   46.2   36.7   5.3

What's Your Trouble?
(Dr. and Mrs. Peale)
15.4   46.2   34.6   3.8

Frontiers of Faith
15.8   36.8   31.6   *15.8*

This Is the Life
6.6   *63.4*   26.7   3.3

Radio Programs

Catholic Hour
9.1   37.2   39.3   14.4

National Radio Pulpit
(Sockman)
3.5   21.0   38.7   *36.8*

Old Fashioned Revival Hour
(Fuller)
7.7   33.3   38.5   *20.5*

Hour of Decision (Graham)
10.8   24.3   *46.0*   *18.9*

Art of Living (Peale)
4.8   19.1   33.3   *42.8*

☐ 0-29 years   ▨ 45-64 years

⊠ 30-44 years   ■ 65 years and over

[a] Percentages italicized when they are five percentage points or more *above* the figures for the total New Haven population.

FIGURE 19. Religious television and radio program audiences: percentage distribution of male heads of households, by occupation

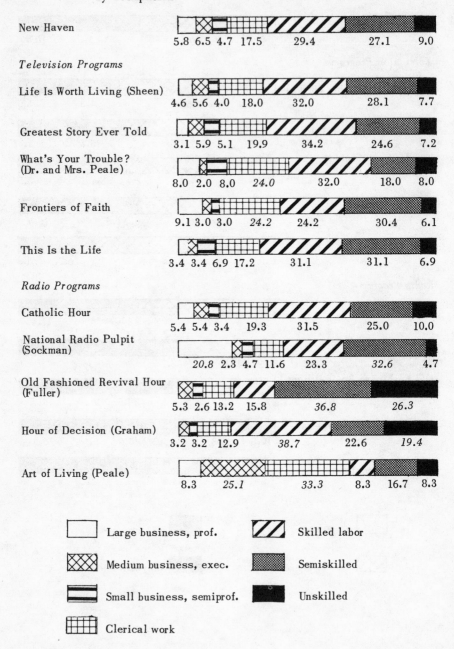

a Percentages italicized when they are five percentage points or more *above* the figures for the total New Haven population.

FIGURE 20. Religious television and radio program audiences: percentage distribution of male heads of households by education

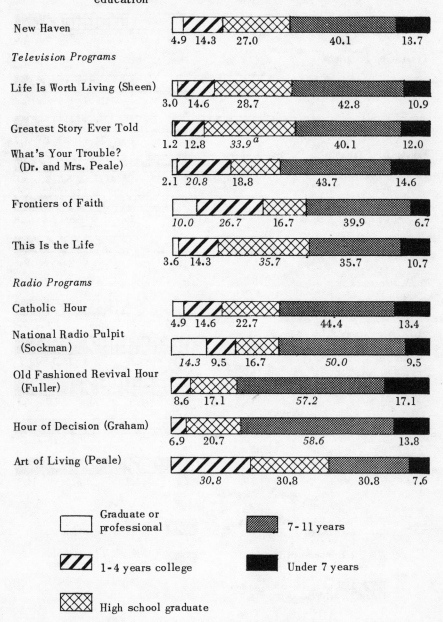

New Haven
4.9 14.3 27.0 40.1 13.7

Television Programs

Life Is Worth Living (Sheen)
3.0 14.6 28.7 42.8 10.9

Greatest Story Ever Told
1.2 12.8 33.9 [a] 40.1 12.0

What's Your Trouble?
(Dr. and Mrs. Peale)
2.1 *20.8* 18.8 43.7 14.6

Frontiers of Faith
10.0 *26.7* 16.7 39.9 6.7

This Is the Life
3.6 14.3 *35.7* 35.7 10.7

Radio Programs

Catholic Hour
4.9 14.6 22.7 44.4 13.4

National Radio Pulpit
(Sockman)
14.3 9.5 16.7 *50.0* 9.5

Old Fashioned Revival Hour
(Fuller)
8.6 17.1 *57.2* 17.1

Hour of Decision (Graham)
6.9 20.7 *58.6* 13.8

Art of Living (Peale)
30.8 30.8 30.8 7.6

Graduate or professional

7-11 years

1-4 years college

Under 7 years

High school graduate

[a] Percentages italicized when they are five percentage points or more *above* the figures for the total New Haven population.

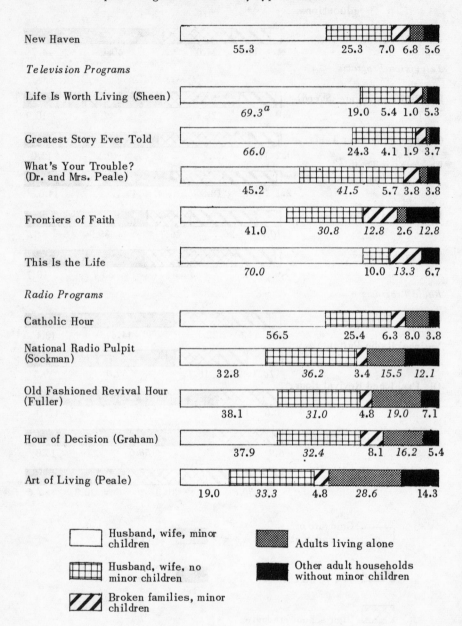

FIGURE 21. Religious television and radio program audiences:
percentage distribution by type of household

New Haven
55.3   25.3   7.0   6.8   5.6

Television Programs

Life Is Worth Living (Sheen)
69.3[a]   19.0   5.4   1.0   5.3

Greatest Story Ever Told
66.0   24.3   4.1   1.9   3.7

What's Your Trouble?
(Dr. and Mrs. Peale)
45.2   *41.5*   5.7   3.8   3.8

Frontiers of Faith
41.0   *30.8*   *12.8*   2.6   *12.8*

This Is the Life
70.0   10.0   *13.3*   6.7

Radio Programs

Catholic Hour
56.5   25.4   6.3   8.0   3.8

National Radio Pulpit
(Sockman)
32.8   *36.2*   3.4   *15.5*   *12.1*

Old Fashioned Revival Hour
(Fuller)
38.1   *31.0*   4.8   *19.0*   7.1

Hour of Decision (Graham)
37.9   *32.4*   8.1   *16.2*   5.4

Art of Living (Peale)
19.0   *33.3*   4.8   *28.6*   *14.3*

☐ Husband, wife, minor children

▨ Adults living alone

▤ Husband, wife, no minor children

■ Other adult households without minor children

▨ Broken families, minor children

[a] Percentages italicized when they are five percentage points or more *above* the figures for the total New Haven population.

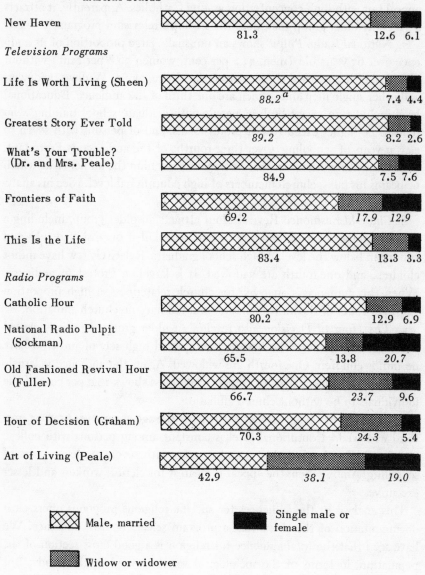

FIGURE 22. Religious television and radio program audiences: percentage distribution of heads of households by marital status

New Haven   81.3   12.6   6.1

Television Programs

Life Is Worth Living (Sheen)   88.2[a]   7.4   4.4

Greatest Story Ever Told   89.2   8.2   2.6

What's Your Trouble? (Dr. and Mrs. Peale)   84.9   7.5   7.6

Frontiers of Faith   69.2   *17.9*   *12.9*

This Is the Life   83.4   13.3   3.3

Radio Programs

Catholic Hour   80.2   12.9   6.9

National Radio Pulpit (Sockman)   65.5   13.8   *20.7*

Old Fashioned Revival Hour (Fuller)   66.7   *23.7*   9.6

Hour of Decision (Graham)   70.3   *24.3*   5.4

Art of Living (Peale)   42.9   *38.1*   *19.0*

◻ Male, married   ◼ Single male or female

▨ Widow or widower

[a] Percentages italicized when they are five percentage points or more *above* the figures for the total New Haven population.

6. *The Catholic Hour*, like Sheen's television show, has quite general appeal but with high concentration among Catholics. Apparently, it attracts a generally older group than does the Bishop's television program.

7. *National Radio Pulpit* shows an unusually large proportion of its audience over 65 years old (men, 33.2 per cent; women 36.8 per cent) without children, either married couples or persons living alone. Widows, widowers and other single men and women are one-third of the audience. Educational level includes an excess both of people with graduate school training, who tend to be higher executives or professionals, and of persons with seven to eleven years of schooling. Over three-fourths of the audience is Protestant. It is noteworthy, however, that Sockman is reaching the audience at which he beams his talks, church members of high educational level. (See his analysis of objectives, Chapter 6.)

8. *The Old Fashioned Revival Hour* attracts an older group, including a sizable number over 65, tending toward semiskilled or unskilled jobs and education below the level of high school graduate. Relatively few have minor children, and one-fourth are widowed. It is largely a Protestant audience. When this audience is analyzed for church relatedness, a high proportion (33.3 per cent) of the individuals are found to have no church affiliation.

9. *The Hour of Decision* also reaches an older group, especially skilled and unskilled laborers who have not completed high school and who have no minor children. One-fourth are widowed. Again the audience is largely Protestant, but the analysis of church relatedness shows 18.9 per cent of the individuals to be without church affiliation.

10. *The Art of Living* reaches particularly the age group over 65, over one-third widowed.[4] Educational level is constant among persons with college training, high school graduates and persons with seven to eleven years of schooling. Among men, the appeal is greatest for clerical workers and lesser executives.

This analysis of the audiences for specific religious programs offers clear documentation of the thesis that a program selects its own audience. We have seen that the *total* audience for religion is a good cross section of the population, in terms of the sociological variables used in this study. But *specific* program audiences, in most cases, are far from cross sections. They vary in size, religious composition, church-relatedness, social class, education,

---

4 This finding may be a function of the smallness of the sample (21 households), in view of the audience for What's Your Trouble?, Peale's television series. The Art of Living was not being aired in New York City or in New Haven during the time of the study. Listeners had to be real "fans" who sought the program on distant stations.

occupation, type of household, marital status and number of children in families. They vary, also, in the degree in which they are concentrated in specific groups or draw widely from a number of groups.

The facts presented in this chapter do not, of course, explain reasons for listening-viewing or nonlistening-viewing. At best, they only provide clues for further study. Sheen's drawing power, for example, is substantial in all groups, but there are still three households that do not watch his program for every household that does watch. Sockman's audience may consist largely of Protestants over 45 years old, but in this group there are far more non-listeners in the population than there are listeners. Fuller and Graham may appeal to older, working-class Protestants, but, again, there are many more of these persons who never hear these preachers than there are who do. The mistake must not be made of assuming that because a given program draws its audience from a particular segment of the population, that segment is, therefore, adequately provided with religious programs that suit its tastes and needs. As an analogy, it may be pointed out that a small sect may draw its membership almost exclusively from factory workers, but there would be few religious leaders outside that sect who would claim that it alone was adequate to minister to an entire working-class population.

Pursuing this point further, we would point out that the sociological characteristics of an audience are, as a rule, significant rather than accidental, but the nature of their significance varies a good deal. The audience for the Rosary Hour, for example, is likely to be drawn from among social class IV families, not because the program appeals to factory workers as such, but because it is directed at Roman Catholics, and Catholics are largely found in social class IV. Why does Peale's radio program appeal to older people and those without children? Probably because it is directed at anxious people and anxiety is more a characteristic of age and of childless adults, and because these people—in New Haven—are less likely to have television sets than are families with minor children and are, therefore, more likely to be radio listeners. Why does The Greatest Story Ever Told appeal to Protestant families with minor children? Undoubtedly, the answer will have something to do with the attitude of the Protestant parent toward the religious training of children. Why does National Radio Pulpit (Sockman) reach older, better educated Protestants? Undoubtedly, there is a connection between the content of the message and the program format and the tastes of well-educated Protestants of advanced years.

We have reserved for the last chapter a discussion of the implications of the data, but it is important to stress here that the design and content of a program seem to set definite limits upon the audience it will reach. Ideally, it seems possible to predict with some precision what kind of audience will be created for any program the basic characteristics of which are known, in any population which itself is known in some detail.

PART IV

Depth Studies of Individuals

CHAPTER 12

Procedure in the Depth Studies

Lengthy nondirective interviews were conducted with representative families as a basis for a "depth" analysis of the needs and values of the public in relation to religious television and radio. Each of these interviews lasted from two to four hours; some were even longer. They were held in the homes of the respondents and were recorded on tape. The technique of depth interviewing was tested in a pilot study in Kansas City, and interviews taken there were included in the analysis procedure for the depth studies.

The families chosen for the depth interviews do not constitute a subsample of the 5 per cent population sample. It was obvious to the planners of the study that an acceptable probability sample of the population would be so large as to defeat the purposes of the interviews. The staff required to collect the interview information from such a sample was beyond the budget capacity of the Communications Research Project. Moreover, even if the budget had been large enough to permit the drawing of such an interview sample, the sensitive analytical procedures which were contemplated would have been hampered by an unwanted profusion of interview cases. It was recognized early in the study, therefore, that a nonprobability "chunk" of the New Haven population was desired for the interviews.

The chunk was designed to include representation from the principal cultural variables relevant to the purpose of the study. Approximately half of the chunk was drawn from listeners-viewers of religious radio and television programs and half from persons who did not see or hear such programs. Within those basic categories, judgment was exercised to obtain a desirable spread on the following additional variables:

1. Religious affiliation
2. Occupation
3. Education
4. Age
5. Number in household
6. Income
7. Radio and television set ownership
8. Race and nationality

The families in the interview chunk have been considered always within the framework of the characteristics of the whole population of New Haven, as represented by the 5 per cent sample; but they are seen as particularizing the population in the views and actions of individuals. Fifty-nine families have been chosen from the depth interview cases to constitute the chunk used for analysis, and subsequent material and conclusions are drawn from their interviews.

Appendix E, Table 1, compares the characteristics of these families with those of the total population. The interview chunk, compared with the New Haven population, is overweighted with high income, college-trained, social classes I and II, Protestant families, with household heads more than fifty years old and either professionals or executives in large or medium-sized businesses. The chunk is underrepresentative, for New Haven, in families with minor children, where the household heads have high school education or less and are employed in white collar, skilled or unskilled jobs, with income of $3,500 and under. Even so, enough interviews were conducted in the underrepresented cells to provide basis for analysis of the attitudes and interests of such persons.

The writers conducted more than 75 per cent of the interviews used in the analysis. Appointments were made with respondents. Husbands and wives were interviewed together. Children were included if they were present. The interviewer, upon arrival, set up his tape recorder, plugged it into the house circuit and adjusted it. The members of the family usually were interested in observing the operation of the recorder and an easy conversational rapport was established through inviting them to hear their voices in the preliminary casual conversation.

The interviewer then told the family that he was interested in how they felt about radio, television, movies, newspapers, magazines and books—what they liked about them and what they didn't like about them. He explained that he didn't know the "right" questions to ask and that anything they might feel like saying would be useful. He assured them that he didn't care who talked first, or how long they talked. If necessary to get them started, he repeated these preliminary remarks. Then he lapsed into a friendly, relaxed silence and waited for them to begin talking. The procedure was that no matter what the respondents said in the period before they "ran down," the interviewer would nod sympathetic understanding and encourage them to continue. Occasionally respondents would ask direct questions of the interviewer concerning what they had just said: "Was this what you wanted?" To such questions the interviewer said, "I'm interested in anything you feel like saying about radio, television and such like." If respondents lapsed into silence, the interviewer often echoed back the last remark to start the conversation again.

The interviewer tried in this fashion to keep the conversation respondent-centered until manifestly the family had run out of things to say in the absence of further stimulation. At this point the interviewer's procedure was to introduce a series of standard "probes" as a means of eliciting attitudes toward a minimum number of identical topics on the part of all respondents in the depth interview chunk. Some of the probes referred to television and radio:

News and Commentators: Feelings about Edward R. Murrow, Fulton Lewis, Jr. Some people like certain types of news, such as about politics, or wars, etc.

Drama: Crime programs. Daytime serials. Do the people in them meet the same kind of problems that face people in real life?

Sports: What about the sport appeals to one? Wrestling; boxing; participant sports.

Quiz and Stunt: How do you feel about programs where people answer questions or do stunts for prizes? Groucho Marx?

Religious programs: As to radio ministers: How do you feel about ————? What idea do you have as to ———— [the minister's] denomination? What do you feel ———— [the minister] would say about race relations? About communism? About sending missions to China today? Some people talk about Bishop Sheen's program; I wonder how you feel about it?

Probes on conditions of listening or viewing religious programs: Alone or with others? Just sit and listen (look) or do other things at same time? In addition to going to church, or in lieu of same?

Still other probes dealt with other media, such as newspapers:[1]

Papers read: Attitude toward; length of time spent reading; when read; which sections read in what sequence?

Columnists: Attitude toward Dorothy Thompson, Westbrook Pegler, Drew Pearson, Walter Lippmann.

Magazines:

Magazines read: Attitudes toward; length of time spent in reading; which sections read in what order; when.[2]

Books:

Books read: Attitudes toward; length of time spent in reading. Titles.[2]

[1] Listings of newspapers and magazines read regularly in each household in the 5 per cent sample were obtained in the first interview with the family. However, it was ascertained early in the survey that information about reading of books could not be obtained in door-to-door or telephone interviews. No questions were asked of the general population sample about their use of motion pictures.

[2] See Footnote 1.

Motion Pictures:

Movies seen: How do you feel about motion pictures?

Other probes referred to non-mass media attitudes:

Corruption in politics; communism; race relations; morals; children and their problems: We hear a lot about ——— these days. I wonder how you feel about it? How can (or what should) an individual do about ———?

Human relations: What kind of neighborhood is this? What sort of people live in it?

Ego images: What do you want your children to be like when they grow up?

Schools: How do you feel about the public school system?

Other Faiths: How do you feel about other faiths?

When this phase of the interview was completed (usually in from two to four hours), the interviewer collected from each member of the family of teenage or older two sets of answers to structured questions. The first questionnaire was addressed to the history of the senior members of the family, to their organizational affiliations and activities, to their interest in all sports and leisure time activities, including vacations, and to the parallel affiliations, activities and interests of their children. The second questionnaire was a modified form of the F-scale, adapted from *The Authoritarian Personality,*[3] and intended to reveal something of the authoritarian or antiauthoritarian structure of the respondents' personalities. Lastly, the interviewer sought to engage the co-operation of each member of the family in maintaining a time-use diary for eight days. This diary was in the form of a checklist by quarter-hour intervals for 24 hours per day and provided 28 precoded categories of time use.

Immediately after the interview, the interviewer dictated his visual impressions of the respondents and their home and explanations of events which might not be understood from the playback.

Analysis of the Interviews

The depth interviews have all been analyzed by several methods, each designed to elicit, primarily, material that would throw light on (1) how the respondents went about forming opinions, and the role of religion, television and radio in this process; (2) their attitudes toward specific ethical and moral problems, the actions they advocated, the action they took, and, again,

---

[3] T. W. Adorno, Else Frenkel-Brunswik, Daniel J. Levinson, R. N. Sanford, *The Authoritarian Personality* (New York: Harper & Brothers, 1950). The items taken from the F-scale were from Forms 45 and 40 as described at pp. 255–57. One item was modified and seven additional items to be described later were added.

the influence of the mass media and of religion; (3) their personal problems, hopes, aspirations; (4) the function of religion in their lives, and their function in the religious life of the community; (5) the place and function of religious television and radio in their lives, and the potential of such programs for future influence; (6) what the respondents could articulate as wanting from religion and religious broadcasting that they do not now get from them.

The interviews were conducted to elicit both sociological and psychological data. The interviewers used a nondirective technique, but they did not feel that a client-therapist relationship existed between them and the respondents. Rather, the relationship was one between two or more equals, one of whom was seeking opinion and information, but not trying to structure the form or the scope of the subject matter. The adoption of this methodology predicated certain limitations upon judgments exercised in the analysis of data. It was, of course, necessary to evaluate what the respondents said and to form opinions about their personalities, their veracity, their fund of information, their attitudes and their interpretation of their actions. In analyzing the interviews, we had constantly in mind our own Protestant rationale and our understanding of the social situation in which both the interviewers and the respondents were operating. For example, when Mr. Manson, whose interview is analyzed later, boasted of his business acumen, his statements were not accepted at face value. The analysts attempted to maintain a reasonably sophisticated attitude toward what the respondents told the interviewers, without trying to project any basic theory of psychological motivation onto the persons who had been interviewed. The analysts quickly became aware of the ease with which they could slip into interpretations and projections they were not competent to make on the basis of their knowledge of the respondents. This danger was met by adopting several forms of analysis which were applied serially, and by subjecting the interviews both to group analysis and to individual analysis by a succession of persons. Nevertheless, evaluation of the interviews was never easy. The analysts—the writers, plus psychologists, sociologists and educators who assisted—often found themselves diverging somewhat from one another in interpreting motives, attitudes and actions of the respondents. The final opinions, reported here, were not always reached unanimously. Time and again we received graphic evidence of the validity of the Biblical admonition, "Judge not that you be not judged." When one human being attempts to judge another, he cannot wholly divorce himself from his subjective evaluation of the self.

The first analysis of the interviews was made by a panel consisting of the writers plus guests invited because of their expert knowledge. The interviewer would summarize orally the situational information concerning a respondent family. He would then play the recording of the interview in its entirety, stopping to replay any portions that other panel members wished to study and discuss. During the playback, notes were made under the following standard categories:

1. *Sociological identification.* Descriptive information on occupation, income, education, age, social class, size of family, ethnic factors, organizational activities and interests.

2. *Social orientation and behavior.* Attitudes and interests in the family, the neighborhood, minority groups, politics, et cetera.

3. *Psychological pattern.* Types of needs and values; strategies for perceiving and using information from the environment; conceptions of self, authority; emotional and intellectual factors.

4. *Religious background, behavior and attitudes.* Attitudes toward the church; church background; church activity pattern; conception of the role of the church in society; hopes as to what respondents and their children should obtain from religion; their concept of their own role in worship, religious education, evangelism, daily religious living.

5. *Attitudes toward the mass media in general.* Attitudes toward the mass media and particularly radio and television in light of attitudes toward leisure time use in general; the pattern of viewing and listening; their interest in and attitudes toward types of mass media content and toward specific programs, pictures, et cetera; their suggestions for changes in media content; their attitudes toward children's programs on radio and television as related to their attitudes toward children.

6. *Attitudes toward religious radio and television.* These attitudes viewed against the background of media attitudes, religious life and interests and their interests in general; their use of specific religious radio and television programs and the values inherent in such listening; the accessibility of the family to organized religion as presented through these media, particularly in contrast with other more conventional methods (preaching, church school, calling, et cetera) used by the churches in effecting changes in attitudes and behavior or developing attachments to the church.

At the conclusion of this playback, one of the panelists made an analysis based on his notes under the descriptive categories. Amendments, exceptions and amplification were then stated by other panelists and a discussion ensued. Recordings were made of this analysis and were subsequently transcribed.

Several dozen interviews were analyzed by this procedure. By then, we had developed sufficient familiarity with the typologies of the respondents that analyses en banc were not yielding enough new insights to justify the effort. Remaining interviews were then assigned to individuals for analysis, along with a sampling of the interviews already analyzed by the panels.

A third, and final, analysis was made to record detailed behavioral information uniformly from all respondents as preparation for exposition of findings. Both the en banc and the individual analytical procedures dealt in broad issues and conclusions. They were too loose to yield minor data of uniform comparability as between interviews. Procedures and a form were, therefore, designed to draw a systematic summary of data from each interview. The writers themselves processed 25 of the interviews, using this final analytical procedure. The remaining interviews were processed by junior staff members.

CHAPTER 13

People: Their Interests
and Preoccupations

The narrow separation between certainty and uncertainty in reaching conclusions in attitude studies is too well known to need documentation here. Furthermore, the state of psychological theory is still far too unsettled to permit any degree of confidence that any single model of psychological theory of behavior will resemble very closely either reality or the comparable theory of a generation hence. Both of these thoughts were held constantly in mind as warnings while the depth interviews were evaluated.

The necessary kit of tests and categories which would be needed to analyze all of the psychological variables that affected the depth interview respondents was in no sense ready at hand when the study was undertaken. Our investigation, therefore, necessarily proceeded with the concepts and the tools that were available. J. J. Stein prepared a preliminary analysis of psychological patterns among respondents in the interview chunk. This analysis was concerned with the problem of discovering any general personality and phenotypical patterns among two classes of respondents, listeners-viewers of selected religious programs and nonusers of religious radio and television. The semantic differential tests developed by C. E. Osgood of the University of Illinois were administered to a selected group of respondents and to several religious broadcasters in an attempt to discover the psychological relationships between the broadcasters and members of their audiences.

Some help in identifying categories was derived from E. C. Tolman's Psychological Model[1] (Figure 23). Tolman described behavior in terms of dependent, intervening and independent variables. The behavior with which we were concerned was the use of television and radio, and especially the listening to and viewing of religious programs. The listening-viewing

[1] Reprinted by permission of the publishers from T. Parsons and E. A. Shils, editors, *Toward a General Theory of Action* (Cambridge, Mass.: Harvard University Press). Copyright 1951, by The President and Fellows of Harvard College.

FIGURE 23. Tolman's Psychological Model

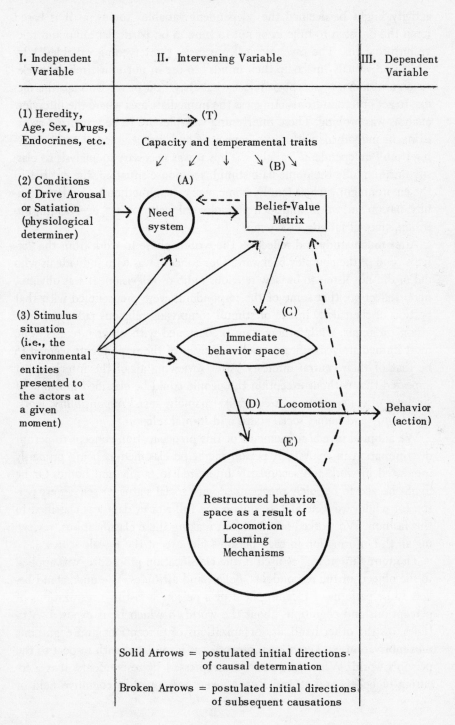

I. Independent
   Variable

II. Intervening Variable

III. Dependent
   Variable

(1) Heredity,
Age, Sex, Drugs,
Endocrines, etc.

(T)

Capacity and temperamental traits

(B)

(A)

(2) Conditions
of Drive Arousal
or Satiation
(physiological
determiner)

Need
system

Belief-Value
Matrix

(3) Stimulus
situation
(i.e., the
environmental
entities
presented to
the actors at
a given
moment)

(C)

Immediate
behavior space

(D)   Locomotion

Behavior
(action)

(E)

Restructured behavior
space as a result of
Locomotion
Learning
Mechanisms

Solid Arrows = postulated initial directions
                    of causal determination

Broken Arrows = postulated initial directions
                    of subsequent causations

activity might be deemed the "dependent variable" for us, as it is based upon the decision to tune in or not to tune in on particular radio and television programs. The psychological processes ("intervening variables") by which individuals "make up their minds" to use or not to use religious television and radio, to accept or reject what they hear or see through the media, to act or refrain from acting was the immediate area where the interview analysis was probing. These intervening variables are to be visualized as existing in individuals with given capacities and temperamental traits deriving from "independent" variables. Thus it was necessary in analysis to classify meaningfully the immediate stimulus-response situation, the entities in the environment such as family, home, work, neighborhood, social community, nation and world, and such physiological factors as sex, age, health, nutrition, state of fatigue, et cetera.

After much study and reflection the writers chose to work from the "effects" end of the complex backward. Our concern was with individuals who did or did not listen to or view religious radio or television. It was obvious, upon reflection, that some of the respondents were preoccupied with that portion of their daily intake of stimuli comprising religious radio and television programs, while others were preoccupied with other interests. The most immediately significant level of analysis of the respondents seemed to be that of their central interests. After reviewing all of the interviews, it appeared that without exception the people could be classified into one of six areas of concentration or centrality: namely, social responsibility, work, self, family and home, social status and formal religion.

We adopted several refinements of this preoccupation concept to permit discrimination in analysis. A person might be classified as being primarily interested in work and secondarily interested in family and home. Or he might be said to be solely preoccupied with social status, or self. Every person for whom we were able to obtain the full run of data was classified in this fashion. We worked as a group in making these classifications, reviewing all the information in each person's file, except the F-scale scores.

The term "interests," as used in the classification procedure, was applied to the objects of the respondents' beliefs and attitudes. We understand beliefs to be patterns of meaning held by a person as lasting organizations of perceptions and cognitions about the world to which he is exposed. Attitudes, on the other hand, are organizations of perceptions and cognitions plus motivations and emotional processes as formulated with respect to the person's world. When judgments are expressed by respondents, it is a focusing of beliefs and attitudes on a given perceptual or cognitive field or situation. *Opinions* are a product of perceptions, beliefs and attitudes. They remain stable for some time. Beliefs which the person regards as verifiable may be thought of as *knowledge;* those which he regards as unverifiable may be considered matters of *faith.* These concepts have been defined here for convenient reference. Each of them is regarded by some psychologists as representing processes within the group of intervening variables in the Tolman model—located, presumably, in the areas designated as need-system, belief-value matrixes, immediate behavior space and reconstructed space.

The Patterning of Interests among the Persons Interviewed

The 59 interviews in the chunk included 89 adult respondents. What kinds of people were these respondents, with what spread of interests? Qualitative considerations are pre-eminent in dealing with these persons. No stress should be laid on the proportions in such a nonprobability chunk of the population. Nevertheless, suggestive clues to behavior may be missed if one fails to observe the bulk relationships among these 89 persons. The significant data concerning them is presented in Appendix E, Table 2, classified by the primary or sole preoccupation of each individual.

The largest interest groups are *family and home* (25 persons), *social status* (19 persons) and *self* (19 persons). The first two of these groups have certain similar characteristics.

It is not surprising to find that the people who are preoccupied with family and home and social status are the youngest of the interest groups, with median ages for the heads of the households of under forty. They are in families which are somewhere on the individual and social progress "ladder" and in the process of establishing personal and social group identities for themselves. Significantly, they contain the bulk of the skilled workers in the chunk. About two-fifths of the family and home group are skilled workers, while almost half of the social status group are drawn from the same occupational class. In income these two classes are about average for the country ($3,501–$5,000). In educational background these respondents have fared a little better by contemporary standards than their peers generally in the United States. The median members of both groups have finished high school and had several years either of college or of business school training. The chief distinction between the social-status group and the family and home group as derived from these gross data appears to be the greater frequency of children in the households in the family and home group; 64 per cent of the people in that interest group are in homes with minor children while only half of the individuals in the social status group have minor children. Both groups are four-fifths saturated with television sets and all the families have radios. As might be expected from other aspects of the study, the majority of Roman Catholic respondents (five out of seven) are in the family and home group.

The third among the large groups is the one termed *self-preoccupied*. This group is dominated by a disproportionate number of females (three-fourths of all the persons in the group) and contains almost all the persons whose only occupation is "retired" or "housewife." The self-preoccupied persons are also the oldest group (median age of head of household, 68), and the group with the lowest average income ($2,001–$3,500). Only two of the self-interested people are in families where there are minor children, and, proportionately, more of them are in the husband-and-wife-alone, the adults-living-alone and the other-adult households. One is perhaps justified in inferring that the self-interested people are those who have neither children nor material means to interest themselves in external objects. Lacking diversions outside themselves, they may be also relatively poorest in internal resources. Their educational backgrounds are the skimpiest of all the groups, averaging only ten years of formal education for the heads of the households.

The *work-centered* individuals comprise a fourth group of thirteen persons. This group is evenly split between families where the head of the household is in a profession or is a large business owner or business executive, and where he is the owner of a small business or is a semiprofessional. It is an older group with median age of fifty for the heads of the households. There are more husbands and wives living together alone than there are mates with minor children. The income level of this group is higher than for the family- and status-centered persons, averaging $5,001–$7,500. The median social class for the group is II, indicating well-to-do families lacking substantial inherited or acquired wealth but with junior professional or fairly high managerial status. The median head of the households in this group had been through the third year of college.

Social responsibility is the center of interest for a fifth and smaller group of eight persons. The median social class rating is I (wealthy families, leading business and professional men). This group is dominated by professionals and the largest business owners and executives, with a median income of $10,001–$15,000. The median education of household heads is a full four years of college. It would be a mistake to think of the people whose interests centered on social responsibility as being people past the prime of life. The median age of the heads of these households is 46 years (third from lowest for the six groups), and three-fourths of the households consisted of husband, wife and minor children.

The sixth and last of the preoccupation groups is that where *formal religion* appears to be the center of interest. It is small, consisting of five persons, and for this reason not much can be said about it. The median social class appears to be low—class IV. The median years of schooling of the heads of the households is completion of high school, the income median is $3,501–$5,000 and the median age is fifty. Three of the five families represented in the group consist of husband, wife and minor children.

Persons as Illustrations of the Interest Groups

The general characteristics of each of the interest groups are, of course, the sum of the characteristics of individuals. A short description of one person [2] from each of the groups will serve here to communicate the flavor of the interview situations and to demonstrate the kinds of people under each classification. Detailed analyses of selected interviews have been reserved for succeeding chapters.

SOCIAL STATUS: MRS. RICHARDSON[3]

Mrs. Richardson is the dominant member of an upward mobile, working-class family (class IV) who would rather be "right" than be happy. She was reared in a lower class home in Boston. She attended and graduated from a New England college, where she majored in nursing. Afterward, she was employed as a general duty nurse, prior to her marriage. At 34, she has three children, girls 7 and 4 and a boy 5.

Richardson is a master tool and die maker—a craftsman who is one of the aristocracy of skilled workers—earning between $5,001 and $7,500 a year. He is 37 years old and is work-centered. The prestige and ego-satisfaction of his work provide him a satisfying life, taken in conjunction with his wife, children and home. He is high school educated. He has no drive for social advancement, but his wife does.

Mrs. Richardson is the spokesman for the family. She invariably uses "we" in voicing opinions. Frequently, she attributes opinions and beliefs to her children and her husband which are obviously her own. Self-improvement of a strictly individualistic species is a pervading force for her. She

[2] In all descriptions of interview respondents, names, occupations and other data that would identify individuals have been changed.

[3] The Richardson family is also included in the detailed analyses of families using religious radio and television. The inclusion of this interview in both forms of reporting should help the reader understand the process of analysis.

idealizes the virtues of the home, attributing idyllic virtues to the children, her husband and herself. She idealizes the values in "education." Both husband and wife idealize personal economic independence as typified in the bank account and private property, epitomized in home ownership. She idealizes the role of the church in providing help to individuals—but no correlative privilege of giving help to others nor of worshiping and glorifying God through the church was manifestly realized. She idealizes upper middle class disrespect for politicians, government and labor unions, with a corresponding respect for "business" and for advertising. She even is troubled as to whether, morally, she has a right to disapprove publicly of commercial advertisements on television—even though she feels they are factually distorted—when she does not buy the product of the sponsor. She has ambivalent attitudes toward television; simultaneously feeling that she must disapprove of it as "low brow" and withal revealing that their television set is almost always in use.

Mrs. Richardson is strongly inner directed,[4] though it is not suggested that all social status-centered persons necessarily are. She is driven by the "Yankee" ethic in a relatively pure form—hard work, thrift, piety and personal improvement. She has developed her own conception of what it means to live like a "proper Bostonian" and she has a strong compulsion to reach that level.

In striving for social status, Mrs. Richardson struggles against severe obstacles. She and her husband belong to no peer groups that could advance their social fortunes. The only such group to which they have made half-hearted overtures is one of the upper class Congregational Christian churches. The occasion for initiating this move was the arousal of an interest in religion in the Richardson children through contact with neighborhood Roman Catholic children. The Richardson children were told that the catechism was a "secret" and valuable. Mrs. Richardson had been raised a Methodist, then detached from churches, but the curiosity of the children about the catechism alarmed her. She began sending them to the Congregational church school about six months prior to the interview. At the same time the husband and wife became regular attendants at the worship service of the church. At the time of the interview, she considered that the minister of the church had neglected them by failing to make a parish call. They had not applied for membership in the church; but subsequent to the interview they joined.

The only other organization to which Mrs. Richardson belongs is the

4 In the sense suggested by David Riesman, *The Lonely Crowd* (New Haven: Yale University Press), 1950.

PTA. He belongs to none. Both of them have a number of hobbies at which they are competent and which seem to consume a great deal of time. He works in photography, woodworking and gardening and plays golf. She works with wood, knits, embroiders, crochets, sews and gardens. Both of the Richardsons have compulsions, but his are satisfied largely in his work, while hers come out in minute attention to details in response to her frustrated social ambition.

The Richardsons own their home, a side-by-side duplex located in an old mid-town residential area into which Italians and Negroes are migrating. The house and neighborhood are a constant source of irritation to Mrs. Richardson. She dislikes her neighbors and is full of clichés of a critical nature with respect to Italians and Negroes. She longs to move to an upper class suburb and build a modern house among neighbors she would like and respect. But the heavy weight of prejudices the Richardsons carry marks their distance from the social class goal of the wife.

FAMILY AND HOME: THE CROMWELLS

The Cromwell family consists of husband, 39, wife, 37, and eight children of whom two are children of Mrs. Cromwell's sister. The oldest child is a boy 17, who is in the Army. After him come a boy 15, a girl 14, a boy 12, a girl 9, a boy 4, and two infants less than a year old, one of whom is the sister's child. Cromwell was born in Hartford, his wife in New Haven. He spent some time in the Navy and has lived briefly on the West Coast, but his life has mostly been spent in New Haven. His wife has lived only in and around New Haven. The husband never attended school after the eighth grade but the wife completed high school.

The Cromwells are in social class III. At the time of the interview, Cromwell operated a battery repair service in a suburb where he owns his home. Previously he had held numerous odd jobs. He worked on WPA during the depression, has driven oil trucks, pumped gasoline in service stations. When business is bad in his battery repair service, he closes it down and finds a laboring job somewhere in the neighborhood. He has no employees in his shop and rationalizes this situation by priding himself on thus avoiding all the red tape and taxes that go with being a businessman of any size. Mrs. Cromwell supplements her husband's income by working at such jobs as factory machine operator, waitress, baby-sitter and clerk in the neighborhood grocery. The only organization to which either Cromwell belongs is the local PTA. In politics, he is a nominal Republican, she a nominal Democrat, but neither has much party loyalty.

Neither of the Cromwells belongs to or attends a church, although he was reared as a Methodist and she as a Roman Catholic. They were married by a Roman Catholic priest, but were indifferent toward church attendance. Indeed, they became hostile toward Roman Catholicism because they resented the attempt of a priest to get them into his church.

Cromwell is of British-American stock and is imbued with the accepted Yankee individuality, free enterprise business doctrine and social-cultural pattern. But for him, the system has brought something far short of success. The Cromwells have always been economically insecure. Nor have they ever achieved any marked degree of social status, even though their suburb has, until recent years, been small and semirural and he has operated his own business. It is understandable, then, that the Cromwells should consciously reject social status as a value in life, just as they regard work as an unfortunately necessary means to an end. Their attitudes toward the business society and toward community organization and community institutions in general are strong in cynical rejection.

On the other hand, the Cromwells' attitudes toward people are warm and empathetic. Their good deeds to neighbors in trouble are generally known in the community. Among themselves, this large and socially rebellious family is at once close- and loose-knit. The various members go their own ways with great self-determination, but they move within a well-defined framework of interpersonal relations based on mutual respect. This respect is based on a self-prescribed morality similar to the lower class morality of nineteenth-century New England.

The family members participate in many common activities. The chief object of family interest—individually and collectively—is sports of all kinds. Fishing is the most popular and seems to have some therapeutic value in both personal and family problems. Other participant sports such as hunting, baseball, football are valued highly. The Cromwells prefer to participate in sports, but contests and reports on television, on radio and in magazines and newspapers are followed with only slightly less avidity than are the active forms of sport.

While Cromwell has had little formal education, his analytical powers, vocabulary and articulateness are considerable. Presented with the sympathetic, neutral ear of the interviewer he gave penetrating observations on a wide variety of topics a considerable social distance from him, such as the relative roles of capitalism and communism in Asia. Mrs. Cromwell is a pleasant, energetic woman who tacitly acknowledges the male function of speaking out on policy issues to outsiders, though her participation in the interview left no doubt that she is articulate in her own right.

The Cromwells present a united cohesive front against persons, practices and institutions in the community that represent authority. Included are such varying elements as the school administrators, policemen and churches —the latter two conceded to be useful for weak people. Cromwell scorns organized religion on the theory that it is controlled by hypocrites; but he makes it clear he feels he will not be accepted as a peer by church people in his community. On the other hand, Cromwell stated a concern with the hereafter and with worship. He said he prays by himself each night. Actually, both Cromwell and his wife do appear to be personally devout. They have given no religious instruction to the children, but are permissive as far as church attendance is concerned. As a consequence, the children have shopped around with their friends among both the Protestant and Roman Catholic churches of the community. None of the children has affiliated with a church or church school. No one in the Cromwell family listens to religious programs on the radio or sees them on television.

SELF: MRS. STUART

Mrs. Stuart, at the time of the interview, was a widow, aged 74 and living alone. Her home on the ground floor of an old house in a deteriorating mid-town residential area is plainly furnished but is clean and orderly. Her education and vocational background place her in social class III, but her income is about $2,000 a year.

Mrs. Stuart is a native New Englander and was raised a Congregationalist in the cultural climate of Emersonian liberalism. She completed two years of college, then studied art. From 1902 to 1909 she taught art in a medium-sized New England city. Then she married a YMCA secretary. Her husband died in 1925 after sixteen years of apparently happy married life, spent mostly in the Middle West. There were, by then, three children. Mrs. Stuart supported by the children by teaching art in the public schools of a small Middle Western city. Each of the children went through college and on to graduate study, and each is now engaged in a profession. Mrs. Stuart retired in 1942 and has lived alone most of the time since, though in the summer she visits her married children.

Life for Mrs. Stuart now revolves largely around her interests in her church, the YMCA, her reading and her radio listening. Membership in church groups and in the World Fellowship committee of the YMCA is her principle means of social contact. She belongs to three church organizations, a women's prayer group, a Bible class and a women's society. Her life apart from these groups is apparently quite solitary. She spends a great deal of time listening to the radio. She has no television set. She has a wide variety of program interests, ranging through news, general drama, daytime serials, comedy drama, quiz and religious programs. Her religious listening is indiscriminate. She will listen to any religious broadcaster, even if she does not agree with his theology. Her interest centers on National Radio Pulpit (Sockman), Art of Living (Peale) and The Greatest Story Ever Told, and she listens to those programs regularly.

Her regular reading is saturated with religious periodicals, *Christian Herald, Clear Horizons, Today, The Upper Room*. She also reads religious books such as *A Man Called Peter* and *Mr. Jones, Meet the Master*.

Mrs. Stuart lives in the YMCA tradition, with a scale of values that rates "service" highly. Her attenuated Emersonian ethic of humanist self-improvement gives her a purely individualistic view of mid-twentieth-century society. She is constantly striving for self-improvement, especially in matters of religious faith. She believes people can improve through their own efforts, and that they should help one another toward such improvement. Here her ethic of service manifests itself in a quality of condescension—which she would scarcely recognize as condescension. She feels a duty to help suitable inferiors to "rise" to an appreciation of the values of her kind of culture. Her social distance from others is scaled according to race, color, nationality and creed, although she is dimly aware of conflict between these feelings and her own doctrine of Christianity.

Her style of life today resembles that of the other-directed [5] adventurer on the frontiers of taste, except that for her the sampling takes place on the frontiers of religious faith. She is accessible to consideration of any and all religious views. All beliefs have for her primarily a personal reference, however. She does not practice this permissiveness in the social arena. She is not affiliated with any action-seeking social group—not even a political party—and she seems oblivious to the social problems associated with contemporary society. She has discharged her duty to her children and to her dead husband and is, in effect, living in her own personal past while preparing for a future in another life.

WORK: MR. WALTON

Walton was classified as work-centered, his wife as family-and-home-centered. He is in social class II, a college graduate in his forties, holding an

[5] See Riesman, *ibid*.

executive post in a large business. His income is between $7,501 and $10,000. He was born and raised in a small New England town. Now he lives in an upper class suburb, in a substantial, well-kept and tastefully furnished house. He has three children, two boys and a girl.

Job attitudes pervade Walton's whole life. He is obviously fascinated by his vocation and works hard at it. Public relations are important in every job in the company for which he works. Walton lives by the "line" which is worked out among his job peers and superiors. He accepts this viewpoint as a guide for his conduct, while at the same time maintaining his concept of himself as a poised, independent person. Since he is in the upper junior executive level of his company, he must be constantly on the *qui vive*, constantly efficient. He may soon face the possibility that he has reached his ceiling in the management hierarchy. As yet, he appears to nourish the expectation that he can rise farther.

Throughout the interview, he revealed an uncritical acceptance of stereotyped opinions current among his peers. Where they were undecided, he was undecided. For example, he is a Republican in politics. When the interview was taken, just prior to the party convention in 1952, he was unwilling to commit himself as to whether he favored Taft or Eisenhower for the nomination. (His wife had no such qualms.) He stated that this choice was currently an open matter in his office peer group.

Walton has a variety of organizational attachments, all in keeping with his vocational position. He belongs to a fraternal society, is active in the PTA. He is especially interested and active as a leader in organized sports for small boys. He is a member and a conspicuous worker in one of the oldest and socially most desirable Protestant churches in New Haven. (He was reared in a different denomination, which also has churches in New Haven.) He attends church regularly. He is attracted by the ceremony and by the fact that church attendance permits him to see and be seen by "people . . . you don't see at other times."

Among other church activities, Walton has participated in the social action program of his local church. His views on social action are rudimentary —he doesn't know what restrictive covenants are—but antagonistic. He regards the social action program as a "lost cause in my estimation, and chiefly because there doesn't seem to be an understanding of what the purpose of it is. . . . My own personal opinion is that some of the churches, probably a good many of them, have been carried away by this socialistic idea that seems to have been prevailing in the last ten or fifteen years. . . ."

Walton does a moderate amount of regular television viewing. He likes such programs as Groucho Marx, I Love Lucy, Studio One, Philco Play-house. His television-radio news sources are Today, Swazey and news bul-letins on local radio stations. He watches Sheen on television to find out what he is talking about. Walton thinks the Bishop is unbiased in his treat-ment of subjects. The whole Walton family watched The Greatest Story Ever Told while it was on television. They listen intermittently to this pro-gram on radio.

Walton regards himself as a warmly loving father and husband, and all indications are that this affection is returned by his family. But the manage-ment of the home and the bulk of responsibility for the children is left to the wife. This arrangement, too, is a vocational division of labor.

SOCIAL RESPONSIBILITY: MR. FRAMPTON

At the time of the interview, Frampton was 22 years old and nearing grad-uation from Yale Law School and induction into the army, both of which he faced with equanimity. He is in social class II, married to a beautiful young woman. They have no children. His income, when interviewed, came partly from his wife's earnings as a teacher, partly from an allowance from his father, a prosperous businessman.

The Framptons lived in a modest, two-room, mid-town apartment. The furnishings showed sophisticated taste, but the apartment was markedly un-tidy. They owned a good quality radio-phonograph combination, but no television set.

Frampton's interests are broadly diversified in the social sciences, philoso-phy and the arts. He prizes his personal integrity and freedom and is ac-cessible to self-examination. He has been sheltered by his family background from having to commit himself to the outside world. He was educated in preparatory school and Columbia University before coming to Yale. As an upper class, nonmobile, he has developed a further sheltering range of inter-ests in consumption. He savors his leisure and employs it in sampling as widely as possible in food, drink, movies, sports, holidays (visited Mexico the previous summer), handicrafts (works expertly in ceramics), art, music, radio, newspapers, radio commentators and newspaper columnists, maga-zines and books. While his orientation is palpably other-directed, Frampton is able to laugh at his bohemian foibles and to evaluate critically his adven-tures on the frontier of taste. More or less unconsciously, he follows in the Emersonian tradition of seeking personal completeness through as wide as possible a variety of experiences, though a relativistic viewpoint bars him from integrating them into a systematic philosophy. He recoils from self-alienation and tries to protect himself from it.

His thirst for experience is combined with a conscious program of social action. Abstractly, his policy toward social problems is to weigh carefully matters of principle, which he grasps with maturity beyond his years. Concretely, he has opposed race and class discrimination and is active politically. When interviewed, he was in process of organizing a group of graduate students to support Stevenson for President. Again, on the abstract level, he was able to verbalize his own choice of the course of expediency when confronted with the dilemma between principle and self-interest in a hypothetical legal case where he might risk social ostracism as the price of defending an unpopular client. He candidly admitted that expedience would rule: a candor which amounted almost to cynicism. Whether, faced with reality, he would act out his opportunistic views is, of course, an open question.

In religion, Frampton also is an explorer. His parents are Jews who have rejected Judaism to participate in the Ethical Culture Society. He has had no training in Judaism and has no interest in Ethical Culture. He has read an appreciable amount in the works of Protestant theologians. He is neutral toward religion, except for Roman Catholicism which he opposes because he believes it is authoritarian. (His wife is a former Roman Catholic and citizen of a Latin American country.) He listens regularly to one religious program on radio, Religion at the News Desk.

FORMAL RELIGION: THE HALLS

The Halls are in social class IV. They are in their fifties, with two grown daughters. Both husband and wife completed high school. Hall is a clerk in an industrial establishment, with an income of $3,501–$5,000 per year.

Hall's position in relation to nonreligious institutions is best described as anonymous. At work he has only petty status. He is a clerk and accustomed to a lifetime of order-taking from organizational superiors. In relation to politics, he is full of anomie. He regretted the necessity for the political speeches which in 1952 interrupted his favorite television programs. He is frankly bewildered by the political process in which apparently equally acceptable authority figures present somewhat different claims, based on the same issues. He does not know whom to believe; nevertheless, he is a Republican. This bewilderment over where authority really lies, over how to make a choice extends into all areas of sociocultural decision making.

In no sense is it hyperbole to state that for the Halls religion is their shield and buckler—their security framework. Their life outside the home is centered in the church. They belong to a Lutheran church, although he was raised an Episcopalian and she a Congregationalist. In the church he has status—for he has been a deacon and chairman of the board of deacons—and so does she—for she is a past president of the ladies' aid. They attend the Sunday services of worship regularly, and look upon the sermons and other pronouncements of the pastor as authoritative guides for conduct. Both of them belong to all of the church organizations for which they are eligible, finding their social as well as their religious lives centering there. It seems obvious that with advancing age their attachment to the church is growing greater. Earlier he had been an active Mason and a member of the foremen's club where he worked, and she had been a member of Eastern Star. All of these affiliations have now been dropped, while church-centered activity has been increased.

Their religious beliefs, as revealed in the interview, are interlarded with authority stereotypes. Hall cherishes the fact that he was baptized "in water that actually came from the Jordan river." He would like to see Protestant church unification, but only on the basis of Lutheran doctrine and polity. He feels that Protestants should be represented by one—or at most two or three—powerful leaders who would be strong, recognized public figures like Sheen or Spellman—figures who would focus loyalty and group spirit, and who would appear publicly in vestments. He thinks there should be a Protestant television program of the same type and "as good as" that of Sheen. His bias towards religious authority was revealed in a change in attitude toward the interviewer when—in response to a direct question from Hall—it was revealed that the study was being conducted under religious auspices. Previously, Hall had been polite and cooperative (but not to the point of overriding his wife's decision not to turn off the television set during the interview), but after the revelation of sponsorship he became extremely deferential toward the interviewer.

A secondary center of security exists for Hall in his home. It is clean and attractive, furnished in conventional style. When the interviewer arrived, the blinds were drawn on all the windows, perhaps symbolically, although it was not yet dark on a spring evening. And the family was watching television raptly. Hall proudly showed the interviewer through the house. He had finished the basement as an elaborate recreation room, so his daughters might have a place for themselves and their friends within the home and under the watchful eye of himself and his wife. One analyst felt that, in a Freudian sense, the home—and also the church—were likenesses of the womb, into which the Halls had retreated at a much earlier age—if indeed they ever ventured far from them—for the emotional security they knew not how to develop in society.

Both the Halls were born and reared in New Haven in working-class families. No class mobility took place for either of them. She followed him into the Lutheran church after marriage. Mrs. Hall's attitudes were manifested in the interview as cynical and bitter. Her interests are limited to the church, her home and television. The Halls had owned a television set for more than a year at the time of the interview, but they were still engrossed in it and could be classified as saturation viewers. They did no radio listening.

CHAPTER 14

People: Personality Types and the Use of Religious Programs

The purpose in probing into the ideas, tastes and habits of a chunk of the individuals in the population sample was to identify some of the dynamics of personal orientation and behavior that might help explain selection or rejection of religious programs and the effects of such programs on people. In Chapter 13, these dynamics were described in terms of the *major interests* or *preoccupations* of the interview respondents. Now, the chunk is to be further dissected in terms of individual attitudes toward authority, which will be related to the respondents' preoccupations and to their taste in religious broadcasting.

Attitudes Toward Authority

THE RATIONALE OF THE ANALYSIS

The authoritative element in religion is basic to most faiths. The idea of God has some authoritarian meaning for all theistic religions. The concept of authority in Protestantism is a powerful one. It varies from one Protestant group to another, but the locus of authority is in the individual and the religious group, as they exist in relation to God. Authority, for Protestants, is characteristically manifested in ethical standards and positions.

In this authority sense, the religious faith and practice of the Protestant is more the product of an *internal* process than is the faith and practice of the Roman Catholic. Leaving aside doctrines of the church, it seems fair to say that faith and practice in Protestantism depend less on a social institution (the church) or the authority of religious specialists (the clergy) than they do in Roman Catholicism. True it is that Protestants, like all value-oriented groups, have a multiplicity of values associated with their faith, which are perceived as being tied up with their religious group associations. It is equally true that, within Protestantism, there are wide differences of opinion as to the nature of the authority of both the church and its clergy.

But it is still clear that Roman Catholics are generally distinguished from Protestants by the type and extent of authority they attribute to the church and its priesthood and by the relatively lesser importance they reserve for the internalization of authority by the individual. Jews, in general, hold concepts of authority in their religious faith roughly analogous to those of Protestants, but place even less emphasis on the authority of an institution and its professional staff, and consequently more emphasis on the internalization of authority in the individual and the group.

In view of the place of authority in theistic religion, a study of the attitudes of the depth interview respondents toward authority seemed essential. However, the question of "authoritarianism" in personality was approached with considerable caution. T. W. Adorno's work on *The Authoritarian Personality*[1] was published and began to be widely discussed when the Communications Research Project was in its formative stages. As a result of extensive testing and appraisal of the techniques embodied in *The Authoritarian Personality*, social scientists appear to have a working consensus that these techniques produce valid results when their limitations are understood. In planning our own research into attitudes toward authority, we could turn to Adorno's method and theory (and almost nowhere else) for a set of tested instruments backed by a rationale of the meaning of their findings. We decided, eventually, to use certain Adorno tests as supplements to the rest of the depth-interview analysis, to relate them to other kinds of data concerning the families and individuals under study and to use our best judgment in interpreting their meaning.

The research looked for material in the interviews that might relate attitudes toward religious authority to the authoritative aspects of religious radio and television programs. We borrowed the F-scale test from *The Authoritarian Personality* for the measurement of attitudes toward authority, revising one item in it and adding five new ones which were designed to measure attitudes toward religion.[2]

---

[1] T. W. Adorno, *et al, op. cit.*

[2] The five items added were:

"Most people who try to run their lives according to the teaching of the Bible find that Bible principles are not practical in real life."

"The minister (or priest or rabbi) should be the final authority on the way we should act and what we should believe."

"In order to obtain Divine assistance in life's crises, it is necessary to get it through your church (or priest, pastor or rabbi)."

"There is little hope of getting along with people of foreign countries that are not Christian."

"Sending missionaries to Communist China would help defeat communism and save our way of life."

It will be useful for the reader to recall the current status of research in the area of personality and attitudes. Only within the past fifteen years have American psychologists attempted a quantitative exploration of total personality in relation to attitudes. Adorno's work pioneered in a new territory here and set off many subsequent studies. Adorno and his associates were attempting to learn the nature of the needs and drives which predispose the individual to receive fascist ideology favorably (including such correlates as punitiveness, prejudice, et cetera) when he lives in a political situation where it is possible to make relatively free choices. To accomplish this aim, they studied "the reverberations of social patterns within the most intimate realms of individual life," including a person's perceptions of self, family, in-groups and out-groups, "leaders" and "underdogs," social and political and economic institutions, parent-child relations, sexual attitudes and behavior, personal aspirations, religious groups and the whole complex of interactions that occur within a person's "life space" that condition his attitudes and personality. Out of this research came many provocative hypotheses and some useful tools, one of the most widely known of which is the F-scale, which, in the light of subsequent research, appears to measure a conception of the world which characterizes fascist ideology.

A recent evaluation of the significance of the F-scale sums up the available evidence as follows:

. . . It did discriminate between individuals who displayed behavior which was authoritarian in interpersonal relations rather than politically. Individuals high on the F-scale tended to be condescending toward inferiors, resistant to scientific investigation, more sensitive to superiors than peers, and more prone to project their own attitudes upon others. . . .[3]

Upon the basis of available data, it may be concluded that the general point of view regarding the relationship between personality characteristics and ethnic prejudice developed in The Authoritarian Personality has been substantiated by subsequent research. . . . What might be termed the lowest common denominators of the personality attributes of the prejudiced person . . . are a relatively low level of mental functioning (probably partly due to low IQ and partly due to inadequate utilization of actual capacity), a hostile view of the social world and a degree of fear of the physical one, an inability to release successfully emotional affect in interpersonal relations, and an inability to accept oneself. These are uncomfortable people in an unpleasant and unpredictable world.[4]

[3] Richard Christie, "Authoritarianism Re-examined," in Richard Christie and Marie Jahoda, Studies in the Scope and Method of the Authoritarian Personality (Glencoe, Ill.: The Free Press, 1954), p. 193.

[4] Ibid., p. 166.

THE F-SCALE AND RELIGION

After studying the scores on the F-scale of 1,249 individuals, predominantly on the Pacific Coast, the authors of *The Authoritarian Personality* concluded that those "who profess to some religious affiliation express more prejudice than those who do not; but mean . . . scores for all the large denominations are close to the theoretical neutral point."[5] No significant differences appeared between the members of larger Protestant denominations, although Unitarians and a group of minor Protestant denominations showed significantly lower scores, and persons who never attended church averaged lower scores than those who did attend. The authors of *The Authoritarian Personality* speculated that religion in America has been so far "neutralized" that church membership has little significance in differentiating prejudiced from nonprejudiced persons. They summarized the meaning of acceptance or rejection of religion in the attitudes of the individuals as follows:

The psychological factors which appear most important are much the same as those which came to the fore in preceding chapters: conformity, conventionalism, authoritarian submission, determination by external pressures, thinking in in-group-out-group terms and the like versus nonconformity, independence, internalization of values and so forth."[6]

The Adorno group treated religious authority in the same manner they did human authority, applying the same tests and drawing conclusions that equated divine authority with human authority in its influence on the person. On several items in the F-scale dealing with divine authority where the Adorno group judged that agreement with their statement indicated prejudice, a practicing Christian or Jew could conscientiously answer only in the affirmative. The Adorno staff exhibited what may most charitably be called naïveté in their analysis of how an individual acts in relation to his loyalty to God, as distinct from his attitudes toward human authority-figures.

When religious attitudes are being studied there are levels of meaning in the concept of "authority" that neither the F-scale nor the particular items added by the writers to the F-scale to measure "religiosity" may be sensitive enough to identify. What is the "authoritarian aggression" or "authoritarian submission" reaction of a particular personality to be when the authority sanctions are divine as opposed to authority sanctions that are human? Obviously, one's answer to this question depends on basic theological presuppositions about the reality and validity of divine sanctions. There are certainly cases in history where the familiar human hierarchy of aggres-

[5] Adorno *et al, op. cit.,* p. 220.
[6] *Idem.*

sion-submission has been turned upside down by submissiveness to divine sanctions. An individual may be resistant to established authority in the human sphere precisely because he acknowledges an authority superior to human authority. Macaulay cites the example of the Puritan. "The Puritan was made up of two different men, the one all self-abasement, penitence, gratitude, passion; the other proud, calm, inflexible, sagacious. He prostrated himself in the dust before his Maker, but he set his foot on the neck of his king."[7]

We do not intend to say, then, in certain of the materials that follow, that a high score on authoritarian attitudes toward certain of the institutions or symbols of religion—the church, the clergy, the Bible—is in the minds of the researchers to be equated with what the authors of *The Authoritarian Personality* consider "fascist" attitudes in human relations. These relationships to divine authority are complex and subtle, being compounded of loyalty to doctrinal positions as well as of personality factors and convictions concerning social organization. They need, therefore, to be evaluated from a different base from that used to determine relationships in the human authority sphere.

F-SCALE SCORES

Other studies have indicated that results and meanings of F-scale scores have been found to be different in various sections of the country and in varying subcultural groups. In other words, in interpreting the following comparisons, it must not be assumed that the scores in *The Authoritarian Personality* represent a carefully determined national average, or that even if they did, higher or lower scores in the present research would represent a variation from a theoretical norm.

In the present study the mean score for the 62 individuals in New Haven tested with the F-scale was 4.04. *The Authoritarian Personality* reported the following mean scores for various groups tested:

482 students	3.66
154 middle-class women	3.62
53 working-class women	3.86
69 middle-class men	3.69
61 working-class men	4.19
total of 2,099 individuals tested	3.78

[7] Thomas Babington Macaulay, *Milton.*

Two other groups tested by one of the present writers (Smythe) gave the following mean results:

179 University of Illinois students   3.32
19 ministers of the United Church of Canada   3.29

The net difference in mean score between the New Haven group and the Berkeley (Adorno) group was not significant, but the differences in scores on certain of the subscales were significant. The New Haven group was significantly higher on authoritarian submission, authoritarain aggression, power and toughness, and destructiveness and cynicism (see Figure 24). The median score for the New Haven group was 4.10.

The New Haven chunk from whom F-scales were obtained was not a balanced representation of the population for several reasons. The most unbalanced aspect of the F-scale material is the faith composition of the group tested. It consisted of fifty Protestants, one Roman Catholic, and eleven persons with no religious connection. F-scale medians for these groups were as follows:

50 Protestants   4.11
1 Roman Catholic   4.38
11 No affiliation   3.74

The F-scale scores from New Haven show somewhat better distribution by social class. The number in each class and the median score was:

6 social class I   2.27
15 social class II   3.52
18 social class III   4.10
18 social class IV   4.93
5 social class V   5.41

These results showed a significant correlation between social class level and median F-scale scores, which increase as social class declines. This result confirmed what other studies have suggested.[8]

The New Haven group who provided F-scale scores were not as well distributed in relation to the major preoccupations discussed in Chapter 13 as they were in social class. Persons preoccupied with formal religion numbered only two (in the same family), while persons primarily preoccupied with

[8] Leo Srole has demonstrated that among less educated, lower income persons, there is a close relationship between anomie (or social distance) and prejudice, while for highly educated, high income persons the factor most closely associated with prejudice is authoritarianism. In our present study social class I individuals were relatively free from both prejudice and authoritarianism. See discussion in Christie and Jahoda, op. cit., pp. 174–75.

FIGURE 24. New Haven interview chunk: comparison of subscale
scores (mean) for the F-scale with *The Authoritarian
Personality* [a]

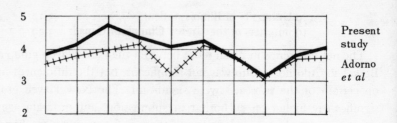

	Power and tough- ness [c]	Destr. and cyni- cism	Auth. subm.	Conv.	Auth. aggr.	Anti- intra.	Sup. and ster.	Sex	Proj.	Total
Present [b] Study	3.94	4.18	4.70	4.34	4.09	4.21	3.71	3.11	3.80	4.04
Adorno, et al [a]	3.55	3.74	3.96	4.18	3.21	4.09	3.78	3.05	3.78	3.71

[a] Note: A score of "1" represents emphatic disagreement; "7" emphatic agreement.

[b] Based on 295 individual scores.

[c] The subscales are described as follows:
   Power and toughness: Preoccupation with the dominance-submission, strong-weak,
leader-follower dimension; identification with power figures; overemphasis upon the
conventionalized attributes of the ego; exaggerated assertion of strength and toughness.
   Destructiveness and cynicism: Generalized hostility, vilification of the human.
   Authoritarian submission: Submissive, uncritical attitude toward idealized moral
authorities of the in-group.
   Conventionalism: Rigid adherence to conventional, middle-class values.
   Authoritarian aggression: Tendency to be on the lookout for, and to condemn, reject
and punish people who violate conventional values.
   Anti-intraception: Opposition to the subjective, the imaginative and the tender-minded.
   Superstition and stereotypy: The belief in mystical determinants of the individual's
fate; the disposition to think in rigid categories.
   Sex: Exaggerated concern with sexual "goings-on."
   Projectivity: The disposition to believe that wild and dangerous things go on in the
world; the projection outwards of unconscious emotional impulses.

   Source of data: Adorno, *op. cit.*, (270-71, 255-57).

social responsibility numbered only five. The number of individuals in each group, together with the group mean score, were as follows:

2	Formal religion	5.43
15	Self	4.93
20	Family and home	4.10
12	Social status	3.95
8	Work	3.28
5	Social responsibility	1.76

Again, there was what appeared to be a significant relationship between median F-scale score and the variable *major preoccupation*. Those preoccupied with self show a considerably higher median score than those preoccupied with work or social responsibility. Further, a cross-tabulation of these scores by social class and major preoccupation (see Appendix E, Table 3) shows that these two variables have a significant degree of independence from each other. Persons in social classes II, III and IV were fairly evenly spread among the four significantly large interest groups: self, family-and-home, work, and social status. We are not dealing with a spurious relationship in the correlation of F-scale scores with either social class or major preoccupation.

Figure 25 pursues this line of investigation one step further. It presents the median scores on each of the subscales for each of the social classes as represented in the interview chunk. It is at once apparent that the median F-scale scores we have been considering do come from class profiles which for the most part are quite different from one another. Our data here support the hypothesis in *The Authoritarian Personality* that the potential for fascist attitudes is strong in the wage-earning, high-school-educated portion of the population. We find, for instance, that the highest scores among the subscales for social classes IV and V were registered on the subscale measuring the tendency to identify with authoritarian aggression. Similarly, the susceptibility of the "middle class" to fascist ideology is strong in the scores that measure submission to authority, which were highest for social classes II and III. Social class I individuals registered highest on conventionalism.

Figure 26 presents a corresponding analysis of the subscales for the New Haven group when they are organized in major preoccupation groups. The groups with the higher scores—self-centered, family-and-home-centered, work-centered, and social-status-centered—all registered their highest single score on the subscale measuring authoritarian submission. The next highest subscales for these preoccupational groups, in rank order, were as follows:

Self: authoritarian aggression, destructiveness and cynism, sex.

Family and Home: conventionalism, anti-intraception, power and toughness.

Social Status: anti-intraception, conventionalism, authoritarian aggression.

Work: destructiveness and cynicism, conventionalism, superstition and stereotypy.

There seems to be a logic in these subscale profiles that deserves more intensive analysis than could be devoted to it in this study.

FIGURE 25.　New Haven interview chunk: median subscale scores for the F-scale by social class [a]

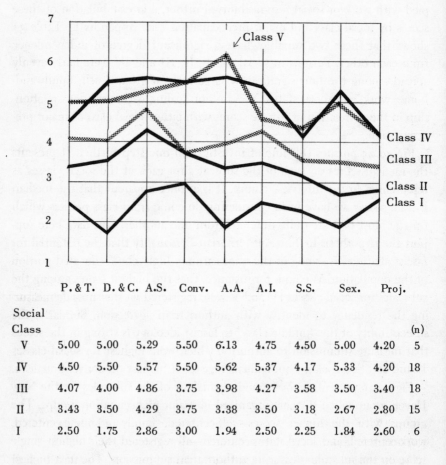

Social Class	P. & T.	D. & C.	A.S.	Conv.	A.A.	A.I.	S.S.	Sex.	Proj.	(n)
V	5.00	5.00	5.29	5.50	6.13	4.75	4.50	5.00	4.20	5
IV	4.50	5.50	5.57	5.50	5.62	5.37	4.17	5.33	4.20	18
III	4.07	4.00	4.86	3.75	3.98	4.27	3.58	3.50	3.40	18
II	3.43	3.50	4.29	3.75	3.38	3.50	3.18	2.67	2.80	15
I	2.50	1.75	2.86	3.00	1.94	2.50	2.25	1.84	2.60	6

[a] Note: A score of "1" represents emphatic disagreement; "7" emphatic agreement.

AUTHORITY IN RELIGION

Three of the items added to the F-scale measured attitudes toward authority in religion. They were:

1. Most people who try to run their lives according to the teachings of the Bible find that Bible principles are not practical in real life.

2. The minister (or priest or rabbi) should be the final authority on the way we should act and what we should believe.

3. In order to obtain divine assistance in life's crises, it is necessary to get it through your church (or priest, pastor or rabbi).

FIGURE 26. New Haven interview chunk: median subscale scores for the F-scale by interest groups[a]

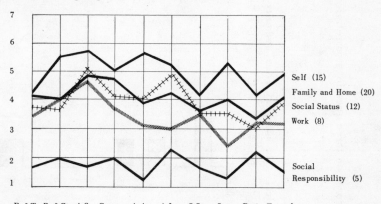

Interest groups	P.&T.	D.&C.	A.S.	Conv.	A.A.	A.I.	S.S.	Sex	.Proj.	F.total	(n)
Formal religion	5.21	4.25	6.29	5.50	6.07	5.50	4.75	5.50	5.20	5.43	2
Self	4.43	5.50	5.71	5.00	5.62	5.25	4.18	5.33	4.20	4.93	15
Family and Home	4.14	4.00	4.86	4.75	3.92	4.25	3.67	4.00	3.40	4.10	20
Social status	3.85	3.75	5.07	4.12	4.00	4.87	3.50	3.50	3.00	3.95	12
Work	3.43	4.00	4.85	3.75	3.07	3.00	3.50	2.50	3.30	3.28	8
Social responsibility	1.57	2.00	1.71	2.00	1.25	2.50	1.66	1.33	2.20	1.76	5

[a] Note: A score of "1" represents emphatic disagreement; "7" emphatic agreement.

A technical discussion of the discriminating power of these items is given in Appendix F. Figure 27 shows the median scores on these tests according to religion and major interest of respondents.

The over-all reaction of the New Haven chunk was one of moderate disagreement with the first proposition, that the Bible is not a practical guide

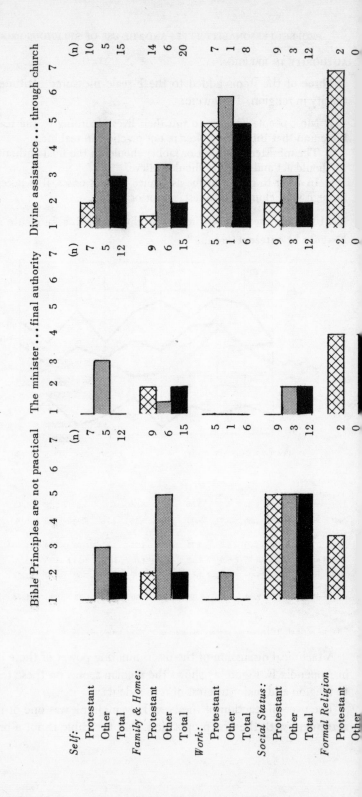

FIGURE 27. New Haven interview chunk: median scores on three questions on religion by Protestants and others in interest groups [a]

	(n)
	3
	2
	5
	45
	17
	62

Social Responsibility

Protestant	3
Other	2
Total	5

Total New Haven Chunk

Protestant	35
Other	17
Total	52

[a] Note: A score of "1" represents emphatic disagreement; "7" emphatic agreement

FIGURE 28. New Haven interview chunk: median scores on three questions on religion by social class [a]

Bible Principles are not practical · · · · The minister...final authority · · · · Divine assistance...through church

Social Class	1 2 3 4 5 6 7 (n)	1 2 3 4 5 6 7 (n)	1 2 3 4 5 6 7 (n)
I	6	6	6
II	13	13	15
III	12	12	18
IV	16	16	18
V	5	5	7

[a] Note: A score of "1" represents emphatic disagreement; "7" emphatic agreement

to living (median 2.5, or halfway between slight and moderate disagreement). There was considerable difference between Protestants and non-Protestants here, however, Protestants recording favorable views of the practicality of the Bible (median 2.0) and non-Protestants generally unfavorable attitudes (median 5.0). The least acceptance of the Bible was in the social-status-centered and social-responsibility-centered groups where the median scores were 5.0 (moderate agreement with the proposition). Self-centered and family-and-home-centered groups had attitudes of moderate acceptance of the Bible as a practical authority (median 2.0, or moderate disagreement with the statement), and the work-centered group accepted the Bible strongly (median 1.0, or strong disagreement with the statement).

The interview group disagreed strongly with the second statement, that "the minister (or priest or rabbi) should be the final authority on the way we should act and what we should believe," with Protestants and non-Protestants alike recording a mean score of 1.0. The only persons who indicated any agreement at all with this proposition were among formal-religion- and family-and-home-centered Protestants and self-, family-and-home-, and social-status-centered non-Protestants.

The third item, concerning the necessity of securing Divine assistance through the clergy, showed considerable discriminating power in the New Haven chunk. For the total group, the median score was 2.0 for Protestants and 3.0 for non-Protestants, indicating moderate or slight disagreement. There were significant differences between interest groups. The work-centered group had the highest degree of agreement with this authoritarian proposition, with a median of 5.0 for Protestants and 6.0 for others in the group. Self-centered individuals disagreed slightly (median 3.0), Protestants here disagreeing moderately and non-Protestants agreeing slightly. The family-and-home-centered and the social-status-centered group both registered a median of 2.0 (moderate disagreement), and in both cases the Protestants disagreed more strongly than did the others in the groups.

Other data in this report have indicated that social class status has a good deal to do with attitudes. The median scores for the interview group when they are arranged by social class are revealing and even disturbing from the point of view of policy (see Figure 28). Acceptance of the Bible as a practical authority was apparently fairly common in classes I and II; while in classes III, IV and V the Bible as a practical guide to living was rejected moderately or strongly by the median individual. The median social class V individual registered moderate acceptance of the clergy as the final authority on belief and action and strong acceptance of the church as the exclusive means of gaining Divine assistance. It should be remembered that the persons in class V had a median score of 6.13 on authoritarian aggression and 5.29 on authoritarian submission. Class IV individuals, the largest group in the chunk and in the population, had mild to moderate agreement with the exclusive prerogative of church and clergy to dispense Divine assistance. They are also individuals with high authoritarian scores. The other social class groups registered substantial rejection of the second and third propositions.

Major Preoccupations and Use of Religious Programs

We turn now to our central concern: the relationship of personality type to the use of religious programs. First, we will discuss this question in relation to personality types as described in the preceding chapter, grouped according to major *interests* or *preoccupations*.

Table 83. New Haven interview chunk: number of religious programs regularly seen or heard, distributed according to major preoccupation of respondents

Religious Programs	Family and Home	Self	Social Status	Work	Formal Religion	Social Responsibility	Total
Sponsored by National Council of Churches:							
Total	10	19	8	8	3		48
Peale	6	11	4	3	2		26
Sockman	4	6	3	5	1		19
Bonnell		2	1				3
Roman Catholic Programs:							
Total	16	6	9	3	2	3	39
Sheen	13	6	9	3	2	3	36
Other	3						3
The Greatest Story Ever Told	13	2	6	7	2		30
Other Programs	7	11	2	5	8	3	36
Total Programs Used	46	38	25	23	15	6	153
No Use of Religious Programs	4	2	6	2		6	20

Information concerning regular listening on radio and viewing on television was carefully secured from each person interviewed. The same information had been secured in preliminary doorstep and telephone interviews. However, in the course of the depth interviews a substantial number of respondents furnished much more detailed information about listening and viewing habits than they had given in the original interview. The depth interviews proved to be more reliable and more fruitful in obtaining basic information about the respondents than did the listening-viewing survey conducted through the less rigorous technique of relatively short direct question-and-answer interviews.

Table 83 shows the number of regular uses of religious programs by the persons in the chunk. Respondents are classified according to their primary preoccupaton or interest.

FREQUENCY OF PROGRAM USE

The first thing to be noted is the relative frequency of use of religious programs by the different interest groups. Classified according to major preoccupation, the interview groups used the following average number of programs per person:

Total all groups	1.7 programs
Formal religion	3.0 programs
Self	2.0 programs
Family and home	1.8 programs
Work	1.8 programs
Social status	1.4 programs
Social responsibility	0.8 programs

INTEREST GROUPING AND PROGRAM USE

The next framework for analysis of these data is the extent to which the interest groups turn to different kinds of programs on radio and television. These data appear in Appendix E, Table 4, expressed in terms of percentage of total uses by each group. We shall discuss here the tastes evidenced.

It will be recalled that the *family-and-home-centered* group was the largest in the chunk. It was also the youngest (along with the social-status-centered), with more than half of the families having minor children. Two-fifths of the families were those of skilled workers. The incomes were about average for the country and the median social class rating in the group was III. Heads of families had high school education or slightly more. Five of the seven Roman Catholic respondents were in this group. It contains the largest number of religious program users and one-third of all programs used were Roman Catholic. Sheen's program represented one-fourth of all programs reported. The Greatest Story Ever Told held equal rank with Sheen. Programs sponsored by the National Council of Churches appeared to have relatively little interest for these people, with only ten uses out of a total of 46.

The next largest group in the interview chunk were the *self-centered* persons. These individuals were predominantly older (median age 68), consisted three-fourths of women and had the lowest median education of any of the groups (tenth grade) and low income (median $2,001–$3,500). There were no Roman Catholics in the group and few families with minor children. This group seemed to concentrate on the National Council programs, which provided one-half of all religious programs seen and heard regularly. The Peale programs provided 11 of 38 mentions, and "other Protestant" programs collectively another 11. The Greatest Story Ever Told and Roman Catholic programs had relatively little appeal.

The *social-status-centered* persons were like the family-and-home-centered group in social composition. Equally young, but with fewer minor children, nearly half of the family heads were skilled workers. Median income was average, median social class was III and median education was fourteen years. The group consisted of seventeen Protestants and two Jews. It is noteworthy, therefore, that Sheen's was the most frequent single program used (9 out of 25 mentions). Second place was taken by the National Council programs, with eight uses, of which Peale accounted for half. The Greatest Story Ever Told was reported six times.

The *work-centered* group was composed largely of major and minor business executives, professionals and semiprofessionals. The median social class was II, and incomes averaged $5,001–$7,500. Median age of the household head was fifty, and husbands and wives with no children or with children who had grown up and left home were more common than were families with minor children. There were no Roman Catholics. In this group, National Council programs were used most often (8 of 23 uses). This is the only category in which Sockman listeners outnumbered Peale listeners. The Greatest Story Ever Told had nearly one-third of all mentions.

The *social-responsibility-centered* group was dominated by wealthy executives and professionals. Income, education and social class level were higher than for any other group. Nevertheless, median age was relatively young (46 years). Half of the people in this group did not listen to or view religious programs. There were no Roman Catholics, but the religious programs reported were divided among three persons who watched Sheen and three others who used a miscellany of Protestant programs.

The *formal-religion-centered* group had the lowest social class median (IV). Education averaged high school level (twelve), median age was fifty, and median income was $3,501–$5,000. Two of the seven individuals in this group were Roman Catholics. Over half of all programs used by this group were miscellaneous Protestant and nonsectarian, with the remainder distributed almost equally among National Council sponsored programs, Roman Catholic programs, and *The Greatest Story Ever Told.*

PROGRAM AUDIENCE COMPOSITION

The third general analysis of the data in Table 83 deals with the composition of the audience for each program or group of programs. Since the interview chunk was not a probability sample, the data do not show the actual proportions of each interest group in the audiences. They are useful for comparing the proportions in the audience for one program or group of programs with those in another. Appendix E, Table 5 shows the percentage of the audience for each program that is drawn from the different interest groups in the chunk.

The largest concentration of the regular audience for programs produced by the National Council of Churches falls in the *self-interested* group of persons (40 per cent). Only 21 per cent of the persons in the chunk were classified as self-interested, but they make up 42 per cent of the Peale audience and 32 per cent of the Sockman audience, and in the cases of both men, are the largest single group listening to them.

Appreciable proportions of every interest group used Roman Catholic programs—meaning, primarily, Sheen. This audience was distributed in close proportion to the division of the chunk in interest groups. The *family-and-home-centered* people predominated. They constituted 41 per cent of the audience for Roman Catholic programs, while they comprised 28 per cent of all persons interviewed. This distribution parallels the data in Chapter 11 which show the Sheen audience to be concentrated heavily in class III and IV families with minor children. Self-centered persons made up only 15 per cent of the audience for Roman Catholic programs. Since there were only seven Roman Catholics in the interview chunk—five of them family-and-home-centered and two formal-religion-centered—it is obvious that most of the use of Roman Catholic programs by people in those categories and all of it by individuals in the remaining four interest categories was by non-Catholics.

The audience for The Greatest Story Ever Told is separately listed in the tables because of its size and because it is a unique program type in character and sponsorship among the religious broadcasts. Like the Roman Catholic programs, its appeal is fairly representative of all religious groups, except for its very slight appeal to the self-centered group and its strong appeal to the family-and-home-centered group. It found no audience among those persons in the interview group whose major interest was social responsibility.

The "other Protestant, Jewish, and nonsectarian" programs are a diverse and miscellaneous collection consisting of the following fourteen programs:

Name of Program	Number of Regular Users
New Haven Council of Churches (A Mighty Fortress, Evensong)	6
Religion at the News Desk	4
TV Chapel (DuMont)	4
Billy Graham	4
Salt Lake City Tabernacle Choir	4
Old Fashioned Revival Hour	4
Columbia Church of the Air	2
Youth on the March	2
Unity	2
Lamp Unto My Feet	2
Lutheran Hour	1
The Eternal Light	1
Frontiers of Faith	1

It is notable that the two largest segments of the audience for these programs were the self-centered people (30 per cent) and the formal-religion-centered people (22 per cent). In most cases these persons were multiple-program users, and the programs listed were part of a group of religious broadcasts to which they listened regularly.

These data may be summarized as follows. The largest interest group, the family-and-home-centered, were proportionately most numerous in The Greatest Story Ever Told audience and the audience for Roman Catholic programs, and relatively least numerous in the "other Protestant" program audience. The self-centered interest group was second largest in the total audience, was best represented in the audiences for National Council and "other Protestant" programs and least numerous in the audience for The Greatest Story Ever Told. The third largest group, the social-status-centered, were best represented among the people who used no religious programs and were also well represented in the audience for Roman Catholic programs and The Greatest Story Ever Told. The work-centered group was most interested in The Greatest Story Ever Told and least interested in the Roman Catholic programs. The formal-religion-centered group made its largest relative contribution to the "other Protestant" program audience and its smallest to the group who used no religious programs. The social-responsibility-centered people were very light users of religious programs and the

FIGURE 29. New Haven interview chunk: median scores on F-scale and on authoritarian aggression and authoritarian submission subscales of regular users of specified religious programs [a]

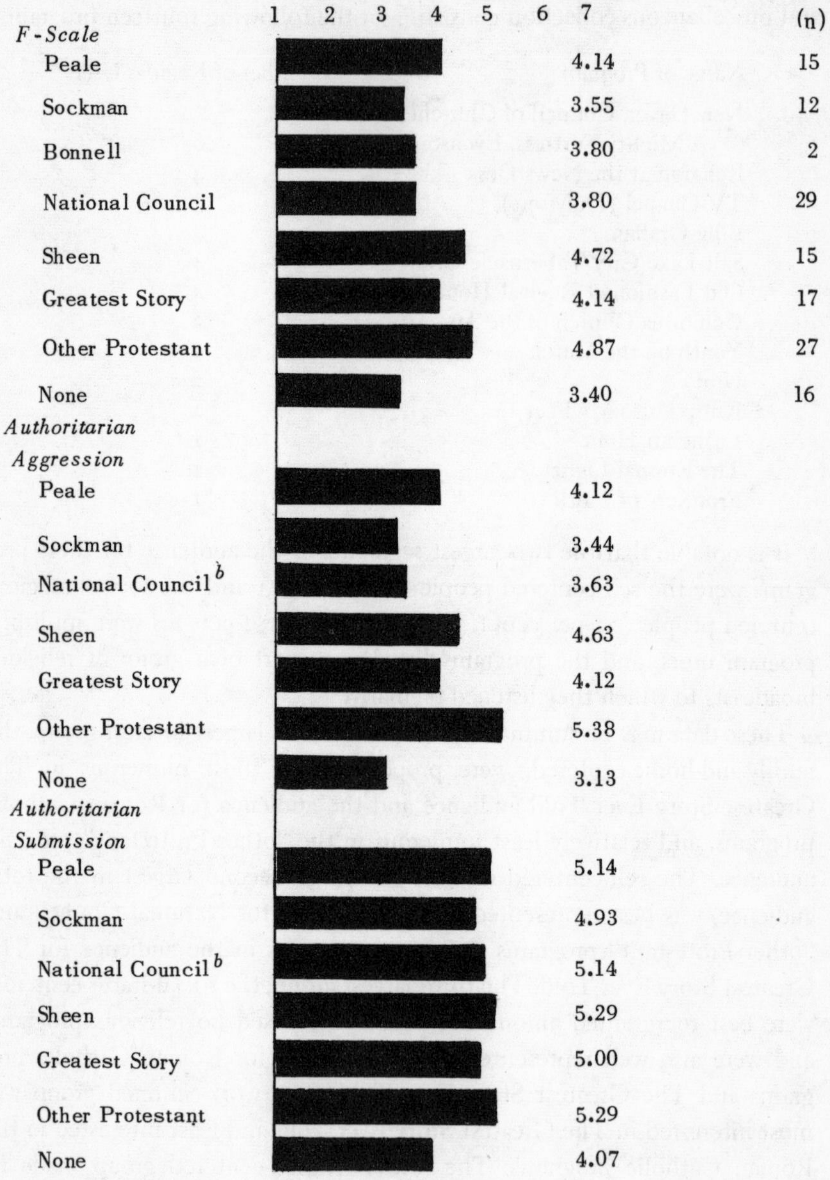

	1	2	3	4	5	6	7		(n)
F - Scale									
Peale								4.14	15
Sockman								3.55	12
Bonnell								3.80	2
National Council								3.80	29
Sheen								4.72	15
Greatest Story								4.14	17
Other Protestant								4.87	27
None								3.40	16
Authoritarian Aggression									
Peale								4.12	
Sockman								3.44	
National Council [b]								3.63	
Sheen								4.63	
Greatest Story								4.12	
Other Protestant								5.38	
None								3.13	
Authoritarian Submission									
Peale								5.14	
Sockman								4.93	
National Council [b]								5.14	
Sheen								5.29	
Greatest Story								5.00	
Other Protestant								5.29	
None								4.07	

[a] Note: A score of "1" represents emphatic disagreement; "7" emphatic agreement.

[b] Bonnell omitted.

only audience they provided was a few users of Roman Catholic programs and a few of "other Protestant" programs.

Attitudes Toward Authority and Their Influence on Use of Religious Programs

The analysis of attitudes toward authority provides a second major framework within which to study the personality types of the interview respondents. How were these attitudes related to the selection and use of religious radio and television programs? Median scores for several of the measures of authoritarianism already discussed (subscales of the F-scale) were calculated for each of the major program audiences. They are the basis of the discussion that follows. The over-all F-scale scores for these audiences and the scores on the subscales of authoritarian aggression and authoritarian submission are presented in Figure 29.

TOTAL F-SCALE SCORES

With due regard for the small numbers involved in some of these scores, this analysis seemed to justify the following inferences:

1. Individuals who use no religious programs have the lowest identification with authority.
2. The Sockman audience has the lowest identification with authority of the audiences analyzed here.
3. The Sheen audience and the audience for "other Protestant" programs have the highest identification with authority.
4. The audience for Peale, the combined audience for all National Council programs, and the audience for The Greatest Story Ever Told stand in a neutral position with respect to authoritarianism.

By Social Class

Having already discovered at a number of points in this research that generalizations of this kind, while statistically accurate, might be misleading unless examined in relation to social class, we proceeded to analyze these data further by the social class composition of these audiences. The statistics are given in Appendix E, Table 6. They lead to the following modifications of the foregoing inferences.

1. Individuals who use no religious programs are more heavily concentrated in the upper social classes, where authoritarian attitudes as measured by the F-scale score are low. However, nonusers in classes III and V have F-scale scores as high as the median for their entire group.
2. The low Sockman audience score is accounted for by his audience in social classes II and III; the one social class IV user had a higher than average score.

On balance, however, one would still conclude that the Sockman audience has little identification with authoritarianism.

3. The Sheen audience is consistently higher in identification with authority than are most of the other audiences. The differences vary by social class, with class III users ranking lowest (4.07) and class IV users highest (4.93). The "upper class" Sheen audience is more authoritarian than most other religious program audiences, and is especially more authoritarian than the audiences for National Council of Churches programs. In the "lower classes," Sheen's audience is not more authoritarian than other religious program audiences, or those who use no religious programs.

4. The audiences for "other Protestant" programs, The Eternal Light and the nonsectarian programs show no real consistency, as one might expect from the heterogeneous nature of the programs involved in this grouping.[9]

Detailed analyses were also made by social class of the scores on the "authoritarian aggression" and "authoritarian submission" subscales. Variations from the pattern described above were minor. Scores generally mount for each program audience as one moves from social class I to social class V. The sole exception to this trend is for class IV users of The Greatest Story Ever Told, whose scores on the authoritarian aggression subscale are lower than for any other social class.

Authoritarian aggression scores for users of the various religious programs, distributed by social class, are presented in Appendix E, Table 7. The parallel dissection of the social class composition of the audiences when they are analyzed for scores on authoritarian submission has been omitted. It indicates that the "no program use" group is significantly lower in authoritarian submission, even in classes IV and V, when compared with people in the religious program audiences. The scores for the program audiences are not significantly different from each other, either between or within social classes.

ANALYSIS BY INTEREST GROUPS

Appendix E, Table 8, gives the detail of the authoritarian characteristics of the religious program audiences when they are arranged according to major preoccupations or interest groups.

The formal-religion-centered respondents, it will be recalled, had the

[9] There is evidence, however, that scores for this group reflect to some extent the characteristics attributed by sociologists to adherents of minor sects within Protestantism, which in New Haven, as previous data have shown, tends to mean working-class families beyond middle age with less than high school education. These people seem to be characterized by relatively high F-scale scores, and in these data would be the audiences for Billy Graham and The Old Fashioned Revival Hour, both with high scores. On the other hand, the audiences for "other" religious programs also include listeners to Religion at the News Desk and The Eternal Light, with low scores.

highest F-scale median score (5.43), but since only two individuals in this group provided F-scale data, it must be considered too small for significant analysis.

The next highest median score (4.93) was in the *self-centered* group, with fifteen members for whom F-scale scores were available (eleven Protestants, four no religious affiliation). This group predominantly uses the National Council programs. Within the National Council audience, they have higher scores than the family-and-home-centered group, but lower scores than the work-centered group. The self-centered group also has a substantial number of Sheen viewers, and they have a higher median F-scale score than any others in the self-centered group except the audience for "other" programs.

The *family-and-home-centered* people had the next highest median F-scale score (4.10) about average for the entire interview chunk. They were fourteen Protestants, one Roman Catholic and five without religious affiliation. They were distributed as an audience representatively among the five audience categories (National Council, Roman Catholic and "other" programs; The Greatest Story Ever Told and nonusers). The family-and-home-centered audience for The Greatest Story Ever Told had the highest median F-scale score (4.72). Roman Catholic program users (4.38) and persons who did not use religious programs (4.37) also were relatively high. The audiences in this group for "other" programs and National Council programs were relatively low in this measure of attitudes toward authority (3.52 and 3.42).

The *social-status-centered* group, with a median score of 3.95, consisted of twelve Protestants. They had a median F-scale score of 3.95. None for whom F-scale scores were available listened to or looked at National Council programs.

In this group, The Greatest Story Ever Told audience scored high in authoritarianism (4.33), with Sheen's audience following (4.07); nonusers scored 3.39.

The *work-centered* group consisted of eight Protestants, whose F-scales scored a median of 3.28. The scores of listeners and viewers of National Council and Roman Catholic programs were highest. The median score of each group was 4.87.

Social-responsibility-centered individuals for whom F-scale material was available numbered only five, of whom only one indicated he regularly used a religious program ("other"). His score was low (1.45), lower even than the median for the four nonusers (1.78).

The pattern of these data is decidedly less clear than that of the preceding analysis based on social class:

Median Scores for Users of Specified Programs

Major Interest	Median Group Score	National Council	Roman Catholic	The Greatest Story Ever Told	Other Programs	No Programs
Self	4.93	4.62	4.83	3.40	4.93	4.52
Family-home	4.10	3.42	4.38	4.72	3.52	4.37
Social Status	3.95		4.07	4.33	2.79	3.39
Work	3.28	4.87	4.87	3.47	3.97	2.55
Social responsibility	1.76				1.45	1.78
Total	4.10	4.07	4.72	4.14	4.87	3.40

Only the people who use no religious programs at all show median scores that are consistent in their relationships with the median score for the total group. All program audiences show considerable variations from the scores of the total chunk when examined from the point of view of primary interest. We may assume that these variations are partly a function of the small numbers involved, but in view of other general consistencies of the data, they would appear to be due also to the characteristics of the interest groups as they have been previously described.

AUTHORITARIAN AGGRESSION VERSUS AUTHORITARIAN SUBMISSION

One further analysis of interest, among many that were done, is that of the relationship of authoritarian aggression subscales to authoritarian submission subscales of the program audiences when divided into interest groups. The subscales are:

Authoritarian aggression: Tendency to be on the lookout for, and to condemn, reject and punish people who violate conventional values.
Authoritarian submission: Tendency to submissive, uncritical attitude toward idealized moral authorities of the in-group.

The mean authoritarian submission score for all the respondents is 4.70 as compared with a mean authoritarian aggression score of 4.09. Table 84 shows the relationship between these two scores for the different segments of the religious program audience. (The absolute scores will be found in Appendix E, Table 9.)

At the one extreme we find the social-status-centered persons whose authoritarian submission scores are consistently higher than their aggression scores, as might be expected of a group oriented to upward social mobility. At the other extreme are the self-centered users of the National Council programs, whose aggression-submission scores are approximately equal, as might be expected of a Protestant group of advanced years with a primary concern for the needs of the self. The family-and-home-centered group were nearly as consistent in showing an excess of submission over aggression as were the work-centered group.

Sheen has an audience with submission scores considerably higher than aggression scores. National Council programs have audiences whose scores are approximately equal. The Greatest Story Ever Told and "other" programs have audiences where submission scores are generally higher than aggression scores.

Table 84. Relative level as of median scores on authoritarian submission and authoritarian aggression of members of interest groups who regularly use specified programs

Program	Self	Family and Home	Work	Social Status	Social Responsibility	Total
Peale	0	+	0			+
Sockman	0	+	−			+
Bonnell	0	−				0
Sheen	+	+	0	+		+
Rosary Hour		0				0
What One Person Can Do		0				0
The Greatest Story Ever Told	+	0	+	+		+
Other Programs	0	+	+		0	0
No Programs	+	0	+	+	+	+

+ means authoritarian submission median score is more than 10 per cent higher than authoritarian aggression score
− means authoritarian aggression median score is more than 10 per cent higher than authoritarian submission score
0 means the two scores were within 10 per cent of each other

RELIGIOSITY AND AUTHORITARIANISM

Figure 30 details the results for the three items added to the F-scale to measure attitudes toward religious authority. (See page 257.)

The median listener to the three National Council programs—Peale, Sockman and Bonnell—flatly rejected all three authoritarian propositions. The largest amount of agreement with the proposition that the Bible is not a practical guide to living was found in the Sheen audience, none of whom was a Roman Catholic, where the median score was 5.00 (moderate agree-

FIGURE 30. New Haven interview chunk: median scores on three
questions on religion, distributed by regular use of
religious programs [a]

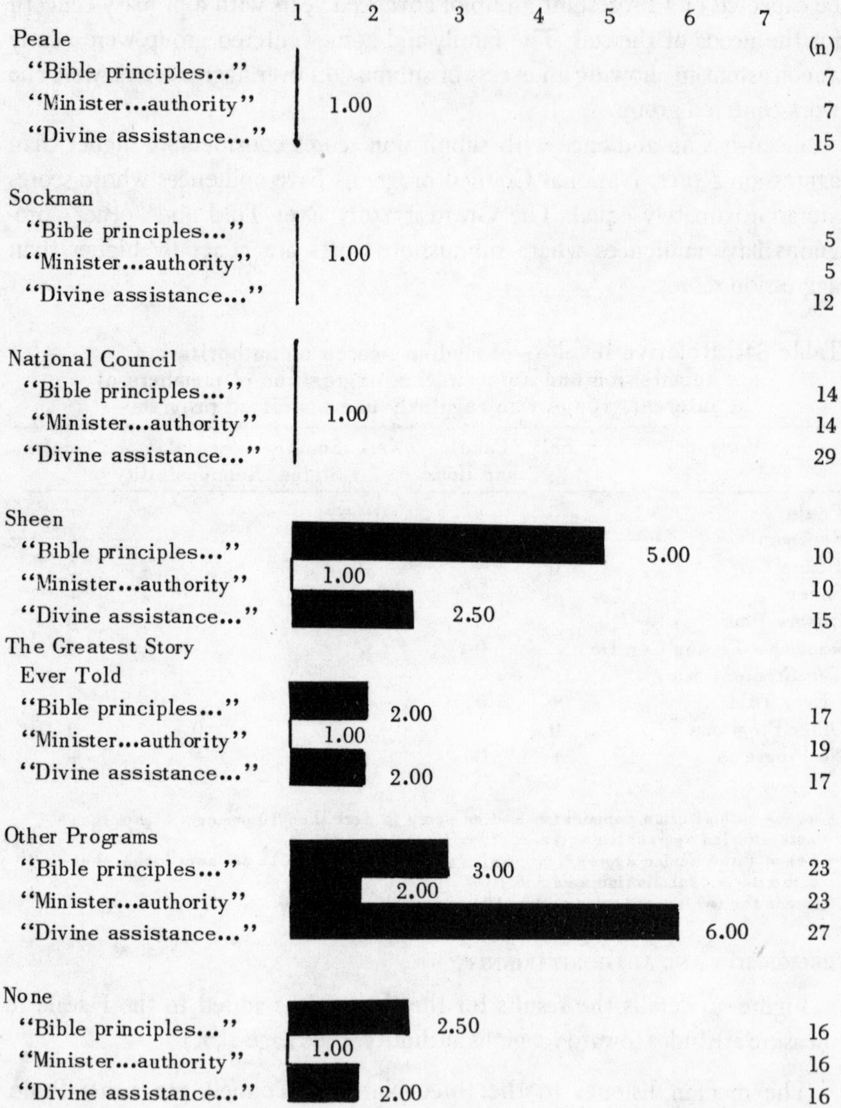

	1	2	3	4	5	6	7	
Peale								(n)
"Bible principles..."								7
"Minister...authority"	1.00							7
"Divine assistance..."								15
Sockman								
"Bible principles..."								5
"Minister...authority"	1.00							5
"Divine assistance..."								12
National Council								
"Bible principles..."								14
"Minister...authority"	1.00							14
"Divine assistance..."								29
Sheen								
"Bible principles..."					5.00			10
"Minister...authority"	1.00							10
"Divine assistance..."		2.50						15
The Greatest Story Ever Told								
"Bible principles..."	2.00							17
"Minister...authority"	1.00							19
"Divine assistance..."	2.00							17
Other Programs								
"Bible principles..."		3.00						23
"Minister...authority"	2.00							23
"Divine assistance..."					6.00			27
None								
"Bible principles..."	2.50							16
"Minister...authority"	1.00							16
"Divine assistance..."	2.00							16

[a] Note: A score of "1" represents emphatic disagreement; "7" emphatic agreement.

ment). The least amount of disagreement with the second proposition was found in the audience for "other" programs, although the actual median score was 2.00 (moderate disagreement). The audience for "other" programs registered strong acceptance of the third proposition, median score being 6.00. This score reflects especially the opinions of the audience for Billy Graham and The Old Fashioned Revival Hour. The Sheen audience also measured only slight disagreement with this proposition, median score being 2.50.

CHAPTER 15

Personality Traits in the Sheen Audience

Introduction to the Analyses

The depth interviews were held, primarily, to find out what role religious programs play—or might play—in the lives of persons and families. This information can be had only from individuals and only through a deep comprehension of their personalities, tastes, attitudes, behavior, relationships and general life style. While religious broadcasting was the central concern of the research, it was seldom the focal interest of individuals in the audience. Therefore, it was necessary to learn a great deal about people to develop perspective on an activity that was usually peripheral or incidental to the major emphases of their living and their use of the mass media.

Reporting on the people, as individuals, is also difficult, not only because of the great amount of data in each interview, but also because each analysis must attempt to give insights into personality without, in the process, being so selective as to bias the general findings. This report of personality attributes has been organized on the basis of "typical" members of the audience for leading religious programs. This "typicality" is sociological; that is, among the depth interview respondents, the people in the descriptions that follow represent the median attributes of the audiences identified in the probability sample in terms of social class, religious affiliation, age, occupation, education, family type and so forth. We also attempted in our selection to be faithful to what had been discovered about preoccupations of different audience segments, even though these findings were not based on a probability sample. There is no guarantee, of course, that these people are in any sense "typical" in terms of personality or character attributes, for which we had no probability sample—if, indeed, such a sample could be drawn. Consequently, in the character sketches that follow, we have no statistical "class" or "religious" or "ethnic" behavior pattern or interest. We do have a conviction, based upon the interview experience, that within each individual described there are hopes and fears, ambitions and determinations, likes and dislikes, attitudes and motivations and a sense of selfhood which are his or hers alone. While these attributes may be influenced by sociological position in the environment, they may not be wholly attributed to it, and may be expected to spark a resistance to environment in some instances.

We have prepared character sketches intended to be illustrative of the audiences for religious programs. The sketches are of *real people*. They are not composites of several interviews, nor has anything been changed in any interview to conform to any pattern or theory. Names, of course, are fictitious—though ethnically accurate—and certain facts that might identify individuals have been omitted or masked. And, we repeat, while these people may not be accepted as being representative in a rigorous statistical sense, we have taken every precaution the data would permit to select cases that would accurately reflect the life situations of the major blocs of families in the respective audiences.

Now, a word about bias. The basic Protestant value orientation of this research was set forth honestly in the Introduction, and while the research staff has been scrupulous in adherence to the disciplines of fact-gathering and analysis described, judgments are contingent upon value orientation as well as upon facts. The value structure of the writers has been clear at several points. We do not pretend, for example, that a research staff with Roman Catholic hypotheses concerning man and society would have necessarily come to the same conclusions that we did about the Sheen programs.

The summary evaluation of people in the audience is an even more delicate matter. While there is no intention here to judge people, judgment is often implicit in the critical analysis of character, or where it is not implicit, it can easily be read into an analysis by the reader, who has his own standards concerning character. The sketches are a scientific description and analysis of what people said, and how they said it. They may reflect the relative lack of confidence in human nature found in standard techniques and terminology used in probing beneath surface behavior for motivations and tensions that lie behind behavior and its rationalization. Indeed, the two clergymen involved in these analyses first reacted to the sketches that follow—even the ones they, themselves, had prepared—with the opinion that the reports were too "uncharitable." In all but a few instances the interviewers had reached a cordial rapport with the respondents and had enjoyed the contact on a friendship basis. The clergymen thought the respondents were "better" people than the analyses would indicate. Yet, after re-examination of all the data and rehearing of the interview tapes, there was little they could

change. The analyses appeared to be valid and the misgivings of the clergymen tended to reflect their desire to be optimistic about the familiar character structures found in middle class American Protestantism more than they
did the handling of the interview materials. This experience underlined the
dictum, "All have sinned and fall short of the glory of God."

With these observations—or perhaps confessions—by the writers, we turn
now to the character sketches.

The Sheen Audience

It is appropriate, in view of the fact that Sheen's audience is the largest
by far of all the followers of religious radio and television programs, that we
start with several illustrations from it. The median viewers of Life Is Worth
Living are Roman Catholics, between 30 and 45 years of age, with from
seven to eleven years of formal education, married with minor children, and
in social class IV—which means employed as semiskilled workers, with
income between $3,501 and $5,000. Such a family from among those in the
interview "chunk" is that of Mr. and Mrs. Jack Voskuil.

The Jack Voskuils

Background Data

Social Class: IV
Own home
Own television and radio sets
Income: $3,501–$5,000

	Husband	Wife
Occupation:	Factory electrician	Housewife
Education:	Completed eighth grade	Completed eighth grade
Age:	34	29
Religious background:	Roman Catholic	Roman Catholic
Church attended:	Roman Catholic	Roman Catholic
Preoccupation:	Family-and-home	Family-and-home

Children: Son: 4; Daughters: 10, 6

The Voskuils live in one of New Haven's working-class suburbs. He has
worked for the same company for thirteen years. He appears to conceive of
himself as a God-fearing, hard-working man whose prime interests are his
wife and children. His interest is in loving and cherishing—not in exploiting
them. He sees himself also in stereotypical terms as a lower class son of
Ukrainian immigrants who is enjoying the blessings of living in a free,
democratic country. While his entire employment experience has been dur-

ing conditions of economic prosperity, this aura of the "melting-pot" view of American society has not displaced completely his identification with the working class. He speaks and thinks of himself as one who will always be an employee and who assumes that the interests of his class are to a substantial degree opposed to those of the employers.

Voskuil's Ukrainian parents came to the United States shortly before World War I. He was born in New Haven in 1918 and has lived all his life there. One of a large family, with four brothers and four sisters, he was forced by economic necessity to go to work full time when he finished the eighth grade. While he does not blame anyone for this fact, he wistfully wishes he could have had more education and that perhaps he could have become an electrical engineer. As might be expected under such conditions, he has considerable respect for people with "an education." Paradoxically, he also has an anti-intellectual bias. Rather than attempt to improve himself through extension courses or night school, he accepts his "lot," devoting his leisure time to his family. Now, he works six days, including Sunday, and looks forward as if to a utopia to the day which he thinks is not too far off when a man like himself will be able to support a family through working only six hours a day for five days a week. Prudently, he scorns some of his acquaintances who work at two jobs. He says,

Some of them are tryin' to live beyond their means. So they have to have two jobs—to support their families. They're killin' themselves.

Voskuil's employment history includes a brief term as a milkman and a year or so of work in a munitions plant. He is a member of the CIO United Electrical Workers union and sympathetically regards his one experience of a strike, lasting three weeks, as successful. In respect to shop talk about politics, he says,

People are funny. They get all riled up about something for a few days and then they get cooled off. They look at things from how they affect their jobs.

Shop talk also includes gossip to the effect that new industries are prevented from entering New Haven by Yale, which the men feel runs the city. This interpretation, which he accepts, arose from conversation in the shop when the men were "pinched a bit" by unsatisfied demands for wage increases.

Voskuil's working-class viewpoint is not obtrusive. He stays out of most political discussions at the plant. He manifests no particular interest in news or national affairs. He is anything but an "inside dopester" in relation to commentators. His views on communism are conventional. However, it is interesting that he volunteered, in talking about New Haven, the remark that the "cops" aren't like they used to be. Formerly, the Irish New Haven cop was friendly and respectful toward people on his beat; nowadays, Voskuil feels, the cops are not friends of the ordinary people.

The Voskuil home was furnished well. It was neat and indicated constant repair and redecorating. The kitchen, which he had installed, was modern and well-equipped. Such chores keep Voskuil occupied in his leisure time.

The family has two television sets—an older one with a ten-inch screen and a radio-phonograph in a handsome cabinet, and a newer larger screen set. The older set was retained for the benefit of the children, both because they might want to see different television programs than do the adults, and because of the children's phonograph record collection which the parents encourage.

The family has lived in its present home for seven years. The Voskuils say they bought it because of the possibility of their children growing up where there was room for some grass and flowers, and space for them to play outdoors off the street. The interviewer remarked, toward the end of the interview, that it looked as though the children were the center of their lives, which prompted the Voskuils to say:

Mrs. V.: Yeah!
V.: I couldn't have what I wanted when I was a kid. So. I want mine to have those things. Probably spoil them a little bit.
Int.: Was this because you had such large families?
V.: Yes, and times were hard . . . that's why I had to quit school and go to work.

Voskuil was raised in the Ukrainian Roman Catholic Church and served voluntarily as an altar boy between the ages of ten and fourteen. He believes that a devout religious life is essential, and wishes to see his children grow up with similar attitudes. He said that it was good for him to be an altar boy because it sort of "tamed him down." The impression conveyed is that he was expressing a felt need for submission to spiritual authority. When he was single, he attended church regularly, but because of his Sunday work it has been impossible for him to go to church except on work holidays and holy days.

Mrs. Voskuil, who is now only 28, was married at 17 after very brief employment as a press operator in a doll factory and a short experience as a baby-sitter. She is attractive in appearance. Her voice is heavy and coarse, whereas her husband's is gentle and subdued. She is one of a number of children of Italian parents. Her father is a retired automobile salesman. She met her husband as a friend of her brother's. Every Sunday she and her husband take their children to dinner at her parents' home, and in the summer they all go on family outings. The picture presented of her self-image is of a working-class wife and mother whose interests are limited to her home, her peers and her own parents and brothers and sisters. This is, perhaps, a typical self-image of an American of Italian descent in the second generation. She was conventional, with the "proper" manners of the American middle class, in performing the introduction of a neighbor woman friend who "dropped in" while the interview was underway. She tried politely to provide suitable answers for the many questions addressed to her during the interview, though she had great difficulty in finding any words at all for expressing her tastes in television programs. Her answers were fluent and enthusiastic, however, when she talked about her neighborhood. She perceives it in glowing terms. It consists of Irish, Polish, Italian, German working people—all of them "very friendly." It is not only the Roman Catholics in the neighborhood who are friendly; the Protestants are just as nice, just as friendly.

THEIR VIEW OF SOCIETY. Mrs. Voskuil has worked out a personal policy for getting along that meets her needs well. When the interviewer commented on her friendliness, she explained:

I don't like trouble. I don't like to make trouble. I mind my own business and stay out of trouble.

This personal policy can be summed up in the familiar term, "children-kitchen-church." But she does not feel circumscribed or pinched in her social relationships. She is a member of the public school PTA and enjoys it, because she finds herself among her peers there. She belongs to a church-affiliated social group, St. Theresa's Guild. She also is a member of a four-woman informal sewing club which meets regularly to socialize as much as to sew or embroider. But where social contacts and activities tend to be impersonal, Mrs. Voskuil loses interest. For example, she volunteered she had not registered to vote:

I should, but I felt my vote would probably put the wrong man in. I don't know about those things. Next time I'm goin' though.

Differences in attitude between Mr. and Mrs. Voskuil were revealed in their views on the education and potential future of their children. The older daughter, like her mother before her, is being educated in a Catholic parochial school. The second girl, however, was entered in public school, "because the parochial school was too crowded." Both parents are happy with the public school for this child, and would not transfer her to the parochial school. Her religious training in released-time classes is considered satisfactory.

When the Voskuils were asked, "What do you hope for your children?" the question elicited the following colloquy:

Mrs. V.: Nothing special. Just that they grow up to be—[pause]—good citizens, 'n' honest, 'n' decent. That's all. I don't want them to be anything else out of this world.
V.: [quietly and seriously]: Just a little better than we are.
Mrs. V.: Just a little better than *I* am [laughs self-consciously].
V.: Well, they'll have more of a chance than we—than I did, anyway.

Mrs. Voskuil evidently respects her husband and recognizes his unfulfilled capabilities. But she does not want his discontent transmitted to the children. She accepts the policy, which he initiated, of having one child in the public school. But it seems likely that she wants her children raised in her own image (she doesn't want them to be "out of her world"), whereas her husband's ambition is to see them more class mobile. This inference is supported by the fact that while her husband verbalized his wish to have had professional education, upon being asked in that context whether she has any dreams of a better life, she replied: "No, we have a satisfied life."

Lest this portrait appear to present Mrs. Voskuil in unfair terms, let it be said that she seemed to have less ethnocentrism than her husband, though neither of them is unduly prejudiced.

Int.: Do you feel that being a Ukrainian made any difference here in New Haven in opportunities offered or in financial offerings?
V.: It didn't make any difference.
Int.: Do national and minority groups get along pretty well?
V.: Yes, they do. . . . We have a lot of Negroes, you know. And since this new law has been passed that they can move out to any place they want, a lot of them are begrudged a lot of things. . . .
Mrs. V.: I don't see why they shouldn't have them. They're human. They have to live just the same way we do.
V.: Of course, they live a wilder life than we do.
Mrs. V.: Not all of them. There's a lot of white ones that lead just as wild a life as the Negro.
V.: There's a lot of them that are afraid of them more than anything else.
Mrs. V.: If you don't bother them, they're not going to bother you.

When it comes to economic ethnocentrism, the Voskuils agree. They said that she seemed to have less ethnocentrism than her husband, though Negroes, when as Mrs. Voskuil stated, "a lot right up here need those jobs. They don't have to get outsiders."

LEISURE TIME AND THE MASS MEDIA. It has been noted that Voskuil's chief leisure-time activity is maintaining his house, while his wife finds time for a church social organization and a sewing club. She also works on their yard. Voskuil remarked during the interview that he preferred living in the more spacious suburban area to the downtown city of New Haven because he was "sort of the outdoor type." He also reported that his favorite sports, when he got the time for them, were fishing, hunting, bowling and horseshoes, while his wife enjoyed fishing, swimming and horseshoes. In the preceding year he had seen one baseball game and the two had gone to the races "a couple of times." Their motion picture attendance was estimated at two or three movies in the preceding year. In the summer, Mrs. Voskuil went to the city beaches "almost every day," and she and her husband went to an amusement park two or three times. On his last vacation, he remodeled the house.

The Voskuils' mass media intake consists of great quantities of television, daytime radio, a daily paper and several magazines. On occasion both television sets are simultaneously in use. They consider television a blessing; they "wouldn't be without it." It took the place of moviegoing which the presence of children had made relatively difficult in recent years. Their tastes in television are undiscriminating and difficult for them to verbalize. They spoke of the popular television programs with favor, in fact seemed to like everything on television, except significantly, that no news reports or news commentators were ever mentioned. Mrs. Voskuil said that she had been "bored" by the broadcasts of the political conventions. Mrs. Voskuil reported listening throughout the day to popular music from a New Haven station—the only radio listening now done in the family. Apparently television also is kept on pretty constantly until sign-off on the local station.

Children's viewing time is estimated at about 28 hours per week. As with many parents, the Voskuils find nothing but good in television for their children. She feels that the children's programs are suitable for them. She revealed a totally permissive policy toward children's television viewing:

Int.: How do you feel about children's programs on TV?

Mrs. V.: They're good. Lots of people don't care for Howdy Doody. They say it's noisy. But that's not for adults, that's for children. It's not meant for grown-ups. And we have our programs that they don't care for.

Int.: Who decides what to listen to?

Mrs. V.: When the children come out of school until the time they go to bed they listen to what they want to listen to and when they go to bed we listen to what we want. Usually the adult programs go on at that time anyway—around 8 o'clock.

Int.: There's a program, I don't remember what the name of it was—it was about a school—

Mrs. V.: Oh, you mean Ding Dong School. Oh, he [the 4-year-old] just loves it. He always listens to that. He sits there on the floor. Even me, I like to listen too. I go in there and watch it. It is very good. They all like it, even my nieces; yes, they all like it. The ones that don't go to school, they figure that they are going to school by sitting and watching it here.

Her husband said that television keeps children from running around. He remarked with tolerant amazement that the youngest one even comes running downstairs so as not to miss the cartooned commercial advertisements. Hastily, he added, "It's educational, too." Mrs. Voskuil said that her children did not enjoy the mysteries or horror programs and voluntarily turned them off and went outside to play when they came on. She reported viewing the mysteries and quiz programs and singled out I Love Lucy and Red Buttons as favorite programs. By way of explanation she said: "I Love Lucy is so natural, it's like the people next door."

In their use of newspapers, the Voskuils display a consistent pattern. He reads the first page and the sports page. She mentioned first the advertisements, and then, one suspects with self-respect bias, asserted that she reads the whole paper. Asked if she reads the columnists, she first replied ambiguously, "Ummm." On being asked if she likes any of them in particular, she reluctantly said "Yeah," then confessed that she did not know what the term "columnist" means. The magazines subscribed to include *Parents*, *Popular Science* and *Popular Mechanics*, but the interview is silent as to the meaning of such material for the Voskuils.

RELIGIOUS TELEVISION AND RADIO. Before television the Voskuils listened to Roman Catholic radio programs. Voskuil listened to early morning masses on radio and found them satisfying when he was unable to go to church. Now, the only religious program watched by either of them is Sheen. It is interesting to note their separate views on this program because the subject came up first before the husband came home and then afterward. Mrs. Voskuil volunteered that she watched the Bishop whenever she had time. When asked directly what there is about the program that she likes she said:

The way he talks—[long pause]—I can't explain it [long pause]. It's what he says and the way he says it. Everyone in our family likes him. . . . The way he talks makes you sit there and look at him.

Her husband was able to verbalize more easily. He likes the Bishop very much:

V.: There's a man who's well educated. I don't believe there's anybody who dislikes him.

Int.: Is it what he says?

V.: It's *what* he says and *how* he says it. How he puts it over. I believe he's one of the greatest speakers I ever heard.

Int.: What is it that is so appealing about him?

V.: Well, in the—as far as Bishop Sheen's concerned, he's a man—he's a great man. He doesn't have to sit down and write a script for him to read from. What he thinks, he speaks. One thing after another. He must have a very good education. He can keep going for hours from one subject to another.

Sheen's frequent brief allusions to philosophers, books and abstract concepts have tremendous prestige value for Voskuil. They embody the "education" which Voskuil sorely feels the need of. Such "tags," in what is essentially a stream-of-consciousness discourse, which otherwise might be assumed to attract intellectuals to Sheen, here are disclosed as attracting a man of no competence in this area.

The influence of Sheen on the Voskuils can best be assessed in the light of their opinion-action-forming pattern. Outside of the labor union, his peer group in the factory and his immediate family the interview did not reveal any sources of information and authoritative opinion for Voskuil other than television and the New Haven *Register.* Mrs. Voskuil is limited to her family, her neighborhood peer group and television. Even on television, both Voskuils are dominantly concerned with entertainment. Between them they watch all sports, quiz, drama and variety shows indiscriminately, but neither one watches a single news program regularly, nor do they listen to news on radio.

In the light of this isolation from opinion-forming media and persons, the preoccupation with Sheen, especially apparent in Voskuil, assumes major importance. Mrs. Voskuil's relation to Sheen is more obscure than her husband's. She can miss the program without disturbance. He cannot. It seems safe to say she will shape her attitudes toward the Bishop in terms of her perception of her own and her children's interests. She is essentially a non-reflective person who is uncritically attached to the existing social order, but is overtly anomic about it. Voskuil also is overtly anomic, because of the drain on his energies of his job and his family and his preoccupation with them, but he has a real potential for action in relation to the social order.

He yearns to participate in such action, especially if it will improve his own status and that of his group.

Voskuil's feeling of educational and cultural inferiority limits his ability to reason through problems and make independent decisions in the socio-cultural and religious spheres. He has standards, but they are not self-generated. An outside observer would judge that these standards work successfully within the family and probably in his other personal relationships. Voskuil, too, knows they work, knows his relations are happy ones, but his knowledge does not give him intellectual security. The blend of religious authoritarianism with intellectual authority found in Sheen's program has a powerful appeal for a man like Voskuil. Within limits, he can be led by such a program. The latent anti-intellectualism—revealed by repetition of the gossip about New Haven being dominated by Yale—can be developed and exploited by Sheen's antirational policy. Voskuil's ties to his religion, made tenuous by his work schedule, can be maintained and even strengthened, since Sheen typifies the authority of the church Voskuil welcomed in his youth. It would be rash, however, to hazard a guess as to how far Voskuil would go in following an authority figure. The interests of his family, perceived in its social class setting, are his dominant concern. If they were to come into conflict with the Bishop's policy, Voskuil's loyalty to his mentor would be severely strained.

SHEEN AND PEALE LISTENERS

The Elmer Jacksons

Background Data

Social Class: II
Own home
Own radio set, no television
Income: $2,001–$3,500

	Husband	Wife
Occupation:	Retired teacher	Retired teacher
Education:	High school	Two years college
Age:	74	70
Religious background:	Protestant	Protestant
Church attended:	None	None
Preoccupation:	Self	Self
Children: None		

The Jacksons listened regularly to The Catholic Hour when Sheen was speaking and to The Art of Living.

This childless couple was married late in life, when Jackson was 53 and Mrs. Jackson, 49. They had been fellow teachers in a New Haven high school. He taught mechanical drawing; her subject was music. At the time of the interview both were retired, living in a substantial, attractive suburban home with well-kept, wooded grounds.

Jackson's self-image is that of a man who has failed to rise in the social class scale in accordance with his capabilities. Consequently, he feels defeated in relation to himself and balked by his environment. The attitudes of frustration manifested in the interview are supported by his F-scale ratings, for he is moderately authoritarian with a total score of 5.69. On the subscales, he is close to the maximum in power and toughness (6.71) and sex (6.67), while he is nearly as high on authoritarian aggression (6.25), superstition and stereotypy (6.17), authoritarian submission (6.00) and projectivity (6.00).

Jackson said little about his childhood, but it appears he was born of native Anglo-American stock in New Haven. He has lived his life in New Haven and its environs, apart from brief teenage periods of residence in New York, New Jersey and Ohio. Indeed, for 51 years—from 1897 to 1948—he lived in the same house in New Haven. This static symptom is significant in relation to his frustrated class mobility ambitions. As a young man near the turn of the century, he had been employed in the automobile industry in its pioneer phase. He worked for ten years in the budding industry, was even sent to Europe by one early automotive manufacturer to study European techniques. He shifted to teaching as a stopgap when he lost his job in the brief depression of 1908. Eventually it became a permanent career.

He was vehement in stating:

One of the biggest mistakes of my life was getting into teaching. I simply got into it during the 1908 depression, that was all. I took it with no idea of staying in it long. [Rattling a bunch of keys vigorously.]

Evidence of dissatisfaction with teaching appeared frequently throughout the interview. He complained bitterly about the low pay and the fact he could not risk expressing personal opinions for fear of arousing the wrath of his pupils' parents.

Jackson's timidity in climbing the economic class ladder is to be considered in relation to his timidity in other directions, at least since he retired from teaching in 1946. He indicated he has been active in local ward politics as a Republican; however, he had refused to run for alderman because of the expenses he felt he would incur in the post. It seems probable that his late marriage indicates timidity in relation to the opposite sex, although little direct evidence on this was available.

The tactic of being an "inside-dopester" fitted easily this man whose ambitions outran his courage. He could, and did, practice inside-dopesterism in relation to his community peer group and the mass media. In using this tactic he easily identifies himself with individuals in the social class to which he has aspired but not reached. Thus, he often quoted "Yale men" as authorities, "the top European engineers," and the currently ruling member of the Henry Ford dynasty. It has been but a short step from relying on such comfortable authority figures to accepting superstitious authority symbols. Jackson made frequent, incidental, references to the forecasts of astrologers, Nostradamus, Balthazar, and palm readers in his interpretations of the world around him. The F-scale rating of 6.17 on superstition and stereotypy is no accident.

HIS VIEW OF SOCIETY. Jackson perceives people outside his immediate family in ethnocentric terms. However, this ethonocentrism is more latent than evident. He expressed no racist prejudice, and emphasized that in teaching he

. . . absolutely refused to talk politics with my boys and absolutely refused to talk religion with them. I might say something that immediately gets me in dutch with the family.

You've got to be very tolerant with them. We frequently get asked to some Jewish service and to Catholic churches on occasions.

This "broad-mindedness" on which he prides himself masks the unconscious view of social process as being a matter of in-groups, where "one is known." Unacceptable people should not push themselves into places where they are unwanted. Thus, confronted with the hypothetical situation of a minister in a metropolitan community when strained race relations break out in violence, he said:

I think ministers could do a great deal of good in their own church, but I don't think they would do much when they got out where they weren't known.

Carried further afield into hypothetical issues concerning the responsibility of Christians in relation to China today, he revealed a total lack both of information and capacity to understand the issues and forces at work there. On issues such as political corruption in the United States, he believes that the only thing the individual can do is to take some action at the local level, that the only thing the churches can do is to "educate their members." In the economic area, he believes that business cycles take place with "clockwork" regularity and links the prospect of a future depression with soothsayers.

The handwriting is on the wall—like Balthazar—no one seems to recognize it.

Jackson's political views were conservative Republican. He had favored Senator Taft as the candidate for President. He opposed political and social action by churches; suspected the higher officials of some Protestant churches —naming the Methodists particularly—of being inclined toward communism. He disapproves of the general conduct of organized religious groups.

RELIGION IN HIS LIFE. The few facts volunteered by Jackson concerning his childhood related to religion. He attended Methodist church school as a child and later, as a young adult, he was secretary of his Sunday school. His father and grandfather had been lay ministers in the Methodist church. One suspects that resentment against his father underlies his present negative attitude toward churches.

My father . . . was one of these real shouting Methodists, you know that they used to have in the early days. So I got my fill of that too, when I was young, you know. . . . My grandfather had a marvelous voice. I wouldn't wonder but what you could hear him for a half a mile and understand what he was saying. . . . It was marvelous to hear him shouting at somebody. He worked outdoors; he was a builder and contractor in his early days.

The vigor and masculinity of his father and grandfather simultaneously attracted and repelled this rather less vigorous man. Thus we find him regretting "there doesn't seem to be the spirit in the church that there used to be lots of times." But he belongs to no church, and he dislikes spirited presentations in religious radio and television programs. His personal brand of religion is "broadmindedness." He showed no interest in salvation or the Gospel.

Mrs. Jackson's image of herself is of one who has a right to be satisfied with her life, insofar as her teaching career is concerned. She is frankly proud of the fact that every year while she was teaching her pupils took prizes. A lack of evident emotional warmth in the domestic side of her life may be traceable to the fact that she married late and had no children. She shares to some degree her husband's feelings of frustration and superstition about the outside world. The F-scale material supports this analysis. Her total score is neutral (4.31) and much lower than that of her husband. Her destructiveness and cynicism score is quite low (2.50). The subscales in which she scores higher than neutral are anti-intraception (5.75), projectivity (5.40), and power and toughness (5.00).

Mrs. Jackson was born in a small town in Illinois but moved before the age of twelve to Danbury, Connecticut, where she finished her formal education with graduation from high school. She began teaching school almost immediately and continued, apparently uneventfully but satisfyingly, until her retirement two years before the interview.

HER VIEW OF SOCIETY. Mrs. Jackson, like her husband, is full of ethnocentrism.

If a colored family is acceptable, it's all right for them to move into a housing project, but if they aren't, and many of them aren't, then they have no business moving into a place like that. No matter what the nationality or who the people are there's certain places you know you have no business going into if you're brought up right. It's usually the ill-bred class of foreigners that will try to do that sort of thing.

Her attitude toward the civil structure of society is anomic: "There is nothing that the individual can do. It's a closed corporation." Like her husband, she had hoped that Taft would be nominated for the Presidency. She echoed rather routinely Jackson's stereotypical political views.

RELIGION IN HER LIFE. Mrs. Jackson again echoes her husband in the feeling that in her younger days she "got too much religion." As a consequence, she has no church affiliation and has rejected one consistently since reaching maturity. In her early years, her mother had sent her and her brother and sisters to an Episcopal church every Sunday. Her father, who had been raised a Roman Catholic, had rejected that faith despite the fact that his oldest sister was a nun. This aunt had, however, helped the family move from Illinois to Connecticut and had arranged for Mrs. Jackson to go to parochial school. There she was oppressed by the profusion of religious ceremonies and now attributes her aloofness from church to the resentment generated at that time.

LEISURE TIME AND THE MASS MEDIA. The pattern of living for this retired Protestant couple is pleasantly varied. Apparently there is little conflict between them. Jackson belongs to the Masons, while she finds that a ceramics club, child welfare work and music take up much of her time. She visits art and clay exhibits in New York, and attends the Metropolitan Opera. She also likes recorded music and uses her radio a good deal for music, listening to all serious music programs.

They make extensive use of the mass media. Radio receives their joint attention every evening from six to eight, when they listen to all the news programs and commentators, of whom they named eleven. While their list includes Murrow, they have no comment on him. They dislike Elmer Davis for his "nasal voice." Their highest praise is for Fulton Lewis, Jr., whom "we never miss." Next highest praise is given to George Sokolsky, who has "a very pleasing voice—so much sincerity." He also appears to the Jacksons to have had "the most experience of all the commentators." Drew Pearson is heard, but "we don't take much stock in him—I just generally sneer at him."

The Jackson's taste in radio drama runs to crime programs and the Lux Radio Theatre. In comedy-situation drama programs, they regularly hear The Big Show, People are Funny, Millie, Life with Luigi, and Ozzie and Harriet. They hear two quiz programs, Groucho Marx ("He has a nice way when he talks to people," said Mrs. Jackson), and Dr. I. Q. Boxing is their only regular sports broadcast. Mrs. Jackson said:

Sometimes I like to listen to the fights—I want to see who wins—but I get every hit, every poke in the jaw I get. When it's over I'm worn out.

In the daytime, besides music, they listen regularly to This Is New York and Martha Dean.

The Jacksons realize that radio is supported by advertising, but they are critical of the amount and type of advertising carried. They feel that commercial announcements on radio are getting longer and more offensive as time passes and that they should be curbed by a law. They also feel strongly that certain advertising of drugs should not be permitted, and hold the Pure Food and Drug Administration and the medical profession jointly responsible for existing advertising which they feel is misleading or in poor taste.

The Jacksons read two newspapers, the New York Herald Tribune and the New Haven Register. Jackson reads the columnists before the news. He generally approves of what Westbrook Pegler says, but feels that "he doesn't ride the Roosevelt family half hard enough." In referring to his reading of Walter Lippmann and the Alsops (of whose views he inferentially disapproves), Jackson remarked:

Anyone who's been out and around and goes to school beyond the reading stage, they don't agree with everything they see and read. A lot of times we don't know about things. Everyone ought to be as well posted as they can be on what's going on.

Mrs. Jackson implicitly agreed with her husband's views on the columnists with the exception of those on Pegler who she thinks "occasionally rides the Roosevelt family too hard."

The only other portions of the newspaper referred to by this family were the comic section and letters to the editor. Jackson reported a preference for Sad Sack and Dagwood, while Mrs. Jackson preferred Henry among the comics.

One might expect that former schoolteachers would have an interest in books, either of the fiction or nonfiction variety. This expectation is substantially unfounded as far as the Jacksons are concerned. Mrs. Jackson reported that she belongs to the Book-of-the-Month Club, but nowhere in the interview did she refer to any particular book. Jackson's only reference to a book was that Dante's *Inferno* had been one of his favorite readings when he was younger.

Magazines are the Jacksons' main source of reading material. They regularly buy *Automotive Industries, Popular Science, Popular Mechanics, Collier's, Saturday Evening Post, Redbook, American* and four astrology magazines (of which they named but three, *American Astrology, Horoscope* and *Astrology Guide*).

Jackson volunteered somewhat sheepishly:

I read things I shouldn't read—a good many detective stories—the true, not the imaginary ones.

I read most anything I can get my hands on—don't make much difference what it is. I'm especially addicted to technical subjects naturally—automobile engine work, jet propulsion, anything in that line.

But his real love appears to be the astrology and soothsaying literature. He reeled off a list of the "forecasts" that had come true—World Wars I and II, Pearl Harbor, Truman's election in 1948. He described how a palm reader had forecast his trip to Europe, then had told him he would never want, but would never have any money. "He was absolutely right." Jackson also made forecasts based on Nostradamus and other "seers."

The Jacksons used to go to the movies as often as three or four times a week. While it may be due to the fact that they are now advanced in age, they reported that now their moviegoing is limited to less than one movie a year on the average and that the reason is that "movies got so poor."

RELIGIOUS RADIO. The taste the Jacksons display in religious radio programs is keyed to Jackson's antipathy to vigorous (i.e., revivalistic) expression of religious beliefs, which we noted earlier was linked to his relation with his father. The fact that programs select their audience members was pointedly illustrated by Jackson's opening remarks on this topic:

Well, of course some of the religious programs, one or two of them we turn off about as quick as they come on if we happen to be tuned in on that station because of that, that they, whoever is doing the talking at that time seems to be ranting and raving around with a high pitch, and a loud voice, you know.

He implicitly recognized that a program is in reality a totality of explicit and implicit material, for he went on to an insight that reveals that the quality of the voice *implies other features* of the program that are repellent to him:

And I wouldn't exactly say they were going back to the days of Hell and Purgatory, you know, and all that stuff, that if you don't watch your step you are going to be damned anyway, but it's the—the voice and the attitude of the speaker seems to indicate that. Whereas some of the other programs that you listen to are—the minister or sometimes probably a layman doing the talking that has a very smooth delivery, and it is a pleasure to listen to the program— ideas and voice and everything about the program.

Jackson said that voices on religious radio programs should have the qualities of sincerity, cheerfulness (as against mournfulness), good tone quality, and be neither too high nor too low in pitch. His over-all evaluation of religious broadcasting was:

I think, without any question, probably the radio does a tremendous amount of good in broadcasting services because they get to a lot of people that under no circumstances could you pry loose from their home and get them into church.

He made it plain that he and his wife were in this category.

Jackson was interested in The Catholic Hour only when Sheen was broadcasting.[1] He approves of Sheen, of whom he said,

Sheen is very interesting . . . he's very sure of himself when he speaks. He don't want you to doubt anything he says.

Mrs. Jackson is slowly becoming deaf. She cited the advancing deafness as a reason—or an excuse—for not going to church.

I can't go up and sit in the front seat where I could hear him, or sit right beside the pulpit, you see, and hear everything anyone says that way, but I can tune the radio in, and that's what I like.

So her sole contact with religion is through her bedside radio, though she is not a "fan"—cannot be counted upon to listen every week.

She mentioned Peale's broadcasts as having helped her. It is important to establish just how this took place.

---

[1] In a subsequent interview, Jackson reported that since Sheen has left radio, he goes to the home of a Roman Catholic friend to watch him on television. The Jacksons still have no television set.

Mrs. J.: The first time that I heard Dr. Peale, I was very nervously tired. I had just given up school, and I had had a very hard year, and a rather unsatisfactory year [apparently marred by conflict with some woman in her school] and the very first time I heard him, he said, "Now I think we had better all relax." And he went through this—just how to relax. Told you just how to sit, and just what to do, how to hold your eyes, and how to hold your head, and how to hold your arms, and by the time he had finished I was completely relaxed, and then he said, "Now as you sit here you ought to be relaxed, and you ought to be willing to listen." And he said, "Supposing Jesus was sitting beside you. What would you ask him?" I think that impressed me more than anything I've ever heard a minister say. And from then on I was writing to Dr. Peale. And I listened to him every Sunday for a long, long while. I can't tell you—why I just wouldn't miss him, you know. He seemed to do a lot for me.

Int.: How about you, Mr. Jackson?

J.: I don't remember hearing him at all—to tell you the truth.

Mrs. J.: I had been sort of running my own life without much thought, and he sort of gave me the idea that with proper thought in your relationship to God that He was—in other words, I felt as though God was much more real to me than He had ever been in my life. And that if you sat right down and talked, as you would talk to Him if He were sitting beside you, that you would get direction in your life—inspiration to—just what to do. I had never had anybody impress me the way he did.

The interviewer pursued the matter by asking what difference it made in her feelings about herself and other people:

Mrs. J.: I think a much more tolerant feeling about other people. If they do things that are particularly disagreeable to you, maybe you don't know what's inside their minds and their thoughts about these things. And maybe they don't intend to react to you that way, and I think I had a far better feeling towards particularly one person that I had to deal with a lot in my work, you know. Changed my viewpoints. It didn't make me like her any better, but it made me—

Int.: More tolerant?

Mrs. J.: Yes.

J.: If anyone could be tolerant to her.

Mrs. Jackson wrote to Peale for a pack of the "How" cards[2] and appears to have used them while she was listening regularly to the program. She visualized Dr. Peale as "tall and slim and very athletic looking. He might have just graying hair, but he doesn't have an ounce of flesh on him that he doesn't need, because he talks in such an active way." She supposed he might be a Congregationalist.

2 "How to Relax," "How to Say Your Prayers," "How to Go to Church," "How to Make Your Work Easy," "How to Solve a Problem," "How to Forgive," "How to Break the Worry Habit," "How to Get People to Like You," et cetera.

Peale's program did not lead her to a personal attachment to a church, or even to continued use of religious radio programs.

Mrs. J.: Dr. Peale seems to think you ought to go to church. You ought to be affiliated with a church, and you ought to go to that church every Sunday. I don't agree with him on that. Not that I think, you know—I think that's all right—I think that—I think if I was very much younger I would do that too, because I think it's a fine thing for anyone to feel that you belong to a certain church, but I don't think that church seems to mean so much to people any more. It doesn't seem to me it does.

Int.: You haven't listened regularly to other religious programs besides Dr. Peale?

Mrs. J.: Not regularly, no.

The combination of Sheen for Jackson and Peale for Mrs. Jackson stems logically from their character traits. Jackson's need for a masculine authority figure—at the opposite pole from his father and grandfather—vigorous and certain; eminently respectable but still ready to view with mistrust much that is popular or "progressive" in the social order, is admirably met by Sheen. Jackson's attachment to Sheen is an ego-building experience. Mrs. Jackson, more secure in her ego-image and more satisfied with her role and accomplishments, needs, rather, the kind of help that will take her through immediate problems and temporary difficulties in relationships. Peale evidently gave her the techniques that could restore her to a normal emotional balance, where her inner resources keep her at a stable level of adjustment.

The Jacksons' responses to the supplementary F-scale statements underlined their personality differences. Jackson strongly agreed that divine assistance must come through the church or the clergy; his wife moderately disagreed. Jackson feels the clergy are the authorities on belief and behavior; his wife strongly disagrees. Jackson strongly feels that Bible principles are impractical in daily living; his wife takes the opposite view.

How may we evaluate the role of religious radio for the Jacksons? It seems fair to say it is improbable any program will induce them to participate fully in church. Spiritual comfort can be brought to them via radio through programs featuring well-performed, nonrevivalistic music and speakers who are not overtly emotional. Because they are looking for authority figures on which to lean and because they are so interested in news and commentary, a program like Religion at the News Desk, with a less liberal bias, might engage their interest. Their age makes it doubtful that their basic social attitudes and behavior would be changed by either type of program.

The William Richardsons

Background Data

Social Class: IV
Own home
Own television and radio sets
Income: $5,001–$7,500

	Husband	Wife
Occupation:	Toolmaker	Housewife
Education:	High school	Graduate work (M.A.)
Age:	37	34
Religious background:	Protestant	Protestant
Church attended:	Congregational Christian	Congregational Christian
Preoccupation:	Work	Social status

Children: Son: 5; Daughters: 7, 4

The typical listeners to The Greatest Story Ever Told are a Protestant family with minor children, the parents of whom are between 30 and 44. They have had between seven and twelve years of schooling and are in social class IV. The Richardsons, a brief description of whom was presented in Chapter 13, are such a family.

The Richardsons' values are centered in conventionality—epitomized in the family as an institution. Mrs. Richardson unconsciously views herself as superior to her present status and is driven to rise in the social class scale. Her husband's image of himself is of a highly skilled workman whose competence and economic security are established. We classified him as primarily preoccupied with his work; his wife, primarily with social status; both of them as secondarily preoccupied with family and home. The self-imagery of both the Richardsons is scanty. Inwardly these are barren people.

The interview materials (there were two long, discursive interviews with this family) clearly portray the social status and work preoccupations of this couple, but superficially their primary expressed concern is the home—the house, the garden, the children and especially the children's welfare. This viewpoint dominates largely because Mrs. Richardson is the spokesman for the family and does most of the talking. She is compulsively concerned with all the details of life. Her forte is organization of the detail of the life of each member of her family. She is domineering. Richardson is submissive in the home situation. Both of them are humorless.

In the light of the attitude structures found in both of them, it is perhaps surprising that their F-scale scores are as low as they are. Mrs. Richardson's over-all F-scale score is 2.79. Richardson's is 3.97. Her highest subscale scores are in conventionality (4.25) and authoritarian submission (4.00). His highest subscale scores are in destructiveness and cynicism (6.00), authoritarian submission (5.29), and conventionality (4.75). Her lowest scores are in suspicion and stereotypy (2.00) and anti-intraception (2.25). His are in authoritarian aggression (3.00) and anti-intraception (3.25).

THEIR VIEW OF SOCIETY. The Richardsons' conventional idealization of the family as an institution conceals the fact that they are isolated. They referred to no friends or social activities. They are completely divorced from political activity. They do not vote. Except for the minutiae of conducting a household, they even seem to be isolated from each other. One is justified in carrying the thought one step further; individually, they are alienated from themselves, except as tools for social advancement or work.

The alienation from society shown by the Richardsons extends to individuals. While they report, superficially, quite "correct" (i.e., enlightened middle class) attitudes toward Negroes, their ethnocentrism comes through plainly in their contemptuous attitudes toward Poles, Italians and Roman Catholics, both in the neighborhood and in his shop. Even in discussing the mass media, both Richardsons made derogatory comments about almost every television character. The Richardsons' ethnocentrism must be distinguished, however, from the blind, undiscriminating negativism of people like Mr. Manson. The Richardsons were rather well-informed; for example, he used correctly and with outward sympathy the name "National Association for the Advancement of Colored People." We interpret this gentility as part of their upward-mobile strivings. They have identified themselves with the ideology of laissez-faire individualism of the nineteenth-century variety. They do not respect individuals. This aggressive attitude is coupled with their idealization of property, especially the importance of owning their own home in the "right" neighborhood. We may suppose that their economic history in part explains this drive. They were adolescents during the depression of the Thirties. Both of them came from working-class homes where the meaning of economic insecurity was painfully apparent. Both chose vocations that promised personal economic security—he, through an apprenticeship leading to his skilled machine-tool occupation, she, through four years of college education, followed by graduate nurse's training. Economic security was thus achieved by both of them without group help. Neither has ever asked for or received anything from unions or government. It is logical, from their viewpoint, that they are both antiunion, and antigovernment.

RELIGION IN THE LIFE OF THE RICHARDSONS. The Richardsons' religious experience, like other parts of their collective life, expresses their preoccupation with class conventionality. Richardson was raised in Scotch Presbyterianism. As a child, he regularly attended church. Mrs. Richardson grew up in a lower social class Methodist church in Boston. In that context we find the origin of two of her adult values: her extreme dislike of emotionally demonstrative religious activity ("We don't like the spectacular type of religion.") and her drive to emulate the rigorous social standards of upper class Bostonians. As is often the case with middle class Protestants, the Richardsons drifted away from church in their adolescence. Their return to church was made just a few months prior to the first interview and originated also in conventional class feelings. They live in a predominantly Roman Catholic neighborhood, and their children

. . . would find their playmates studying catechism, and why—they came home with the idea that it was a privilege to be allowed to read their little playmates' catechism! . . . So we figured, well, as long as the children are interested in meanings, and knowing, they might just as well have their own Protestant books to read, and their own Protestant Sunday school to teach them what we believe.

Spurred, as he put it, by this incident, the Richardsons

. . . spent a lot of time looking for a church that satisfied our needs—for the family. . . . It's amazing the few churches that do. We felt we wanted to attend church as a family. *We felt it was the right way to do.* [Emphasis supplied.]

They selected an upper class Congregational Christian church. Superficially, the reason given for this choice was that the church school and worship service are held at the same hour, and the transportation problem was solved by this arrangement. Substantively, it is clear from the whole interview that the class composition of the church was the compelling consideration. The explanation of "what we feel in our hearts religion is" was as follows:

Mrs. R.: Well, I suppose we feel basically, at least I feel, that religion is—well, I don't know what it is. But it just gives a person what he needs to meet and face life, and what it is, and to live with one's neighbors, and with one's family, and the whole society in peace and harmony. And I think that while I have seen and come in contact with so much quarreling among families, and people who have lost something basic on which to build their life, and the life of their family around, I, in my own heart, when I sat down and thought it all over, I couldn't find any better place for it to lie than in religion. Some kind of a unit that would give a family stability and peace and—well, happiness, yes, very definitely the happiness that they need. And I think we have found it. I know we do. I know I feel a lot better since I've been going to church. And I don't think it's just the fact of going to church either. But, as I say, I think I'm easy to live with. Am I?

R.: I guess so.

Mrs. R.: And I hope I am—and I really feel in my own heart that going to church has done a lot for me.

R.: It gets us out together, and to my way of thinking, things have changed a great deal since I was a boy. It seems now that there is—well, I can't say about my own family, because we are always together—but it seems that there isn't as much family life any more like when I was a boy.

The purely ideal statement of an appropriate attitude toward religion, given by Mrs. Richardson, is not supported by any evidence in their behavior or attitudes that religion has actually that deep a hold on them. They manifested no interest in, nor support of any part of the church's program, be it missions, worship, religious education, preaching or whatever. They talked only of what they expected to get *from* religion; never about what they might give to someone else. There was little grasp of spiritual concepts. But there is the evidence, quoted above, that the compelling force is conventionality, and their own ethnocentric aversion to having their children "trapped" by the Roman Catholics whom they consider an inferior group. The emphasis, time and again during the interviews, on the family-unity significance of religion is overdetermined and reveals a sense of the disunity of their family group. This disunity is suggested plainly by her coupling of religion with her being "easy to live with" and his ambiguous reply.

LEISURE TIME AND THE MASS MEDIA. The Richardsons reported no social contacts other than those involved for him in his work, and for both of them with his parents—apparently a weak and unsatisfactory relationship. Their only organizational attachment is her membership in the PTA.

Richardson works six days a week, so necessarily his leisure time is less than usual. The interview suggests that his social contacts at the plant are the locus of a major share of his interests in life. He plays golf regularly, presumably with men from his shop. And he reveals a systematic pattern of conversational interchange with men at the shop on all sorts of topics, including religion and politics.

Both Richardsons have hobbies, in addition to the physical upkeep of their house. His interests are photography, woodworking and gardening on their small lot. Hers are woodworking, knitting, crocheting, embroidering, sewing and gardening. In answer to the question, "Where did you spend your last vacation?" they answered glumly, "None." They drive out to the open country about six times a year, go to amusement parks about twice a year and to the movies twice a year. Both of them swim in the summer.

Both of them formerly played tennis and Mrs. Richardson formerly played basketball and baseball.

The Richardsons had owned a television set for a year and a half at the time of the interview. When they first got it, they watched indiscriminately. They claimed in the interview that their use of television had become selective and was interspersed with listening to radio and records, and reading, when hobbies and housework permitted. The evidence is persuasive, however, that they use television more than they will admit. They had comments to make on almost every program broadcast on the two stations which they can tune in. It is reasonable to infer that as a release from the fatigue caused by long hours of work at the shop and around the house—a release which he cannot find in the company of his wife and children—Richardson sits and watches television every evening after the household chores are done. Mrs. Richardson, who is hard-of-hearing, enjoys television more than radio because of the visual element which makes it more comprehensible.

The pattern of television use which the adults in the house follow includes a number of sports. They both watch football, baseball, wrestling and boxing. Mrs. Richardson evidently works off a lot of her ample store of aggression while watching boxing, for she reports that she can knit the whole foot of a sock during one ten-round bout. She also says that she gets excited while watching wrestling matches. They dislike serial dramas on the television and radio, but report regular viewing of Philco Playhouse, Studio One and the Robert Montgomery drama program. In variety, they like the Godfrey, Murray and Sullivan programs. Groucho Marx is the only quiz program they watch—probably because of its punitive content, since they lack a sense of humor. Their taste in music is "schmaltzy." They like the light music of the Firestone program. Richardson uses his automobile radio to hear popular music on his way to and from work. Jive and bebop music are too unconventional for their taste. They make little use of news programs on radio or television, listening to only two local radio newscasts.

One cannot leave the subject of their use of television without comment on their ambivalent attitude toward advertising. They resent and criticize the length and frequency of commercial interruptions of programming. In part this disapproval is a middle class attitude which they ape, but in part it is because advertising offends their compulsive attitude toward the content of the programs. While disliking advertising excesses, they feel that it is not proper for them to criticize them because they do not buy the products whose advertising annoys them.

Mrs. Richardson estimated that the children spend twelve hours a week before the television set. She regulates the use of television strictly—programs, hours when viewing is permitted, even the volume of the sound. The children may not tune or adjust the set. They are forbidden to watch television after 8:00 P.M., their bedtime. During school vacations, the children are permitted to watch selected portions of late evening shows which their playmates report they see regularly. The television regulation is apparently a settled routine.

When the television set was first installed, the children wanted to watch it all the time. As a consequence, Mrs. Richardson forbade them to watch it at all for a while. They now see such children's programs as Howdy-Doody, Tom Corbett, Gabby Hayes, Roy Rogers, Hopalong Cassidy, Super Circus, Big Top and Kukla, Fran and Ollie. They are also permitted to watch Godfrey and Groucho Marx. We defer discussion of their use of religious programs.

The Richardsons read one newspaper, the New Haven *Register*. Richardson turns to the comic strips and sports and pretty much lets it go at that. Mrs. Richardson reads the front page, then turns to the obituaries! She also claims she reads the editorials. Richardson reported—to his wife's somewhat shocked surprise—that he reads two New York tabloids at the shop.

The Richardson magazine reading is consistent with their attitudes. They subscribe to *Reader's Digest, Good Housekeeping, Better Homes and Gardens, Popular Mechanics* and *Home Craftsman.* Richardson forthrightly said that he likes the "stories" in the fiction magazines, while Mrs. Richardson stoutly maintained that she likes only the articles. Again we observed her compulsive attachment to self- and home-improvement materials.

Neither of the Richardsons buys or reads books. She tried to make much of the fact that they give Book-of-the-Month Club type books to each other as presents but no books were seen in their downstairs rooms.

A curious reverence for books was volunteered in a discussion of Bibles. The possibility that the children would deface books was a powerful deterrent which had kept the Richardsons from giving them a Bible. The origin of the feeling was traced by Mrs. Richardson to a ruling by her parents that books per se were never to be mistreated. This item supports the portrait here drawn of her as permeated by upper middle class values, while realistically living at a much lower level.

RELIGIOUS RADIO AND TELEVISION. The religious program which most interests the Richardsons is The Greatest Story Ever Told. It has values for all of them, as the following excerpt haltingly delivered by Richardson early in the interview reveals:

We're very much taken with that program. We think it's very, very good from the standpoint of explaining Biblical stories to the children, and well, there's a lot of things about the stories that have slipped your mind. Small parts of the stories have either slipped your own mind or something about them that you never did fully understand is pretty well explained in those stories. . . . It brings back to you very vividly stories that you learned in Sunday school when you were children, and, well, the Bible—it's quite a book to become intimate with, and the average person has no, well, I won't say no desire, but he just never seems to get around to reading it. And I think that these stories recall a lot to the adult, and I think they are very instructive to the children too.

Mrs. Richardson added that her children get so engrossed in The Greatest Story Ever Told that they are oblivious to what goes on in the living room, even when their names are called. She was asked how much she thought the children (aged 7, 5 and 4) understood of the program. She said:

I think the older girl understands quite a bit; she is quite a reader. She has a very fine vocabulary for her age and she seems to have a good understanding of things. I don't think the other children understand too much of it, like, for instance, the story of the Good Samaritan—they had an idea what was going on, and they were very concerned that he was left by the wayside there and that the others passed him by. They were quite concerned as to what was going to happen to him and why the other men didn't stop and help him out. For that reason I think they get quite a bit although they possibly don't get as much of the other stories as the older girl does. She is apt to talk things over after a story like that is on. It seems to make quite an impression on her as she does talk about it. For that reason alone, I think they are good for the children. They see the cowboy stories and they see some of these other lighter things, and then you don't hear any more about them. But stories like The Greatest Story Ever Told they will talk about it and ask why did this person do a certain thing and why didn't he do a certain thing. It evidently gives them quite a bit to think about.

The essential identification of their religious attitudes with their moral code was nowhere more clearly stated than in their appraisal of Sheen's television program. Their first reaction to him was in terms of their children:

Mrs. R.: We did tune in one Sunday and saw Monsignor Sheen. The children were a little bothered with his dress, and his style, and they didn't want to watch it. But I watched it. I saw the whole program, and the children, as I say, while they wanted it turned off at first because his dress was different from what they had been accustomed to, I noticed that they were listening a bit too, at times. And, as I say, I listened to the entire program even though I am not a Catholic, and I don't believe in the Catholic religion.

Thereupon followed an extremely significant colloquy:

R.: Of course his program isn't—
Mrs. R.: Catholicism.

R.: It isn't purely religious. I don't know just how—

Mrs. R.: It is religious, but it isn't religion in only the Catholic way. It's more of a general religion.

R.: Well—he isn't actually preaching religion. He is preaching—

Mrs. R.: Goodness.

R.: Goodness. It's hard for me to explain but I don't think in the programs that I saw that he made any reference to one religion or the other. It's just more or less generalized.

In the light of the marked Roman Catholic flavor of Sheen's program, this passage establishes firmly the conclusion that the Richardsons' Protestantism and their aversion to Roman Catholicism are grounded in prejudice rather than in any doctrinal or policy concepts that may separate the two faiths.

Protestant programs on radio and television have never appealed to the Richardsons, primarily because they have an aversion to preaching. Richardson's comment is sufficient to dispose of their attitude toward such programs as those of Peale and Sockman:

We—from time to time we have listened—I can't recall anything offhand. To me it's pretty hard to concentrate on a radio sermon. Most people probably aren't like that, but I just happen to be one that doesn't like presidential speeches, or political speeches, or things like that.

Mrs. Richardson agreed with him that "sermons on the radio are hard to follow."

The Old Fashioned Revival Hour once caught Richardson's attention and appealed to his nostalgic fondness for the revival hymn-singing that was an almost daily event in his childhood fundamentalist Presbyterian home. He does not listen to the program regularly, though.

The Richardsons' involvement in religion is typified by their responses to the three supplementary statements on the F-scale. Husband and wife answered identically. Both disagreed strongly with the statement indicating that the church or the clergy are exclusive channels to divine assistance, and equally strongly with the statement indicating the minister is a final authority on matters of belief and behavior. Both, however, agreed that the Bible is not a practical guide to daily living. They are, in other words, conventionally Protestant in their stress on the independence of the individual in his own religious life, but they do not complement this Protestant belief with its traditional counterpart: reliance on the Bible as a textbook for living. This makes somewhat suspect their assertions concerning the value of The Greatest Story Ever Told as a vehicle for Bible teaching, either for themselves or for their children. If the Bible is not a practical guide to living, why should Bible teaching be of value? Probably for the Richardsons the honest answer is that this is one more conventional value to which they adhere as part of their class image. There is little evidence of serious interest in either love of God or love of neighbor in the Richardson ménage.

A pertinent concluding question is: Can religious programs on television move the Richardsons in the direction of a more meaningful relation with religion? As far as Richardson is concerned, the sort of program that might have this effect would have to be couched in dramatic form, preferably with nostalgic music of the revivalist type. Most important, the content of such a program would have to present Protestantism in authoritarian terms. Even though he said in the interview that he had seen Sheen only a few times, he several times alluded admiringly to him as "having a lot on the ball," et cetera. Richardson is more submissive to authority than he is a rebel against it. Probably the theme of such a Protestant program would have to be the authority of the Protestant conscience—a theme, by the way, also reminiscent of his Presbyterian youth. The ideal Protestant program for Mrs. Richardson would be one that would present Protestantism as the epitome of respectability and security. She would be grateful for a chance to accept directives from such a program. An alternative to the approach via television would be a concerned pastor who, through skillful counseling, might generate a more fertile stream of attitudes and interests in her, and through her, in the whole family. Mrs. Richardson is psychologically the key figure in this family. If the anxieties and inner conflicts that drive her compulsively were relaxed, either by a television program or by her church, then the house might become a home rather than a collection of people and things, which now, for lack of human warmth, it is.

The Kevin Boyles

Background Data

Social Class: II
Own home
Own television and radio sets
Income: $7,501–$10,000

	Husband	Wife
Occupation:	Sales manager	Housewife
Education:	High school	Partial college
Age:	50	41
Religious background:	Roman Catholic	Roman Catholic
Church attended:	Roman Catholic	Roman Catholic
Preoccupation:	Formal Religion	Family and home

Children: Son: 14, Daughters: 15, 10, 6

A second interview with users of both the Sheen program and The Greatest Story Ever Told provides a picture significantly different from that of the Richardsons. The Boyles rank higher in social status, in education (Boyle went to business college; Mrs. Boyle had nurse's training) and in income than do the typical audience members for these programs.

The Boyles live in a new suburban area, a continuation of an older upper class New Haven suburb. Their neighbors are upper middle class families, one of whom maintains a forty-foot yacht. Both Boyles are devout Roman Catholics, although their neighbors are largely Protestant.

Boyle was not present for the interview. Mrs. Boyle is physically attractive. Psychologically, she is in a state of turmoil and inner conflict. She sees herself as a woman who is struggling valiantly to discharge the duties of her role of mother and wife—duties which exhaust her and make her ill. She only half conceals from herself the fact that she often wishes she had never accepted this present role but had instead pursued the professional career of teaching nursing for which she had been trained. But her family background and religious beliefs lead her to repress such wishes. She is driven by her values to live up to her role.

Her husband is the personification of the ideal male counterpart to this wife-mother role. Implicitly, and we suspect in many ways explicitly, he dictates the details of their joint life style; though he is benevolent, albeit exacting. It is as if, in the person of her attractive husband with his "perfect disposition," she has a faith like a tiger by the tail and cannot let go. She absorbs most of her resentment psychosomatically ("I never knew what it was to be sick until I was married. And then it was just one thing right after the other.") She has a tactic for minimizing this resentment: in her selection of entertainment she chooses only material that makes her laugh. Thus, she avoids television and motion picture dramas:

I like anything that I can laugh [at] because I figure all day long it's one problem after another. I like anything I can just relax with. It's—the same when I pick out my movies. I don't want to go to anything that I have to go through deep drama and feel when I come out that I just—oh, sobbed my heart out. I don't want that because I think life in itself is bad enough when you stop and think about it. And I figure I'd just as soon get a laugh. [Emphasis supplied.]

She also discharges part of her resentment vicariously through empathizing with boxing matches on television. She insists on watching them although she says it "gives her children fits."

It would be unfair, however, to create the impression that this was a ruthlessly selfish woman. On the contrary, Mrs. Boyle is compulsively devoted to caring for her children and husband. She is permissive to a surprising degree in dealing with her children—considering the religious code to which she adheres. And she respects the integrity of all individuals to an extent we found among few other persons of any faith.

Mrs. Boyle's personality is also affected by her social class situation. She comes from a middle class home in a city near New Haven. She had aspired to professional status and chose nurse's training because she felt it offered a woman the best chance to achieve that standing. Her parents were comfortably well-to-do merchants. Her mother's parents were French Canadian, with a tradition for education. Her grandfather was a college graduate and an uncle was a Roman Catholic archbishop. Her father was of German Lutheran stock, richer than her mother's parents, but of a cultural tradition that esteemed a trade and derogated an education. There was no conflict over religion between her parents. The children were made Roman Catholics but her father remained a Lutheran.

And I wouldn't have changed him for anything in the world. He was just the most wonderful Dad a person could have, Protestant or Catholic. He brought us up with a very liberal mind. . . . They were married in a Catholic parish— not in a church, in a rectory. And . . . we were taught to believe that the Protestants were just as good as we were; only that they were brought up differently. They believed in the same God, and that's the way we were brought up. But they never, I never remember hearing religion discussed in our house, other than on a decent basis. I mean there was never any comparing or anything.

While her parents were permissive in religion, her mother exercised positive behavioral controls that irked her deeply. She was forced to take piano lessons for ten years, and singing lessons, for which she commuted to a nearby town. In her teens, when she dated boys, her mother forced her to get home early and otherwise held the reins strictly on her.

Even before she met her husband, Mrs. Boyle valued her faith so highly that it broke up several romances. On one occasion she and a young Protestant were getting seriously interested in each other when she severed relations bcause she "could never give up her religion" and it "would have been unreasonable to expect him to give up his." On another occasion she could have married a wealthy young man who was a Presbyterian and who wanted her to "turn."

I would never have known what it was to lift my fingers to dust or wash, but he was a Presbyterian and wanted me to turn. I came very near it. I was on a train and was going down to New York to be married. . . . I got off here in New Haven. I couldn't go through with it.

While this incident may have been reconstructed in retrospect for sake of heightened dramatic impact, the fact remains that the anecdote illustrates her attachment to her faith.

Her parents seem to have hoped she would be able to move into higher social circles and endeavored to equip her for such mobility. She resisted this parental direction. Now there is no piano in her house and she expresses complete distaste for the idea of a singing career. In a home where the father did not value college education highly, and certainly not for a girl, she formed her plan for a professional career in nursing. After a two-year post graduate course she was ready for nursing teaching. She had already gained experience in several types of nursing duty. As a last stage of preparation she began private duty nursing. One of her first patients was the man she was to marry. Her professional career ended when she married at age 25. Her present recollection of the transition expresses her underlying resentment:

I still say it was too early [she laughed). Marriage at its best is a hard life. It's all professions in one. You have to be a nurse. You have to be a book-keeper. You have to be a psychiatrist [laughing again]. There's no two ways about it. You do. And, why you have to be a maid. You have to be a cook. You have to be a seamstress. You have to be practically everything there is in the book, all rolled in one. It's a *hard* job [laughs], to do it right. It's a *terrific* job. [Emphasis in original.]

The light laughing touch did not obscure the staccato emphasis with which she voiced this criticism. After seventeen years of marriage, Mrs. Boyle has a comfortable home with four normal children and an apparently devoted husband. Yet there are indications that her upward social mobility wishes are frustrated. Her husband's income is less than that of their neighbors, many of whom in addition to higher income enjoy the class perquisites of being Yale faculty members. At his present age (51) and type of employment (branch sales manager), Boyle is probably receiving as much pay as he ever will. But in recent years as the family multiplied and living costs rose, it has not been too ample. True, they are able to rent the same summer house "at the shore" that they have used for years. And Mrs. Boyle takes pride in pointing out that they are not spending all their income. With unconscious acceptance of male chauvinism, she says:

We are looking forward to giving all of our children as high an education as they'll be able to take. If they're not smart enough, we won't push them. But if they are, we'd like to see even [sic] the girls have a college education.

The Boyles maintain, within their income, a rather higher standard of living than their financial resources would lead one to expect. Besides the costs of home maintenance, there are two children in parochial schools and the family does considerable entertaining. Mrs. Boyle spends a lot of time in planning new and attractive dishes for buffets and dinners when her husband's business friends and their wives are invited in. She gets much help from cooking programs on television, ("I've had things here that people raved about."). It has been possible for the Boyles to stretch their income to cover all these demands, but at considerable emotional and physical cost to Mrs. Boyle. She said:

I'm not active in clubs and I don't go out card playing like a good many of them do. And I busy myself right here in the house. One time I had a woman who took care of the two older children, and a housekeeper, and I was getting so that I had more aches and pains than a woman ninety. And it was for the simple reason that I didn't have anything to do. . . . I was driving everybody crazy—running to the doctor. And I was just getting to be nothing but a neurotic. I had nothing to do but think of myself. . . . I found myself doing more and more work all the time. And I'm very contented. I don't have half as many aches. . . . When I do it, I know it's done and done right.

Despite this statement, Mrs. Boyle, at the time of the interview, was convalescing from a major surgical operation which had hospitalized her for weeks. This was one in a series of major and minor illnesses that plague her constantly. There is reasonable evidence in the interview to relate her illnesses and her neurotic anxiety to conflicts revolving around her professional career drive, her social aspirations and her duty role as mother and wife. We have already mentioned her preparation for upward mobility. She has achieved some of her goals, but has not been able to feel comfortable with the behavior and values of her neighborhood and its social groupings—especially where those values run counter to her religious beliefs.

RELIGION IN THE LIFE OF THE BOYLES. Just what is the meaning of religion for Mrs. Boyle? It is mysticism. It is the assurance of authoritarian support. She explained the "meaning" of her faith thus.

Well, you see over there [pointing to rosary]. I say that every day. I haven't skipped that in years. And I have a very deep feeling. I have never once asked for a thing—I don't ask for the impossible and I don't ask for a million dollars or anything crazy—when I ask for anything—it might be for good health or it might be for a neighbor that is carrying a child that is not expected to live because of a toxic condition or something, or it might be as I did for my Dad, a speedy and a happy death, he was suffering so terribly. I have never yet asked for anything that it hasn't been granted. And I have so much belief in my

prayers and in my beads—my rosary—that I know that I couldn't have had it
in any other religion because nobody else believes in those beads nor do they
believe in those Novenas that we say.

The recent surgery had required 37 days in a hospital and at times she was
near death. She credited her survival to a "miraculous medal" that she wore
around her neck and refused to let the nurses remove. She concluded: "How
could you drop that faith? . . . I've always felt that way."

Mrs. Boyle's religion appears to be devoid of conceptual, theological content. No hint of such meaning appeared in the lengthy interview. But her
religion does include more than confidence in the efficacy of prayer. It is a
moral code, sanctioned by arbitrary, if mystical authority. She is an obedient
follower of this code. She had a priest come to bless their house when they
moved in. She attends Mass every Sunday and says her rosary every day.
She listens to Catholic broadcasts on radio and television.

One of the values she derives from Sheen is significant to our analysis of
his many-layered approach. Sheen's most important function for Mrs. Boyle
seems to be his ability to settle her doubts about actions of the Church that
conflict with her personal moral standards—such as the sanctioning of
divorce by the Church in certain cases:

He clears up a lot of ideas that I may have had. There's quite a few different
things that I question. About different people getting divorce or separations—
I can't see it. When the Catholic Church believes in one thing and you read
about something else, then I will question those things. And he'll inevitably
come out with it two or three weeks afterwards and clear up these things that I
had been wondering how the Church could excuse a person like that, you know.

Kevin Boyle, the husband, is unusually zealous in his religious life. He attends Mass and Communion every day of the year; has done so for 24 years.
She says it is "as natural for him as smoking is for some people." She obviously admires—almost reveres—her husband. She feels his good qualities
are grounded in his devotion to religion:

If I had his disposition that's all I'd ask for. He doesn't change from one day
to the next. Very easy-tempered. Very easygoing. . . . Everybody says he should
have been a priest. . . . He wouldn't have it if you said he was religious [laughs
proudly]. No, he wouldn't have it at all. The day hasn't begun for him, you see,
until he has gone to church. . . . I'd say he is far more religious than I. He
makes two retreats a year. He goes in November, and he goes to a monastery in
either April or May. And he has the most wonderful disposition I think God ever
gave any man.

Mrs. Boyle accepts the Roman Catholic woman's subordinate role to her husband as well as to the Church. Her husband's dominance in the home is epitomized by his ruling about Mass:

He makes all of us go to Communion [on Sunday]. I mean, even if we didn't want to go [laughs]. But he thinks it's a good habit to install [sic] in the children. He thinks that they—like he acquired the habit of going every day, he feels that if he makes the children go every week they will acquire that habit.

While Mrs. Boyle believes devoutly in the Roman Catholic ritual, she reveals unconsciously the fact that she has implicit reservations about its basis. She abruptly rejects the notion of "getting friendly" or "fraternizing" with her priest. She thinks priests should be kept "at a distance" socially. She was anxious that we not misunderstand; she believes in giving as much money as possible for contributions for the poor, and cakes for cake sales. But she doesn't believe in inviting priests to dinner. To do so would be to perceive them as human beings, not as symbols in ritual:

Once you get too friendly, I think you're missing out on a lot of what they really stand for.

This feeling that the sacrosanct nature of the religion would not withstand too close scrutiny again was reported in relation to nuns. She said that she has some very dear friends who are nuns and that she takes them out for rides. She will not, however, invite them to her home because:

I don't want them to be discontented. By the time you become too friendly with them and take them into your home, they figure they're missing something, where if they don't see anything but what they're used to, then they're satisfied in their surroundings. And why, you know, spoil that illusion?

Mrs. Boyle's ideas about her children's religion teach an observer a great deal about her own beliefs. The children are not being trained in religious ethnocentrism. They recognize that there are Methodists and German Lutherans and others who are "every bit as good as us." Mrs. Boyle does not demand that her children shall marry Roman Catholics. This policy and her essentially nonrational conception of religion are clear from her statement:

If Ann was to marry tomorrow and wanted to marry a Protestant, I wouldn't say anything—as long as I knew he was decent, you know. Because I've seen it work out, and I know it can work out, because it did, right in my own family. But, of course, as they say, there is a feeling. But I think we're getting more educated about it all the time. I'd hate to think that we weren't. I think it would be terrible, because after all, if you believe in God at all, you know that there is one God. It's just that you've been brought up a little bit differently.

It's like if you were French and you were brought up to eat certain foods. And if you're German, you're brought up to eat German foods. You're brought up in religion, and it's just that you're brought up that way, that's all. It's hard to change, that's all.

It does not follow that she would willingly see her children "turn" from Roman Catholicism. She frankly says that her influence, for what it was worth, would be brought to bear to prevent such action.

HER VIEW OF SOCIETY. Mrs. Boyle has an unusually high degree of respect for individual integrity. This quality comes out in many ways.

She gives every evidence of appreciating the unique and diverse qualities found among her four children. Her boy, she said with wry amusement, is so interested in sports of all kinds that she half suspects he may want to choose a coaching career. Her twelve-year-old girl has an encyclopedic curiosity about the physical world (weather, rocks, et cetera) that embarrasses her because of her own inability to give the required information. Consequently, she is glad that this girl finds much information (on which she takes systematic notes) in the travel documentaries seen on television. Reacting violently against her own parental controls as a child, we find Mrs. Boyle able to go to sleep before her oldest daughter comes in from a date, although her husband "stays up and frets" until she comes home.

Mrs. Boyle's attitudes on interpersonal issues are colored by her resentment against social class distinctions. She feels that ability, rather than social position, should be the test of acceptance in peer groups. For example, she thinks the social caste requirements for membership in the New Haven Junior League are:

. . . terrible. I wouldn't join it for all the money in the world. They tried to get me to join it.

She has a related feeling about the public schools in the neighborhood where she now lives. She thinks they are bad for her two children who attend them because her children get ideas of living from their playmates that are "over their heads." She especially deplores the lack of uniforms for girls in school, which she feels opens the way to unfair discrimination in the social life of the children, based on the ability to buy clothes. She also objects to the excessive lack of discipline in the "progressive" public school. She is anxious, for all these reasons, to have her children attend parochial high schools.

Consistently, Mrs. Boyle applies the same logic to her relations with minority races. She feels that Negroes in New Haven are subject to more disadvantages than other groups.

[They] are restricted to custodial jobs and this is wrong. If they're good they should be allowed to do it. I mean, they didn't ask for their black [skins]. It could have been me as well as they that had the black skin.

Her experience with Negroes has been limited to having a Negro servant in the past who "was perfectly wonderful—if she went home without kissing the children good-by, they used to cry and carry on." She balances these remarks with:

I'll grant you there's some of them that you've got to be very careful of. But those of them that I've come in contact with—I mean—I've always felt they were just all right. . . .

And on Negro housing problems:

They're not allowed but only in one section and, uh, I think they firmly believe themselves—they'd rather be together in their own section. There's—it's true you might find one or two who would like to get out and mix in but they don't as a whole. They'd rather stay in their own little group. But you don't often see those people getting any kind of a break as far as conditions are concerned—not here anyway.

Significantly, Mrs. Boyle herself raised the ultimate question to test her race views: would she want Negroes living next to her? She frankly expressed uncertainty as to what her reaction might be. She hoped she would take it as a matter of course:

I've always been brought up to believe that you pay attention to who lives in your own house. If you're doing what's right in your own house, you're not supposed to pay any attention to what they're doing over there. You've your own worries. That's what I think I'd be. I don't know.

This is a half-view of the Christian concept of love; while respecting the rights of other persons negatively by refraining from hurting them, she seemed to say that she has no obligation to help them. In social terms, her attitude amounts to a sort of upper middle class anomie. Such an anomic position is indicated by the absence of any comments on issues of a political nature in the long interview. While we know the Boyles are Republicans, we were left in the dark as to what, if any, attitudes they might have on domestic or international political issues, or for that matter, local issues in New Haven.

LEISURE TIME AND THE MASS MEDIA. The Boyles' leisure is organized around television, radio, spectator sports and participant sports. There was no evidence that they read any books. They do read a number of magazines—*Life*,

Look, Good Housekeeping, Sign, The Catholic Digest. Their only newspaper is the New Haven *Register.*

Television is "just a part of our way of living." They had a convincing demonstration of this the preceding winter when during an ice storm they were deprived of electricity for three days:

We were near crazy. My husband said, "What did we do before we had television?" He said, "Well, can't you play cards? Why don't you color? Why don't you read a book? Read a book!" Everybody around here was just *lost.* They didn't know what to do.

Their television set has had a "terrific workout" in the three years they have had it. In that period they have worn out three picture tubes.

We have already noted Mrs. Boyle's liking for boxing and comedy programs. She dislikes violent crime programs.

Those killing things—I just can't stand it! Some of them are so terrible! [The children disagree and she does not actively oppose them.] They sit here just glued to the set. And I don't think that is good. There's not much that I do about it. If I'm in here I'll switch it. I won't let them look at it. But if I'm not home, they'll watch them all.

When her husband is home, Mrs. Boyle will leave the living room when the crime shows come on after 10 P.M., but he will watch them until the stations go off the air about 2 A.M. Both of the adults said they watch Swazey and one other news program, Studio One, the Kraft Theatre, Philco Theatre, and Starlight Theatre. Comedy programs they particularly like are: I Love Lucy, I Married Joan, My Friend Irma, Beulah, Colgate Hour, Godfrey, Gracie Allen, Amos and Andy, and Martin and Lewis. Mrs. Boyle dislikes television soap operas for the same reason she prefers comedy to serious drama:

I can't see it. Life is troublesome enough without seeing this wife take this man from this other wife and the mother-in-law making it so hard for the daughter-in-law. I just don't go for it.

She also avoids Strike It Rich, Break the Bank and similar shows. Her daytime viewing is limited to cooking programs ("You'd be surprised, with the parties I give, the ideas I've gotten from TV. And I got that cookbook over there through the TV."), and ball games. She and her husband watch all television sports except wrestling. The children are left free to choose their own programs. The youngest enjoyed Ding Dong School and was also interested in the Kate Smith hour, Garry Moore, all puppet programs and all commercials containing cartoons. For evening viewing the children preferred Godfrey, Amos and Andy, Gracie Allen, Groucho Marx, Ed Sullivan, Martin and Lewis and all crime shows. They did not like Eddie Cantor or Caesar and Coca. Milton Berle was disliked by all except the youngest.

The Boyle children have a complicated pattern of interweaving homework with viewing of particular programs, beginning about 4:30 with the Early Show. If this program is good on a particular day, they'll come downstairs, leaving their homework, which they begin on arrival home from school, and watch for an hour. Then they study until dinner is ready. They get back to the television immediately after dinner. The price of seeing evening programs is that they have finished their homework. Bedtime for the two youngest is 8:00 and 8:30 respectively in the winter and 9:00 in the summer. Mrs. Boyle reported she has little trouble getting the children to bed:

I just tell them to go and they go. I'm not kidding myself by saying they don't give me an argument about it, but I don't listen to the argument. I just say, "That's enough and you've got to go!"

The children supplement their television viewing by using their individual radios to hear popular music while studying in their rooms. They do only a moderate amount of comic-book reading. Mrs. Boyle permits them to read the Bugs Bunny, Humpty-Dumpty, Archie type, but forbids them to bring those of the Batman variety into the house.

The whole family has many outside-the-house activities. Boyle is a member of the Knights of Columbus, the Holy Name Society and the Retreat League. Mrs. Boyle belongs only to an Association of Nurses and the PTA. Neither of these organizations takes much of her time. She swims, bowls, skates and hikes, while formerly she enjoyed golf, tennis, basketball and bicycle riding. Boyle plays tennis, swims, bowls, skates, hikes and rides bicycle; formerly he also enjoyed golf, horseback riding, basketball and football. Both enjoy spectator sports. They attended two football games, one baseball game and three or four basketball games the preceding season. They go to the movies and the legitimate theater four times a year each. They drive out to the country to get away from the city about every other week. Summer vacations are regularly spent at the seashore. The children are members of the appropriate peer groups, such as Boy Scouts, Girl Scouts, et cetera, with the curious-minded twelve-year-old girl belonging to a scientific club.

RELIGIOUS RADIO AND TELEVISION. The Boyles hear The Greatest Story Ever Told, though Mrs. Boyle did not indicate this program has a serious hold on their interests or effect on their beliefs. The children watch an unidentified Sunday morning program which deals with "questions on the Bible." The whole family watches and enjoys Frontiers of Faith:

We listen to the Protestant part. And the Jewish. My goodness; a lot of the time you'd swear that you were listening to your own. And in the Presbyterian there—it was just the same, almost as a Mass. In fact one day we were watching and we thought it was.

Here, as in her general view of religion, an interest in ritual obscures the conceptual content of religion.

The Boyles also had watched the National Council programs of Bible puppets:

I liked it very much. And so did the children. We all stayed right there and saw all of them. We enjoyed it very much.

Here again the technique (puppets) rather than content appears to have attracted their interest.

We have already noted one important use Mrs. Boyle makes of the Sheen program. The whole family watches him regularly, as a matter of religious loyalty. What is their attitude toward him?

Of course, being Catholic, we're a little prejudiced. We don't miss him, unless we have to. If we don't get him on a Tuesday night we get him on Sunday, on a rebroadcast.

Like the Richardsons the Boyles perceive Sheen's content to be generally religious rather than Roman Catholicism:

He's not preaching the Catholicity of everything. He does on some phases, but I mean, I think he's speaking to a whole group, the way many of the ministers do. When they get up they don't, uh, definitely stay with one religion. They're just talking about God and the whole, and His principles.

According to Mrs. Boyle, the whole family enjoys Sheen. Her explanation of the appealing qualities in his program is mostly based on her face-to-face perception of him in devotional services:

Int.: What is it about him that you like?
Mrs. B.: Well, it's—that he holds your interest, I mean. And there's something about him—he doesn't use words or language that's not understandable, even to the younger ones, I mean. And if he does use a word that is a little bit vague, or thinks he does, and you don't understand it, he will definitely break it down. And of course I like him because I have met him personally and have listened to him a good many times in person when he came here to do devotionals and things like that. And, of course [laughs], he's a lot more dynamic if you can see him in person. Oh, it's just—I don't know what it is. It just seems

as though he hypnotizes you, and I think he could talk on any subject and you'd sit there and you don't care how long he takes, where with most people, regardless who they are, after an hour passes you're on edge. But not with him. I don't know why. Maybe it's the tone of his voice, or the way he presents it. I don't know but I know that you just go right along with him. And when he could hold my seven-year-old daughter's attention, there's something [laughs]. I don't think she understands half of it, but she'll sit there and just watch him, you know.

It is plain from Mrs. Boyle's analysis that the multilayered idea patterns of the Bishop are welded into dynamic unity by the personality that presents them. Whereas with some viewers (e.g., the Voskuils) Sheen stands for knowledge and the intellect, for the Boyles he stands for infallible advice on the proper style of life. It is eloquent of the intimacy of the relation between Sheen and his audience members that he creates the illusion of two-way communication. Note how she said that if he uses a word that is a little bit vague "and you don't understand it, he will definitely break it down."

Unlike some of the families we have interviewed and analyzed, the Boyles are firmly committed to religion. The religious radio and television programs they use, regardless of the sponsorship, are perceived in ways that agree with and strengthen that commitment. The chance is remote that Mrs. Boyle would change her religious outlook because of radio or television programs. Her faith is compounded of mysticism, uncritical acceptance of "given" moral attitudes and voluntary subordination to an authoritative dogma that casts her in a subordinate role as wife-mother. Her belief that this role is divinely ordained provides the rationalization for driving herself compulsively beyond the limits of exhaustion. In a sense, her faith enables her to tolerate a life that the same faith makes intolerable.

The only chink in this close-knit faith structure is in her conceptual view of the individual; here she operates in rational rather than in emotional terms. Here, if anywhere, the Protestant concern for the dignity of the individual human being may have a specific appeal for her. We have not stressed the fact that Mrs. Boyle made it clear that some of her happiest recollections as well as her most deep-felt values are tied to her memories of her Protestant father. Her resentment of manipulation by others, her feeling for the rights of persons who are exploited, her discomfort with some of the neighborhood values, her fear that her children may not experience the few things from her childhood she sees as meaningful and honest—these are bound up with her memory of a father whose faith she rejected, but whose values are basic in her attitudes.

How do we view Mrs. Boyle in relation to the essential postulates of

Protestantism adopted for this study? We concluded that Mrs. Boyle does not accept the premise that an individual deals directly with God. She depends upon earthly intermediaries in the person of the Roman Catholic hierarchy; although she recognizes implicitly that the mediation is somewhat illusory. There is no evidence that she accepts the Bible as a guide. Only in relation to her concept of the person is she accessible to the Protestant viewpoint. She is wedded to her faith and her role within it. The possibility of personality change is almost nonexistent. The physical and psychological forces that make her partly resentful of her fate will continue to operate until her children mature and she is released from her motherly duties. Then a change may be in order as she may be free to renew her professional life.

A COMPARISON

The Richardsons and the Boyles have similar tastes in television programs and both families are heavy viewers of television. They share an attitude toward Sheen, both believing that he preaches "goodness" or "religion in general," not Roman Catholicism. Thus, both identify religion with middle class morality of a conservative sort. Here, with television, the resemblance between the two families ceases. The Richardsons are isolated socially; the Boyles are not, and the Boyles are friendly with non-Roman Catholics. The Richardson home is cold and empty of spirit; that of the Boyles is warm and full of the values compatible with their faith. The Richardsons regard their children as mannequins to be manipulated; the Boyles view their children as persons with unique qualities to be enjoyed and personalities to be nurtured toward a full life. The Richardsons would control their children tightly; the Boyles have a much more permissive policy, even in tolerance of other religious beliefs. Interestingly, both families seem to be consciously trying to mount the ladder of social mobility. The climb wears least on the Boyles.

CHAPTER 16

Personality Traits in the Audience for Protestant Programs

The Peale Audience

The combined audience for the Peale radio and television programs would be typically represented by a childless Protestant household in social class III. The household head would be in his thirties, with a high school education. The interview chunk did not include any Peale listeners who precisely fitted that pattern. We have chosen for analysis two persons who supplied clear-cut evidence of being helped by Peale in ways that pinpoint the influence and effects of his programs. Both of these persons also represent substantial groups in the Peale audience.

The George Clarks

Background Data

Social Class: IV
Rent apartment
Own television and radio sets
Income: $3,501–$5,000

	Husband	Wife
Occupation:	Factory worker	Clerk
Education:	High school	High school
Age:	59	51
Religious Background:	Protestant	Protestant
Church Attended:	None	Congregational Christian
Preoccupation:		Self
Children: None		

Only Mrs. Clark participated in this interview. Her image of herself is of a tired, apathetic and resigned person of middle age who craves the human warmth of love and whom life has frustrated in many ways. The chief frustrations are a husband she considers inadequate and her childlessness. The marriage seems to be a cold relationship between weak individuals who lean on each other without either of them getting much support from the other. Status and convention have important influence on Mrs. Clark. She has many of the earmarks of the tradition-directed person. She accepts—resentfully—her place in life. Any desires to improve her social status seem to have been submerged by her marriage. She is submissive to authority and identifies herself with it. Politically, she is convinced that in the light of world conditions we can only "pray for the right leader to be elected." Spiritually, she is routinely active in her church. Personally, various signs indicate she has sexual drives that clamor for release but are repressed with conventional strictures. Her psychological strategy seems to be a rationalization that a drab life is all she is entitled to—that it is righteous and just, and that anything better or different would be sinful. She therefore does not permit herself to contemplate ventures which might relieve the monotony of her existence but would entail the possibility of criticism either from others or from her own conviction of what is right and proper.

These conclusions are supported by interview material. They also are consistent with her scores on the F-scale. Overall her score is 5.35—considerably higher than the average of the interview chunk. Her highest score is on conventionalism—6.75, with other high scores being registered for authoritarian submission (6.57), anti-intraception (6.25), sex (6.00) and authoritarian aggression (5.62). Significantly, in view of the impotent role we perceive Mrs. Clark has adopted for herself, her lowest score is on power and toughness (4.14).

Mrs. Clark's parents emigrated from Chicago in the 1890's, prior to her birth. They had been Congregationalists in Chicago and joined the Congregational church in their new neighborhood. Mrs. Clark grew up in this church and has never attended any other. She began teaching in the church school when she was sixteen. She was married at 23, and for the next eighteen years, while she was a housewife, she was superintendent of the junior department in the church school. She greatly admired her minister of this period and valued his friendship. She reported he was quick to perceive— "from the expression on your face"—the onset of personal problems and quick to offer his help. Mrs. Clark frequently sought his counsel.

When she was 40, Mrs. Clark began to experience a series of crises. She realized she would be unable to bear a child—a bitter disappointment. Her husband fell seriously ill. She found work as an office clerk when she was 41, although she had never worked before. Her minister resigned and was replaced by a man whom she thought was both unperceptive and unapproachable. But she continued to attend church regularly and to teach in the church school.

Mrs. Clark stated frankly she was not happy in her job. She had difficulty getting along with several supervisors. By the time she was 48, she was in an emotional crisis. She was in bitter conflict with her supervisor whom she was convinced was persecuting her. She was "in a bad mental state" concerning the office situation which was "entirely out of my hands." She wanted advice from her minister but felt, since he had not perceived she was in trouble, he would neither be interested nor understand. She stopped teaching in church school, feeling her agitated mental condition made her both an unworthy and an ineffective teacher.

The crisis also included the "forced" sale of the Clark house to Negroes and movement to an apartment. Mrs. Clark did not associate this incident with her mental distress and bitterness. Such dissociation was typical of her.

It was in this condition that Mrs. Clark began to listen regularly to Peale on the radio. She wrote for his literature. She had heard Peale intermittently before, but the pertinence of his message led her, in extremity, to make his program a central feature of her life in her crisis. Peale gave her relief from her anxiety. He made her see that other people faced the same kind of interpersonal problems she did. She looked around and discovered that literally this was true of persons in her own office. She lost her feeling of isolation in her anxiety.

What was it about Peale's program that helped her?

I was quite interested in his program because of the actual experiences it seemed to me he could give. And the firmness of his voice made me have belief. I do think he has a wonderful voice and a clear speech that makes you have confidence in what he is telling you. And he related so many experiences similar to what I was going through. And then also they would—at the close of the program—give the announcement about this booklet. So immediately I wrote, thinking it would help me.

When the booklet came I found it most valuable. I used it and it helped me a great deal in working out my own problems. It was a little selfish, maybe, in me, but it was what I felt I needed and I continued to listen to him each Sunday until I went back into my church work again. Now I'm teaching and have to leave home at nine, so I don't get to hear him, and I haven't for a year now. But up to that time his programs meant a great deal to me [pause] and my husband also.

All told, she heard Peale's program each week for about a year. In retrospect she analyzed it further in these terms:

Mrs. C.: I do think his program was most helpful to people with a disturbed mind. We think sometimes we're ill. And it's mental—purely mental—you're confused. You don't know why you get that way sometimes. And it's only through the spiritual that I think we can combat it. That's the way I feel—from my own experience [nervous laugh].

Int.: And you feel that the elements in the Peale program which were helpful to you were the appropriateness of the messages—

Mrs. C.: That's right.

Int.: Plus the firmness and the inspirational quality of the voice.

Mrs. C.: Um hunh. Yes, sir.

Int.: I wonder how it would be if you had exactly the same words but a different voice. Would it mean as much to you?

Mrs. C.: Well, I've wondered about that. Because I do think that firmness of his—well, when he speaks I just feel that he knows what he's talking about. And a lot of times I think that when we listen to our own ministers in our own church, we wonder sometimes—I have—about the sureness of their thoughts on these things. But it seems like I've never had that feeling with him. I just always thought: Well, he said so and he knows. And it was just that firmness that made you have confidence in him and what he said.

The psychotherapy derived from Peale was described when the interviewer asked her about her actions after listening to him.

I did take different actions, but I took them all within myself. I was to blame a good deal for my own personality problems. I had to change my way of thinking entirely to cope with the situation. I'm still in the process of working it out, hoping I haven't hurt myself to humble myself too much. Sometimes we get angry within. There is a righteous anger as well. We have to stand up on our own—up for what we think is right. . . . But if we do it in an understanding way, it's better for both parties. And as he has often said, we have to pray for them as well as ourselves—which is not so easy.

The role of religious radio has been introduced out of the customary order early in the analysis of this interview because of its central position in the life of Mrs. Clark. In analyzing her relation to religion, it is necessary to raise certain questions not dealt with in the discussion of the interpersonal problems on which she obtained help from the Peale program. It is plain that Peale's role was that of the husband whose wisdom and authority could be relied on to solve interpersonal problems. Apart from her work-centered problems on which she obtained help from Peale, what other problems and attitudes in personal relations did she have?

We have noted that Mrs. Clark is uncertain about her relationships with herself. Her concern and confusion over whether she had gone too far in humbling herself in the office situation showed she does not have a sure, confident self-image. Her ego is so submerged in conventional attitudes she has difficulty identifying it. She has systematically compartmentalized the conflicting elements in her attitudes and behavior. Such unconscious dissociation could only produce anxiety.

RELIGION IN HER LIFE. Mrs. Clark's lack of certainty extends to the one area where she feels some degree of competence—religion. She reads the Bible every day. Each Monday she begins preparing the next Sunday's church school lesson. But, in the interview, she was unable to describe or define her religious convictions. Her lack of certainty about them extended to an unwillingness to commit herself on the "religiosity" items on the F-scale. Her church school teaching is descriptive; she avoids interpretation.

Her religious beliefs are conventionalized. Witness her conception of the role of the minister. One cannot escape the conclusion that her relation to the church is social and temporal, not spiritual. Religion provides a form for social activity; it is not a functional power in her inner-life process. Mrs. Clark seems never to have grasped the inner meaning and the life of the Christian Gospel.

The weakness of spiritual values was noteworthy in the Clark husband-wife relationship, as she described it. Clark is a factory machine worker. He has held the same job in the same plant for thirty-two years. He has never joined the union, nor sought to rise to a supervisory rank. Mrs. Clark's words and intonations as she described her husband and his work showed that she thought him to be an inadequate husband. He has failed her in the three critical functions of a husband. He has not given her a child. He has not provided economic security: she has had to take upon herself part of the man's role of wage earner. He has not bolstered and extended her social prestige; he does not even participate in her social world, the church.

The interview gave no evidence of warmth, respect, mutual sharing, deep affection between husband and wife. Their tastes are divergent, even in their use of their leisure time watching television and on vacations. Both the Clarks appear to be weak and convention-bound. Their mutual support emotionally is as tenuous as their perceptions of themselves as persons.

HER VIEW OF SOCIETY. Mrs. Clark is anomic in relation to society at large. She has voted Democratic regularly simply because it was her husband's wish. But she voiced no attitudes on national or international affairs, except for the most trite clichés. She had no views on corruption in government. When the question of the possible influence religion could have on corruption was raised, she said vaguely that the churches should "stick together" and do something—she did not know what—about it. She eschewed any discussion of the issues in the pending national election, saying, "That's bigger than I'm able to think of, but we should pray for the right leader the next time." When the issue of Asia and communism was raised, she gave, as if by rote, the view that continued mission work there would be desirable. To stimulate her, the interviewer posed the issue as one of taking bombs or Bibles to the Asians, to which she responded:

Bibles may be slower but in the long run will be better . . . *we can't let our feelings get the better of us.* [Emphasis supplied.]

Her aggressive tendencies, thus thinly overlaid with religious slogans, are apparently shared by her husband, for she reported that he sometimes says "we should get it over with in Asia"—presumably by all-out warfare.

The aggressiveness toward out-groups, revealed in relation to Asians, was confirmed by her attitudes toward minority groups in the United States. Mrs. Clark opened the interview, even before the tape recorder was connected, by apologizing for her three-room apartment. She explained they had lived there only a few years; that they had been forced to sell the home they occupied for twenty-five years, because Negroes came into the neighborhood; that when they sold their house (at a low price) they were the last whites in a black block. She reported at length on this incident. Her friends had talked to her about the "un-Christian" nature of her feelings toward Negroes. Yet she was frightened at night and frightened at the thought that should she need help there would be no one but Negro neighbors who would come to her. She feels that cities should prevent the Negroes from doing what they did to her. Cities should provide segregated housing for Negroes.

Not all Negroes are bad. The "better class" of Negroes are "all right." It is the "others" who "cause trouble" and "we've got to educate them." Projecting her own hostility, she said that Negroes resent whites as much as whites resent them. She reported unenthusiastically on her minister's exchange of pulpits with a Negro pastor three years previously. The response to the Negro preacher

. . . was not too good. Some were generous but many were opposed.

"Generosity," incidentally, is a word she used in such contexts with disapproving overtones.

The interviewer asked Mrs. Clark what she thought Dr. Peale and Dr. Sockman would say about her housing problem in relation to the Negroes. She first avoided the question in relation to Peale, saying she had "wondered about it" and changing the subject. When the question was reintroduced, she replied in very apathetic tones that she thought

. . . he would say Negroes had as much right in this world as we do and we have to meet it [the housing problem] some way.

As for Sockman, she responded promptly that he would be

. . . very generous—he more often talks along that line than Peale—I think Peale talks more about personal problems.

Mrs. Clark has a consistent pattern of prejudice in personal relations which is more open than latent. Crystallization of the prejudice, as with other persons interviewed, centers in the problem area where economic and social competition between the out-group and the in-group has been sharpest—in this instance, in housing. Rather symbolically, she put a signature to the portrait of her ethnocentrism by telling us that she organized and was president for two terms of a chapter of a secret women's fraternal organization within her church.

LEISURE TIME AND THE MASS MEDIA. The Clarks have an automobile. He has a hobby, fishing, and ties his own flies. Mrs. Clark takes pictures with a Leica and does handwork, such as knitting. Fishing is a bone of contention between them. On their last vacation, they spent half of it fishing (to please him) and half of it visiting friends (to please her). She was slightly acid about the problem.

The Clarks' principal leisure-time activity, except for weekends, is television watching. Reading is secondary. On weekends they visit friends and relatives or entertain. Then canasta playing is a favorite activity.

The Clarks had owned a television set more than a year at the time of the interview. Clark bought the set and, at first, Mrs. Clark "couldn't stand it." Gradually, she came to like, then to be captured by, television. Husband and wife watch each night from six to ten o'clock. They would like to watch more, but they go to bed at ten. She said, resignedly, "When you work, you don't have much time."

They view a wide variety of programs. Mrs. Clark likes musical shows, such as The Hit Parade and Fred Waring; variety and quiz programs; some drama. She watches Swazey every night. He is her chief news source, though she "glances through" the evening Register. Significantly, Ted Mack is one of her favorites ("He's so gracious—so kind to everyone."), and she dislikes Groucho Marx ("I don't admire his sarcasm. He's very unkind to people."), but watches him regularly. She described her enthusiasm for Juvenile Jury in the warm tones of affection she always used for children.

Clark likes crime shows; Mrs. Clark does not. ("There's so much bad in the world that when I'm home relaxing I'd prefer not to see something like that to think of.") Clark greatly enjoys boxing and baseball and watches them whenever he can. Mrs. Clark dislikes them, but sometimes watches. She reserves the time when he watches wrestling for work on her Sunday school lessons.

One incident from her television viewing pointed up the degree of anomie and conventionality in Mrs. Clark's thinking. She described a documentary on communism that she had watched. She detailed the political theme of the drama; but she did not perceive it in political terms, but as a moralistic tale designed to show that young people who experiment with unconventional behavior will be seduced before they realize what is happening to them.

RELIGIOUS RADIO AND TELEVISION. Listening to Peale has been Mrs. Clark's most significant use of religious broadcasting. She also hears Sockman from time to time, and likes him "very very much." She knows the schedule of programs sponsored by the local council of churches and listens intermittently. She has heard Fuller a few times—not enough to form a judgment on him. She was a regular Sheen listener when he spoke on The Catholic Hour and has transferred her interest to his television program.

Sheen makes "very good statements . . . they make you think a great deal." Mrs. Clark was impressed by Sheen's description of the training given to Roman Catholic priests. She did not know about the graduate education of Protestant ministers. She admires the readiness of Sheen—and every priest —to speak with authority on any topic, in contrast to the tentativeness of much Protestant clerical opinion. The priests "take the thing world wide," are dependable sources and power centers.

We concluded that religious television and radio programs are an important source of information and opinion for Mrs. Clark. They are also a yardstick against which she can measure the performance of her own minister. They have not led her to an understanding of the Christian Gospel that comprehends its absolute demands for commitment and conduct, nor have they advanced her theological orientation. On the other hand, listening to Peale renewed her sense of responsibility to her church—especially to the children—and brought her back to resume her Sunday school teaching. Quasi-clinical help of the kind provided by Peale, which will reduce her fears and anxieties and provide useful guides for conduct, is an important function of religious broadcasting in Mrs. Clark's life.

John West

Background Data

Social Class: I
Owns home
Owns television and radio sets
Income: Over $15,000
Occupation: Owns business
Education: College graduate
Age: 55
Religious Background: Protestant
Church Attended: Congregational Christian
Preoccupation: Formal religion—self
Children: Adult daughter

Our second Peale listener is a very different type of person from Mrs. Clark. While the Peale audience is centered in the lower middle class, a number of his listeners are high-ranking business executives. Well-to-do Protestant businessmen seem to find Peale's message relevant to both their spiritual and their business lives. John West is a striking example of this group.

Despite the fact that he had agreed to the interview, a half hour of patient persuasion was necessary before West would permit the tape recorder to be used. He would not fill out an F-scale.

West is a handsome, tall, heavy-set man with a powerful bass voice. (He says his wife complains, "I roar like a bull.") He walks with a spring, exudes vitality, looks younger than he is. Upon acquaintance, he is friendly and attractive.

West owns a large appliance business and holds a franchise from one of the largest companies in the field. He has spent most of his adult life in this business, first as a salesman, then as a franchised dealer. He has enjoyed eighteen years of profitable business as a proprietor and is now wealthy.

As a precollege youth, West had been a regular churchgoer. He and his wife were baptized in the same church, and were in Sunday school together to the end of high school. But throughout his adult life West had not attended church at all until two years prior to the interview. Then he heard Norman Vincent Peale speak at a dealers' convention and underwent a conversion. Our problem is to inquire as to the meaning for Mr. West and our society of this conversion experience.

West is vague as to just how Peale won him:

[I] can't recall anything he said. It was a cumulation. . . . It was his delivery, his sincerity, his just plain horse sense . . . his philosophy—and incidentally, not a soul got up and left in that large auditorium when he talked and that's un-usual. It was straight . . . and plain, to the point, and he talked in language we can understand.

I like him very, very much. I think he's doing a splendid job. I think he does a job of reawakening people and making them a little more conscious of their church life. I think that took place in my wife and myself.

West became vigorously interested in Peale and his writings and sent for literature offered on the radio program. At the same time, he rediscovered the Bible:

The other thing, I think, was I came back and bought a transalation [sic] of the Bible, and—uh. Having not very determinedly tried to read the Bible in the past, I had picked it up and become very easily discouraged and laid it down. So coupled with Dr. Peale and the transalation which I believe anyone can read and enjoy and understand—that was an added impetus for me to become active in the church.

Still following Peale's advice, he and his wife began to shop around for a church connection. They found a suitable upper class church and joined. By the time of the interview his name was being placed in nomination for one of the official posts in the church. He now reads his Bible regularly, under-scoring it as he goes. Apparently his wife reads the Bible along with him. For background, West also reads Oursler's *Greatest Story Ever Told*, and *Greatest Book Ever Written*. The Bible is a continuing source of inspira-tion:

It's made a tremendous change, I think, in my thinking, in my actions, in her [his wife]—and [pause] I think that if everybody would read a transalation. . . . The only reason a man isn't a Christian is that he hasn't read the Bible, I be-lieve. Setting down [sic] and—in your home or in your office, and reading the Bible—the translation of the Bible—you find an awakening in yourself. Now Dr. Peale's booklets that he puts out could be classed in that same category. . . . If you don't have a Bible, pick up one of his pamphlets. It's almost a transala-tion—in one form. . . . It might be kind of your first primer—books to start on to awaken an interest in you. Dr. Peale's pamphlets are—uh, when you read those books, they're very interesting reading. They're not quite so heavy and they awaken an interest. And then you pick up your Bible. And you've got a sort of a spark there [that will spur you to] want to go through. It kind of in-trigues you to read it. And then . . . you can't help being impressed, reading those books.

This impassioned, if incoherent, testimonial goes on to summarize, very cor-rectly as we shall later see, the effects of the reading:

It—I think, stimulates self-analysis. You begin to study yourself a little better. You have an awakening of conscience—your own conscience. I—it seems that that's the one—the inner man, that has to be awakened, not the outer man. . . . That's what I think happened to me.

Adopting the position of a "reformed rapscallion," he says his "thoughts and actions are now different."

Mr. West's interest in the Bible did not stop with his church relationship. He first bought and gave copies of it to the key men in his business and then to all his employees. Sales meetings of his staff include references to Peale's pamphlets, and sometimes to the Bible, which generate extensive discussion of religious matters:

It has brought me closer understanding of my employees and I think perhaps they know me better. We think nearer alike. We have more—I think—admiration or—we think more of each other. I think there's a cementing relationship between us. . . . I even have used Dr. Peale's little booklets for sales meetings. . . . I think they enjoy them thoroughly, for there's so many things applicable to a businessman in his church and Dr. Peale's sermons—*why we're both dealing in people.* They're different paths but I think their reaction is about the same. That if we'll follow the teachings of the church and apply them to our business with these people, I think we gain the respect and admiration from our customers. Of course, with that as the basis, the foundation of all sound business—as people who have confidence. I have a lot more confidence in my employees because they can't help read this book—the Bible—this transalation, without it reflecting in their actions towards our customers. It *builds business because they reflect to the customer that we're—uh, a good Christian firm and that our dealings are based on the Christian faith.* [Emphasis supplied.]

While West concedes that this new direction in his life, like the "reawakened interest in church" on the part of others, may be influenced by the stress of the times, the process he describes as having taken place in himself is internal and subjective.

The preceding self-portrait is the self-image that West now presents to the world. It is what an open-ended interview based on directive questions would elicit as the effects of Peale's sermons and booklets and the Bible. The *real* needs and values in West, which emerge with clarity from the nondirective portions of this interview, have sufficiently general significance to make him a classical type for his sort. Psychologically his personality is accessible to more precise analysis than are most of our interviewees because his internal dynamics are so clearly delimited. What are the essential need-value processes operating in West?

The nature of the internal conflict which had prepared West for his conversion experience and what followed it can best be described by relating the story of how he came to have watertight compartments or dissociations in his values and behavior.

West's childhood included the implantation of Calvinistic values. He went to church and Sunday school, and there began his romantic attachment to the girl who became his wife. At college he was an enthusiastic fraternity man—in the early twenties when the fraternity social values rated drinking, athletics and heterosexual play highly. It does not appear that he got much out of the academic side of college. After college he tried out different styles of life. He did construction work. He worked in lumber gangs. He was a short-order cook in a restaurant. He was an automobile mechanic.

His mature life was largely centered on his work. Starting with labor on a production line, he progressed to being a salesman and then, after a ruthless struggle, acquired his own dealer franchise. The ethics of his business, then as now, were as close an approximation to the all-out aggressiveness of "rugged individualism" as could be found in our society. He played this business "game" ably, for he prospered.

Given his robust health and extroverted play habits developed in his youth, it was inevitable that his nonbusiness life would include elements of dissociation later to cause him anxiety. At some point along the way he married his childhood sweetheart and they had one child about 1925—a girl. He told us nothing of what either the daughter or wife looks like, or of their personalities or interests. We never even heard their names. It is probable that his parental function during the girl's childhood was limited to providing the high standard of living appropriate to his class, community and neighborhood, together with token participation in her recreation. Lack of concern with, and essentially, lack of respect for both wife and child may be inferred. His social life followed the pattern developed earlier. Drinking parties with "the boys," golf, fishing, football and baseball games, horse races, boxing and wrestling matches occupied his time away from the office. He was the sort of man who could enjoy his associations in the American Legion (including its stag parties), his fraternity alumni association (he still subscribes to and reads its magazine), luncheon clubs and the dealers' association. He participated enthusiastically in all of them. Riesman would say that he followed (and occasionally led) in using his leisure according to peer group patterns of taste formation. In all of this he was other-directed, doing what was approved by his peers, with hardly a backward glance at his childhood conscience values associated with religion and strict morality.

Shortly after World War II West's daughter met and fell in love with a young South American businessman. He was of good family and a Protestant. West stated he could find nothing objectionable in the young man. Yet he refused to consent to his daughter's marriage. She was firm in her intention to marry. Stalling desperately, West wrote to a reputable U.S. citizen in Latin America, asking him to check on the fiance and his family. West's last defense against the marriage was demolished by a report that son and family were of impeccable social, religious and business standing. The marriage ceremony was performed in a Protestant church in the Latin-American country, with Mrs. West present. She returned to the United States completely satisfied with the marriage and with her son-in-law and his family.

She came back so impressed on how intelligent they were and what Christian people they were and if we knew them better we would have entirely different impressions of those people. And she found that true. She came back with a very kindly feeling for the people. She couldn't understand why we could have wars if we knew those people. And I expect that's true. [Emphasis in original.]

West implicitly recognized the "loss" of his daughter as being the trigger that set in motion the events that led to his return to active church membership. He related how his daughter had asked him to become active in the church when she was in her early teens—long before her marriage. He had refused, and as a result she had joined a church of her own selection rather than his own. West was convinced that had he joined the church when his daughter beseeched him to do so, she would not have married as she did. Consequently, he felt guilty. In voluntarily introducing the narration of the marriage incident, he prefaced with:

That's quite a story and I don't like to tell it [pause] but I'll tell you.

He feels that he neglected his daughter. This feeling called forth the companion feeling that he had neglected his wife. The corollary of these feelings is that he feels guilty over having been a "rapscallion," his summary term for his deviations from what he now regards as proper husband-and-father-behavior. It was in this frame of mind that he said he was "awakened" by Peale. This "awakening" he understands as being that of a conscience which had slumbered too long.

This account of how his need and value system became neurotically dissociated is cast entirely in West's own frame of reference. It is appropriate now to examine it analytically. What is the strategy and what are the tactics of West's personality as religion touches it? We have the material in a five-hour interview to supply explicit as well as unconscious clues.

West needed to find a strategy to cope with a complicated fear-guilt situation. He had passed his fiftieth birthday and had his first real intimations of his mortality—he was nearing old age. He had accumulated all the money he could ever need, by means that troubled his conscience. He had maintained a conventional domestic establishment with wife and daughter, but had never functioned fully as husband and father. Instead he had found companionship and entertainment outside his family. He came near to losing his dealer franchise because of heavy drinking. His energies were beginning to wane and he became sated, or bored, with the endless round of business contacts and parties. His daughter's unwelcome marriage constituted the catalytic agent around which he focused his guilt. The strategy he adopted was thus motivated by guilt. Our problem now is to determine the source of that guilt and the meaning of the strategy which it impelled him to adopt.

It is clear that the guilt was *not* based on a quasi-sexual interest in his daughter, as crude applications of Freudian theory might suggest. West was never, as far as the interview discloses, close enough to his daughter to justify a suspicion of this sort. Such a source for his guilt would require that he have had a warm relationship with her; the fact is that the relationship was shadowy in the extreme.

Was the guilt inspired by his early indoctrination with Calvinist theological notions about sin and salvation? We think that is one of the sources of it. He may have disregarded his religious code of ethics during most of his adult life; but face-to-face with life's end, his transgressions of that code plague his conscience. There is a substratum of this kind of guilt in West, but it is by no means strong enough to account for all the facts. He makes much of promoting religion through church attendance, Bible reading, pamphlets, the mass media, but there is nothing in his strategy to indicate a real recognition of guilt in the inner-directed, conscience-driven style of Calvinism. Instead he implicitly takes the position that there is really nothing wrong with being unchurched; it's just that such people are missing something, as a family without a television set or an automobile is said by the dealer to be missing something. What West, prior to his conversion, had been missing was the practical, down to earth version of religion which did not force him to reject anything as positively *bad*, but instead told him in substance, "It's your negative thinking, not your actions, that makes you uncomfortable. You've just not developed all of your potentialities."

A second possible source of West's guilt is his conviction that he violated the ethical standards of his peers, including his business friends who were active in the church and the "they" who could remove his dealer franchise. This sort of other-directed censure became sufficiently palpable to West by the time he reached fifty that he began to heed it. When the heeding took him to church, he who had been "lost" and thought himself "found" was in truth still only at the beginning of his conversion experience. For basically, the theology of his church which he considers sacrosanct is couched in a language different from that of his peers who brought him there. "Sin" and "personal maladjustment" are not interchangeable. It may be questioned whether his church was better prepared to understand his terms than he was to understand its terms.

Sin-consciousness and peer-group disapproval might be taken together as a sufficient explanation of West's guilt. However, we think that another source for his guilt exists, one in which he approaches a theological under-standing of "sin." He is aware he has been wrong in reducing human beings to the level of commodities ("We're both [Dr. Peale and himself] dealing in people").

Manipulation, whether it was by subtle conditioning, by cajolery, by puffery or by forceful aggression, was the principal means by which West built his business fortune. A parallel mode of manipulation and exploita-tion underlay his treatment of women. Tenderness and understanding of women were conspicuously absent from his long interview. Most of his life he has been implicitly contemptuous of women and has used them rather than negotiated with them as individuals with personal dignity and integrity. We think it is a belated recognition that he was wrong in depriving people of their innate integrity which spurred his conversion. His guilt over neglect of his daughter has valid human meaning in this context. Similarly, he can now respect his wife as he never did before. He could even report, deferen-tially, her view that war would be unthinkable if "we" could get acquainted with foreigners as she did. Whereas previously they were without common interests, now he and his wife can share their introduction to religion. He can confess, as he does in the paragraph quoted below, that "there's good in pretty near everybody."

West extends this belated recognition of the rights of individuals to his business life, but apparently only through projection to the ethics of others than himself. For example, he was indignant that his appliance manufacturer had told its dealers during the war to dismiss their salesmen when civilian goods were not being produced and had added in substance the advice: you aren't responsible for them any more than we're responsible for you. West likewise now feels that big corporations, like big government, are likely to "walk over the rights of the people and they would destroy the rights of the people if they had a chance."

On balance, we feel that the heaviest loading of his guilt feelings comes from the disapproval of his peers, with anxiety from his commodity-concept of humanity and from conviction of his sinfulness, following in that order.

The strategy designed to cope with West's guilt is the promotion of Peale's approach to religion. His policy is to devote himself to religion as he understands it. He will participate fully in his church, through attendance, financial support and service. In so doing, he will operate at the level of business manager of a spiritual enterprise, the profit-and-loss statement of which will be measured in terms of Bibles distributed and members gained. At the same time, he will "apply" his version of religion in his business, and to his financial profit there; for as we noted in an earlier quotation, the reputation of being a moral, Christian establishment will be a valuable asset for an appliance dealer. Through this policy, he expects to expiate his guilt feelings.

This solution to his guilt problem—to the extent that it is a solution—has the convenient advantage of permitting him to integrate the previously dissociated areas of his life while only superficially turning away from his previous philosophy. Christianity for West at his present stage of religious development bears a noticeable resemblance to the values so clearly stated for Babbitt by Sinclair Lewis and for Christ by Bruce Barton a generation earlier. Christ does not ask him to give up his business or even reduce his profits. Quite the contrary; the essence of Christianity is a sales technique which permits a man to square his conscience with God, through the forms of religious observance in company with his peers, and simultaneously to build a more profitable business, with employees tied closer to employer.

West was precise in his plan for the promotion of religion. He would extend the salesman ethic technique to the church:

A direct selling appeal may raise barriers. But get on the other side and let him [the prospective customer] answer his own questions. I think it [the Bible] will stir up within him—he'll take a pretty good look at himself, and he can't help if he's got anything good in him—and I think there's good in pretty near anybody—I've never met a really bad man, or very few of them, all the way through—that will kindle that feeling. Because I look at myself. Boy, I was a rapscallion [laughs] and mabe I still am.

"Churches are staid, cold places for a stranger to walk in." He would have them physically as warm, comfortable and attractive as a well-appointed sales display room. Inside, the down-to-earth practical religion would be made available in a friendly, warm, courteous atmosphere. Rather than high-pressure the customers with promises and threats, he would have the church approach the prospect delicately. Have you ever read a translation? We don't blame you for not being able to read the King James Version. Do you know there is a version you can read? When the customers read the Bible it will work on them and they, too, will attend church regularly.

We've got very few people going to church compared to those on the outside. If we could get those people into the church, the coffers of the church would be far fuller than they are now, even with small contributions.

And with the larger funds derived from more members, the church could open more branches with more modern equipment, and distribute more Bibles to more unbelievers who in turn would come to church and further swell the coffers. The plan is identical with that for selling appliances except for the substitution of Bibles for appliances.

West's strategy may be evaluated in terms of the fundamentals of Protestantism. West accepts fully the postulate that man should deal directly with God without the necessity of an intermediary. He probably always accepted this view although he may be able to verbalize it better since his conversion. The postulate concerning the use of the Bible is one that West has accepted only since his conversion. The practice of using it and of attending church may lead to substantive growth in his understanding. The possibility certainly exists of such growth. The probability of such growth depends on factors associated with his view of human beings.

This turns us to the third essential postulate, that of the God-given integrity of the individual. We have noted that West's business, social, family and now religious areas of life are largely based on a denial of this postulate. The probability of major change—learning—in this area of interpersonal relations on the part of a man in his mid-fifties probably is not great. His accumulation of liabilities here is substantial. We have already described how he lacked respect for men and women, in business and in play. To this we must now add other evidence of his lack of understanding of people. He is full of prejudice, which is to say that he organizes his perceptions of people ethnocentrically, with his own in-group in the center. Businessmen in his own church and their equals are this in-group. Politicians he places a long distance away from it, for he holds the conventional stereotype of the goodness of the private businessman and the essential badness of the politician. The story of his daughter's courtship by the "foreigner" illustrates his ethnocentrism. Even the fact that the son-in-law is a Protestant, a private businessman vouched for by West's own authority, could not qualify him for acceptance. West avoided probes for his views on race relations. However, he was openly patronizing toward workingmen. He assumed, as a matter of course, that all unions are radical and dangerous. He seems to place all minority groups on lower rungs of his value ladder. Lastly, West's conception of his relation to civil authority is naïve and does not show an understanding of civic responsibility. He accepts uncritically the cliché often used by political demagogues but seldom believed by them:

We should get back to our Constitution. I'd be very happy, and I think anybody would that's in business today if our government would get out of business and get back to the Constitution of the United States and act as they are authorized by our Constitution to act.

Any broadening of West's understanding of the nature and integrity of persons will depend in large part upon the influence of his minister and his church. Arguing from a psychological base, one might say that growth in human understanding is now possible, but unlikely. But the power of the Gospel to change lives may not be measured in terms of probabilities. When the Gospel takes hold, it forces spiritual growth in the most unlikely subjects.

If such growth does not take place as a consequence of his new relation with the church, the Bible and his wife, then what has appeared to be West's conversion will turn out to be only a "reconditioning" which did not wear well. In this event, the effect of Peale will have been like that of aspirin: it will have temporarily deadened the pain of anxiety without being a specific. If, on the contrary, West does learn a new and clear understanding of the will of God and the nature of human dignity, the effects on him will be really chastening. Then, for the first time, will he realize the extent of his previous sin. Then will he come face to face with his real guilt. Then will a genuine conversion take place.

LEISURE TIME AND THE MASS MEDIA. It will be useful to close this analysis with a summary of West's attitudes toward the mass media. His consumption of them is conventional and limited. He reads very little in books, except for his new-found interest in those by Oursler and Lloyd Douglas. He reported reading Life, Saturday Evening Post, Kiplinger's, Guideposts, and his fraternity magazine. His wife reads Harper's Bazaar. He reads the local New Haven Register casually.

West does not see religious programs on television. He does watch one drama, the Philco Playhouse, and two news programs, Swazey and a local roundup. Among variety programs he mentioned only Godfrey; among quiz programs, Juvenile Jury, Ted Mack and Groucho Marx; among musical programs, only Fred Waring; and among public issue programs, only Meet the Press. He enjoys football and boxing on television.

It appears that with his extroverted personal pattern of life, West has not had much time for the mass media. "Dealing in people," he is anything but isolated from them or dependent on vicarious contact by means of the media. His taste in mass media fare is as conventional as his season seats at the legitimate theater to see the New Haven tryouts of Broadway productions; both equally are peer-group dictated and productive of conversational small change for use in his social and business relations.

It is interesting, finally, to speculate on the reason for his nonuse of religious radio and television. It is possible that he, who practices manipulation of people by advertising and the mass media, is desensitized to such manipulation as far as his own perceptions are concerned. If this be true, then it would seem that Peale's effectiveness in reaching West came partly from Peale's personal magnetism, experienced in person, and partly from the fact that Peale was simultaneously being accepted by West's fellow businessmen. For such people as West, the radio or television program, whatever idea it was presenting, would seem powerless to convince unless backed up by the sanction of their peer-group approval.

West, like Mrs. Clark, was helped through a period of anxiety by Peale. In both cases Peale returned his listeners to a local church and a local pastor, where they took on active responsibilities as church members. And in each case the listener believes that the key to the solution of personal and interpersonal problems is to be found in Christian teaching.

The writers have indicated their suspicion that the therapy offered by Peale was shallow in both the spiritual and the psychological dimensions, and this is a criticism of Peale's approach that is quite widespread in religious circles. It is well to call attention to the fact, however, that within the dimensions where Peale seems to operate, he accomplished things that the churches and pastoral ministries to which these two people were related had failed to accomplish. He spoke to anxieties in terms that these anxious people recognized were relevant to their situations, and he relieved those anxieties in such a way that both persons became accessible to the deeper and more permanent ministries of the local pastor and the local church fellowship. West correctly understood that Peale did a good "selling job" on him, and as a selling job, it accomplished its purpose.

Radio and television have played the role of salesman for many products besides religion, and it may well be that this is what these media are best adapted to—getting the potential customer out to the nearest retail outlet for the product offered. It is of course ridiculously inadequate to try to reduce religion to sales jargon. But it is equally shortsighted for churchmen to pretend that spiritually immature minds do not need simple, even oversimplified truths to capture their imaginations. The role of a Norman Vincent Peale deserves some careful and constructive thinking by church leaders who are willing to think of radio and television as part of a larger strategy in which the local pastor can play the final and ultimately most important role.

The Sockman Audience

The general listener to Sockman on the radio is in social class I or II, elderly, Protestant, with some college education. Typically, he has a church background and orientation, although he is not necessarily a church attendant. Widows and widowers bulk large in this audience. But Sockman also appeals to married couples—and especially to men—of late middle age. We have chosen to analyze two classes of Sockman listeners, one a widow, the other a married couple. The widow was among the persons interviewed in Kansas City, Missouri, during the pilot phases of this study. Her type was duplicated in several instances in New Haven.

Mrs. Clara Wakefield

Background Data
Social Class: II
Rents apartment
Owns radio set, no television
Income: Over $15,000
Occupation: None
Education: Finishing school
Age: 71
Religious Background: Protestant
Church attended: None
Preoccupation: Self
Children: Four adult sons; one adult daughter

Mrs. Wakefield is a large-framed, handsome woman with a warm, outgoing·personality and a capacity for smiling at her own foibles. She lives alone in a four-room apartment with a panoramic view of the city. Her husband, a prosperous merchant, died in 1932, leaving her more than comfortably well off. She does not live luxuriously, but it is evident she can easily afford what she chooses to do. One of her choices is to contribute generously to her local Presbyterian church—which she never attends—Presbyterian missions and the Sockman program.

Mrs. Wakefield is enjoying her later life. She has been the wife and companion of a successful, self-made businessman—a man of power. She has seen her five children grow into well-adjusted adults, marry and establish secure, satisfying families. She played her role of wife and mother with happy zest. Her memories are sweet and she has no apparent regrets. She has long since adjusted to the loss of her husband. She now holds the position of benevolent matriarch to her children and grandchildren, accepting and returning their love and attention, but assuming no responsibility for their problems and decision making.

Her "duty" done, Mrs. Wakefield now feels free to indulge herself in the social life of her own age group—visiting, card playing, dabbling in art and art criticism, an occasional drink of sherry or even a highball. Except at one point she has no guilt feelings about her living and her little adventures, for her lifelong role has embodied solid, sober upper middle class virtues. But she volunteered she felt guilty for not setting her grandchildren an example of regular churchgoing.

Mrs. Wakefield's psychological poise and balance includes even the orientation of herself and her family within a historical perspective. She has written and published a brief autobiography for the benefit of her children and grandchildren. It is the life story of her family and its part in the pioneering development of the West. She regards a high standard of living as the natural reward of the pioneering efforts. How did she come to this belief?

Mrs. Wakefield was born in Detroit of Scotch-Irish Presbyterian parents. Her grandfather had been one of the first elders of the Presbyterian church in Detroit. The family moved by day coach to Kansas City in the late 1880's. There she was reared in a rather stern, God-fearing home. Her father would not permit liquor in the house. Church attendance and family prayers were compulsory.

In her late teens she was sent to New York City for finishing school. Her Midwestern values showed plainly in New York, for, as her autobiography tells us, she felt "like a revolutionary" when she sat in Central Park and watched the rich women drive past in their carriages with their tiny dogs on their laps.

She was twenty-one years old at the end of her second year in New York. It was time to marry her sweetheart in Kansas City. He was twenty-six years old and made his living selling bicycles on commission and organizing college fraternities. The year was 1901. In the next fifteen years the Wakefields had five children. Wakefield opened his store in Kansas City and prospered. The family was the center of her life while her children were growing up. Her autobiography presents a picture of psychologically healthy relationships between parents and children, as witness this passage:

War comes and finds us [in 1917] plugging away with youngsters going to both kindergarten and college. And our eldest stepping out into the world with parents too busy to supply the mature understanding that boys need so much. We were constantly demanding the oldest to act like a grown man instead of a wistful youth looking for excitement and thrill, trying to make his dreams come true. Too bad parents can understand certain children only when they are not pressed for time and by all the hurry and worry of sessions with children's diseases.

The Wakefields enjoyed a high standard of living. There were servants, and care of the family never meant drudgery for her. They had a summer home large enough for twenty guests.

When Wakefield died in 1932, all of the children were grown, even the youngest being in college. With no family responsibilities left, Mrs. Wakefield progressively relaxed her inner-directed style of life. Even her activity in her church—where Wakefield had been an elder and she a women's leader—dropped off. Two bouts of major surgery gave her the excuse for stopping church attendance. She substituted weekly listening to the Sockman program.

RELIGION IN HER LIFE. Mrs. Wakefield's concern with religion has been unobtrusive, but it has been an essential part of her life. She has always belonged to the local church her family joined when they came to Kansas City. She dutifully—and cheerfully—served first as primary teacher, then as Sunday school superintendent over a period of almost twenty years. She was also a church caller, specializing on new families in the community. She has always taken Presbyterianism to be her religion as a matter of course. ("There's no reason for us to be Presbyterian. We're just born that way.") But her views on church affiliation are not parochial. She said:

I'm just fed up with denominations. . . . Well, I think that they major so much on denomination that they forget Christianity. And I've been places where they sort of force the idea of what denomination you are. What difference does it make? . . . I believe that's one reason why I'm enjoying this radio program. Because there's no yak-yak about a denomination. That's a dreadful thing to put in here. [Laughing and pretending exaggerated horror at her language.]

She told a story about "a little old lady" of whom she asked, "Why do you go to church?" and who replied, "Oh, Mrs. Wakefield, I like to go through the religious motions." Mrs. Wakefield does not like the religious "motions" at all. The overt emotional quality of spiritual or social fellowship is unattractive, indeed repellent, to her. Religion is both subjective and rational for her. She views the worship service as a place to gain both spiritual renewal and direct guidance for conduct in the succeeding week. There is no evidence that she ever felt the need for personal or spiritual guidance from a minister. Therefore Sockman, whom she may never see, is just as satisfactory a pastor as is the minister of her local church—perhaps more so, since he can make no demands on her time or her emotional resources.

HER VIEW OF SOCIETY. Mrs. Wakefield talked freely about her religious convictions, but she was reticent about expressing opinions on political, economic and similar problems. The views she voiced were typically what one would expect to hear in the home of a conservative American businessman. She is a Republican and she does vote. In race and minority group relations, her attitude toward Negroes and "foreigners" was not actively hostile; rather she showed conventional stereotypical beliefs.

Mrs. Wakefield's F-scale scores confirm these conclusions about her social views. Her over-all score was 5.23, appreciably higher than average for the depth-interview chunk. Her highest scores were on destructiveness and cynicism, 7.00, anti-intraception, 6.75, sex, 6.33, and conventionalism, 6.00. Her lowest score was on superstition and stereotypy, 3.67, with power and toughness next to lowest, 4.43. She was strongly Protestant in her attitudes toward relationships between God and man and the concept of the Bible as a practical aid in the solution of day-to-day problems. She also indicated a high degree of respect for the sanctity and dignity of individual personality in interpersonal relationships. This respect for persons was apparent throughout the interview; even her group prejudices were divorced from individual relationships.

LEISURE TIME AND MASS MEDIA. All of Mrs. Wakefield's time is leisure time and the style in which she uses it has already been described in general terms. The mass media definitely do not dominate. She rejects television:

I wouldn't have the television thing—it's sort of commercial business. I don't like commercial business.

She is what might be called an incidental radio listener. She listens five to six hours a day when she is home.

Daytime serials are a favorite type of radio program for Mrs. Wakefield.

She does not listen every day, "only when I think of it." But she thinks of it enough to keep up with the story line on Against the Storm, Pepper Young's Family, Brighter Day, Road to Happiness and One Man's Family. She showed no embarrassment in admitting her enjoyment of the soap operas. The interviewer asked whether she thinks the solutions to interpersonal problems presented in such programs are realistic. She replied that some of the solutions are "perfectly splendid"—hardly a relevant response.

Another preferred type of program is the evening drama. She listens regularly to Lux Theatre, Theatre Guild and Hollywood Star Playhouse, and thinks they often present "perfectly wonderful" plays. Sometimes she enjoys a mystery show. She *reported* that she listens regularly to news programs and commentators, but was unable to name a single news commentator. She dislikes popular music and has only a perfunctory interest in symphonic music and opera on radio.

Except for radio, her chief interest in the mass media is in books. She was one of two persons in the depth interview sample who read books regularly. Mrs. Wakefield and her friends were in a "Great Books" class and were systematically plowing through that meaty agenda. The week following the interview they were to begin reading Karl Marx.

She claimed: "I read everything I can get ahold of." She subscribes to *Reader's Digest, National Geographic, American* and *Woman's Home Companion*, but did not comment on their content. She subscribes to and goes "straight through" the two Kansas City newspapers. She "used to go a lot" to movies in earlier years; now she sees not more than one or two a year. She still goes to the legitimate theater about three times a year.

RELIGIOUS RADIO. Mrs. Wakefield's interview was biased by the fact that it was taken during a pilot study and she had foreknowledge that the interviewers were associated with the National Council of Churches. On the one hand, this was an advantage, since Mrs. Wakefield went out of her way to explain carefully her relationship to the Sockman program and its effects on her. On the other hand, this knowledge led her to adopt a strategy of apologizing for her abandonment of church attendance by portraying herself as too ill and feeble to go to church. On the surface she presented a picture of a shut-in for whom Sockman's program was a satisfying but definitely inferior substitute for the experience of attending divine worship in church. She described how she listened to Sockman as she lay in bed each Sunday morning, leaving the interviewer to infer her reasons for not getting up.

The pretense of disability broke down progressively as the interview proceeded. Partly this happened because one of Mrs. Wakefield's friends, a widow sixty-five years old, was present and needled her with humorous gestures and giggles when she overplayed the shut-in role. Partly it was because Mrs. Wakefield is too honest and salty to endure such a role as a weakling long. The day after the interview she telephoned to apologize for all "the alibis I gave you yesterday about why I don't go to church."

Early in the interview she reported she had been listening to National Radio Pulpit since she heard Cadman in the 1920's. She said she had begun to depend upon the programs for her religious guidance and experience at the time of her first operation, soon after her husband's death. Her two operations, she said, had hit her hard.

And a person in that condition isn't able to get up and go to church. And then the crowds of people—the groups of people made me so weary that I just started listening to the radio. And it's just a perfect blessing to me.

Stung by the interviewer's summation that she was physically unable to attend church, however, she later "came clean":

It isn't a matter of being able to go out. I'm able to go anywhere in the world I want to go, whenever I want. It isn't that at all. It's a matter of being able to worship here on this radio and that, that satisfies me. And, uh, there we are. I'm perfectly content and happy to listen to this program. And that's my church activity.

Mrs. Wakefield considers Sockman to be her minister and said:

Dr. Sockman is tolerant and Christlike. And he leaves you something at the end of every service that you can work over in your mind during the following week and use, definitely.

It is the word which counts for her, and the simplicity with which Sockman says it gives the basic value to his program. Unlike any other person interviewed, she commented on other parts of the program besides the sermon, particularly the benediction:

There's no one that gives the benediction just like Dr. Sockman. You really feel blessed. But I expect that's because years ago somebody told me to relax and listen and really be blessed. And then you really are.

Once in a while, Mrs. Wakefield listens to other religious radio programs, but not regularly. She sometimes listens to Peale:

. . . Although his voice [laughs and gesticulates in protest toward the tape recorder]—his voice is not at all attractive. But what he has to say is very worth while, definitely.

She has heard the Old Fashioned Revival Hour and rejected it forthwith, although she remarked that when she was much younger they had gone to hear Billy Sunday and "loved to hear him" (presumably as a form of entertainment). She also listened for a brief period to a local program from the Church of Latter-day Saints. Occasionally she hears The Catholic Hour. She did not comment on the substance of either program.

Sockman's program serves a terminal function for people like Mrs. Wakefield. These older people may not attend church services for a number of reasons, not the least of which is that National Radio Pulpit is not only a satisfactory substitute but superior to what they feel they would receive in their own church. Their use of the program is subjective. It does not spark action or change personal convictions. It does provide comfort and a real reassurance of the importance of spiritual values already held.

If Riesman is right in his appraisal of modern society, inner-directed oldsters, like Mrs. Wakefield, will die and be replaced by aged people who are other-directed. If that occurs, Sockman's programs may be expected to have a declining audience of older people.

The Roland Austins

Background Data

Social class: III
Own home
Own radio set, no television
Income: $5,001–$7,500

	Husband	Wife
Occupation:	Office manager	Housewife
Education:	College graduate	College graduate
Age:	53	51
Religious background:	Protestant	Protestant
Church attended:	Methodist	Methodist
Preoccupation:	Primary: Family and home	Primary: Family and home
	Secondary: Work	Secondary: Formal religion

Children: Son: 17; Daughter: 14

The Austins are a pleasant, quiet couple who appear to be chiefly concerned with the everyday affairs of family and job and a small group of acquaintances, centering mainly in the church. Austin is a long-term employee of a corporation with nation-wide interests and has been subject to frequent transfers. The family has lived on the West Coast in both Oregon and California and in the Middle West. He has been in his present post longer than any other, has risen to a senior clerical position and may well have found his permanent niche. If no further promotions come, he probably will not feel frustrated or unduly disappointed. He likes his job and finds continuous satisfaction in handling its minutiae.

Respectability seems to be the central value in the images Mr. and Mrs. Austin hold of themselves and the society they live in. Respectability may fairly be defined as conformity to the practices and values of their peers— his office associates and the social group to which they both belong, stemming from the church. Religion has a great deal of influence and importance in their lives, but is subordinate to their conventionality and is used to buttress their concept of acceptable behavior.

And how do the Austins behave? In such a way that they will neither hurt nor exploit other persons nor positively dominate nor change any social situation they are a part of. No surface conflicts appeared in their relationship to each other. The children were not in the interview, but from the parents' report there is a warm bond of love within the family. They transfer their peer-group standards to the children. They will be satisfied if the girl contracts a marriage and has a family "like ours"; if the boy "marries a good girl" and reaches his father's vocational status. Their attitude toward persons outside the family are ethnocentric in the style of middle class people who rationalize their in-group versus out-group perceptions of people as being based on differences that justify resulting prejudices. Austin's F-scale score is 3.42, while hers is 3.07—both considerably lower than the 4.04 average for the sixty-two individuals in the interview "chunk" for whom this information was available. It is consistent, in the light of the portrait later to be drawn in their own words, that we find the highest subscale score for each of them is in authoritarian submission (5.14). His other subscale scores are about or below average. The scores indicate that Mrs. Austin is much tougher and more destructive and cynical than he, while Austin is much more projective and interested in sex than she is.

RELIGION IN THE LIFE OF THE AUSTINS. Austin was born in a small town in Kansas. His family were Friends (Quakers). Their church employed a minister, though, and he said, "the branch from which I came you would possibly recognize as a Presbyterian or a Methodist service for the most part." Austin voluntarily classified himself as a "fundamentalist"—i.e., opposed to "modernism" in theology. But he frowned on the use of revivalistic techniques as being beneath the dignity of the church. He emphasized strongly in various contexts his feeling that religion should be "practical" for everyday living. Austin discoursed at length on sectarian differences in worship technique. In spite of his extensive discussion of religion and his undeniably active church life, the interview revealed little substantive religious faith on Austin's part, and certain evidence suggested a real deficiency in understanding. For example, Austin has heard Sheen a good many times and reported:

There's a lot we agree with him on. He doesn't particularly deal with the doctrine of the Catholic Church. It's a matter of daily life with him.

Mrs. Austin was born in a small town in Minnesota. Her family were Methodists and a brother entered the Methodist ministry. "I just grew up in the church," she said. "I don't even remember when I became a member." She, like her husband, prefers conservative theology and preaching that is grounded in the Bible to "modernism." She shares his feeling that revival meetings are outmoded; but she reported her children have attended meetings of the Youth for Christ organization and enjoyed them. She said:

We might have at their age. That's what we're trying to figure out. But listening now we don't appreciate it particularly.

The Austins are members of the Methodist church "in our immediate community," a middle to lower middle class neighborhood where they own a seven-room house. Austin sings in the choir and plays the piano for a men's Bible class. He greatly enjoys both activities. Mrs. Austin is more active and more involved in the church leadership. She also sings in the choir. She is chairman of the junior department in the Sunday school and teaches a fifth-grade class. She is a member of the board of the Women's Society for Christian Service. She is a member of a prayer group that meets weekly and also participates in the city-wide World Day of Prayer service. Mrs. Austin estimated she spends one week day and two evenings in church, as well as Sunday morning. She reads the Bible daily, following one or another plan for consistent Bible study.

In spite of her active church life, Mrs. Austin, like her husband, showed little evidence that the compelling absolute of the Christian Gospel affects her thinking and action in significant ways. She made no reference to ways in which her faith had guided her in solving problems of living. She made no avowal of adherence to particular Christian ideas or doctrine, although one cannot disregard her attention to the Bible.

THEIR VIEW OF SOCIETY. The Austins apparently do not participate in civic affairs, nor do they seem to be interested in the larger spheres of politics, economics, international affairs, the United Nations, atomic energy and similar matters. Even in the church, their interest does not go beyond their local congregation. They are indifferent to missions, social action and the general affairs of Methodism. They showed no interest in the World Council, National Council or state and local councils of churches. The few opinions they ventured on the civil structure of society revealed conventional attitudes and a general lack of basic information.

We have suggested that the Austins' attitudes toward people are implicitly based on an assumption of "difference" that separates social groups in expedient ways. These "differences" embody skin color, language, religion, physical fitness, social class and numerous other factors. Their ethnocentrism and their Christianity are compartmentalized by the Austins; and they do not know that these two beliefs, which comprise the foundation pillars of their respectability, are in fundamental conflict.

The Austins' in-group versus out-group views were elicited by the query: "How do you feel about your neighborhood?" Austin volunteered:

It seems nice to hear the English language when you walk on the street, which you didn't always hear on the Coast. That's sure.

He then added:

A.: Natives here generally do not like the Negroes.
Int.: They don't? You mean folks who were born and brought up here. And you have a different attitude toward them on the West Coast?
A.: Somewhat. I wouldn't want to live amongst them.

Mrs. Austin was willing to confront the conflict between the Christian view of race relations and her own, although her husband was not:

Int.: I'd be curious to know what your impression would be of what Dr. Sockman would say if he were preaching on segregated schools.
A.: No, I wouldn't know what he would say.
Int.: Is there ever anything that he says that would lead you to make definite judgments about social problems?
Mrs. A.: Well, now that segregation business. I think, uh, uh, that we could very safely say that ideally Christ wouldn't approve of it. And I think probably Dr. Sockman would speak out that way. It seems to me that's the Biblical teaching. *But in our present day life we have to have certain tolerance for different groups and get along with each other.* And as I look at the colored folks and segregation, it seems to me they're much happier in their own group rather than mingling with too many white people, or thinking about intermarriage, for instance. And the white people the same. I believe that is true of most of the races or nationalities. Of course, we're finding the intermarriage of the boys who go to Korea and we're finding the same thing—well, the Germans of course are white. But, I think the color isn't what matters. [Emphasis supplied.]

By an unsubtle switch, the Biblical injunction to love your neighbor is perverted to a watered-down doctrine of tolerance between groups which she assumes to be based on vague "differences" that inevitably must set them apart. It is interesting that she states that the color is not what matters, for her rationalization of racial differences explicitly extends to other nationalities of whites (Germans) and to Jews.

Int.: How about a group that is of the same color but of a different religion, such as the Jewish group?

A.: You'll find just as much prejudice against the Jew as you do against colored people.

Int.: Here? Do you find—do you have neighbors who are Jews?

A.: One block over we have one Jewish family.

Mrs. A.: The back yard adjoins the corner of our lot.

Int.: Do they have any difficulty because they are Jewish?

Mrs. A.: I don't think so. Uh, there seem to be some characteristics of the Jew that stand out. The children thought the little [Jewish] girl was different in a way. She might have had some comments made that would hurt her. But she seemed to be the kind of person who wouldn't care what was said. And I just wonder if they develop that kind of *thick shell.* [Emphasis in original.]

The condoning of the cruelty of the neighbors toward the Jewish child was evident, both from what Mrs. Austin said and from her shrill emphasis on the "thick shell." The rigidity of the Austins' principle of "differences" on which they organize their perceptions of people comes clearly from the passage that followed immediately:

Int.: You mean a kind of a cultural trait. Something that comes from their religion or the family, or—

Mrs. A.: Or whether it is just a shell of defense, because they realize there will be some persecution. But you find the same thing true with the little girl who lives next to them. She isn't Jewish but she has a handicap. And the children are just as cruel about what they say about her. I think that's just the difference that is recognized.

There was no hint in this lengthy and nondirective exchange that the Christian should mitigate or strive to eliminate the calculated cruelty of treating people in this way. Ethnocentrism is assumed by the Austins to be natural and inevitable. Its unchristian nature is not recognized.

LEISURE TIME AND MASS MEDIA. The Austin use of the mass media consists of a moderate amount of radio listening and reading of the local newspaper, general circulation magazines and several religious journals. They seldom go to the movies. They have no television set, largely because they could receive only one channel from their location, but also because they are suspicious of the effects of television. Austin said:

I suppose if there were more channels so you could pick your own programs, it'd be less objectionable. There's good and bad in TV programs, same as in radio and everything else.

The Austins' leisure is much more occupied with serious music and with hobbies than with the mass media. He does a great deal of color photography. They like to hike; they spent their last vacation hiking and fishing in Canada. They have an extensive collection of phonograph records, consisting largely of opera and classical music.

Their radio listening is primarily to the "better" music programs. They follow the WQXR network, symphony concerts, opera. They remembered hearing the Robert Shaw Chorale under Protestant Radio Commission sponsorship.

The Austins get their news in capsule form from radio and the newspapers. He reported, "I get most of my news from the radio, except for financial news, which I get from newspapers." She summarized their newspaper reading as, "We read the headlines, maybe, pretty well." Mrs. Austin has no interest in radio news programs, but he listens regularly to news broadcasts and to several commentators. Drew Pearson is his favorite, "because he presents facts you seldom see in the newspapers and because I enjoy his predictions." He likes and believes Fulton Lewis, Jr. He listens to Murrow less frequently than to Lewis.

The only other regular radio listening is to dramas and sports, especially football, basketball and baseball. The whole family hears evening dramatic programs, and all enjoy them. Mrs. Austin rather shamefacedly admitted that she listens regularly to daytime serials, but refused to name the ones she hears.

They take five general circulation magazines, Reader's Digest, Life, Good Housekeeping, American and Pathfinder. Mrs. Austin reported, rather proudly, that they subscribe to the International Journal of Religious Education and to the Christian Herald. They read the Herald from cover to cover, she said. She is especially interested in its reviews of religious books: "Oh, no, I don't have time to read the books, but I like to know what's going on." They read no books at all.

RELIGIOUS RADIO. The Austins are real Sockman "fans." For years they listened together "practically every Sunday morning" until she became active in Sunday school in their present church. They were grateful when Sockman was switched to the afternoon on the local NBC outlet. However, they view Sockman in their own image, reading their own conservative views into what he says:

A.: I've enjoyed Dr. Sockman more than I have the summer speakers. For some reason or other his approach to a subject seems to be a little more to my liking in some respects. It is so realistically practical in his application of the Scriptures.

Int.: Can you give some examples?

A.: Well, offhand, probably not. It seems to me that his talks are always on everyday living life subjects, more than just a comment on what the Scripture says. It is application of what the Scripture means to our everyday life.

Mrs. A.: Well, he isn't neglecting the Scriptures, because he states a fact and then he goes all the way through the Bible finding the Scriptural basis for whatever he is going to say. Whereas some might just take a Scripture passage and describe what it means and where it came from, and give some application to our life.

Int.: Is he a better preacher than most of the preachers you have heard in your own churches?

A.: I would say, yes.

Int.: Would you say that he preaches a Gospel sermon?

Mrs. A.: Yes I would. I was particularly impressed one Sunday when he decided he was going to use some old-fashioned terminology and he did it on purpose.

Int.: Old-fashioned terminology?

Mrs. A.: Telling about his Savior, for instance. He was making it far from what you would think of as modernism.

A.: I wouldn't [call him a modernistic preacher]. I know some people do. I think because he doesn't use certain phraseology that they have been used to. I don't know altogether what his doctrine might be. I haven't heard anything that would make me think he was anything but fundamental and orthodox—a Gospel minister. . . . We could eliminate conservative, anyway. I would consider him fundamental.

There is no evidence they have used Sockman's teaching in solving their life problems. However, within their own context of what religion means, they have given a great deal of thought to what he says.

The Austins are interested in two other religious radio programs. One is Back to the Bible, a daily program of "straight Bible teaching," which is evidently transcribed. Mrs. Austin "likes very much" the music of the small chorus on the program. They classify this program as "fundamentalist." The other is the Old Fashioned Revival Hour which they like for its music. They do not listen to Fuller's talk, because

it is at a time of conversation . . . and we can hear the music without actually stopping conversation; but if you are going to hear a sermon, you would have to stop and concentrate.

Sockman, Sheen (whom they will watch on television if the opportunity is offered), daily fundamentalist Bible teaching and gospel music form the pattern of their use of religious radio. This is a great deal of listening, compared to the fact that most people hear or see only one religious program regularly. It may not be exceptional in their case, bcause the Austins are committed to a life style in which religious *practices* occupy a central position. National Radio Pulpit and any other program they can construe as fundamentalist can be fitted into this schema. The *content* of their religion is rigidly conventional within the framework of their social group. Even their "fundamentalism" is a conventional self-designation rather than a militant faith. They could not designate Sockman a "fundamentalist" preacher if they understood the content either of his message or of Protestant fundamentalism.

The Austins derive strength and satisfaction from their religious practices, but their experience seems to be subjective and selfish. Conventionality and conservatism make religion—and religious radio—for them a matter of taking, not giving—essentially a one-way street. When pushed, they will admit a conflict between certain of their attitudes and the Gospel as preached by Sockman; and when this happens Sockman quickly loses the battle to rationalizations so adept that they must reflect some history of the internal conflict of ideologies. One may hope that Sockman will continue to attract these good churchgoers with his technique, so he may have an opportunity to disturb them with his message; for this eminently reputable church family seems to understand most of the Christian Gospel except the central teaching concerning love of God and love of neighbor.

The Billy Graham Audience

The study found a small but significant audience for the Billy Graham program on radio and television. Radio listeners exceed television viewers. The Graham audience is heavily weighted with persons of not more than eleventh-grade education, persons over 65 years old and households where the male head is a skilled, semiskilled or unskilled worker.

The Nels Swensons

Background Data

Social class: IV
Own home
Own television and radio sets
Income: $5,001–$7,500

	Husband	Wife
Occupation:	Cabinetmaker	Housewife
Education:	Eighth grade	Eighth grade
Age:	68	66
Religious background:	Protestant	Protestant
Church attended:	Lutheran	Lutheran
Preoccupation:	Self	Self

Children: Adult daughter

The Swensons meet the specifications of the Graham audience. They also typify the Scandinavian immigrant population of New Haven. Both of them were born in rural Sweden. Swenson came to America and New Haven when he was eight years old, his wife when she was seventeen. His eighth-grade education, supplemented by correspondence courses, is not a fair measure either of his mental capacity or his skill at his trade. Still employed full time at 68, he can set his own retirement age.

The Swensons are lifelong, active Lutherans. They are in church every Sunday. Swenson was a church trustee for more than thirty years.

Both of the Swensons see themselves as "proper" people. They accept the Lutheran concept of divinely appointed vocation, and they are obedient to their "places in life," to their duties and to the will of God as it is interpreted to them through their church. They are moralistic and conventional in their judgments and attitudes. Both of them have high F-scale scores—higher than average for persons with their central interest—self. Swenson's total score is 4.72; Mrs. Swenson's 4.93. Significantly their highest scores on subscales were on conventionality, 6.24 for each of them, with the next highest being between 5.50 and 6.00 on authoritarian submission, destructiveness and cynicism for Mrs. Swenson, and on authoritarian aggression and authoritarian submission for her husband. This man and woman, despite their rigidities, are well-matched. They have long since adjusted their lives so tensions between them are minimized. All evidence in the interview indicated that they love and respect each other.

Physically, Swenson is large and rugged, with an abundant store of energy. Mrs. Swenson is short and stout. She suffers from eye trouble that limits her capacity to read, but her physical vigor is unimpaired. While Swenson works as hard as he ever did, both of them are relaxing somewhat psychologically. They have brought their daughter to maturity and seen her safely and happily married. Now they can enjoy certain pleasures of old age and relaxation, supported by the feeling that they have always done their duty.

RELIGION IN THE LIFE OF THE SWENSONS. Religion, above all else, has shaped the Swenson's way of life. They began with a strict Lutheran upbringing in Sweden which implanted an unswerving loyalty to the church. They transferred this loyalty to the church in New Haven of which they have been lifelong members. They had nothing but good to say of their church, and especially of the present pastor:

S.: We have a very good minister. He's almost like an evangelist. . . . I have never heard such a man.
Int.: Has he been with you long?
S.: About two years. He's a young man, too—about 35 years old, I guess. Strong voice. Kind of a slight fellow, but my goodness, what a voice he has!

On the content of his sermons, Swenson said:

He gives the Gospel a lot of new angles. He isn't like old-fashioned preachers.

Their appraisal was thus based on the authority and technique of the minister, and on his ability to attract new people to the congregation. The Swensons were not sophisticated in their ability to analyze the theology of their church. Like the Richardsons, they did not detect any fundamental cleavage between the doctrine preached by their own pastor and that of Sheen. They perceived Sheen as preaching a morality common to all faiths, without doctrinal content:

S.: I've heard Fulton J. Sheen on the radio and on television and as far as he preaches you wouldn't know that he was a Catholic. I mean like, if you converse with other Catholic people, over at work and all that.
Mrs. S.: They are all trying to get to the same place eventually —
Int.: —but by different roads?
Mrs. S.: Different roads.
S.: The way he preached last week was almost like Lutheran ministers would preach. He was talking about the Prodigal Son.

On issues relating to church activities the Swensons have conventional attitudes consistent with their upbringing. They were critical of the content of Sunday-school curriculum, feeling it should include more teaching of the Bible and less project work, singing and handwork. They recalled Swedish practice, where religion was taught for two hours a day in the school system. They regret the fact that the Lutherans do not have the widespread opportunities in the United States that the Roman Catholics do to teach religion in parochial schools. They feel that the churches are powerless to do anything about corruption in public life in the United States, except through preaching basic morality. On the other hand, the

Swensons feel that the church has the obligation to educate people against communism. Swenson, to be sure, revealed an insight into the causes of communism that was not shared by his wife who relied merely on stereo-typed formulas in her thinking on the subject. He said that communism won't make much "headway in this country. We live pretty well. When they get hungry, they think the rich fellow gets it all."

Most of the Swensons' moralistic judgments have a religious base. They are conscious of the possibility of sinning through their interest in television programs. Such sin may occur from overuse of the medium—although this worry over stewardship of time has not cut down their television viewing—or from what is watched. Swenson likes variety shows, especially those with pretty girls in the cast, but feels guilty about watching them. (He scored 5.35 on the sex subscale of the F-scale, indicating a moderately high degree of suppressed sex interest. Mrs. Swenson scored a neutral 3.00.) He justified his interest defensively by saying, "Some things in a lighter vein won't hurt you once in a while"; to which his wife responded dourly, "Well, we all have different opinions on radio and television." They consider smoking and drinking to be sinful—although neither is banned by Lutheran doctrine—and are critical of radio and television for broadcasting advertisements of beer, wine and tobacco.

Their morality is part of an authoritarian religious code by which they have governed themselves. The authority stems from the church, to which they have uncritically, and probably willingly, subordinated their own per-sonalities. Both of them expressed emphatic agreement with the F-scale statement, "In order to obtain divine assistance in life's crises, it is neces-sary to get it through your church. . . ." But the church is something more than an authority source. It has provided the Swensons their friends; their sure anchorage in a social group; a blueprint to guide every life activity; and now, in old age, the blessed assurance that life has not been lived in vain and that death is only the beginning, not the end.

Although the Swensons share the same religious beliefs, there was an in-teresting difference between them in their responses to the other two "re-ligiosity" items added to the F-scale. Swenson strongly feels that the minis-ter should be the final authority on belief and behavior and that the Bible is not a practical guide to living. Mrs. Swenson completely disagrees with him on both counts.

THEIR VIEW OF SOCIETY. The Swensons' relationships with other people are conventional ones for persons of their class. They have many friends and enjoy them very much. They are active in standard social organizations; the

Masons and Odd Fellows for him, Eastern Star and The Order of Vasa for her. He has belonged to a pinochle club for forty years and Mrs. Swenson to a bridge club for half that time; the social contacts being more important than the card playing. They have run the gamut of official and social organizations in the church.

Swenson is a member of the carpenters' union, AFL, but like his associates in the trade, he is a rugged individualist. Neither of the Swensons has ever been identified with a political party. Service as an air-raid warden during the war is the only quasi-public interest he has had.

Their attitudes on civil affairs are also conventional. Swenson repeated the clichés current in 1952 about the operation of the two-party political system:

> The Democrats have been in power too long. They need to be chased out and get a house-cleaning done. If the Republicans stay in too long it might be the same thing. It's a good thing for this country to have a two-party system and change over.

He conceded this "change-over" would not prevent corruption entirely, but entertained the vague hope that "it will stop it from getting too big, I suppose." He took a middle-of-the-road position on foreign policy. We should be "out of Korea," but he favored a unified Korea. As a long-run solution for Asian problems, he suggested:

> The people have not been educated on how to till their soil to raise food for themselves—that's the main trouble in China and India.

Mrs. Swenson betrayed a much more punitive frame of mind in such matters. She thought it was "too bad we didn't let MacArthur finish it while he was [in command in Korea]." She was also much more vocal than her husband about communism in the United States. She was particularly puzzled and incensed that so many professors, "people who should know better," have been disclosed as communists. It was as if this discovery led her to mistrust the authority figures she had always regarded as sacrosanct.

The Swensons preserved for the most part a carefully "proper" and neutral position on race relations: "Negroes are just as good as other people," etc. The only revealing break was his disclosure that she dislikes seeing Negroes boxing with whites, and her embarrassed admission that this was a fact plus the defensive remark, "That's my way of thinking."

We concluded that the Swensons adhere to conventional attitudes in their peer group on social and political issues, and that a well-defined ethnocentric view of people underlies their veneer of conventional tolerance.

LEISURE TIME AND MASS MEDIA. The Swensons' friends, social organizations and the upkeep of their neat, attractive home obviously take up a great deal of their leisure time. They also have hobbies; he does woodworking and she crochets and knits. Their use of the mass media is mostly confined to television. Radio and newspapers occupy a secondary position. Magazines and books are practically neglected. They used to attend motion pictures frequently. Swenson, in particular, enjoys movies. While his daughter was living at home, he would often go to the movies alone. He does not do this any more, since Mrs. Swenson would be left alone. He always goes to the circus, though, when it plays in New Haven.

Television is solely responsible for their dropping the movies. It has become a major factor in their lives:

S.: We miss it sometimes when it has gone on the bum for a week or so, and we don't know what to do with ourselves.

The Swensons have differing television tastes. Swenson's runs to variety shows—laughs and girls. Negatively, he has an escapist attitude toward television, as did Mrs. Boyle and others. He doesn't like "sob stories—hard luck. I think there's a lot of problems to life anyway, without looking at it on television."

Mrs. Swenson emphasized her interest in programs "you ought to watch," such as discussions and public issues. We deduced a number of reasons why she concentrated on these program types: (1) She cannot get news and opinion through reading, because of her weak eyes. (2) She is genuinely interested in self-improvement; in fact her conscience drives her to it. (3) She is worried about the violence and threats of violence in the world about her and she gets some release from tension from finding out what is going on in world and national affairs. (4) She knew she was being interviewed by a college professor and wanted to make an impression.

The Swensons watch television together, for the most part, compromising their divergences in taste. Their "check list" of programs watched regularly indicated they view a minimum of 34 hours per week, all of it concentrated in the hours between 4:00 and 10:30 P.M. They also do a lot of casual viewing. They had not been asked to prepare a list of their favorite programs in advance; but each of them clipped the daily television program logs from the newspaper and checked the programs he watched regularly. The two batches of clippings were presented to the interviewer as soon as he arrived.

Mrs. Swenson's list featured news, which she "likes best," but he agreed with a large number of her choices including Swazey, See It Now, American Forum, Meet the Press and America's Town Meeting. Swenson reported he regularly watches practically every variety show and comedy drama on the air. He and Mrs. Swenson agreed on Godfrey and Toast of the Town. Her choice in drama includes The Big Story, Lux Video Theatre, Westinghouse Theatre, Philco Playhouse and all mysteries. Paradoxically, she objected to the violence in the crime programs:

I don't think there ought to be so much shootin' and killin'. I don't see how that can be good for the young generation.

The only drama they agree on is Mama.

Swenson likes popular music programs like the Hit Parade. She does not. But they both watch and enjoy semiclassical programs such as the Firestone Hour, James Melton, and Paul Whiteman.

Quiz shows interest both of them and they agree on What's My Line, Twenty Questions and Strike It Rich. They perceive the latter in these terms:

S.: They do a lot of good.
Mrs. S.: I think that's a wonderful program. It helps a lot of people—needy people.

Mrs. Swenson likes Life Begins at Eighty best among the quiz shows. Swenson chooses Groucho Marx, whom she dislikes thoroughly because she thinks he is cruel.

Swenson likes animal programs, like Zoo Parade, and all sports. He watches boxing and wrestling regularly. Her aversion to seeing whites fight Negroes has already been noted. She is contemptuous of wrestling of which she said:

I don't like any of it. I don't want anything to do with it. How can anybody enjoy seeing people bat themselves almost to death?

Both of them believe public issues should be aired on television. Mrs. Swenson was enthusiastic about the Kefauver crime hearings. "It was good for people—it aroused them," she said. She would like to see important Congressional debates televised: "People should be informed on what's goin' on." Her husband told of learning what the issues were in the controversy over color television standards from a broadcast featuring Commissioner Frieda Hennock of the Federal Communications Commission. Both of them followed and enjoyed all of the political speeches by the presidential nominees.

Television has not completely displaced radio in the Swensons' leisure-time practices. They listen to radio news every morning and to Fulton Lewis, Jr., Walter Winchell and Prescott Robinson. Mrs. Swenson listens to daytime audience participation programs and serials, especially while she washes and irons.

Swenson reads the New Haven *Register*. He habitually starts with page one and skims through the paper, reading the headlines. "If I think it's interesting I read it, otherwise I don't bother." He skips sports news; his interest in sports is in action, not in post mortem or prophecy. He reads and approves of Sokolsky and Winchell. "Almost all of the comic strips" receive his careful attention. He reads the health column, but felt some embarrassment in so reporting.

Magazine reading is limited to *Life*, *Saturday Evening Post*, *Woman's Home Companion*, *American Home* and the *Lutheran Companion*. Since Mrs. Swenson cannot read magazine text, Swenson skims the periodicals and reads occasional stories and articles aloud.

RELIGIOUS TELEVISION. Billy Graham is their mainstay among religious programs, although, as noted, they also watch Sheen with approval, and Mrs. Swenson watched the Du Mont TV Chapel. They had never seen or heard a National Council sponsored program, other than Du Mont Chapel.

They approve of Graham's message, so much so they do not feel the need to discuss it. He says the right things. Their only complaint: "He don't preach long enough, that's the trouble." As with Sheen, they equate what Graham says with what they hear in their own church. They also like the music on his program, although it is radically different from what they see and hear in church.

Both the Swensons feel Graham should be supported by contributions from his television audience. "You see, they don't have commercials so they have to get money some way," Swenson said.

Graham seems to fulfill for the Swensons the same function that Sockman does for his listeners, support and reinforcement of well-entrenched religious views. Essentially, the Graham and Sockman audiences are the same in character, older people with a long history of church affiliation. But there is one point at which Graham is highly deficient in relation to Sockman; that is intellectual spread. Fifty-nine per cent of Graham's audience has seven to eleven years of schooling, but only 7 per cent has any college training. While 25 per cent of Sockman's audience has college training, another 50 per cent is in the seven- to eleven-year category. Sockman not only has a larger audience than Graham in New Haven; he has a much wider appeal.

What prognosis should be made for the Swensons in relation to religious broadcasting? As Swenson's energies fail him, it is likely both of them will depend more on religious television for reinforcement of the values religion has given them. These values are primarily moralistic and ritualistic. They seem to view Christianity and their own church only in moralistic terms. They evinced no interest in missions, social action, worship as reverence to God, prayer. They hold no clear-cut theological opinions. Therefore, it may be expected that such programs as those of Sheen and Graham will serve them as well as any others. They are more likely to continue to accept them with satisfaction than they are to seek out other programs that will be nearer to the interpretation of Christianity they hear in their own church.

The Fuller Audience

Almost two-thirds of the audience for the Old Fashioned Revival Hour is more than 45 years old, and one-fourth of it is more than 65. The heads of two-thirds of the households in the audience are semiskilled or unskilled laborers. Ten per cent of the audience members have less than seven years of schooling, and an additional 50 per cent only seven to eleven years. One-third of the audience has no church affiliation.

The Arthur Mansons

Background Data

Social class: IV
Rent apartment
Own television and radio sets
Income: Under $2,000

	Husband	Wife
Occupation:	Printer (retired)	Domestic
Education:	Less than 7 years	Less than 7 years
Age:	72	68
Religious background:	Protestant	Protestant
Church attended:	None	None
Preoccupation:	Self	Self

Children: None

The Mansons illustrate the older, poorly educated, nonchurchgoers who listen to Fuller. They also watch Graham and Sheen on television regularly.

The Mansons were married, both for the first time, when he was 43. They met in the factory where he was a semiskilled printer and she was an unskilled machine operator. They have had no children. We can say relatively little about Mrs. Manson, because she deliberately stayed away from the apartment during the interview, except for ten minutes at the end. She did complete the F-scale, however, and with a great deal more facility than her husband.

Manson's image of himself is of a man who has been ill-used by his fellow men all his life. He has learned to "take it" and does not expect anything pleasant to happen to him. He now sits out his old age before a television set for upwards of fifty hours a week. He is not really as dissatisfied as his verbalized opinions and attitudes make him appear to be. He is extremely ethnocentric and full of hostility which he discharges at no one, except probably his wife. His F-scale score is 5.21—definitely on the authoritarian side. His highest subscale scores are on sex, 6.33, and authoritarian aggression, authoritarian submission, destructiveness and cynicism, and anti-intraception, 6.00 each.

Manson's childhood is something of a model of the failure of a child of proletarian parents to achieve the start in life that could have developed a self-respecting, rounded individual. His father was a machinist and toolmaker of French-Canadian origin who died when Manson was nine years old, leaving a widow and three children. Manson was the middle child. The other two were girls. His mother, who was of English descent, started a boarding house which was to support her three children, after a fashion. "She was a hard-working woman. Years ago she must have gone to church, I guess," he said.

Manson's back was injured seriously when he was ten years old. Two years later a friend, who nursed in a church-operated hospital for crippled children, arranged for his entrance into the hospital. For the next year and a half he lived in a cast in the hospital. Evidently he was made to go to church and engage in religious studies there without either adequate preparation or the feeling that his religious experience was part of a loving concern for his well-being and recovery. During this period, he became estranged from religion and hostile to it. Since leaving the hospital, he has never gone to church. At 72, he summed up his views of the church in these words:

If you behave yourself, if you live right, it isn't the person that goes to church every Sunday that's the good person. A lot of them go to cover up stuff.

Manson's mother apparently continued to provide him with his main source of emotional support—his references to her were considerably more numerous than those to his wife. He referred with satisfaction to a visit to Florida with his mother, shortly before her death in her eighties. Economically, however, his mother was unable to help him much. His vocational career included a number of unskilled jobs, mostly in Connecticut. Finally, at age 41, he started working for a large factory in New Haven where he was employed as a printer in the plant printing shop. This work began in 1921. Twenty-five years later he was retired on a pension that he bitterly considers to be too small, not having succeeded in rising to the rank either of compositor or foreman. Mrs. Manson was a fellow employee who had begun working in the plant when she was thirteen. When they married, he forced her to stop working. Now that he is retired, he makes no effort to supplement his pension by working. His wife, however, goes out to do housework despite the onset of a heart condition that prevents her from doing the heaviest domestic work. In addition, the burden of shopping, which they do by bus in downtown New Haven to take advantage of advertised special prices, and of housekeeping is left entirely to her.

HIS VIEW OF SOCIETY. The moderately low intelligence and the cunning which has served Manson's survival have not provided him with an enduring, clear view of civil authority, any more than of spiritual authority. His conversation was studded with references to "they" or "them" where authority figures are concerned. He does not vote and does not know the residence requirements for voting. He is against labor unions, but bitter toward his recent employer. He is skeptical about the good faith of politicians in general and of both major political parties, with a single exception—Franklin Delano Roosevelt, for whom he still cherishes a strong attachment. He had considered himself a Republican until the New Deal came along, at which time he switched his allegiance to Roosevelt. Now he is not sure whether Roosevelt did a lot for people, or only fooled them. "I thought he had done a good thing for the working peple." He has been influenced by attacks in the mass media on Roosevelt's actions in the Yalta conference.

While Manson thinks we should "kick out the communists," he considers Senator McCarthy a bad influence who stirs up a lot of trouble. A residue of his New Deal point of view appears in the frank doubt he feels about the talk of the large numbers of communists in the government.

A lot of them people are sayin' this man is a communist. How do they know he is? Some of them probably are. Look at the stir they made in Hollywood. Did they prove it? On some of them?

Manson is skeptical about politicians in general. He thinks both parties are crooked. Corruption angers him. He said, "We ought to clear it up. Both sides are crooked, the Republicans and Democrats." But he has no idea

about how corruption originates or what should be done about it. He agreed
with the interviewer that it is no worse to receive a bribe than to give one;
but when queried as to who gives bribes, he answered, "Crooks, I guess."

Manson and the interviewer held a long discussion of how a bribe is given
and received. Manson told of a friend in local politics who receives gifts of
large quantities of produce from people with whom he deals in his office.
Manson felt he would not call the givers crooks, "but they are looking for a
favor." He finally decided that the vegetables were payment for favors, but
he would not call that graft. Later, however, he readily conceded that the
payment of a $50,000 retainer fee for the passage of a bill is graft; and he
finally decided that the giving and receiving of the vegetables is crooked, too.

Manson has little faith in the honesty of individuals, in either business or
government. It is apparent he has not hesitated to be dishonest himself
where it was necessary to further his job interests. Once he used another
man's name without permission to get a job cutting brush along a highway.
In fairness, we believe there is a vast difference between this sort of dishonesty in a man like Manson who has always been on the ragged edge of
survival and the dishonesty in even minor government corruption.

Manson has little faith in people because nobody has given him cause for
confidence and faith. He feels you cannot get people to become more honest
than they are. That has been his experience. On the other hand, he is shrewd
enough to know that charges against a person do not constitute proof of
guilt, as witnessed by his statement on communists in government.

Manson is loaded with ethnocentrism. He apparently has no friends. He
is suspicious of any nationality or racial group with whom he has contact. He
is convinced that most of "the crooks that you read about" are Jews and
Italians. He is especially resentful of the Negroes and Italians who impinge
on his own effort at survival. He claimed that he sold a house where he
previously lived because Negroes moved into the neighborhood. He resents
the fact that Negroes are mixed with whites in the municipal housing development where he now lives in an apartment, and the fact that many of them
have automobiles while he has never had one. He feels that Italians have gotten a better break in housing than people like himself. After he had voluntarily expressed open admiration for the race segregation in Florida, where the
boss could call "Hey nigger, come here," Manson was asked what he thought
should be done all over the country about the problem of Negroes. He responded with typical ambivalence:

M.: Why you can't do nothin', because the gov'ment has passed this no discrimination. You've got to like it.

Int.: You don't think that's a good thing?

M.: Why the colored people are all right—in their place. . . . President Roosevelt said you shouldn't show any discrimination. That's good enough for me.

He is an example of how potentially intolerant people can be discouraged from overtly punitive behavior through the influence of benign power figures.

This portrait of Manson's present misanthropy should not be left without the indication that at an earlier age he was more socially accessible. He had been a member of the Odd Fellows and the Moose.

LEISURE TIME AND THE MASS MEDIA. All of Manson's time is now leisure time. He spends most of it within the walls of his apartment and mostly in front of his television set, pieced out for relief with listening to his radio. Until recently he had gone to movies several times a week but the rise in admission prices led him to eliminate this expenditure. The television set had been his for only seven months; before that he listened to the radio all day. He "tuned around." "You get sick of the same station all day."

He began listening to the Old Fashioned Revival Hour when he had only a radio, and has continued since getting the television set. The rest of his religious programming is on television, except for Sockman, to whom he listens from time to time. He thinks Sockman is "all right."

Manson seems to have been attracted to the Old Fashioned Revival Hour by the music. The gospel hymns evoked pleasurable nostalgic memories, possibly of his supposedly hateful days in Sunday school. He commented softly, "They sing old religious hymns—old pieces." He had nothing specific to say about Fuller's sermons.

He volunteered without prompting that he watches Graham ("That's a religious program.") and Sheen ("He is really interesting.") regularly.

These religious programs obviously provide him mainly entertainment. But they are also a source for ideas that square with what he considers to be the line being taken by the authorities he designates as "they." They are, therefore, in themselves authorities. At his age and with his experience, it is improbable any religious program would bring Manson into close connection with organized religion. It is possible, though, that should a Fuller or a Graham interpret the Gospel persuasively on the topic of race relations, it would ameliorate Manson's otherwise violent race hatreds.

Manson's general taste in television is undiscriminating. He watches everything on WNHC-TV, the only station he can receive. He would like to be able to get more stations, to have some program choice. Meantime, he uses everything as entertainment, seeking little in the way of information or orientation. He thinks most of the programs are satisfactory. There is nothing he will not accept and watch. He likes wrestling, but said, "It looks as if they hurt each other, but I have heard it's all tricks." Again, he is not quite sure whether or not "they" are manipulating him, and he will not actually commit himself to an opinion. He is quite sure, though, that television boxing is "on the square," and watches regularly with enjoyment. He could not articulate why he had decided the fights are honest.

His use of news programs and of the local newspaper is largely for the raw material for gossip. He reads the gossip column in the *Register*, the "advice to the lovelorn" column, the health and fix-it columns. He also reads the comic strips. Paper-backed mystery stories are his only reading material in book form.

In this welter of undiscriminating media use, Manson manifested a continuing concern over technology. He particularly emphasized his fondness for Norman Brokenshire's fix-it program. He bemoaned the way WNHC "bungles up" technical details of broadcasts and looks forward to the opening of a second television station in New Haven.

Manson is an old man and might be dismissed as being of no importance. Needless to say, we consider him important as a human being, in spite of his vegetablelike existence. His entire life has been that of a poor, downtrodden individual who has never been able to master his fate. He comes to the end of life, sitting it out before a television set, not particularly dissatisfied, not even very much puzzled about what comes next. He has learned to endure the slings and arrows of fortune; does not expect anything good; therefore will not be disappointed. But he has no hope. One is tempted to speculate on the authoritarian potential of Manson were he fifty years younger in times like these and possessed of his present attitudes. His life might also be tragic, but in a much more telling way. Such a man would present raw material for rank-and-file membership in a dictatorial authoritarian movement. He has a potential for aggressive destructiveness that is startlingly high. He has balanced a relatively low intelligence with a great deal of cunning developed in the struggle for survival. This cunning is coupled with a reservoir of lack of information, misinformation and superstition on which he bases his decisions. He has no moral code. Survival and the satisfaction of his basic self-desires have been his motivating forces.

This condition is not necessarily a condemnation of Manson as a person, but of the system of charity medical care, inadequate schooling, the lack of job training and the poor labor relations that let him develop as he did.

Manson's attitudes are negative ones, but they are balanced by a caution resulting from many defeats and by an awe and fear of authority. Therefore, his present aggressive tendencies are neatly balanced off by his practice of submitting to authority, and Manson ends up a man who lives on dead center, unable to decide any issue pro or con, or to initiate any action above the survival level. But a younger Manson in the hands of a dynamic authoritarian leader might have been another matter. The most telling revelation of both the F–scale analysis and the interview was that Manson is antisocial, but has an extremely egocentric personality that craves a position of dominance. Since he is resigned to a social and educational class status near the lower end of the scale, he accepts superior authority, but yearns to exercise authority on his own. His prejudices against others are not the conventional exploiting of group differences based on skin color, nationality or religion. They are deeply personal, envy rather than prejudice—envy of anyone with a car, a house, clothing, a job that Manson cannot own. In the old man, this prejudice-envy appears as harmless griping that at most could erupt into a neighborhood quarrel. A younger Manson, properly inflamed with hatred for his more prosperous fellows, would be a likely candidate for the launching of a savage pogrom.

CHAPTER 17

Personality Traits of Nonusers of Religious Programs

Forty per cent of the households in Metropolitan New Haven do not listen to religious programs on radio or view them on television (Chapter 10). These nonusers, like the people who listen regularly to religious programs, are a representative cross section of New Haven population. Differences between users and nonusers are individual ones; they cannot be charged to group association, but are dependent upon the background and experience of the individual family and its members.

Among Protestant households in the population, there was a significant difference between users and nonusers of religious programs, based on social class. A majority of the households in classes III and V was in the audience for religious programs, while only a minority of the households in classes I, II and IV listened or viewed regularly. Since approximately half of the New Haven population is in social class IV, we have chosen a family from that grouping for analysis as representative of the nonusers.

The Paul Haupts

Background Data

Social class: IV
Rent apartment
Own television and radio sets
Income: $3,000

	Husband	Wife
Occupation:	Laborer	Housewife
Education:	High school	High school
Age:	23	23
Religious background:	Roman Catholic	Protestant
Church attended:	None	Church of the Nazarene
Preoccupation:	Primary: Family and home	Primary: Family and home
	Secondary: Self	Secondary: Self
Children: None		

Paul and Dorothy Haupt were both born in New Haven, Haupt is of German-Irish parentage; Mrs. Haupt comes from "Yankees from way back" of English and Irish origin. Haupt is husky and rough in manner. She is blonde, pretty and comfortably feminine. They live in a working-class New Haven neighborhood, in a four-room apartment that is clean and comfortably furnished in conventional style. Mrs. Haupt was pregnant at the time of the interview.

Haupt has always been an unskilled worker. He was in the Navy for a time, had held jobs as machine operator and clerk in a store. His current job was "ground man" for a crane operator. Mrs. Haupt has held several clerical positions. She had recently quit a job in a utility company office because of her pregnancy.

Haupt's image of himself is that of a "little man" with few resources for coping with a hostile, unscrupulous society. Although he is a common, unskilled laborer, he identifies strongly with employers rather than with workers. He feels the cards are stacked against him because he lacks "pull" based on family connections, educational associations, wealth or political influence. He summed up this view with "You're nothing unless you've got pull." His only assets in the economic struggle are physical strength—now at its prime—and his wits—only average in quality. Making the best of these resources, he cultivates the pose of a "tough guy" who talks gruffly and quickly and who knows what is what in the world, but who is also reasonable.

He presented a quite different face to his wife, toward whom he was considerate and tender. But toward the rest of the world he is ethnocentric, cynical, destructive, conventional and anomic.

Mrs. Haupt's image of herself is that of the young matron-to-be who is the normal wife of a normal "little man." She is happy in her pregnancy and looks with confidence to the birth of the child. She presents to the world the outer shell of Judy Holliday's dumb blonde—who in reality is anything but dumb—using the same nasal accent and speech mannerisms. Peacefulness, normality, cleanliness, prettiness and affection are the central values in her images of self and society. While her husband mistrusts people, she feels at ease with them and values "friendliness" highly.

Mrs. Haupt's over-all F-scale score is a little lower than Haupt's, 4.24 as against 4.59, both being above average. She is less conventional than her husband, 3.75 as against 5.75; less destructive and cynical, 2.50 as against 5.75. She is also more accessible to critical self-examination, anti-intraception score of 2.75 as against 4.75. However, she is more projective than he is, 6.40 as against 5.40, and more submissive to authority, 4.86 as against 4.14.

Both are equally high on authoritarian aggression, 4.62, and approximately the same on superstition and stereotypy, 3.67 and 3.83.

The Haupts can best be described as living a normal life, dominated by their youth and love for each other. Their home is the center of their lives. She likes to get up at 5:00 A.M. to make breakfast and eat with her husband. And she enjoys housekeeping. Haupt likes to fuss with the mechanical problems of the household and its appliances.

What kind of life would Haupt like his child to have? He reflects his own private world in his thinking about the child. "He can't live without fear. That's for sure," he said. And, "He should stay out of politics. . . ." He was sure there would be few things he would force his child to do. One thing he will not force on him is religion. Religious guidance and training will be Mrs. Haupt's job.

Mrs. Haupt's hopes for her child were expressed in these words:

I'd like him to have a normal, peaceful life—be able to live without—[pause, then slowly and discouragedly] I don't know. The way things are now you wonder what kind of life they'll have. . . . He should have a good education . . . you'd want him to be a little better off than you are.

RELIGION IN THE LIFE OF THE HAUPTS. The interview did not reveal a great deal about Haupt's childhood, but one point was clear; a major item in his adolescent revolt was a break with the Roman Catholic Church:

Int.: I wonder what religion means to you.
H.: I couldn't tell you, personally. When I was young, you know when you're in the Catholic religion you gotta—your father tells you to go so you went. And I haven't been very much since 1945 [when he was 16].

Haupt voiced a series of complaints against the authority and constraint imposed upon him by the Church. He had attended parochial school, which he did not like; but he defended the brothers as being better teachers than those found in public schools. Conversely, he thinks religious education for children has no value.

Haupt is especially opposed to ritual and to church worship in general. He railed at the frequency and length of the compulsory worship services during his schooldays. He has a deep dislike for sermons. They bore him, mostly it seems because they are couched in language that he cannot understand. This opposition is not reserved for Roman Catholic sermons. Sometimes, to please his wife, he attends church with her. There, too, the preacher is "too long-winded. He talks over my head."

Haupt, like Richardson and the Swensons, fails to see the conceptual differences between religious beliefs:

They all figure on the same thing, basically; only a different way of believing.

All religions are basically the same—Protestant, Episcopal, Catholic. I don't know about the Jewish Church. Catholics are too strict, that's all.

The churches have lost this man, at least until he can be brought to accept a new set of beliefs and attitudes. The most he would concede religion means is a code of ethics. And he does not relate such an ethical code to his own conscience.

Mrs. Haupt came from a Protestant background and is now casually attached to the neighborhood Church of the Nazarene. Her child will know religion:

Mrs. H.: I think every child should have religious training. After they grow up they have certain problems and if they didn't have religious training they wouldn't know how to solve them.

Int.: What would you teach them?

Mrs. H.: What is right and what is wrong. I think they all should believe in Christ. . . . Know about the Bible—something about it. Most Sunday schools read the Bible to them. They have a Sunday-school lesson and I think that's good for any child.

Int.: What do you mean when you say "believe in Christ"?

Mrs. H.: Well, believe that He came to this earth, and He gave His disciples His—well, He taught them that they could teach the rest of the people about His life, and what they should do, and—well, He taught people to pray when they got—when they have problems and things like that.

Int.: What do you think was the importance of his being put to death?

Mrs. H.: Well, I think it was so that everybody—He sort of atoned for everybody's sins, I think. His death was atonement for everybody's else's sins so that they could be forgiven. I think that that was the main purpose of Him coming to this earth and dying.

She believes one should live by the Ten Commandments. She tries to apply the teaching of the Scriptures to her daily life; though, as will be seen later in her discussion of Negroes, her prejudices are likely to have a stronger influence.

Interestingly, Haupt's rejection of the Catholic Church, while verbally complete, does not extend to acceptance of the Protestant position that divine assistance is available to individuals without an ecclesiastical intermediary. On the contrary, he completely agrees with the proposition that divine help must be sought, if at all, through the church and the clergy. Mrs. Haupt agrees, though less strongly. Both reject the proposition that the clergy are final authorities on belief and behavior. As to the practicality of the Bible as a guide to daily living, Haupt, as might be expected, says no, while Mrs. Haupt says yes.

THEIR VIEW OF SOCIETY. Haupt's image of the civil structure of society is of a jungle struggle for survival in which morality is helpless. "The little man is never goin' to win," he said. He thinks that integrity in politics and business is desirable but that it doesn't pay. He assumes a vague "they" who corrupt government processes, but was positive that his wife was wrong when she said the "they" are businessmen who "don't care what they do as long as they make a little money." The cynical hopelessness of his attitudes and the comparative realism of hers are clear in this interesting passage:

Int.: Suppose that you clear out the men who have been receiving bribes. Is it any worse to receive a bribe, morally, than it is to give one?

H.: As you clean it out, it's not going to do any good. Because the next guy you put in there—he's goin' to say, well this guy made some money. I'm goin' to make some too. In one way it's just as good to leave the thief there rather than put another guy in there and ruin him.

Int.: You feel that there is no way to cure it.

H.: No, I don't think so.

Mrs. H.: People never used to be like that, it doesn't seem to me.

Int.: You think the world is getting worse.

Mrs. H.: It seems that way. Maybe it's because I'm getting old and I hear more gossip. . . .

Int.: It's kind of a hopeless outlook.

H.: All you can do is the best you can do. If everybody did today what was right, we wouldn't have this thing.

Int.: It doesn't offer much incentive to do what's right, does it? You don't get anywhere.

H.: I'm tryin' to make an honest livin', see? So I get $3,000 a year. So here's another guy. He's goin' crooked. He's makin' $50,000. So why shouldn't I take a shot at it? I mean, I have a chance of gettin' away with it, or not gettin' away with it.

Int.: That's my point, exactly. There's no reward for being good.

H.: That's right. You suffer [long pause].

Mrs. H.: With some people, their conscience doesn't bother them, I guess. I think mine would bother me if I did anything that wasn't honest.

Both of the Haupts perceive political policy issues in stereotypical terms. France's weakness is the instability of its governments, said he. Finland is a brave little country that pays its debts, said she. They admitted they knew that 75 per cent of the world population is worse off materially than the families with the lowest income in the United States, but they held that already we are doing too much for the rest of the world. "Foreigners don't appreciate it and don't make any moves to help themselves out of their problems." On Korea: "Call it a police action when there's a hundred thousand casualties?"

He belongs to a union but doesn't know its name.

I joined the union but I didn't know what it was all about at the time. If I could get out now I'd get out today.

Anyone who wants a closed shop is crazy.

Mrs. Haupt, however, views unions in bread-and-butter terms. She belonged to one in the public utility that was effective in settling employee grievances and in getting pay increases. She thinks the union in her husband's shop is a poor one. "It doesn't do anything to protect their members." Haupt did not argue against her point of view. He simply stuck to his statement that pull is necessary in business or government. "If you don't know nobody you can't get along. I've got no use for it. . . . In Washington or anywhere."

Neither of the Haupts belongs to a political party. Indeed the plant union in which he is an unwilling member is their only organizational attachment. They fortify this anomic relation to society by scapegoats: unions and Negroes for him; Negroes for her. The ethnocentrism was open. He said, "Negroes are to blame for their own troubles" by being and acting different from whites.

They come up from the south. There's a lot of things they can't do down there, and they can get away with it up here. And that's what ruins them, see? Right away they go off the handle. And that brings the misery on themselves, and it's their own fault for some of the predicaments they get into. But as far as the nigger moving into this neighborhood. If he could live up to the standards of the rest of the people, all right, I wouldn't have too much complaint. But if he's going to start runnin' around with a knife in his hand, or a beer bottle, or half in a bag, I don't believe in it.

Mrs. Haupt believes rumors that southern Negroes with big families are unduly preferred to native whites in New Haven:

There's an awful lot of them coming up from the south and they go right down and they're on relief right away. Some of us who have been living in the state for several years can't get relief because we have a mother or father or someone to take care of you. It makes them [natives of New Haven] mad because they [southern Negroes] get relief right away.

Int.: Who is this who says that?

Mrs. H.: The lady downstairs; she works in the welfare office.

In her own work, Mrs. Haupt had personal contact with Negro girls, and got along with them. But she confessed she got "that squirmy feeling" when a Negro borrowed a white girl's comb. Nevertheless, she admitted the conflict between her ethnocentrism and her understanding of the Bible:

Int.: Suppose your minister were to talk about the problem of Negroes moving into residential areas. How do you feel he would talk about it?

Mrs. H.: I don't know. It says in the Bible that everybody is equal, that we are really all brothers and sisters no matter what race you are. But I don't know the way some of the Negroes are you really can't live with them, I don't think. I don't know how to live with them. . . .

I think that if the minister was going to talk about that, I think he would say that—uh, that you have to be decent and you have to be nice to people of all races and nationalities, but you don't have to live with them and do what they do. I mean, I think he'd bring that point out that to be nice and considerate to them, but don't go around acting as if you are better than they are. But you don't have to mingle with them. That's how our minister would bring out that point.

Int.: You think he'd be in favor of letting them move into your neighborhood, providing of course, that you didn't feel that you had to invite them into your house unless they wanted to come in and you wanted them to come in?

Mrs. H.: Well, if you didn't, you'd be putting yourself above them.

LEISURE TIME AND THE MASS MEDIA. The Haupts' leisure-time activities are as diverse as their $3,000 income lets them be. Haupt has three hobbies, photography, model-making and gardening. She reported cooking as her hobby. Both of them are sports enthusiasts. They swim regularly. He plays horseshoes and table tennis and bowls. He has also played baseball, football, volleyball and basketball. He skates, goes boating, hikes and likes to camp. She has done some horseback riding, bowling and skating.

They spent a week in Florida on their last vacation before the interview. During the year they saw one football game, went once to a stock-car race and once to "watch the ponies." They go to amusement parks in the summer and drive into the open country every couple of weeks. She goes to the movies more often than once a week, her husband only every other week. Occasionally, she goes to the legitimate theater.

Television has already claimed a large slice of their leisure time and will probably become more important when they face the baby-sitting problem. Their tastes in programs are diversified, but their interests are primarily centered in techniques—plot in dramas, switching operations in news programs and similar technical activities in other shows, interpretation of rules in sports broadcasts. They are interested in program content as role playing of men against women, rather than as development of individual personalities.

Television is their sole news source, and it is limited to two programs, a local news report on WNHC and Swazey. Haupt likes Swazey because "he switches all around and picks up news from lots of cities." He pleases Mrs. Haupt because "he speaks clearly and you can understand what he's talking about."

Mrs. Haupt watches two public-issue programs, Youth Wants to Know and Meet the Press.

Both of them praised I Love Lucy enthusiastically. It is easily their favorite show. Their comments were significant. Mrs. Haupt said, "The men get together and start scheming and the women get together and start scheming." He added, "She's always doing something to get even or vice versa." This is the pattern that is followed when visitors come to the Haupt apartment. The men play cards in the kitchen. The women sit in the living room and talk and look at television. Later the men join them for coffee and to watch boxing or wrestling on television. The Haupts and their friends do not hold the upper middle class view that men and women are conversationally and culturally homogeneous.

The Haupts are selective in their viewing. Mystery programs have no appeal for either of them. Haupt said, "Once you've seen one mystery, you've seen them all." She is equally negative toward daytime serials on both television and radio. "Some of them are kind of ridiculous," she said. "Men and women aren't that stupid. It's so silly." Haupt likes westerns and action dramas. Both of them like a "good musical." She expressed a preference for "a good drama . . . something with a story . . . with a real life situation." They do not like contemporary romantic stories, but they saw and enjoyed a production of "Cyrano de Bergerac."

They see more variety shows than any other type. They like Godfrey and the "good shows" on Saturday night. She is especially fond of Imogene Coca. Haupt likes the Hit Parade because they put on "elaborate shows, spend a lot of money on them." They watch, but dislike, Milton Berle—because he laughs at his own jokes—and Toast of the Town, which is too highbrow for Haupt who said he does not "know what they're talking about on it."

Neither of them watches quiz shows, except for Groucho Marx. Both of them like Marx and approve of him. They praised his ability as a master of ceremonies. They do not feel his humor harms contestants because "they expect to be treated like that."

One of their few disagreements on programs concerns boxing and wrestling. He likes "the fights" and she does not and will not watch them. He is interested in the technique in wrestling ("In Chicago the rules are enforced."); she rejects wrestling ("Same big act all the time."). Baseball on television is accepted by both as a fair substitute for attending games, but they will not listen to baseball on the radio.

The Haupts agreed that he has virtually stopped reading since they got the television set. He had been an Earl Stanley Gardner mystery fan, "because he gets right into the story in the first few pages." He still skims the New Haven *Register*. He may read the *Reader's Digest*, to which they subscribe, because it is "up to date."

Mrs. Haupt reads the *Register*, primarily for local news, comics, the woman's page, the gossip column and the advertising. She likes Dorothy Dix, but believes "sometimes she is a little bitter on life." She also reads the child behavior column. *Reader's Digest* is her favorite magazine because of its capsule content. "You don't have to read all night," she said. She reads *Better Homes and Gardens* and *McCalls* for the recipes and household hints, but dislikes the love stories in *McCall's*.

RELIGIOUS TELEVISION AND RADIO. The Haupts are included in these analyses because they are not regular users of any religious programs. Nevertheless they had something to say about them. They had heard The Greatest Story Ever Told once and had no reaction to it at all. She had seen Billy Graham on television. He impressed her with a talk on corruption in Washington. She perceived the speech as having the moral of urging people to get out and vote to clean up corruption.

What type of religious program might interest such people as the Haupts? The answer is simple: drama. They had once stumbled onto a television play —which they could not identify—that presented the trial and crucifixion of Jesus in political terms. It fascinated them, and they were eager to report the plot to the interviewer. (It is important to note that the Haupts were not aware of the sponsorship of the study.) The flavor of their impression from this play is conveyed in the following comments:

Mrs. H.: When He said He was King of the Jews, the people thought that He was an earthly king, that He was going to take over the other king, take over all his riches—
H.: They didn't understand—
Mrs. H.: —and his land, but that isn't what He meant. That's why He couldn't prove—
H.: I know, but that's the way it was taken on the thing—the program.
Mrs. H.: Yeah—but He couldn't prove to them that He was the King.
H.: He was talkin' in words that they didn't understand.
Int.: How did you like that play?
Mrs. H.: I liked it.

H.: Oh, yes.
Int.: More interesting than a sermon?
Mrs. H.: Oh, yes.
H.: Oh, this was something that would hold your attention.

The prescription for what we think would bring the Haupts into a more n.eaningful relation to religion was given categorically by them:

Int.: Do you reckon that if more religious programs were put on that way that they might be more interesting to people [than sermons]?
Mrs. H.: I think if they used Bible stories, and things like that and showed you parables to illustrate the point—I think it would be better than a sermon—
H.: That would be a lot better than a sermon—
Mrs. H.: —based on one idea, and they go on and on. Some people don't approve of that.
H.: Well, a story like that for an hour would be better than having a service, you know a church service that lasts about an hour, having one of them on the program.

The Haupts do not have any clarity of view about the future. They live in the present, Haupt with cynicism, Mrs. Haupt with hope and confidence. Neither has an abiding spiritual base for his attitudes and beliefs. We hazard the surmise that much of their future character development hinges on the fortunes of economic fate for Haupt. If he should get the sort of "break" he is hoping for and become established in a secure and well-paying job, it is possible the family will move upward socially and simultaneously lose some of the anomic characteristics that presently threaten its future. Just now, Mrs. Haupt has a more tolerant, permissive attitude toward other people than her husband has. Maybe he can improve in this sense, if he achieves economic security.

It seems obvious that what these young people need more than economic security is spiritual security, a faith that will make it possible to meet economic frustration if that should be their lot. A church affiliation should do a great deal to help them attain that faith. If they do not find it, and if Haupt is held to the level of his present job, the future for this young family may not be bright. Then, his cynicism and destructive potential will have the chance to feed on relative deprivation and discontent and bitterness arising from his frustrations. His vulnerability to blind submission to authority then could easily result in his involvement in native fascist movements. Short of this unhappy end, he could easily fall into the anomic pattern of behavior leading to Manson's state.

CHAPTER 18

Significance of Depth Interviews for Protestant Radio and Television Policy

The depth interviews show that religious radio and television, like face-to-face communication, is a process that works on many levels and one to which the audience members as well as the communicator contribute. The essential ingredients are the same in both cases. There is a communicator with something to communicate. There is an audience, potential and actual, composed of individuals with all manner of attitudes and predispositions. And there is the content of the communication, as it is transmitted and received. The content in both cases is a flow of representations in many layers and in many dimensions. Words are only one of the layers of representation —the most honored means in our culture. There are all of the almost countless complexities of pitch, time and intonation. There are all of the layers of meaning carried by visual perception—the gestures, the clothes, the size and configuration of physical objects. Words, which have a high degree of ambiguity, carry meanings of different kinds because of syntax, pace and intonation. It is as if the content were a conveyor belt that carries many different materials to the audience. The audience members bring to the communication as wide a variety of tastes and needs as humans experience in life. What these audience members take from the conveyor belt, what uses they make of what materials they take, how they reshape the materials they take—these processes also are as diverse as the dynamics of the individuals' personalities and life situations.

The wonderful technological devices we know as radio and television do not change these essentials of the communication process. Radio and television do not broadcast magic messages. The amazing feature of these media is simply that they permit so many individuals to see and hear the messages simultaneously.

The six preceding chapters have carried the reader through an investigation of the dynamics of the ways in which the audience members use religious radio and television programs. No one has developed precise methods of analyzing the dynamics of personal needs and values. We have, therefore, necessarily fallen short of achieving a validated theory—if such were possible —that would permit precise prediction of effects of given kinds of programs on given kinds of personalities. We have had to work with rather rough tools; the results are more precise than we expected.

It is not enough, if one wishes to plan for effective development of a religious radio or television program, to know just the size and affiliation of the potential audience. Nor is it sufficient to know its composition in terms of age, occupation, social class, education, race, income and size of family. Useful results may be obtained by wise interpretation of such information, aided by working assumptions as to the tastes, needs and personality structures of the people. Indeed it is at this level that the bulk of research utilized by commercial agencies is applied to the merchandising of products. However, if one seeks to create religious radio and television programs with predictable "effects," more refined tools are needed. Religious programs are not analogous to programs to sell cigarettes. It is to the determination of effects that the so-called depth interviews and their analysis has been devoted.

The depth analysis added to information on age, occupation, et cetera, for each individual the information and insights obtainable from extensive interviews. It classified the individuals on the basis of this information into *interest* groups. We found that in the persons we interviewed the *family and home,* and *social status* interest groups were the youngest with median age of head of family less than forty years. These two interest groups contained the bulk of the skilled workers, with income about average for the country. The chief difference in socioeconomic characteristics between these two interest groups is that the family and home group more often have minor children living at home. The individuals placed in the *self-interest* group were distinguished by their greater age (median, 68 years) and the predominance of females among them. Income is low (median between $2,001 and $3,500) and very few have minor children living with them. The *work*-centered group has about the same distribution according to age, education, income and social class as the total population. The individuals placed in the *social-responsibility*-centered group included a predominant number of professional men and owners and executives of large businesses with incomes above $10,000 and a median education of four years of college. Most of these homes contained minor children. The small group of persons whose interests centered on *formal religion* tended toward social class IV, with only high school education, income of $3,501 to $5,000 and middle age (median fifty years). Knowledge of this kind, based on interests, about a population to be offered religious radio and television programs would be a great deal more useful than simply information about the basic socioeconomic characteristics of the total population.

When we went a step further, we found that the regular use of religious radio and television was significantly related to these central interests of individuals. Those in the *formal religion* groups used the most programs, an average of 3.00 per person, while those in the *social responsibility* group used the fewest, 0.8 per person. Approximately two programs per person were regularly used by individuals in the *self, family and home,* and *work* preoccupied groups, while individuals whose interests centered on *social status* used a fraction more than one, on the average, 1.4.

In our interview chunk most of the *family-and-home*-centered group were regular users of the Greatest Story Ever Told, with almost as large a proportion in the audience for Roman Catholic programs, and the smallest proportion regularly using the Peale, Sockman and Bonnell programs. The largest part of the *social-status*-centered group regularly used *none* of the religious programs, but substantial proportions used the Roman Catholic and Greatest Story Ever Told programs. Of the *self-interest* group, by far the largest portion regularly used the Peale, Sockman and Bonnell programs, with many regularly using miscellaneous other Protestant programs, and the fewest number being found in the Greatest Story Ever Told audience. The largest segment of the *work*-preoccupied group was regularly found in the Greatest Story Ever Told audience and the smallest in the Roman Catholic program audience. The *formal-religion*-centered group used a wide variety of religious programs. This information, however, only partly tells the story.

When the distribution of the regular users for each of the programs was examined, it appeared that the Roman Catholic program users, meaning primarily Sheen's audience, were to be found in appreciable portions in each interest group. The National Council program audience, however, was largely concentrated in the *self*-interest group, with the Peale program showing a higher concentration than the Sockman program. The regular users of other Protestant programs were dominated by the *self*-centered group, and those persons primarily concerned with *formal religion.* As was to be expected, the *family-and-home*-centered group predominated in The Greatest Story Ever Told audience.

We learned more about the personalities of the individuals classified in the several interest groups when their F-scale scores were examined. It then appeared that the groups preoccupied with *formal religion* and *self* were strongly inclined to seek authority symbols. They had median scores of 5.43 and 4.93, respectively, out of a possible maximum of 7.00. Individuals in the *family and home* and *social status* groups occupied a middle position on this scale. Emphatically antiauthoritarian leanings were found in the group centered on *social responsibility*, while slightly antiauthoritarian indications existed for those whose chief concern was *work* (medians of 1.76 and 3.28 respectively).

Quite independently of their central interests, the individuals in the interview chunk were found to be least inclined toward authoritarianism in the social classes toward the top of the social ladder and most inclined toward it in the classes toward the bottom. From this analysis, we were led to expect that the authoritarian leanings of social class IV and V individuals were likely to be *aggressive*, those in classes II and III, *submissive*, and those in class I, *conventional* in quality.

Taking the interest groups into account, again, it was found that the ingredient in authoritarianism on which the highest score was shown was *authoritarian submission* for the *self-*, *family-and-home-*, *work-* and *social-status-centered* individuals. As one would perhaps expect, the second highest subscale scores for these interest groups were found to be *aggression* for the *self-interest* group, *conventionalism* for the *family and home* group, *destructiveness and cynicism* for the *work*-centered group, and *anti-intraception* (inaccessibility to self-examination) for the *social-status*-centered group.

With this background, it then became meaningful to learn that the regular members of the Sockman audience had a predominantly low identification with authority. At the other extreme the Sheen audience members in social classes II and III were found to have quite high identification with authority, while those in social classes IV and V were about average. The Peale audience, the combined audience for all National Council programs and The Greatest Story Ever Told audience stood in a neutral position with respect to identification with authority, and their scores were inversely related to social class. A finding of some general interest was that individuals regularly in each of the audiences for religious radio and television programs had uniformly high average scores on authoritarian submission, in comparison with the neutral scores for those who do not watch or listen to religious programs.

The analyses of the depth interviews, presented in Chapters 15, 16 and

17, disclose the rich diversity of need-value systems that were related to the use of religious radio and television programs. These analyses speak for themselves, for the most part, and need little further summarization. But to carry the analytical process one step further, we have again analyzed each of the interviews to identify more systematically the reasons why the particular radio and television programs had the particular uses for these individuals to which they put them. In this analysis we attempted to identify as briefly as possible three aspects of the problem: (1) What were the underlying predispositions that set the stage for the individual to find use for the particular religious program—why, in other words, was the program listened to? (2) What was the individual's perception of the quality or qualities in the program that made it uniquely able to satisfy this need? (3) What was the nature of the use made by the individual of the program—in other words, what were its discernible "effects?"

Table 85 presents in concise summary form the data about a selected number of the people interviewed, so we may relate personal predispositions to perceptions of the religious programs and the effects of the programs on these individuals.

Peale Audience

Two of the three individuals described from the Peale audience were primarily preoccupied with self and one with formal religion. One each was from social class I, II and III. The anxiety level of each of the three was high and predisposed them to sympathetic reception of the Peale message. In each of the three instances the anxiety was provoked by a problem involving personal relationships. Moreover, in all three cases something approaching panic existed. West was distraught by his guilt in relation to his wife and child and his dissipations. Mrs. Jackson was upset about a work relationship that threatened her lifetime career as a teacher in its closing phases. And Mrs. Clark was in such a "bad mental state" in relation to a work relationship at her office that the problem was, she felt, "out of her hands." All three were in middle age or older. The two women were childless; West had "lost" his child emotionally. All three had F-scale scores at or above average.

These three interviews by themselves would not be enough to support a generalization about Peale. Coupled with the other depth interviews taken in the study, they justify the conclusion that Peale speaks with *authority* ("firmness of voice . . . gave me confidence"), providing his listeners with a philosophy—or method—that relieves the pre-existent anxiety. Different

Table 85. Summary of data on depth interview respondents, their underlying predispositions, perception and use of religious programs, and effects

A. Characteristics of Respondents

Name	Social Class	Age	Major Preoccupation	Religious Affiliation	Man and God	Rating on Criteria [a] The Bible	Individual Integrity
Mr. Austin	3	50	Family-home	Meth.	Prot.	Yes	No
Mrs. Austin	3	50	Family-home	Meth.	Prot.	Yes	No
Mrs. Boyle	2	42	Family-home	R. C.	R. C.	No.	Yes
Mrs. Clark	3	59	Self	Cong.	Prot.	Yes	No
Mr. Jackson	2	74	Self	None	None	No	No
Mrs. Jackson	2	70	Self	None	Prot.	None	No
Mr. Manson	4	72	Self	None	None	No	No
Mr. Richardson	4	37	Work	Cong.	Prot.	Yes	No
Mrs. Richardson	4	37	Soc. status	Cong.	Prot.	Yes	No
Mr. Swenson	4	68	Self	Luth.	R. C.	No	No
Mrs. Swenson	4	66	Self	Luth.	R. C.	Yes	No
Mr. Voskuil	4	34	Family-home	R. C.	R. C.	No	Weak-Yes
Mrs. Voskuil	4	34	Family-home	R. C.	R. C.	No	Weak-Yes
Mrs. Wakefield	2	71	Self	Presb.	Prot.	Yes	Yes
Mr. West	1	56	Formal rel.	Cong.	Prot.	Yes	No

[a] The three criteria here represent the researchers' rating of the persons interviewed on certain criteria that were presumed to be central to Protestant policy. These were:

a. *Man and God* — "Divine assistance in life's crises may be sought and secured directly rather than through a human mediator (priest) or institution (church)." Agreement with this concept is classified "Protestant"; disagreement is classified "Roman Catholic" in this table.

b. *The Bible* — "The Bible is a practical aid in the solution of day-to-day problems." "Yes" means agreement, and is assumed to be a Protestant position. "No" means disagreement. "None" means no information.

c. *Individual integrity* — Respect for the sanctity and dignity of individual personality in interpersonal relationships. Respondents generally classified as evidencing such respect (Yes) or not evidencing it (No).

Table 85 - continued

B. *Underlying Predisposition; Program Use and Effects*

Name	Underlying Predisposition	Perception of Program Attributes	Program Use and Effects — Use or Effects
		Sockman	
Mr. and Mrs. Austin	Highly status-conscious regular church members who make the church the center of their social lives. Neutral F-scale scores. Attitude toward religious radio is that of connoisseurs in religious music, preaching and liturgy.	His preaching style, ability to take a text and work it out in everyday life.	None except for the gratification of their taste in consumption of preaching technique. A genteel entertainment.
		Old Fashioned Revival Hour	
		The old hymns; the revival atmosphere.	Nostalgic entertainment evocative of their youthful experience in revivalistic churches.
		Sheen	
Mrs. Boyle	Torn between personal professional achievement wishes and affection for husband and children; ingrained dependence on the ritual and moral code of the R. C. Church, which gives her means of suppressing wishes. Moderately high anxiety level.	Infallible authority spokesman for R. C. who "answers my questions"; i.e., reconciles church policy and practice on such matters as divorce.	Whenever she questions R. C. moral policies which frustrate her inner urges, Sheen provides reassurance which strengthens her will to submit to exacting faith in face of suppressed desires.

Table 85 - (B) continued

Program Use and Effects

Name	Underlying Predisposition	Perception of Program Attributes	Use or Effects
Mrs. Clark			
	High anxiety level associated with childlessness, cold marriage, focusing on personal difficulties with work associates. Conventional. Anomic. "Bad mental state....out of my hands." Moderately submissive to authority.	*Peale* "Firmness of voice," "actual experience he could give"; "inspirational....gave me confidence."	*Peale* Relieved anxiety; helped her work out office situation. Permitted return to Sunday school teaching. No change in hostility level nor in sterile view of religion.
		Sheen "Very good statements; they make you think a good deal"; the moral code content.	*Sheen* Lessens anxiety by strengthening her adherence to a moral code by means of which she maintains her control over suppressed and unsatisfied needs.
Mr. Jackson			
	An old, frustrated man whose timidity has limited him; closely identified with authority figures; F-scale score moderately high.	*Sheen* "He's very sure of himself when he speaks. He don't want you to doubt anything he says"; aggressive strength in a power figure.	*Sheen* By identification Mr. Jackson gets support for his inadequate self-respect through use of Sheen occasionally.
Mrs. Jackson			
	High anxiety level associated with childlessness, unsatisfactory marriage and focusing on personal difficulties with associates at work. Conventional and anomic. "Very nervously tired."	*Peale* Advice to relax and to pray to an ever-present God for help.	*Peale* Eased anxiety, but effect ended when difficulties in interpersonal relations were ironed out. No further use of Peale or religion. No change in hostility level.

Table 85 - (B) continued

Program Use and Effects

Name	Underlying Predisposition	Perception of Program Attributes	Use or Effects
			Old Fashioned Revival Hour
Mr. Manson	A retired, isolated, embittered, hostile old man who is resourceless to pass the time except for television and radio. Highly identified with authority. Earlier conflicts and anxiety now resolved in hopeless, impotent cynicism.	The old hymns.	Nostalgic entertainment which evokes his youthful pleasures and pains.
			Sheen
		"He's real interesting."	Passes time entertainingly; gives authoritative support to certain prejudices and suspicions about contemporary world.
			Sheen
Mr. and Mrs. Richardson	Highly conventional, compulsive people; he centered on his work; she ambitious for higher social status; very conservative political and economic views.	"Preaching goodness."	In their casual use of this program, it confirms their conventional attitudes and prejudices.
			Greatest Story Ever Told
		Vividness of dramatic form	Their children retain the content enough to ask questions about it. Adults are confirmed in preexisting attitudes toward conventional role of home and church.
			Billy Graham
Mr. and Mrs. Swenson	Tradition-bound, lower-class immigrants with moderately strong identification with authority. Lifelong church-centered social life with liking for revivalist-type preaching technique.	His preaching; wish there was more of it.	Pleasure in the technique of his preaching — a form of religious entertainment.

Table 85 - (B) continued

| | Underlying Predisposition | Program Use and Effects | |
		Perception of Program Attributes	Use or Effects
		Sheen	
Mr. Voskuil	Image of self as in working class and limited to it. Regrets lack of education. Traditionally bound to authority of Roman Catholic Church.	"A man who's well educated"; one of greatest speakers I ever heard"; fluency inexhaustible; power figure.	Program confirms and strengthens his loyalty to church; would influence opinions, especially those not touching V's bread-and-butter interests.
		Sheen	
Mrs. Voskuil	Dutiful, earthy wife and mother in Italian immigrant tradition with interests in children, kitchen and church. Roman Catholicism an unobtrusive part of life-style.	'What he says and how he says it"; "makes you sit there and look at him"; personal magnetism in trappings of authority.	Program confirms loyalty to church and its moral code which she abides by.
		Sockman	
Mrs. Wakefield	In old age, with innerdirected husband dead and large family happily married, she is enjoying herself and has relaxed obligation to attend church. Not a shut-in. Moderately high identification with authority.	The rational, benign style of Sockman provided easy transfer of role of "her minister" to him. His content, especially his benedictions, perceived as of personal value to her.	A terminal substitue for church where religion is a rational, subjective matter with pleasant emotional tones. She supports both Sockman and her old church.
		Peale	
Mr. West	High anxiety level from peer-group censure, fear of mortality and partial awareness of earned guilt, focused on symbolic loss of daughter. Srong identification with authority	Peale's philosophy, sincerity, delivery in a setting where peer-group approval of Peale cued Mr. West to use him.	Relief of some anxiety through conventional activity in church with full realization neither of his sin nor of Christ as Savior.

labels may be attached to Peale's technique. But whether it is termed "sincere," "inspirational" or "relaxing," the effect is generally the same. It is closely analogous to the well-known therapeutic effect of a visit from the doctor, who relieves anxiety by his professional presence regardless of his success or failure in identifying an ailment and prescribing appropriate medication.

The "effect" of the Peale program appears to be psychotherapeutic. Both of the women attributed to it new insights into themselves which permitted them to work out tolerable solutions to their problems. West, likewise, was partly "awakened," though perhaps not so much as he thought he was, and found in church participation at least a strategy for easing his guilt feelings. For all three of these individuals, and for others not reported on in detail here, the ascertainable effect of the Peale program was the solution of such immediate reality problems. Mrs. Jackson's solution left her with no change in her hostility to the person who had provoked the problem and no attachment to religion. Mrs. Clark's solution permitted her to return to teaching Sunday school again but with no change in her previous ethnocentric attitude toward her fellow men and no change in her sterile view of religion. West's future relation to religion is left up in the air, being dependent upon his future relations with his minister and his church.

But it is important to note in every case that although actual "spiritual" progress was limited to a rather narrow range of psychological change, each of the interviewees was left with the conviction that the keys to future growth were to be found in the Bible, prayer and faith. Peale had brought them this far, which was farther than any previous clergyman had been able to bring them, and perhaps further growth must inevitably be sought in relationships with local churches and skillful pastors rather than with any speaker—no matter how winsome and compelling—whose sole contact is through the mass media.

Sockman Audience

It is significant that the two interviews from the Sockman audience selected for depth presentation were in classes II and III and that the age of the individuals was at or past the half-century mark. While anxiety marked the state of the Peale listeners, no unusual degree of anxiety is evident in the Sockman audience. Rather, the state of readiness to listen of these persons is marked by habituation to the ways of middle-class or upper middle-class Protestant churchgoing. These are pillars of the church who for different reasons listen to Sockman. Mrs. Wakefield listens because she has relinquished to a younger generation her church duties and now is luxuriating in the pleasures of life permissible in her social class and age group. The Austins, while younger and still active in church work of all kinds, taste and sample all manner of religious practices via radio. They have the interest of connoisseurs in religious music, preaching and liturgy.

Sockman's appeal for these people is a combination of his personality, his content and his delivery. Sockman is Mrs. Wakefield's rational, intelligent, familiar minister. The demands he makes on her are intellectual and attitudinal only; he does not come down from the Sunday morning pulpit and require behavioral changes in her comfortable weekday life. For the Austins, he is an expert whom they regard with warm, but detached interest; which of his propositions they will accept—indeed, which they will even hear —is their own decision, not the preacher's.

This relationship to the audience seems to be a fundamental attribute of "liberal" Protestantism as it appears in these interviews, particularly in relation to Sockman and Bonnell, who are the prototypes of the radio preachers sponsored by interdenominational Protestantism. They offer ideas and propositions, with the expectation that the listener will make his own selection as to which are valid, appealing to various types of authority—reason, experience, the Bible, the Church. Sheen, on the other hand, delivers pronouncements. He is the authority; his references to other authorities are more in the nature of interesting illustrations than validation of his ideas. The whole difference between Roman Catholic and Protestant concepts of authority underlies the difference in presentation and the difference in acceptance by the respective audiences for these programs.

The effects of the Sockman program appear to be like those of a church service aimed at the committed fellowship. It has no apparent effect in drawing new members, but rather sustains the present ones. Some are shut-in. Others, like Mrs. Wakefield, simply prefer not to attend church. In the Austins we find an illustration of people who hear Sockman as they do their own minister—insensitively and out of long experience in going through religious motions.

Sheen Audience

It is significant that we find a wide diversity of people in Sheen's audience. They are mostly in social classes II, III and IV. In terms of family composition they range from young couples with young children, still in the home-building stage, to elderly, retired people. Their central interests fall into four of our six interest categories. In church attachment, they range from Roman Catholics through Protestants to "none." The Protestant view of man's relation to God and the value of the Bible does not predominate among these people. And, perhaps significantly, only one of them gave evidence of substantial respect for the integrity of the individual human being.

The three Roman Catholics in this group have a common basis for watching the Bishop in their lifelong attachment to the Roman Catholic Church. However, the quality of this attraction is different as between the Voskuils and Mrs. Boyle. The Voskuils typify the lower class immigrants from Europe who are traditionally bound to the Church, but in a rather loose way. They take their dependence on the Church's authority for granted. Voskuil comes to the program keenly aware of the disadvantages he labors under because of his lack of formal education, while his wife brings it only her generalized loyalty to the Church. Mrs. Boyle, on the contrary, typifies the American attitude that stresses the literal observance of both the form and the doctrine of Roman Catholicism. Conflict between her family responsibilities and her personal ambitions makes her need policy advice from an authoritative Roman Catholic source, advice that is beyond the capacity of her parish priest.

The distinctive features of the readiness-states of the non-Roman Catholics who watch Sheen are diverse, although there is a common layer of frustration in all of them. The frustration of the Richardsons stems from their empty, conventional lives and Mrs. Richardson's compulsive efforts to drive the family into higher social status. Mrs. Clark's frustration and anxiety flow from her weak, unloved, childless existence in middle age and her strategy of repressing her unsatisfied needs through moral dicta derived from religious authority figures. Jackson's frustration stems from a lifetime of timidity which he feels robbed him of realizing his full masculine potential in the field of business. And Manson's frustration is the end product of a lifetime of being kicked around by a hostile world.

Sheen speaks to all of these people in harmony with their needs. Voskuil perceives Sheen in terms of his fine education, his fluency and his seemingly inexhaustible fund of knowledge, taking him to be a "great man" who epitomizes the best of Roman Catholicism. Mrs. Voskuil sees Sheen in terms of his personal magnetism which "makes you sit there and look at him." Mrs. Boyle, as would be expected from the analysis of her predisposition, looks for and finds in Sheen's programs moral advice. She finds an infallible policy spokesman for the Church who "answers my questions"— that is he reconciles the seemingly divergent Church doctrine and practice in such matters as divorce. The fact that she is particularly interested in the subject of divorce betrays her conflict between marital duties and her personal development.

Similarly the non-Roman Catholics find in Sheen what they need. The lonely, frustrated Mrs. Clark finds moralistic exhortation. Timid Jackson sees Sheen as positive and aggressive. The embittered Manson, seeking to pass the time, finds him "interesting." The two Richardsons, compulsively concerned with conventional status, find it in Sheen's "preaching goodness."

Congruence likewise marks the uses our eight individuals make of Sheen's programs. Both of the Voskuils use them to confirm their loyalty to the Church. Voskuil learns from Sheen, but it is unlikely he would follow the Bishop if the bread-and-butter interests of his family were thereby imperiled. Mrs. Voskuil uses Sheen's moralizing to support her own values, which are remarkably similar to those preached by the Bishop. Mrs. Boyle gets the reassurance she asks for in her "questions" when she uses the Sheen program for he "invariably" takes up policy issues about the time she becomes aware of them. His infallibility for her is accompanied by the illusion of two-way communication for he seems to her to transcend the limits of television by sensing a viewer's inability to understand an unfamiliar idea and immediately explaining it. Mrs. Boyle makes use of such mystical attributes of Roman Catholicism in very important ways, as our previous analysis of her devotional practices indicates. She uses the Sheen program to reinforce these qualities in her faith and to strengthen her will to submit to her exacting faith as against the suppressed drives that produce her anxiety.

The non-Roman Catholics make similarly appropriate uses of the programs. Jackson, the timid old man, gets support for his inadequate fund of self-respect through the occasional watching of the aggressive strength of a power figure. The anxious, unloved Mrs. Clark uses the moral exhortations to strengthen her adherence to the moral code by which she maintains her control over suppressed, unsatisfied needs. The Richardsons, in their compulsive strivings for self-realization through upward social mobility, use their perception of his "goodness" to confirm their conventional attitudes and prejudices. (Walton [Chapter 13] learns of subjects and viewpoints it is "safe" to discuss and espouse.)

Old Fashioned Revival Hour (Fuller) Audience

The Old Fashioned Revival Hour may be analyzed simply by observing that there is an obvious congruence between the needs of the people who hear it, their perceptions of the program and their uses of it. In all three cases, the readiness-state contains the common experience of childhood or adolescent exposure to old hymns and revivalist-type church services. It is no accident that we find no Roman Catholics here; for the necessary antecedent experience is not found in the Roman practice. It is clear that the features of the program that attracted the listeners were the hymn music and the revival atmosphere. Likewise, Fuller listeners take a nostalgic pleasure in recalling through the aid of this program their childhood or youthful experiences. In Manson's case they are predominantly painful experiences, mixed with youthful aspirations and pleasures brutally mutilated by the reality of a hard world. In the Austins, these youthful experiences have the status of being the ventures of young "amateurs" in sampling religious practices—ventures which Mrs. Austin told us in the interview they have difficulty in reconciling with the pleasure their own children take in attending Youth for Christ revival meetings. They "don't appreciate particularly" this contemporary version as do their children.

Greatest Story Ever Told and Billy Graham Audiences

The Richardsons were the most constant listeners to The Greatest Story Ever Told. Their readiness-state has already been described in connection with Sheen. Whereas, they were only casually interested in Sheen, they were very much interested in The Greatest Story Ever Told. They romanticize their own childhood experiences and are seeking means to impart their quality into their own home, which so lacks human warmth. Bible stories are remembered as being enjoyed in a family setting in childhood. They are therefore predisposed toward something like The Greatest Story Ever Told. They perceive it as having advantages over the Bible stories they remember, for The Greatest Story has the vividness of the dramatic format. The effects of the program on the Richardsons are reported in consistent terms. They saw their children listen raptly. Afterward they asked questions on the meaning of incidents in the stories. The father and mother found a nostalgic pleasure in associating the content of the program with their memories of their own childhood experiences. The program thus confirms and validates for them their pre-existing attitudes toward home and religion. It does not, however, confront them with any Biblical interpretation that may threaten their conventional values. We are forced to omit comment on the meaning of this program to Mrs. Boyle who reported that she listened regularly but failed to give any evaluation of the program.

The Swensons, who watch Graham on television, are the only members of his audience on whom we are reporting. The facts that frame the readiness state of these two older people are simple. They are immigrants from Sweden with tradition-bound, lower-class attitudes. They have had a lifelong attach-ment to the Lutheran church in which they have been active and which has provided them social contacts and prestige among their peers. As was the case with the Austins, they have rather a connoisseur's attitude toward fa-vored types of religious ceremonies, and one of their favorites is the revivalis-tic style of preaching. Congruently, the Swensons appreciate the Graham program for his preaching technique and express the wish that there was more of it. The program gives them pleasure in appreciating it—a form of religious entertainment that passes time pleasantly and maintains the role of religion in their consciousness.

General Conclusions

Not all of the conclusions we have reached are explicitly supported by the depth interview material previously presented in detail. This is inevitable in the nature of the exploratory process. With this warning, we present the con-clusions that may be drawn from the depth interviews concerning the se-lected religious radio and television programs we have been studying.

THE PEALE PROGRAMS

These programs, which are the most popular of those presented by the National Council of Churches, have an undeniable function that they per-form reliably. They offer psychotherapy to individuals whose anxiety levels have risen to uncomfortable heights. The content and style of the pro-grams obviously invites individuals with such problems to "put the shoe on." The content is cast in predominantly market-place language, and invites people with deep-seated personal relations problems to recast them in the limited terms presented by Peale. West illustrates this point. If West's re-sponse to Peale is the general one—and with our present data, we can only infer it is widespread—Peale's program alone is inadequate to meet the prob-lem. Indeed, it may lead to a quasi-solution that in some ways may be poten-tially harmful to the individual and to the church. It can be argued that had West been left in a state of discomfort, facing his peer-group critics and his wife for a longer period, he would have been forced by his anxiety to examine his conscience more fully and more honestly, and thus have re-alized more adequately the full extent of his shortcomings. By providing him an easy out by which he could have his cake and eat it too, Peale may have set back his long-run adjustment to the meaning of the Gospel.

On the other hand, Peale did make a real contact with West, based on the dynamics of his anxiety, and because of Peale's message West did something constructive to relieve his anxiety. There is no evidence that any other re-ligious figure or institution in West's life had been able to accomplish this. But West, like other Peale listeners, has found that Peale's exhortation to go to church, read the Bible, pray, believe, is not as easy to follow as it is to say and hear. The listener who takes Peale's advice finds it necessary to change his way of life.

A second characteristic effect of the Peale program is the tendency, often observed in this study, for the "client" to follow Peale's advice merely as long as his anxiety tells him he has a problem. When the anxiety level drops—because the individual has worked out the interpersonal problem or because other circumstances have disposed of it—the listener drops Peale and his works with no lasting change in religious attitudes or practices. Mrs. Jackson provides an example of this situation.

We have also found in the depth interviews cases where Peale helped a listener with a reality problem, and once it was solved the individual re-turned to an interrupted relation with the church. Mrs. Clark is such a per-son. This is a wholly desirable effect, for so long as she is kept in relation to her church it may be hoped that growth may take place in her grasp of Christian essentials.

We make one other appraisal of the Peale radio and television programs. When they are compared with other programs, notably Sheen's, it is clear that Peale is broadcasting a special-purpose message, appealing to a narrowly selected group of persons. Most of the possible multilayered structure of the Christian faith is left out of the Peale programs. Consequently, the audience that is attracted to them is concerned with only the narrow range of mean-ing carried by the content, and is, therefore, homogeneous in psychological essentials. It follows that a large bloc of the population with other states of readiness to receive Protestant religion is left unserved by the Peale pro-grams.

THE SOCKMAN PROGRAM

Sockman has a loyal and substantial audience that obtains deep satisfac-tion from his interpretation of the Gospel. Predominantly an older audi-ence, its members substantially fall in three groups as far as they were iden-tified in the research. Some of them are shut-ins or others who for various physical reasons are out of touch with their own churches. Some of them are physically able to go to church but prefer Sockman as a less demanding sub-stitute. Still a third group, illustrated by the Austins, find Sockman a stimu-lating, attractive guide to religious knowledge and belief while they participate regularly in the activities of some church. The substance of the Sockman programs is respectable, literate, rational religion of the type familiar in the middle-class and upper middle-class Protestant churches of British-American background. It is what Reisman calls an "inner-directed" type of religion, one which appeals to the strength of the conscience and firm inner purpose of the individual to accomplish change in character or behavior. In view of Riesman's contention that this character type in the population has been progressively outnumbered by the "other-directed" character structure in the past forty years, it is permissible to wonder whether with the passage of time, the Sockman type of program, like its correlative audience, may not tend to decrease in influence. It is certain, as far as this study goes, that the Sockman program has little or no potential in attracting new converts to Protestantism. It performs a useful "holding" function for present practicing Protestants, but it may unintentionally on occasion offer them a justification for avoiding actual church responsibilities.

THE SHEEN PROGRAM

Sheen provides his audience with something they can use on many different levels of meaning. We have observed in the preceding analysis how he can mean many different things to different people. To the uneducated who feel their lack, Sheen is an understandable but superbly educated man who can help lift them toward his level. To the timid, Sheen is a resolute symbol of masculine competence and assurance. To the deprived and bitter, Sheen is at least "interesting," and may be a source of authoritative direction in behavior on political and economic issues. To the conventional and conservative of all faiths, Sheen is perceived as preaching not Roman Catholicism but simply "goodness" and his message is therefore approved and accepted internally. To the prejudiced and bigoted, Sheen offers approval and new ideas in their search for a "progressive" scapegoat on which to vent their undischarged hostility. To the loyal Roman Catholics, torn between personality fulfillment and church-approved morality, Sheen offers an infallible source of authority by which discrepant church program and practice may be happily reconciled and the moral code reaffirmed. To tradition-directed wives, committed to kitchen, children and church, Sheen offers compelling personal magnetism that ornaments their routine religious practice. To upper-class businessmen of conservative leanings, Sheen offers an economic and political program and a symbol that might under certain conditions become the religious counterpart of a native American totalitarian movement. And all this is not exhaustive of what is found in Sheen.

Elsewhere we have observed that the Sheen programs are masterpieces of technical construction. It is no accident that his audience is a legion of types. For he has built a program full of ambiguity, full of cues and symbols on many levels of meaning, carefully put together in relationships and with timing that invite a maximum of disparate interpretations.

THE GREATEST STORY EVER TOLD

The value of the analysis of this program for the present study lies in the demonstration of the kind of audience that may be established for a competently presented program of Bible stories cast in dramatic form. The Peale programs preselect an audience primarily Protestant, usually above thirty years old, beset by problems. Sockman preselects an even older audience, most of whom have long passed their child-rearing period. But the Bible stories in dramatic format preselect an audience distinguished by its high proportion of young parents with children, particularly those parents whose own childhood training stressed Bible study and who feel their children should be receiving comparable training. The dramatic form, in addition to being entertainment in its own right, apparently makes the Bible instruction more palatable to both children and parents. Such a program, based on the best scholarly interpretation of the Scriptures, could well be the cornerstone of Protestant television programming.

THE OLD FASHIONED REVIVAL HOUR

The Old Fashioned Revival Hour, upon appraisal, seems to be, as its title indicates, almost purely an adventure in nostalgia for the audience, a religious version of the old WLS Saturday Night Barn Dance. The entire content and format are a ritual evocation of a kind of religious experience that dominated Protestant America a half-century ago, and the audience appears to consist largely of working-class Protestants whose younger days were spent in an environment with such religious overtones. We may conclude from the evidence that this program also serves a purpose in satisfying the needs of this group for recognition in an urban culture. In a city where Protestants hold the top positions in business and society, the Revival Hour listeners are Protestants who have not climbed the social ladder—they are manual workers—and even the institutions of their own religion have somehow betrayed them by acquiring a "coldness," an urbanity and sophistication, that makes worship in the city a completely different experience from the church in the home town. So they tune in the Old Fashioned Revival Hour and listen to the familiar words with the comforting feeling that at least here, on this important modern medium of communication, the men that "run this country" have had to give some recognition to "our kind" of religion.

The dimension involved here is not merely time, but also space. Revivalistic religion is still familiar in many sections of the country, and the migrant to New Haven may have revival experiences dating back five rather than fifty years. No such person was discovered in the people interviewed, however. It would be interesting to repeat this analysis in a city such as Cincinnati.

THE GRAHAM PROGRAMS

We regret that these interviews did not turn up more information on Graham. There is evidence that his audience rather closely resembles that of the Old Fashioned Revival Hour and that the two programs serve much the same purpose, at least in a northeastern city such as the one we have been studying. Evidence not presented here, however—particularly some pilot interviews taken in Greensboro, North Carolina—hints that while Graham's original and primary appeal is to the evocation of a familiar and pleasant religious experience among Protestants with revival preaching in their background, he builds upon this base a structure of religious orientation and purpose with more dynamic to it than does Fuller. Graham does not confine himself to exhortations regarding the conventional forms of personal morality. He forthrightly treats personal, community, national and international problems, applying his fundamentalist Biblical interpretation to their solution.

PART V

A Strategy for Religious Broadcasting

CHAPTER 19

The Background for
Policy Formation

It is abundantly clear to the reader who has followed the research to this point that this is the kind of study distinguished more by breadth than by precision. By this we do not mean that the research staff has not been precise; we hope it has been adequately demonstrated that we have treated our data with accuracy and our research tools with respect. We mean, rather, that we have considered our problem to be defined by the totality of the situation instead of by the aspects of it which could be put under a microscope. We have tried to tackle a large subject by coming at it from a number of directions and using diverse available research tools that were not always consistent with each other, and certainly not dependent upon each other. Our research design was not in its essence constituted of interdependent methods; the interdependence was rather that of the parts of the problem itself. Thus, different findings have not only different *degrees* of validity, but different *kinds* of validity. The statistics in Chapter 13 are very different materials from the statistics in Chapter 10.

This multifaceted approach to a problem is, in research terms, parallel to the condition of the policy-maker himself, and was designed with this in mind. Policy formation is characterized by the need for making specific decisions at specific times in the context of a complex situation in which some knowledge is specific, but much is composed of hunch, experience, insight, preconception and incidental information. The dissatisfaction of the policy-maker with the researcher is often precisely because the latter defines his contribution so narrowly in terms of that which is "researchable," or amenable to a given methodological procedure, rather than in terms of the more complicated total problem the policy-maker must resolve. We have tried —rightly or wrongly, and with what success the reader must judge—to match research procedures to the totality of the problem; and where the available procedures are inadequate to the complexity of the problem, our findings undoubtedly reflect the fact.

Because we have gone down a number of paths, however, it may be well here to review what has been said thus far. What follows is not a "summary," in the sense of a digest of the preceding chapters, but rather an effort to draw out from those chapters a series of generalizations that form the background for policy formation in this field, as we evaluate the findings.

Chapter 1: Mass communication takes place in a social matrix which is a dynamic composite of religion, national origin, culture and social class. Every given member of the radio and television audience occupies a position in this matrix, and, in addition, is often in the process of changing his position. This position will strongly influence his attitude toward a communicator and the interpretation he gives to the content of a message on radio or television. This conclusion would seem to be particularly true about religious mass communications, which deal so specifically with values.

Chapter 2: The religious divisions in American society reflect to a significant degree the social divisions. The constituency of the Congregational Christian and Episcopal churches, for example, shows a bias toward upper business and professional groups; Methodist toward middle class, white collar occupations; Lutheran toward small business and skilled labor; Roman Catholic toward industrial working-class population, et cetera. Thus, religious affiliation, statistically speaking, tends to be correlated with such other social data as income, education, occupation, housing and type of household and age-sex distribution. It is not a one-to-one correlation (the "working" class is predominant in almost all religious groups, as it is in the population), but it is a tendency sufficiently pronounced so we may assume that in mass communications, a program beamed at a selective *religious* audience will also be selective in such social factors as education, occupation, et cetera. Conversely, a program that selects its audience by education, occupation, family type, et cetera, will presumably find it is religiously selective as well.

Chapter 3: The distinguishing characteristic of the process of communication in the Protestant churches is that, except for the worship service, it is not a "mass" activity but a small group activity. The characteristic program of the Protestant church is a gathering of ten to twenty people in class, club or interest group. The chief exception to this practice is the worship service, which in New Haven is typically a gathering of 150 to 200 people. Aside from the size of group involved, two other distinguishing characteristics of conventional Protestant church program need to be noted, each in specific contrast to the characteristic nature of the secular mass media: (1) the conventional program of the Protestant church has a minimum of professional guidance and leadership; and (2) consciously or unconsciously, the church program seems beamed at groups that are quite selective as to social class, national origin and general psychological orientation.

Chapter 4: Most adults (eight out of nine in this study) appear ready to identify themselves as related to a specific faith group when asked to do so. Those that do not are more likely to be Protestant or Jewish than Roman Catholic, male than female, nonparents than parents. They are also likely to be persons with higher incomes and more advanced education.

Chapter 5: There is little evidence that pastors of local churches have given any serious or deep thought to the impact of radio and television upon their constituents, or the potential usefulness of the mass media as tools in religious education, evangelism, religious public relations and other facets of church program and strategy. Their personal and family use of these media shows no marked difference from the "average" professional; their reactions to religious programming are largely subjective; and their understanding of the religious use of radio and television relegates these media to such peripheral purposes as the ministry to shut-ins.

Chapter 6: The sponsors of religious programs generally state their aims and identify their "target audiences" in broad and sweeping terms, indicating in most cases a failure to focus on specific groups or to delineate specific purposes to be achieved by the programs. The most popular formats for religious programs are talk, drama and the conventional church worship service. Roman Catholic programs tend to be more specific in aim than do Protestant—the aim being the winning of converts—and more ready to give specific and authoritative directives to an audience, even on controversial issues. This practice reflects the Roman Catholic orientation to stronger ecclesiastical authority than Protestants have. Protestant programs tend more to present the generalized principles for ethical, moral and religious living, leaving the listener to make application. Analysis of a number of specific programs showed considerable differences among them in the extent to which they resorted to sharp bipolarization of values or value symbols in efforts to communicate a basic value system.

Chapter 7: Insofar as the concept of "mass" implies a large number of precisely similar discrete units, the term applies to the media rather than the audience. The media present precisely similar stimuli to thousands of people; the people themselves, however, differ markedly in characteristics and reactions. In addition, any audience is almost invariably a minority of the population, and statistical analysis is useful to discover the characterizing traits that differentiate this minority audience from the majority nonaudience.

Chapter 8: Television set owners differed from nonowners in New Haven in the distinct tendency of the set-owning group to be less Protestant (i.e., more Roman Catholic or Jewish) and to be working class rather than upper business and professional class. Radio set ownership was almost universal. Families with minor children are more likely to own television sets than families without minor children. However, television set ownership appears to have rapidly approached near-universality in all groups, judging from evidence secured subsequent to the sample.

Chapter 9: Entertainment programs dominate television (73 per cent) with information programs a poor second (20 per cent) and orientation programs (which include religion) a very poor third (7 per cent). Drama is the most frequent entertainment form; newscasts the characteristic information program. Religious programs get about one in every 100 telecast hours. Crime drama is the most frequent adult drama type, and westerns dominate children's drama. Advertising represents one-fifth to one-fourth of all telecast time. In terms of popularity, the largest audiences watch news, sports, variety, quiz, and general drama programs, in that order, with religion sixth in popularity. On radio, however, religious programs are third in popularity as measured by size of audience. There seems to be no definite relationship between the audience for one program type and the audience for another; viewers of sports programs, for example, are neither more nor less likely to watch religious programs than are viewers of comedy drama. There are, however, some characterizing differences between the audiences for specific program types; viewers of news, sports, variety, general drama, domestic drama, public issues, and crime drama programs, for example, are characterized in each type by some concentration in specific social classes.

Chapter 10: Three out of five households watch or listen to some religious program with regularity. This three-fifths, interestingly enough, is not importantly different from the two-fifths who do not listen in most of the identifying characteristics used in this statistical sampling: social class, income, church attendance, education, age, occupation and type of household. Jews and Protestants are relatively more frequent in the nonaudience, but this condition could have been due to the popularity of a single program (Sheen) at the time of the sample. However, the widespread response to religious programming is evident, representing over half of the great majority of groups in the population studied, however these groups are analyzed.

Chapter 11: When the "audience for religion" is broken down into the audiences for specific religious programs, however, these audiences appear to be much more specialized. Leading Roman Catholic programs have a much larger audience than leading Protestant programs, although the smaller audience for Protestant programs is more diversified (in religious affiliation) than the Roman Catholic program audience. Two programs (Sheen and The Greatest Story Ever Told) accounted for a large proportion of the total audience for religion. The audiences for specific programs, when analyzed, show a considerable amount of bias in religion, social class, age, occupation, education, type of household and marital status, indicating a specialized appeal for most religious programs. The program with the largest audience (Sheen) is also the least specialized by these criteria, except for the preponderance of Roman Catholics among its viewers.

Chapters 12 and 13: The last major approach to the analysis of the audience (and nonaudience) for religious radio and television was in terms of personality types. Here were found the most significant clues to "explain" the use of religious radio and television programs and interpret their role in people's behavior patterns. From the standpoint of understanding and interpretation, the most satisfying approach was the case study. A lengthy nondirective interview, supplemented by certain details of life history and current status and one or two personality tests, can provide the material necessary for a student in this field to state with some assurance the role and effects of religious radio and television in an individual's life style, and to predict reaction to future exposure to such programs. But this is not adequate for the policy-makers who must program for people in large masses rather than as individuals. Therefore, it has been useful to discover that each device used in the analysis of interview respondents has shown that clusterings around *personality types* correlate with use and nonuse of religious programs, and that this use and nonuse can be logically related to personality drives and needs.

One such device was the analysis of people by major preoccupations or interests as discovered in the interviews: work-centered, status-centered, family-and-home-centered, self-centered, formal-religion-centered and social-responsibility-centered. In the case of each group, thus defined, there could be described from actual data something approaching "typical" behavior and attitudes in religion and in relation to the mass media; and there could be projected something resembling "normative" behavior for the ideal types representing each major preoccupation.

A similar situation was found when interviewees were grouped as personality types in accordance with their attitudes toward authority as revealed by the F-scale tests. These test findings were related on the one hand to the respondents' major preoccupations and on the other to their use of religious programs.

Chapter 14: The significance of the findings about personality types and interests is in their unmistakable implication that the policy groups planning the use of the mass media on behalf of the value-impregnated interests of religion cannot master these media unless they take account of the dimension of personality in the audience, in addition to (and in close relation to) the more familiar objective dimensions of age, religious affiliation, income, education, et cetera, by which an audience is more conventionally described. The personality attributes which a clergyman almost instinctively understands and reacts to in face-to-face communication with individuals need to be much more systematically understood and planned for in religious communication addressed to the large, anonymous audience reached by the mass media.

Chapters 15, 16 and 17: These chapters underscored what was said in Chapter 14 by giving detailed analyses of characteristic families in the audiences for specific programs, and by demonstrating in each case that use of a particular program was in no sense accidental, but was related to a position in life and a system of needs and drives that made use of that program a consistent part of a pattern of living. There are logical reasons for listening or nonlistening that go deep into the personality and personal-social situation of audience members, far deeper than their simple identification as Catholics, or Presbyterians, or nonparticipants in any church.

Chapter 18: The programming policy that must emerge from an understanding of the personality complexities of the potential audience, therefore, must of necessity be a policy based upon a well-developed theory about society, community and personality in our time. It must see the potential audience in all the complexity of human dynamics in our anxiety-driven, class-conditioned, striving and mobile age; it must devote at least as much attention to the identification of the groups to whom religion intends to speak via these media as it does to the content of its message; and it must work positively at the task of developing programs beamed specifically at its target populations. It is evident from these audience analyses that religious sponsors are now engaged in a program of broadcasting to specialized groups, but that the specialization is inadvertent and unintentional. The need is for a policy that will permit conscious and intentional specialization in accord with basic religious aims.

CHAPTER 20

A Strategy for
Religious Broadcasting

We approach now the concluding task of this study: an outline of the basic elements which must enter into a strategy for religious broadcasting.

Strategy is at any given time a combination of many factors, some immediate and some long-range. Our procedure here is to move from the immediate to the long-range, from the areas of planning and education where change can be made readily to those where change is a long-term process resulting from careful study, planning and reorientation.

Strategy at the Tactical Level, Where Change Can Be Made Without Change in Policy

1. CHURCHES AND CLERGY USING RADIO AND TELEVISION SHOULD BE MADE TO UNDERSTAND THE NATURE OF THEIR REAL AUDIENCE

Perhaps the most persistent error on the part of religious broadcasters, an error that appears constantly in statements and literature, is the assumption that because the media are almost universal, they therefore deliver to any program an audience representative of universality. This is simply not true; an audience that is a cross section of the available population is a highly unusual achievement, the product of planning, skill and real genius, and it is a rare phenomenon among audiences for religious programs in particular. It is fair to say, on the basis of the evidence presented, that the clergyman who presents on the air a duplication of what he presents from the pulpit will have as his audience about the same group as those who will come to church to hear him. The individuals composing this group will vary from those in his congregation, of course, but as a type, they will be as selective by social class and general social orientation as is the typical Protestant congregation, and the evidence here is that they will be equally selected as to psychological or personality type. Further, for the greatest majority of programs of this type (i.e., the radio or television version of a church service), the audience even in numerical terms in a town such as New Haven does not seem to be much larger than a fair-sized Sunday morning congregation.

In this, research findings are simply a documentation of common sense. The "magic" of radio and television is not the kind of magic that rubs off on the amateur performer, and it contains nothing to add appeal or interest to the clergyman who cannot inspire people in person or in the pulpit. Further, the radio and television audience does not have the motivations of a church constituency, whose group loyalties and commitments may bring them to church regardless of the level of skill of the minister in conducting group services. As a general principle, therefore, if religious agencies wish to use these media to reach a large audience with a message, they would be well advised to select for their spokesmen those persons, clerical or lay, with a demonstrated capacity for capturing the interest and imagination of variegated audiences without these media.

Prestige and position in the church, incidentally, are in themselves no substitute for this kind of skill. This is particularly true in Protestantism, where the important names of any denomination are rarely known outside that denomination's constituency.

2. THE CHURCHES AND THEIR LEADERSHIP SHOULD BE MADE MORE AWARE OF THE TOTAL ROLE OF THE MASS MEDIA IN THE LIVES OF THEIR CONSTITUENTS AND SHOULD GEAR THEIR MINISTRY ACCORDINGLY

The depth interviews presented a great deal of evidence as to the role the media play in the formation of opinions, attitudes, judgments, self-understanding, and, in the final analysis, value patterns. These are critical matters for the churches, and they go far beyond the scope of this study, which is focused on "religious" programming in the mass media. They involve the unprecedented shift in people's attention from opinion-formation groups and agencies that are primary, local and personal to those which are secondary, national and impersonal. It was not too long ago in America that a church member's general life orientation was developed in his face-to-face conversation with neighbors and friends, in his perusal of the local newspaper, in his reading of books—especially the Bible—and in his participation, weekly or more often, in large congregate assemblies in church presided over by a clergyman whose chief purpose was to give him fundamental moral orientation. All these exist today, and are powerful influences in orientation, but superimposed upon them are all the highly developed mass communication devices of our age. Today not only his minister, but Bishop Sheen and Arthur Godfrey and Milton Berle and Edward R. Murrow speak to him of religious and moral matters. Today his picture of conventional or desirable home life is conditioned not merely by what he sees among his neighbors, but by pictures painted by Madison Avenue advertising agencies. Men and women whom he has never met, and never expects to meet, come into his living room under the most calculatedly favorable circumstances to suggest the tastes he should have, the opinions he should hold, the style of life he should follow. A barrage of dramatic shows from Hollywood and New York gives him an implicit image of what the world is like and how families behave and what problems and conflicts he may expect to confront in life situations. Syndicated columnists make explicit a variety of interpretations of contemporary civilization.

The big new phenomenon in mass communication, of course, is television, on which this study has concentrated. We should not exaggerate its influence, even though all tests show it has tremendously conditioned the leisure-time behavior of the American people. But the church must take account of the fact that the people to whom it ministers are also people who devote large blocs of time to watching television. At the most superficial level, this means that if the American people are going to be spending a great deal of time watching television, the churches ought to seek their fair share of time on this medium to communicate what they have to say. At a more basic level, the churches need to understand television as an important part of the lives of their constituents, to discover the pertinence of the Christian Gospel for both the producer and the consumer of television, and to help their clergy to interpret the relevance of Christian belief to this aspect of contemporary life.

The implication of certain of the data in Chapter 5 is that the clergy of New Haven were less exposed to the mass media than perhaps any other professional group, were inclined to discount the influence of the media in their parishioners' lives, and in general were ready to continue to minister as though these media did not exist. If this is a true reflection of their position, it follows a pattern not without precedent in the history of the church. The reputation of the church for conservatism is in part derived from a history of resisting change by refusing to acknowledge its appearance. Television is one more threat to the influence of the church because it is one more secular voice speaking to the public, tempting and wheedling and persuading and informing and arguing and amusing people in accord with whatever interests move the sponsors and managers of the program. It cannot be ignored by the churches; it might, however, be used. Somehow the ministry of the Protestant churches must be made aware of the total role of the mass media in the lives of their constituents, and the machinery of the churches must be geared to a careful and thoughtful educational process to make the constituents conscientious stewards in relation to the use of these media. The principles of Christian ethics apply to both the producer and the consumer of the media, but thus far the churches have made little conscious attempt to think through the obligations of either group.

3. IN SELECTION OF PROGRAMS FOR PRESENTATION, CHURCH GROUPS SHOULD CONSIDER THE MANY DIFFERENT NEEDS AND DIMENSIONS OF THE RADIO AND TELEVISION AUDIENCES.

It is clear that Protestant groups have not understood—or at least have not been able to implement their understanding of—the multidimensional character of the mass audience and the related multilayeredness of program content and format. Most religious programs are singularly one-dimensional. Both statements of purpose and aim have tended to disguise the fact that the typical religious program consciously or unconsciously has been designed to reach only one type of person through one kind of format with one kind of message. This report has surely indicated that potential audiences are not only large, but remarkably varied as to sociological and personality types; that the potential formats for religious programming are limited only by the creative imagination (drama, music, discussion, news, entertainment, preaching, teaching, et cetera); and that the message of the church on the air can take any number of forms according to the types of audiences sought and the needs the programs are intended to serve.

Even without changing policies or changing programs, the agencies responsible for religious programming ought to rationalize what they are doing. Each program the churches sponsor ought to have a clear reason for existence within the framework of the generalized purposes of the Christian ministry. Each program, in other words, should rest upon a statement of policy which defines clearly exactly what the churches are attempting to do in the program and how they intend to go about it. Only then will they have a yardstick against which to measure the program's results.

We have referred more than once to the controversy in Protestant circles over the nature and effectiveness of Dr. Peale's programs and we may use them for illustrations of this point. Without taking sides in this controversy, we would suggest that the programs could be discussed much more intelligently if they were considered against such a policy statement as the following:

We know that American people today are characterized by a high level of anxiety that focuses particularly on interpersonal problems. A symptom of this anxiety is the remarkable reception given to what is called the "peace of mind" cult, which attempts through simple methods of self-diagnosis and self-therapy to alleviate anxieties and induce "happiness." We feel the churches have a serious obligation here in their pastoral ministry. We are aware that the problems related to anxiety are much more fundamental than simple "adjustment" to anxiety-producing situations, and that they involve everything from sin and severe psychological disturbance in the personal dimension to injustice, conflict and social disorganization in the social dimension.

We cannot in a single television series, however, resolve these more fundamental problems. The churches are working on them constantly through their pastoral ministries, their institutional ministries, their programs in Christian social relations and the support of constructive secular programs serving these needs. What we can do in a television series is the following:

1. *Capture the attention of anxiety-driven persons on the basis of their anxieties.*
2. *Direct their attention to the Christian faith as the key to the solution to their problems, both immediate and ultimate.*
3. *Give them specific instructions as to how to make contact with the resources of our faith—the Bible, the church, prayer, the pastors and consecrated laymen—in the confident belief that through these resources they can come to a deeper understanding and eventual commitment.*

For these specific purposes we shall sponsor Dr. Norman Vincent Peale, who has demonstrated an unusual capacity to inspire people to take these first steps.

It must be admitted that such a policy statement at this time is both *ad hominem* and *ex post facto;* it is the rationalization of practice rather than the formulation of new policy. It ignores the fact that a "value-vacuum" exists in counseling programs that gloss over the necessity for fundamental character changes in the treatment of anxiety: that they give the listener less than he deserves and require less than he should give. But it does give a specific policy statement against which to measure practice. We predict that a clear and precise statement of policy in relation to each program now sponsored by religious groups would be a long step toward either making that program more effective or discarding the program as an inadequate means of implementing policy.

4. THE CHURCHES SHOULD GO MUCH MORE VIGOROUSLY INTO THE BUSINESS OF UTILIZING THE PROGRAMS THAT DO EXIST

We have already pointed out that the clergy interviewed were both uninformed and apathetic about religious television and radio. It was not entirely unexpected, therefore, that organized utilization of radio and television programs by the churches was almost nonexistent.

There is an interesting point to be made here. It has been made clear in previous chapters that Protestant programming in general is directed primarily to the like-minded rather than to the secular or non-Protestant public. Sad as this may be for evangelism and outreach, it is often admirably suited to the purpose of enriching the program of the churches, for where is one more likely to find the "like-minded" than among the active members of the church? And these programs would be a rich resource indeed for the local church, for the simple reason that the talent available to the national programming agencies is, as a rule, considerably superior to that available to the local church. The guests on Frontiers of Faith are usually persons of distinction in the church who are not available to the average mission study group; the preachers on the network programs are usually more skilled than the guest preachers available to the average church; the dramatic portrayal of religious and moral problems on This Is the Life is certainly superior to anything comparable that is regularly available to individuals and groups in the local church.

It does not take much imagination to see how a minister or leader, particularly in a small church, could utilize these resources to develop discussion groups or similar activities, if he knew in advance the content of these programs and were given some help in planning programs built around them, such as the manuals for use that accompany films and film strips. Little seems to be done along this line, however, other than leaflets for distribution in churches indicating time and stations for religious programs.

Planned utilization procedures would recognize that audiences tend to be specialized rather than generalized. They would interpret present programs in terms of target audiences and would orient and schedule them accordingly. And furthermore, they would put as much emphasis on recruiting an audience as on getting the program on the air. Any advertiser would pay millions to have a ready-made constituency like the 35,000,000 church members represented in the National Council of Churches, and he would be in a huckster's heaven if he had available to him the elaborate and strongly motivated ecclesiastical structure which is available to the National Council to recruit audiences through the 235,000 local churches that are related to it. It is remarkably shortsighted for the churches to assume they have no recourse but to compete in the open entertainment market for mass media audiences and to be content with audiences composed of people who happen to tune in. If churches were willing to promote the current religious radio and television programs as vigorously as they promote denominational publications or local preaching missions or church school curricula or mission study programs, there seems little doubt that audiences would increase tremendously even if there were no improvement in programs.

5. WITH THEIR PRESENT EXTENSIVE COMMITMENT TO THE USE OF RADIO AND TELEVISION, RELIGIOUS AGENCIES SHOULD BE CONDUCTING A CONTINUOUS AND SYSTEMATIC PROGRAM OF RESEARCH IN THIS FIELD.

One of the most disturbing things noticed in this study—and indeed, the major reason for the study itself—was the fact that the group sponsoring religious programs have little or no validated information about the size and composition of the audiences the programs are reaching or the effects they are having.

Program builders should at least conduct small pilot research studies of the audience for their programs in the areas and at the times when programs are broadcast—or in the case of new programs, where they may be broadcast. They should consider size and composition of actual and prospective audiences as related to adjacent programs in station program structures. There is no need to operate as blindly as has often been the practice, when simple and relatively inexpensive techniques for studying an audience are as ready to hand as is the case today.

The writers of this volume would hope, of course, that future research could go much further than the simple statistical determination of audiences. The role and influence of the mass media in human behavior is an intricate matter; this research has of necessity skimmed much too hurriedly over many questions that deserve more careful and thoughtful analysis. This is especially true in the matter of the communication of values as they relate to character structure and character formation in a society where the mass media seem to play so large and influential a role. Research in considerable depth is essential here if the churches are ever to understand the society in which they work, and even more so if they intend to influence it.

Strategy at the Policy Level, Where Change Must Be More Fundamental

1. It seems clear that the churches are attempting to use the mass media without having clearly determined the role to be assigned to these media in the implementation of policy. Exactly what functions do the churches expect radio and television to perform? This is the question that throughout this study has been left largely unanswered, or has been answered in such generalized and unrealistically optimistic terms (see Chapter 6) as to be meaning-

less for purposes of evaluation. Where in specific cases this research has gone through the lengthy process of determining what function a program *does* perform, there is no concrete statement of purpose against which to compare the empirical evidence in order to assess the success or failure of the program in terms of the intent of the sponsors.

One is tempted to say that religious broadcasting is another illustration of what continental theologians are fond of calling the "activism" of the American churches; the emphasis on program for its own sake, with a rather blind faith that because it is done under church auspices it is "building the Kingdom." Yet surely such activity is useful if it is built around a sense of specific purpose. It is the clear purpose that is lacking, more than any other ingredient—lacking, that is, in any organized institutional sense; there are individuals in this work who can articulate their purposes sensibly and consistently.

What is religious broadcasting intended to do? Win converts? Its effectiveness here could be readily measured, if this were a serious purpose. Prick the conscience of the lagging churchgoer? Present the religious life in attractive terms? Encourage a general attitude of acceptance of religion on the part of the public (i.e., do a "public relations" job for the churches)? Bring the church to the shut-in? Do adult religious education? Bring the "best" in American religion to the average home?

The truth is that religious broadcasting has been promoted through unspecific promises to perform in all the above fields, and many more, but has never been forthrightly tested against any of these promises, nor have the sponsoring churches made their commitments contingent upon performance in relation to specific objectives. Except in rare instances, such as the "One Great Hour of Sharing" campaign, programs have not been planned with specific goals so that the specialists in these media could be held accountable for the achievement of these goals.

We do not mean by this to imply any charlatanry on the part of those who promote and produce religious programs; quite to the contrary, these specialists are themselves the victims of the peculiarly American and Protestant belief in salvation by gadget, which greets each new technique that comes along—the preaching mission, the closely graded curriculum, the every-member canvass, the cell group, or what have you—as the new divinely ordered means of grace, and loads upon it expectations so impossibly unrealistic that no one ever knows whether it has succeeded or failed. Radio and television were greeted with a familiar kind of enthusiasm and have run the familiar course of indiscriminate experimentation without careful evaluation.

There are numerous evidences of increasing maturity among the churches, however, and we may assume hopefully that they have arrived at the point where they can, if they are so minded, state with accuracy and reserve the rationale for their large investment in these media and their understanding of what they consider the reasonable fruits of this investment. Up to now, in the words of S. Franklin Mack, executive director of the Broadcasting and Film Commission of the National Council of the Churches of Christ in the U.S.A., the media technicians have been the tail that wagged the churches' policy dog. Now is the time for the churches to state carefully what they consider to be the proper role of radio and television programs in their over-all policy.

It would be logical here to attempt to interpret policies (the "message" of the church) and then discuss means of implementing policies through the use of the mass media. We shall be illogical, however, and discuss implementation first, reserving our comments on fundamental church policies to the last pages.

2. If the churches are to use the mass media with any effectiveness, their leaders must recognize the fundamental revolution in communications technology that has occurred in our society within the past sixty years. These are the years that have seen the rise of mass circulation newspapers, largely composed of syndicated services; mass circulation magazines; the incredibly prolific comic books; the motion pictures; radio and television. The Protestant churches in the Reformation grasped and used the new technology of the printing press with great effectiveness, and Bibles and books were a chief weapon of Protestant advance. A century ago the Protestant churches borrowed the idea of the tract from—of all places—the French Revolutionaries and used it so effectively as to give the term a permanent religious flavor.

The new revolution in communications technology is just as fundamental and far more widespread in influence than was the printing press. It has meant basic changes in the ways in which American people receive information, develop attitudes and opinions, receive cues as to appropriate behavior, and are generally oriented toward life in our complex modern society.

The elements in this change are many. One, already mentioned, is the decline in the role of the large congregate assembly as the vehicle for structuring public opinion. Another is the disappearance of what communication specialists call "feedback," or the opportunity for the communicator to adapt his message to the audience response, which in face-to-face communication he personally experiences. (Even laughter and applause are "canned" in today's media.) Still another is the rise of huge communications empires that are so powerful as to be practically autonomous, and in which policymakers are many echelons removed from the consumer. Accompanying these are the changes in the American character that students claim to have observed and which have been dwelt on in the preceding text: the increase of anomie and anonymity in personal character and behavior; the "other-direction" of Riesman's new man; the "authoritarian submissiveness" of Adorno, and similar traits that gravely concern those who believe in vigorous and responsible citizenship in a democracy.

The revolution in communications is not something the churches can adjust to by simply tacking on to existing programs a new one called "broadcasting and films." It requires a fundamental re-valuation of all the traditional elements in the church program, themselves the accretion of centuries of evolution through different periods of communications history. We need only read the testimonials of past decades to contrast today's situation with the days prior to the development of the modern mass media.

"I was attracted by the singing and went inside and was stirred by the preacher's message and accepted Christ on the spot." Those were leisurely days when men and women walked the streets in search of simple and inexpensive entertainment—a dog chasing a cat, or an open-air speaker, or a public service of worship. Today not only is the pace of life speeded up, but mass man is deluged with cheap forms of mass entertainment at every corner—the newspaper and magazine stand, the movie theater, the record shop—and the radio and television set in the quiet privacy of his home. No longer are audiences recruited by leaving the door of the assembly hall open —the gathered audience is dependent upon promotional methods that use the mass media—newspapers, radio, television and outdoor advertising.

Or—"I picked up the tract and read it and then and there decided to renounce my evil ways and return to the Christian life." This is from the day when the printed word was relatively scarce, and any scrap of literature was not only read, but passed from hand to hand. Today we are surfeited with print, carefully prepared by writers and artists highly skilled in methods of demanding attention. The traditional tract has little chance alongside the newspaper, the magazine, the comic book.

We need not belabor the point. The means of communication on which the church has relied have not disappeared nor have they necessarily lost their relevance, but they exist in a new kind of culture, and their impact in this new culture must be evaluated in fresh and realistic terms. It is well for Americans to remember that very little of the conventional program of the modern church, by which it communicates its message to people, is as much as a century old, and the media of nineteenth-century religious communication are no more sacrosanct than the morality plays of the Middle Ages.

The reappraisal we suggest here goes deep. It includes not only the rethinking of the relative roles of the physical plant and the mass media as vehicles of communication, but also such matters as the rethinking of the . curricula for training ministers in the light of whatever policy the churches might adopt for the realistic use of available communications media in this age.

3. The effective use of these new media must be based upon a well-thought-out strategy that is in turn based upon a complete and inclusive social theory. Protestants talk a great deal about a program which can be "the Protestant answer to Sheen." The typical concept here seems to be the need for a Protestant spokesman who is personable, dynamic and eloquent. Our analysis clearly points to the conclusion that the starting point for such a program is not to secure a man, but to determine a broadcast program policy based upon, first, a well-articulated theory about contemporary American society, and second, a strategy for applying this theory systematically in the use of the mass media.

Such a theory needs to embrace all social levels, all functional social groupings and all major social institutions. It needs to include a message (content) consciously directed to each social group in the population in terms of its own values, needs and states of readiness. It needs to be developed specifically for intellectuals, for women, for the frustrated operative on the factory production line, for the professional, for the teenager, for the young parent, for the churched and the unchurched.

Such a structured strategy would almost certainly provide not for a single program but for a "team" of complementary programs, with different formats, different themes and different styles, all conceived in relation to each other and to an over-all plan. Such a group of programs might well surpass Sheen's in effectiveness without ever having any single spokesman. Indeed, it is probably not of the nature of Protestantism to voice its message through a single authority figure.

This, we believe, is the central and most important finding of this report: that in programming for religious use of the mass media, the ingenuity and flexibility of the planners must match the complexity of needs and circumstances of the potential audience. It must reflect the diversity of ministry of the churches themselves, and if indeed these media are to emphasize communication to the outsider—which is the claim most often made for them—then their form must be as free, imaginative and uninhibited by conventional church patterns as it is possible to be while remaining within the framework of purpose set by the churches themselves.

And this means that the use of these media must be directed by the top policy-makers of the churches. The mass media are important enough agencies in our modern culture to be servants of policy rather than merely services to other kinds of program. It is true enough that these media can be tremendously useful to existing programs of public relations, religious education, missionary education, fund-raising, evangelism, social action or the multitude of other formal programs under church auspices. But they are not merely useful adjuncts. They are new tools by which man speaks to his fellow man, with a logic and technology of their own which is not subservient to the technique of any other kind of religious program. They should be used by the churches for the communication of whatever is central to the churches' policy, and not merely exploited for the benefit of any religious activity that finds an incidental way to make use of these media. The policy-makers, in other words, cannot evade their obligation to state priorities of church concern, and then to use these media effectively as direct instruments of action in matters of top priority.

4. We are impelled finally to comment briefly in an area where presumably the researcher has no business making judgments: the policies of the churches themselves, to which we have frequently referred. "Policy" has been the neutral word we have used to refer to fundamental questions of ethics, morality and religious belief. We stated early (Introduction) certain premises concerning the religious and ethical message of Protestantism, and the reader cannot have helped noticing that these premises affected our analysis of the content of some religious programs, particularly those of Bishop Sheen. Nor can he have failed to notice that the writers have certain convictions with reference to the question of authority, and that these convictions influenced our treatment of authoritarianism in personality structure.

The most critical and sensitive spot in the ethics of mass communications, we believe, is in the use of these media for the manipulation of people. We have stated our understanding that a fundamental policy of Protestantism is respect for the integrity of the individual—his right to make free and honest decisions in the light of the best judgment of which he is capable and his personal understanding of the faith he holds to. The sanction against manipulation, we further suggest, extends specifically to the manipulation of people for what is presumed to be their best interest.

Here is the danger area for religious groups using the mass media. They are working in an environment where the secular world has elaborately rationalized and even cynically advocated the manipulation of people for the purposes of the sponsor. The entire technology and technique of mass communications is imbued with the psychology of manipulation, of calculated motivation of audiences for purposes that may or may not be made explicit to them. And Protestant religious groups, amateurs at best in this field, may all too easily compromise their own fundamental principles when they believe themselves to be only adapting professional communication techniques to serve the Gospel.

To make the matter even more complex, the churches themselves are far from pure in this regard. Churchmen are not because of their church connections free of the temptation to exploit people for any of many reasons that are remote from the Sermon on the Mount. Indeed, the best evidence and the best analysis of this tendency to sinfulness is in the New Testament.

Finally, we feel it has been demonstrated in this report that the latent content of communication is as important as the manifest content, and that the implicit message of a radio or television program may be even more loaded with value structures than the explicit message.

All this leads us to observe that religious groups using radio and television must develop a sophistication far beyond anything encountered in this research. They must not, through innocence or ignorance, become mere puppets of a medium. More than any other agency using radio and television, the churches have an obligation to use them constructively and in strict accord with the fundamental principles for which they stand.

This would not be so urgent a matter, perhaps, if the churches used these media for some relatively impersonal purpose such as the transmission of information. But it is abundantly clear that religious broadcasters have a much more ambitious aim than this. They intend to use these media to "persuade people to better lives," to "teach the value of Christian character," to "teach individual self-understanding and adjustment in the light of God's word," to "teach Christ as the design for personal living." Unless we are to dismiss these policy statements as wishful thinking, we must believe that the churches—almost alone among the agencies that use radio and television —intend to employ these media to effect fundamental changes in character and in religious and ethical belief.

If so, the churches are committed to a tremendously intricate task in a field of personality development where our best minds confess to uncertainty about both theory and fact. And they are committed to a medium that is dangerously impersonal, where the evangelist or preacher has little opportunity to judge the pertinence of his message for the life situation of the individual who receives it. And finally, they are using media that seem to have tremendous power and influence in society.

The closest parallel in the recent history of the Church would seem to be what has been known as mass evangelism. Most of the pitfalls of mass evangelism apply also to radio and television: the temptation to use spectacular methods; the tendency of the least stable members of an audience to be most responsive; the advocacy of simple techniques as a substitute for the long and sometimes arduous struggle for basic changes in life style; the reduction of the infinite variety of the Christian life to a stereotypical least common denominator; and the failure to attach individuals in an audience to a permanent group relationship or a permanent pastoral relationship that can build a quick emotional response into constructive and lasting character change.

There is not as yet on the horizon of religious broadcasting the program that will compare in "success" with the mass evangelist of earlier days. The danger is that there will be. The danger is that some creative genius will develop the program that is so "successful" by the standards of the commercial users of the media that the fundamental purposes of the Christian church will be ignored or denied. And the sobering fact is that too many church leaders interviewed in this study seemed to be looking for this kind of program—"the answer to Fulton Sheen"—rather than planning a much more diversified, if less dramatic, ministry through radio and television to the varieties of human souls that inhabit this country. In this field as in any other there is no spectacular substitute for the responsible ministry which sees each individual human being as a child of God and speaks to each heart in terms that are relevant to its condition.

APPENDICES

A. Analysis of Program Content
   By Julian N. Hartt

B. Tables Showing Percentage of Television Set-Owning Households Viewing One or More Programs of Specified Types, By Religious Affiliation and Social Class

C. Methods of Testing Statistical Data
   By Vernon Johns

D. Percentage Distribution of Households in Audience for Specific Religious Programs by Religion and Social Class.

E. Background Data of Respondents in Depth Interviews, Covering Various Socio- and Psychological Variables

F. Explanation of "Discriminatory Power" Used in Analysis of F-Scale

APPENDIX A

Analysis of Program Content

NATIONAL RADIO PULPIT; ART OF LIVING; THE CATHOLIC HOUR;
OLD FASHIONED REVIVAL HOUR

By JULIAN N. HARTT
Professor of Philosophical Theology, Yale Divinity School

Theological Positions

THE CATHOLIC HOUR

The Catholic Hour speaker for the programs analyzed was Bishop Fulton J. Sheen. Each broadcast—and the relation between program and program—exhibited a remarkable unity. The opening music, the readings, the prayers, both the content and the delivery of the sermon and the general tone in which each program concluded all appeared to fit into a clearly unified pattern. Presumably The Catholic Hour is designed for a wide audience, an audience more inclusive than the Roman Catholic constituency.

The theological point of view was obviously, and sometimes obtrusively, Roman Catholic. For instance, in a sermon on the Beatitudes (January 20, 1952), the Roman Catholic official pronouncements on marriage and the family were clearly presupposed in everything that Sheen said. The explict position of the Roman Catholic Church on communism also was clearly presupposed. Sheen made no attempt to extend the theological and philosophical analysis of communism beyond the lines sharply defined in the official pronouncements of the Roman Cathilic Church. Hence, we can say that the intent of the seermon was to make as clear and as vividly relevant as possible the official teaching of the Roman Church on matters of great importance in the contemporary world. The way in which this was done was quite remarkably effective. Sheen's mode of address was vivid, it was in places very eloquent and it had a kind of natural poetic cast to it.

The theological argument in The Catholic Hour was simple. It seems certain this simplicity was part of the conscious design of the program. There was no technical philosophical-theological argument. There was a sprinkling of philosophical terms,[1] and philosophers were referred to, but there was no systematic

---

[1] "When He said, 'You have heard,' He included the Mosaic law; Buddha with his eightfold way; Confucius with his rules for being a gentleman; Aristotle with his natural happiness; the broadness of the Hindus; John Dewey, H. G. Wells, Thomas Mann and all the humanitarian ethical groups of our day who would translate some of the old codes into English and call them a new way of life.

"Let Him come into the world that believes in the philosophy of a James, and a Dewey and a Schiller, which denies Absolute Truth, which says that right and wrong are only questions of point of view. . . ."

interpretation of points of view with which the Roman Catholic Church is in sharp disagreement. The listener was encouraged to believe that the Church has taken care of all such opposition.

The Roman Catholic Church believes that its teaching is the perennial and immutable truth; therefore, it is everlastingly relevant to the problems of every society. But Sheen recognizes more or less explicitly that this teaching has to be given a fresh and striking reformulation. The Church does not propose to change its teaching in order to bring it into line with contemporary tastes and standards of judgment, but at the very least it must be given a contemporary flavor. By using incisive and occasionally pungent language, the Bishop tries to show the relevancy of Catholic dogma for the great problems of our day.

NATIONAL RADIO PULPIT

Dr. Ralph W. Sockman had an obviously different approach to the listener than did Sheen; although there was a studied attempt to make a unified impact. The music was well calculated to suggest the tone of the program as a whole. The content of Sockman's sermons, their theological and philosophical presuppositions, and their approach to the mind of the listener were strikingly different from Sheen's.

In the first place, the theological context in which Sockman operated was far less explicit than Sheen's. At one moment the theological background appeared to be "unreconstructed" liberalism with a particular concern for conventional middle-class moralism. But there were also suggestions of a kind of piety which is independent of this piety,[2] a kind of religious experience which does not depend for its validity upon a particular set of theological principles. In fact, theological principles in these addresses of Sockman were pretty hard to extract without the expenditure of considerable imagination. Therefore, so far as theological intellectual content is concerned, Sockman's sermons were far less rigorous and far less clear than those of Sheen.

There are obvious explanations for this. For one, Sheen's theological fences were set up long since by the authoritative fiat of the Church, where Dr. Sockman is free to roam and is under no apparent obligation to pitch a theological tent anywhere. Just as the speaker on the National Radio Pulpit operates outside of authoritarian theological boundaries, so also the listener's attention is not riveted to the production of one clear conviction rather than another. The mind of the listener is left free to extract from the sermon and from the program as a whole whatever seems edifying and morally helpful.[3]

THE ART OF LIVING

Norman Vincent Peale's program, The Art of Living, ran in the same direction as Sockman's in respect to theological clarity; but it reached farther into obscurity and naïveté than did National Radio Pulpit. There was no explicit

[2] See "Fitted for the Future," broadcast on February 10, 1952.
[3] See "The Lift of a Large Outlook," February 17, 1952.

theological perspective in The Art of Living. There was religious language. Jesus was mentioned and always in a complimentary way, but the carefully formulated theological traditions of the Christian Church seemed to play no role in Peale's sermons. The problems with which he was concerned were ones of psychological adjustment in the context of middle class moral norms and aspirations. It was assumed that these values and aims are expressions of God's will; and Peale taught that God's will is significant. But rigorous theological analysis of morality and of the aims of our society was wholly absent from this program. Peale wished his listener to adjust to "plain facts." The actualities of sin and of anxiety which are deeper than concern over one's social status, business success, the esteem of peers, etc., were systematically ignored. The actualities of sin and guilt, or death and transfiguration, played no real part in Peale's approach to the mind of his listener.

Of course, the contemporary mind is obsessed with the fears and worries to which Peale speaks. Ours is a neurotic age and a neurotic society. Whoever speaks a comfortable word to such an age will get a hearing, especially if the word is simple, homely and entirely devoid of barbs and nettles.

OLD FASHIONED REVIVAL HOUR

The Old Fashioned Revival Hour exhibited a kind of unity. The music, the prayers, the vocal quality of Dr. Charles E. Fuller were woven together in a way that would be effective to a mind which was already halfway sympathetic to this approach. There is no great mystery about the kind of Christianity proffered. In the programs which I heard, the more explicit theological aspects of fundamentalism did not bulk large. The other components were present and active—the fundamentally emotional angle, the fundamentally moralistic appeal. Someone looking for a reasoned case for Christianity, and capable of recognizing it when he heard it, would find nothing to satisfy him in these programs. A case was not even made for literalistic interpretation of the Bible. The truth was assumed, and every device was calculated, apparently, to command emotional acceptance of it.

The Role of the Church and Christian Teaching

The authoritarian presupposition to one side, I find The Catholic Hour commendable for the following reasons: (1) Christianity was shown to stand for certain things, and these certain things were shown to require theological and philosophical truths. (2) The things for which the Church stands are persistently and continuously relevant to the problems of human life. I do not accept the particular way in which these two elements were put together in The Catholic Hour. Nevertheless, this kind of approach to the contemporary mind has a great deal to commend it. It creates the impression at the outset that Christianity has an authoritative word to speak to the contemporary mind as well as to all minds in all times and places. Thus, any supposition that one can make of Christianity what one wishes—on the basis of one's own needs, of one's own interest and desires—is struck a powerful blow at the very beginning. Does not every Christian believe that there is truth in Christianity which does not depend upon his personal situation, that there is truth which speaks to his mind and to which his mind must be conformed?

This affirmation is a general assumption which is indispensable to the preaching of the Christian message. This assumption implies that the Church must adopt or assume the role of teacher to the contemporary mind. The Church does not say to people: "You tell us what you're interested in, you tell us what you'd like to hear, and we'll see if we can find something which we can do up in an attractive package for you to take home." No, the Church adopts the role of teacher. There are things that people need to know. Some of these things they have forgotten, some of them they have minimized and some of them they have denied; but these are things which we have got to know, for upon them depends our salvation. The Catholic Hour clearly assumed this role of authoritative teacher.

The Old Fashioned Revival Hour operated with a similar general assumption. The Church has to play the role of teacher. There are truths which modern people have been induced to forget or to deny, truths which are indispensable to their salvation. But Fuller was not nearly as explicit as was Sheen on the role of the Church as the teacher of these truths. Nevertheless, Fuller assumes that our lives are built upon illusion and deceit unless we recognize that certain things are true, whatever our private tastes, opinions and desires may be.

Sockman and Peale did not appear to share this general position. The authority of Jesus, the Christ, was demonstrated by them, if not actually established, pragmatically. Certain things occur that we believe are desirable for our happiness and general effectiveness when we follow the course mapped out by Jesus. The Roman Catholic, on the one hand, and the Protestant fundamentalist, on the other, would not rest their cases on this kind of appeal to pragmatic experience and to religious experience.

The Church as teacher did not cut much of a figure in the content of either Sockman or Peale. Peale, in particular, paid little attention to the Church as teacher, as an ongoing institution, as a community in whose hands authoritative teachings concerning God and man's well-being have been deposited. Both fail to represent the Church as standing over against the mind of contemporary man with a teaching, with a body of truth, which he can neglect or scorn only upon pain of damnation or sore distress.

This warning or threat of damnation need not be vulgar or crude. The Church's authority need not be represented in ways obviously aggressive and domineering. It is not necessary to make crass appeals to authority; it is not necessary to bulldoze the mind into acceptance of these teachings. Subtle persuasions are just as available to the authoritarian such as Sheen, as they are to the spokesmen of gentle reasonableness and religious tolerance, such as Sockman and Peale. The authoritarian approach is not necessarily committed to techniques and devices which outrage the sense of liberty and reasonableness in contemporary man. A great flourish of reasonableness may well be made by the authoritarian. This happened in The Catholic Hour. But the intransigence of the Roman Catholic position also comes to light in The Catholic Hour programs. The Church has defined its position. This position is not open to effective criticism. It stands there for the listener to accept, or as that upon which he can break himself if he will not accept it. There were several suggestions of this attitude in Sheen's addresses.

Fuller tried to drive home the truth of Christianity by a frontal assault on the emotions. He used emotional sanctions to lodge in the minds of the hearers what he regards as the Christian point of view.

Reasonableness prevailed in Sockman's sermons. A fair judgment upon one's experience and upon the experience of the race will show that Christian teaching is the only really adequate instruction concerning our well-being and our ultimate salvation.[4] The ultimate questions, the questions concerning final life and final death, did not get much attention from Sockman. They got less from Peale. As far as Sockman was concerned, reasonableness, persuasiveness of the quality that I have suggested, stood out as the way in which Christian teaching must find its most secure and productive place in our lives.

Peale relied greatly on appeals to experience—experience of emotional distress, and experience of relief from this distress and the resolution of life's problems through believing in the moral teaching of Jesus.[5] There was not present the kind of wider appeal to history, to the consensus of human experience in general, which appeared to be Sockman's fundamental and ultimate argument.

[4] "In Christ we see the key to the riddle of the universe. Our world wears an enigmatic face, a face sometimes ugly as sin, sometimes beautiful as angels, a world as cruel as a sea in storm and as tender as a mother with her babe, a world of snakes and stars, of bribery and bravery, of laughter and tears. But this medley of events has behind it a Creator with a purpose and a program. And these are revealed in the life and love and laws of our Lord Jesus Christ."—"Jesus Christ Our Lord," January 20, 1952.

[5] "Well, this letter is from a man who runs a hotel in Florida, right down where it is sunny and warm and where the palm trees are blowing in the breeze, where people are on the golden sand. In this letter he invites me to come down there and bring my entire family and stay with him free of charge as long as I want to. And this is going to require all the will power I have ever had because I'm not able to go. This hotel manager says: 'When I started to attend your church I was in a fog engulfing me. But by listening to the services I found the way to happiness through Jesus Christ, Our Lord, just as you said I would. And nothing, nor no one will ever make me lose it. I am that well founded in the faith that I now know that all things are possible through God. I have found it to be absolutely so. Every day I ask God to guide me in my business of operating this hotel, and I want to tell you that we are 50% ahead of last year. If more people will take God as a partner, they will find that their business runs smoother and more profitably than when they try to run it through their own simple and feeble efforts. But beyond that, and more important, I found a peace and happiness and a love and a sense of beauty that I would never have believed possible.'

"I would say, wouldn't you, that this man has found the master key to success."—"The Master Key to Success," February 10, 1952.

Intelligibility of Ideas

Intelligibility is a difficult norm to interpret in connection with the content of radio scripts. On the one hand, it suggests that which is understandable or comprehensible in itself; and on the other hand, it suggests that which minds are likely to understand or comprehend at a particular time and place.

Sheen proceeded rather clearly and obviously upon the assumption that Roman Catholic teaching is intelligible in the former sense of the term. It is more difficult to say whether the approach of The Catholic Hour is intelligible in the second sense. In the sermon on the Beatitudes, Sheen started out by asserting that the teaching of Jesus cannot be separated from the authority of his divine person. The moral teaching of Christianity cannot be abstracted from faith in the divine lordship of Jesus Christ. Apparently, Sheen was going to talk about the organic connection between morality and faith in Jesus Christ as Son of God. Actually, he said very little more about this idea until the sermon reached its conclusion. Nor did he undertake to tell us in this program how the divine lordship of Jesus Christ is to be understood, except in terms of the absolute moral supremacy of his teaching over against merely human wisdom. Thus, the problem of the divinity of Christ, which was one of the announced themes of the sermon and which was the real theological problem, was not touched upon at all.

The intelligibility with which Sockman seemed to be concerned was this: How does the Christian teaching illuminate our everyday existence? He answered: "Better than anything else." Sockman's language was adequate for this answer. It was aimed effectively at showing how Christian teachings and attitudes illuminate productively certain areas of our experience. He used no technical terminology.

From time to time Sheen used a philosophical term; and from time to time he alluded to the thought of some philosopher. He did not hesitate to refer to Kant or to Spinoza or to someone else of undeniable importance in the history of philosophy and of religious thought in the Western world. Sockman did not use such references. Perhaps he was somewhat more realistic than Sheen. How many of the people who are likely to listen to a religious radio program know anything about Spinoza or Kant or any of the figures of critical importance in the history of ideas in the Western world? On the other hand, to use philosophical terms here and there and to drop a philosophical or theological name occasionally may seem to lend the program a kind of intellectual tone and distinction which it otherwise would not have. Accordingly, I am reasonably sure at this point that when some people say they find Sockman superficial and rather simple they probably mean that he has not dignified his utterance with an occasional philosophical term or with allusion to some philosophical or theological notable, living or dead.

Fuller was not very much worried about the problem of prestige references. His terminology may be understood in the context in which he operates, by the audience to whom he makes his widest appeal. When I say his terminology is understood, I have to qualify that as follows. The response, emotional and senti-mental, which is desirable in his religious context is prompted by the use of certain words. The emphasis does not fall on understanding these words. It falls upon the production of certain emotional or sentimental effects; therefore he requires an audience trained to react emotionally to his trigger terms.

Peale was even more innocent than the other three in respect to indulgence in philosophical and theological allusions and in use of the names of notables in the intellectual history of the Western world. Occasionally he quoted from Epictetus or Marcus Aurelius, but this hardly lent, and, I suppose, was hardly designed to lend the program an intellectual distinction. Much that he said and did seemed, in fact, to be inspired by a very different motivation. Peale is folksy. Peale is homey and simple. The language he uses is imprecise in the phil-osophical and theological sense. He talks like the wise family doctor, the shrewd and helpful druggist on the street corner, full of everyday sagacity, full of a wis-dom which the philosophers know not but which Jesus apparently knew.

This approach is not at all calculated to arouse the sympathies or the interest of people with any theological sophistication. It is not astonishing, therefore, that seminary professors and seminary students should be filled with undiluted contempt when they hear Peale, and that they should be moved to such rhap-sodical heights in expressing this contempt. His appeal is just not to the person who is interested in theological dialectic or even to the person who has a pri-mary interest in the higher life of the mind. The problems of emotional distress, or mild neurotic symptoms are things that can be taken care of by spiritual medi-cine far simpler than the intellectually complex and emotionally undigestible preaching and teaching of the theologically sophisticated preacher.

Communication and Interpretation
of the Christian Message

How are Christian interpretation and communication understood in these four programs? Interpretation, so far as the Roman Catholic position is con-cerned, is a process by which the true teachings of the true Church are made clear and unavoidable to the minds of men. Interpretation is not an open pur-suit of truth which is too much for any particular mind or company of minds. The truth is available in the Church by the grace of God. The problem of the interpreter is to make this truth clear and unavoidable to the minds of his hear-ers. The minds of the hearers have to be prepared; but in this preparation no apparent concession is made to the philosophies which the secular mind brings to the task of imparting truth.

Interpretation has a somewhat broader and more vague significance for Sock-man. He does not play the role of the teacher. He does not represent the Church in its teaching capacity in any way similar to that adopted by Sheen and the Church which he represents. Interpretation is a matter of elucidating the char-acter of the world and of the human situation in this world. This elucidation draws upon poetry; it employs anecdote and story, whereby the significant fea-tures of our life are disclosed. Significant possibilities for the enhancement and redemption of our life are revealed. Interpretation, so understood, is much more like the pursuit of a truth which is more than the preacher and more than the listener. The truth is a spiritual condition—not a body of doctrine or a system of truths—which the mind is obliged to accept not only for its enlargement or its enhancement, but for the ultimate salvation of the spirit or of the person as a whole.

The difference between The Catholic Hour and National Radio Pulpit can be illustrated in a number of ways. One point of difference is the voices of the respective preachers. Sheen is quite characteristically and consistently incisive and authoritative in his utterance. This incisiveness of language actually may be taken, sometimes mistakenly, as a sign of an incisiveness of mind. The precision and the sharpness of his voice may suggest that back of the voice there is a mind which has gone into all of these complex problems thoroughly and finally. In this case, of course, the mind would not be primarily the mind of the preacher, but the mind of the Church; but the listener may not be aware of this subtle distinction.

Sockman's voice expresses a kind of gentle reasonableness, suggested by a rising inflection at the end of a line, whereas Sheen comes down finally at the end of a line. Sheen's utterance is complete; the Church's teaching is finished; the analysis of the human situation is definitive and clear. No openness of mind, no genuine novelty in the discovery and delineation of spiritual reality are left as real possibilities by Sheen's voice and general mannerism.

Peale's voice suggests, as indeed the program as a whole does, a greater openness and permissiveness than do the others; a still greater indeterminateness so far as formal teaching is concerned. The voice is frequently the voice of the sage, the homely, everyday philosopher, the man whose sagacity can be trusted to see us through our perplexing everyday problems. Interpretation in this context is a matter of making available a certain treasury of homely wisdom. The preacher does not summon his hearer to embark with him on a laborious pursuit of wisdom. The preacher does not demand of his hearer, by voice or by content of utterance, that the listener be prepared to accept truth from on high which he must assimilate, to which he must adjust himself at whatever pain.

Interpretation in the context of the Old-Fashioned Revival Hour is somewhat different again from what it is in Peale's case. There are teachings which the mind must accept. This point is characteristic of what is loosely called Protestant fundamentalism.

We have briefly considered the question of how Christian interpretation is understood in the four programs. There are still more difficult questions. What is interpretation in the Christian context? How adequately do these four interpretations explain Christianity? The answering of such questions demands some evaluative co-ordinates. They cannot take the form here of presenting a systematic theology. We can only indicate certain broad demands which every interpretation of Christianity must acknowledge.

The first of these demands is that Christianity shall be presented as thoroughly realistic. The second is that Christianity should be presented as a religion concerned with the total person and with the whole world.

Interpretations of the Christian Gospel which concentrate upon some particular area of life, such as emotional maladjustment and the confusions of the private emotional life, and neglect the problems of full involvement with the world are inadequate and distorted. Peale's program is a striking illustration of this kind of inadequacy. Sockman's program also sails close to these shoals. One could easily infer from his sermons that there is no problem so deep or so formidable that a kind of gentle reasonableness will not at least alleviate its pain, if not fully resolve it. But Christian theology holds there are problems for which there is no human resolution. These problems are not presented or scrutinized in Sockman's program.

There is also a kind of simplicism (a distortion of the Gospel in the interest of simplicity) in the Old Fashioned Revival Hour. There are great problems that stalk us, problems called sin and death by the Protestant fundamentalist. But these problems can be resolved, the listener is told. They can be resolved by coming under conviction of sin and by accepting salvation in Fuller's terms; and once this is done, apparently the problems are adequately taken care of.

The Christian Gospel stands over against this kind of simplicism. In its light we have to confess that in this life there are problems which we do not resolve, but which the grace of God gives us courage and patience to acknowledge and to live with hopefully. But there is a manifest tendency in all of the speakers but Sheen to present Christian faith as an absolute cure for every affliction. Perhaps this tendency itself reflects an assumption that the radio religious program must always be affirmative and reassuring, or the audience will evaporate.

In effectiveness of communication and techniques used to reach the mind and heart of the hearer, I think that The Catholic Hour is superior among the programs to which I have listened. Its music, for one thing, is rendered by people of professional competence. The speaker's voice is a first-rate instrument. What the speaker says is direct, it is vivid and it frequently takes on a kind of poetic eloquence, which at its best can be genuinely and deeply moving.

Reverence and Worship

Which of these programs is most markedly and persistently religious? By religious is meant: What inducement is offered to evoke a spirit of reverence before the Almighty and Eternal God? An obviously or even subtly manipulative approach will get in the way of this spirit.

The Catholic Hour is calculated to evoke a sense of worship. Reverence before the Almighty and Eternal God is enjoined in hymn and prayer. It is made clear at the outset that religion concerns God and man's relationship to God. The job of the interpreter of the Christian faith is to make clear what man's situation is before God.

The Art of Living is not notably religious in this worshipful sense. On the basis of the Sockman programs which were studied, I should also have to say that man is not summoned forthwith and persistently to humble himself before the Eternal, Almighty God; although I would not pass this judgment on other programs of his which I have heard. But Peale's talks are even further away from this atmosphere of reverence. The programs studied had no summons to bow low in humility and contrition before the everlasting God. The listener was encouraged to use religious resources for the manipulation of his ego and to some extent for the manipulation of his environment. Prayers, the literature of religions, the processes of reflection and meditation—all of these things were marshaled for the achievement of certain rather easily definable and recognizable psychological ends.

The Art of Living is, on the whole, not religious at all except in the use of religious terminology and in the appeal to a kind of piety. There is probably some connection between this absence of a profoundly religious note in Peale's program and its wide popularity. As a people we are not disposed to take seriously anything which calls for humiliation of pride or for a radical displacement of the ego as the center of gravity. A summons to reverence in the deep sense is a demand for humility and contrition before God; and this is a demand which the secular spirit of our world is going to postpone action on as long as it can.

There is a lively problem here. *Can a radio presentation of the Christian message hope legitimately to create a church atmosphere?* Perhaps we are demanding too much in some of the criticisms we make of these programs. The radio religious service obviously operates under some heavy disadvantages compared with the service in the church. Therefore, radio presentation of the Christian message ought to create a distinctive atmosphere, instead of trying to ape the service in the church. The speaker on the radio would not play the role of a preacher, let alone a priest, at all. He would adapt himself to the demands and the possibilities of the medium, and he would also adapt the presentation as a whole to the medium. He would not evoke the moods of piety; he would evoke, among other things, real curiosity as to the content of the Christian message. The tone would not be preachment, it would be discussion. Sheen appears to be attempting this in his television show, but the result seems to me so far to be a hybrid. It is a hybrid with possibilities, however.

Relevancy of the Christian Message on Radio and Television

If a person starts with the Catholic position and if he is knowledgeable, he will grant that in the American scene many people are indifferent to that viewpoint. The doctrines of that Church will seem simply irrelevant. Sheen recognizes that this is the problem before his Church. He grapples with this problem directly. He calls us to confront actualities which are what they are whether we are Catholic or not. He says: "Here are certain things which define our contemporary situation. We cannot deny the existence of these things. Our problem is to find grace to help in this and every time of need." Again, Sheen says: "We know that the secular interpretation and solution of these problems is a bankrupt operation." So he does not begin with a flat enunciation of his Church's position relative to these problems. He begins with our problematic situation in which we have to recognize that the breakdown of standard approaches to the problems is itself part of our present problem.

What could we say in this connection about the other programs? How do they approach the job of making the Christian message (however understood) appear really relevant to ourselves? Obviously, it will not do simply to stay over and over again in a sermon that the Christian message is relevant. It will not do to say you just *must believe* that it is relevant. This relevancy must be dramatically exhibited.

Peale, like Sheen, begins with a kind of invitation to us to see the plight that we are in as individuals. Sometimes there is also an invitation to us to see that a part of our plight is that we have tried solutions other than the Christian solution to our problems. For instance, there is the person who has turned to drink as a solution of his problems, or the person who has surrendered to immorality, or the one who, having made a failure of his life, now becomes a communist. But in general, Peale certainly does not believe that secular solutions are antithetical to Christian solutions provided that the secular view respects established Protestant morality. Nevertheless, in all of Peale's programs, there is acknowledgment of a problem of fundamental importance: how to convince an audience predisposed toward solutions other than the Christian solution, that the Christian word is a timely word, a word of persistent relevancy for the great problems of our time. This problem is dealt with through methods ranging from that of The Catholic Hour, with its faith in a truth that is everlastingly the truth by which the mind of man must be brought up short, to a far looser and vaguer position in Peale's program. But Peale, too, affirms that Jesus Christ is the same yesterday, today and forever.

I am aware that the study of the New Haven population shows that the great majority in Sockman's audience are middle aged or older. I believe that the kind of cultural sophistication which here and there Sockman appears to presuppose is a kind of appeal which would have meaning only for the older segments of our American people. It may be that appeal to such sophistication is something which the younger people may feel has no really important or intrinsic significance in the context of religion. This conclusion is at best a guess. It is hard to believe that younger people find that Peale's program has more bite.[6] They may feel that it has a kind of immediacy of reference and application to their problem. Perhaps just the difference between the everyday religious philosopher, the everyday wise man, on the one hand and of the ostensibly more urbane and cultured approach of Sockman on the other has something to do with it. Perhaps the short-order lunch counter character of Peale's general approach is attractive for the younger section of the audience. Sockman certainly does not consistently create the impression that great problems can be settled by a few moments of meditation and the reading of pamphlets on how to live confidently. Surely we ought not to underestimate the appeal of a simple gospel in our cultured and confused times. Anybody who can say: "Now here is the problem!" even though it is not the real problem; and "Here is the solution!" even though it is not the real solution—anybody who is in a position

[6] I am here discussing the combined audience for Peale on radio and television. The men in the television audience are 53.2 per cent and the women 61.6 per cent, 44 years old and younger.

to say this is going to command at least an initial hearing in our culture. How significant the hearing will be; what this kind of preaching will do to effect a Christian readjustment and reconstruction of life, both personal and social, is a very different question. In our time the spiritual medicine man has at least as wide and as diversified an initial hearing as he ever did, and perhaps even more so.

APPENDIX B

Tables Showing Percentage of Television Set-
Owning Households Viewing One or More
Programs of Specified Types, by Religious
Affiliation and Social Class

TABLE 1. Number of television set-owning households[a]

Religion of Household	Social Class of Household					
	I	II	III	IV	V	Total
Catholic	22	64	265	863	362	1576
Protestant	23	73	178	318	82	674
Jewish	14	55	88	94	15	266
Mixed	1	12	43	110	19	185
Total	60	204	574	1,385	478	2,701

[a] Religion other, none, and unknown omitted from these tables.

TABLE 2. Percentage of television set-owning households
viewing one or more news programs, by religious
affiliation and social class

Religion of Household	Social Class of Household					
	I	II	III	IV	V	Total
Catholic	90.9	81.2	92.8	88.6	82.5	87.6
Protestant	69.5	93.1	87.6	86.7	80.4	86.3
Jewish	78.5	89.0	86.3	88.2	73.3	86.4
Mixed	100.0	91.6	88.3	85.4	84.2	86.4
Total	80.0	88.2	89.8	87.9	82.0	87.1

TABLE 3. Percentage of television set-owning households
          viewing one or more sports programs, by religious
          affiliation and social class

Religion of Household	Social Class of Household					
	I	II	III	IV	V	Total
Catholic	86.3	87.5	85.2	83.6	78.4	82.9
Protestant	56.5	80.8	79.7	79.8	87.8	80.1
Jewish	78.5	80.0	89.7	72.3	66.7	79.7
Mixed		41.6	83.7	88.1	84.2	83.2
Total	71.6	80.3	84.1	82.3	79.9	81.9

TABLE 4. Percentage of television set-owning households
          viewing one or more variety shows, by religious
          affiliation and social class

Religion of Household	Social Class of Household					
	I	II	III	IV	V	Total
Catholic	59.0	70.3	83.3	79.1	79.5	79.3
Protestant	69.5	75.3	79.7	78.6	79.2	78.3
Jewish	71.4	72.7	77.2	75.5	73.3	75.1
Mixed		58.3	79.0	83.6	100.0	82.1
Total	65.0	72.0	81.0	79.1	80.1	78.9

TABLE 5. Percentage of television set-owning households
          viewing one or more quiz programs, by religious
          affiliation and social class

Religion of Household	Social Class of Household					
	I	II	III	IV	V	Total
Catholic	72.7	70.3	81.5	76.2	73.8	76.3
Protestant	60.9	78.1	78.7	82.4	85.4	80.6
Jewish	92.9	70.9	78.4	66.0	60.0	72.2
Mixed	100.0	58.3	81.4	76.4	63.2	75.1
Total	73.3	72.5	80.1	77.0	74.9	76.9

TABLE 6.   Percentage of television set-owning households
           viewing one or more general drama programs, by
           religious affiliation and social class

Religion of Household	Social Class of Household					
	I	II	III	IV	V	Total
Catholic	81.8	75.0	69.0	65.9	59.6	65.6
Protestant	47.8	53.4	73.0	60.3	45.1	60.6
Jewish	71.4	70.9	79.5	59.5	73.3	69.9
Mixed		75.0	86.0	53.6	73.6	64.3
Total	65.0	66.1	73.1	63.2	58.1	64.7

TABLE 7.   Percentage of television set-owning households
           viewing one or more religious programs, by
           religious affiliation and social class

Religion of Household	Social Class of Household					
	I	II	III	IV	V	Total
Catholic	59.0	68.7	66.4	63.2	57.7	62.6
Protestant	47.8	52.0	52.2	51.5	57.3	52.3
Jewish	50.0	29.0	26.1	34.0	53.3	32.3
Mixed	100.0	58.3	55.8	60.9	31.5	56.8
Total	53.3	51.4	55.0	58.4	56.4	57.2

TABLE 8.   Percentage of television set-owning households
           viewing one or more comedy drama programs, by
           religious affiliation and social class

Religion of Household	Social Class of Household					
	I	II	III	IV	V	Total
Catholic	68.1	46.8	52.4	50.7	51.9	51.3
Protestant	30.4	47.9	53.3	47.1	57.3	49.5
Jewish	57.1	50.9	45.4	38.2	26.6	43.6
Mixed		50.0	48.8	51.8	47.3	50.2
Total	50.0	48.5	51.3	49.1	51.8	50.1

TABLE 9. Percentage of television set-owning households viewing one or more music programs, by religious affiliation and social class

Religion of Household	Social Class of Household I	II	III	IV	V	Total
Catholic	50.0	35.9	42.2	39.5	37.8	39.5
Protestant	21.7	46.5	35.9	34.9	35.3	36.0
Jewish	42.8	32.7	34.0	44.6	33.3	37.9
Mixed		33.3	46.5	40.9	42.1	41.6
Total	36.6	38.7	39.3	38.9	37.4	38.7

TABLE 10. Percentage of television set-owning households viewing one or more crime drama programs, by religious affiliation and social class

Religion of Household	Social Class of Household I	II	III	IV	V	Total
Catholic	31.8	29.6	35.8	36.8	37.2	36.4
Protestant	13.0	23.2	42.1	40.2	39.0	37.8
Jewish	7.1	18.1	31.8	24.4	6.6	23.6
Mixed		16.6	34.8	45.4	57.8	42.1
Total	18.3	23.5	37.1	37.4	37.4	35.9

TABLE 11. Percentage of television set-owning households viewing one or more domestic drama programs, by religious affiliation and social class

Religion of Household	Social Class of Household I	II	III	IV	V	Total
Catholic	13.6	14.0	24.1	23.9	26.5	24.0
Protestant	21.7	20.5	19.6	28.9	18.2	24.0
Jewish	7.1	23.6	14.7	31.9	26.6	22.9
Mixed		8.3	27.9	31.8	52.6	31.3
Total	15.0	18.6	21.6	26.2	26.1	24.4

TABLE 12. Percentage of television set-owning households viewing one or more variety programs, by religious affiliation and social class

Religion of Household	Social Class of Household					
	I	II	III	IV	V	Total
Catholic		7.8	3.0	3.9	6.1	4.4
Protestant	8.6	2.7	6.7	9.7	7.3	7.9
Jewish	7.1	1.8	9.1	10.6	6.7	7.9
Mixed			4.7	6.4	21.1	7.0
Total	5.0	3.9	5.2	5.9	6.9	5.8

TABLE 13. Percentage of television set-owning households viewing one or more public issues programs, by religious affiliation and social class

Religion of Household	Social Class of Household					
	I	II	III	IV	V	Total
Catholic	18.1	7.8	6.4	3.2	1.9	3.8
Protestant	8.6	5.4	5.6	4.7		4.5
Jewish	7.1	1.8	7.9	6.3		5.6
Mixed		8.3	11.6	3.6	10.5	6.4
Total	11.6	5.3	6.7	3.8	1.8	4.4

TABLE 14. Percentage of television set-owning households viewing one or more "western" programs, by religious affiliation and social class

Religion of Household	Social Class of Household					
	I	II	III	IV	V	Total
Catholic	4.5		3.0	4.0	5.2	3.9
Protestant	4.3	1.3	2.8	4.7	9.7	4.4
Jewish		1.8	1.1	2.1		1.5
Mixed			2.3	4.5	10.5	4.3
Total	3.3	0.9	2.6	4.1	6.0	3.8

APPENDIX C

Methods of Testing Statistical Data

By VERNON JOHNS

Mathematical Statistician, Columbia University

Summary

The data on the social status, religious affiliations and television viewing and radio listening habits of the 5 per cent random sample of the population of metropolitan New Haven were subjected to the following types of statistical analysis:

a) Certain pairs of variables were tested for mutual independence by the chi-square method.

b) In the cases where the chi-square tests indicated that the variables were not independent, a measure of the degree of association between the variables was computed.

c) Confidence intervals for the proportions of the population regularly listening to (or viewing) various radio and television programs were computed.

d) Chi-square tests were made for various types of television programs to determine whether or not religious affiliation or social class differences produce patterns of viewing which differ significantly from those expected on the basis of set ownership.

Explanation of the Statistical Methods

a) The chi-square test for mutual independence was used to determine whether or not any relationship exists between two variables. If, for example, no relationship whatever existed between religious affiliation and level of education, this would mean that knowledge of an individual's religious affiliation would give no information at all as to his probable educational level, and vice versa. Generally, sociological variables are not found to be completely independent. The ability of the chi-square test to detect small deviations from complete independence increases as the sample size is made larger. In studies such as the present one, in which the sample consists of a rather large number of individuals, the chi-square test is quite likely to lead to the rejection of the hypothesis of complete independence.

The chi-square tests in this study have all been made at the 1 per cent level of significance. This means that in about 1 per cent of the cases where the variables are in fact mutually independent, we may expect the tests to indicate that they are not independent. In order to make this percentage smaller (subject to the limitations of the available chi-square tables), we would have had to reduce the ability of the tests to detect real deviations from independence.

434

It should be noted that these chi-square tests are not independent of each other. A false result in any one case, due to sampling error, is likely to be associated with false results in other cases because of the interrelatedness of the data.

b) As indicated above, we will often expect to find that some degree of relationship exists between the pairs of variables being studied. However, the chi-square test applied to a large sample will often indicate a "statistically significant" departure from complete independence when the relationship between the variables is too slight to be of any sociological importance. Hence, when the variables are known to be related (on the basis of the chi-square test), it is desirable to obtain some measure of the "degree of association" between the variables. The measure of association selected for use in the present study was the square root of a measure (suggested by Cramér[1]) based on the value of chi-square computed in the preliminary test of independence. This measure of association can vary between the limits of zero and one, and will be small when the variables are nearly independent. The measure of association will be unity only when the specification of the value of one variable completely determines the value of the other. For example, suppose that 900 individuals were classified according to two variables, A and B, each of which consists of three classes. Then if the cross-classification of the individuals was as in Table 1 or Table 2, the variables would be independent and the measure of association would be zero. If the cross-classification was as in Table 3, however, the measure of association would be one, since if an individual is known to be in class A_2, for example, then he must also be in class B_3, and similarly for A_1 and A_3.

Table 1

	A_1	A_2	A_3
B_1	100	100	100
B_2	100	100	100
B_3	100	100	100

Table 2

	A_1	A_2	A_3
B_1	40	80	60
B_2	60	120	90
B_3	100	200	150

Table 3

	A_1	A_2	A_3
B_1	300	—	—
B_2	—	—	300
B_3	—	300	—

It is clear from this illustration that it would be very unlikely for sociological variables to produce a measure of association close to unity. The measure of association is not strictly analogous to a correlation coefficient; hence, values of the measure of association which seem small in relation to values usually obtained in correlation studies may still indicate the existence of a considerable degree of association between the variables.

The proportion of the individuals in the sample who listen to a particular program will be approximately the same as the proportion in the whole population who listen to the program; however, there will be some difference because of

[1] Harold Cramér, *Mathematical Methods of Statistics* (Princeton University Press, Princeton, 1946), pp. 443–44. Certain desirable properties not possessed by Cramér's measure of association are obtained when the square root of the measure is used.

sampling variation. Thus, it is desirable to establish an interval around the sample proportion within which we may reasonably expect the true population proportion to lie. The confidence intervals in this study have been calculated with confidence coefficients of 95 per cent. In each case the probability is 95 per cent that the proportion listening to Sheen lies between 22.0 per cent ($= 23.4 - 1.4$) and 24.8 per cent ($= 23.4 + 1.4$). The probability statement may be interpreted to mean that if repeated samples of the same size were taken from the population and confidence intervals were calculated in the same way, then about nineteen times out of twenty the confidence intervals would cover the true population proportions. However, this does not mean that nineteen out of twenty confidence intervals calculated from any one particular sample will cover the corresponding population proportions; if by chance the sample is non-representative, all of the sample proportions will tend to differ substantially from the population proportions.

c) Chi-square tests were used to determine whether or not religious affiliation or social status affect the listening and viewing habits of the individuals in the sample. In these tests, the number of individuals in each religious group (or social class) who regularly view domestic drama programs, for example, is compared with the number who would be expected to view these programs if the tendency to view is assumed constant for all religious groups (or social classes). The expected number of viewers in each religious group (or social class) under the hypothesis of a constant tendency to view was computed on the basis of the sample proportions of individuals in each religious group (or social class) who own television sets.

In each case for which a significant value of chi-square was obtained, we may say that for that particular type of program there is some variation in viewing habits among the various religious groups (or social classes).

Results of the Statistical Analysis

a) In the following cases where pairs of variables were tested by means of chi-square, a statistically significant departure from independence was found:

1) Occupation of Male Head of Household by Religious Affiliation.
2) Education of Male Head of Household by Religious Affiliation.
3) Age of Male Head of Household by Social Class (Catholic).
4) Religious Affiliation by Social Class.
5) Religious Affiliation by Income.
6) Religious Affiliation by Type of Household.
7) Number in Household by Social Class (Catholic).
8) Number in Household by Social Class (Protestant).
9) Number in Household by Religious Affiliation (Social Classes I and II).
10) Number in Household by Religious Affiliation (Social Class III).
11) Number in Household by Religious Affiliation (Social Class IV).
12) Number in Household by Religious Affiliation (Social Class V).
13) Religious Affiliation by Audience and Nonaudience.

14) Set Ownership by Audience and Nonaudience.
15) Income of Family by Audience and Nonaudience.
16) Age of Wife or Female Head of Household by Audience and Nonaudience.
17) Church Attendance of Wife or Female Head of Household by Audience and Nonaudience (Catholic).
18) Church Attendance of Wife or Female Head of Household by Audience and Nonaudience.
19) Age of Male Head of Household by Audience and Nonaudience (Jewish).
20) Education of Male Head of Household by Audience and Nonaudience (Jewish).

b) Among the pairs of variables for which the chi-square tests indicate that independence does not hold, the following pairs showed measures of association exceeding 20 per cent (which indicates a substantial amount of association):

1) Number in Household by Religious Affiliation (Social Classes I and II).
2) Number in Household by Religious Affiliation (Social Class III).
3) Number in Household by Religious Affiliation (Social Class IV).
4) Age of Male Head of Household by Audience and Nonaudience (Jewish).
5) Education of Male Head of Household by Audience and Nonaudience (Jewish).

The following pairs of variables showed measures of association between 13 and 20 per cent, indicating a moderate amount of association:

1) Occupation of Male Head of Household by Religious Affiliation.
2) Education of Male Head of Household by Religious Affiliation.
3) Age of Male Head of Household by Social Class (Catholic).
4) Religious Affiliation by Social Class.
5) Religious Affiliation by Income.
6) Number in Household by Religious Affiliation (Social Class V).

The remaining pairs of variables show measures of association grading from 12 to 2 per cent.

c) Refer to the tabulated results.

d) The chi-square tests of the effects of religious affiliation and social status on television viewing habits indicated the existence of statistically significant effects in the following cases:

1) Religious Affiliation (Crime Drama).
2) Religious Affiliation (Religious Programs).

APPENDIX D

Percentage Distribution of Households in Audience for Specific Religious Programs by Religion and Social Class

TELEVISION

Sheen

Religion of Household	Social Class of Household					
	I	II	III	IV	V	Total
Catholic	1.5	4.1	16.0	40.1	13.8	75.5
Protestant	0.5	2.0	4.1	5.5	1.3	13.4
Jewish	0.1	1.0	0.6	0.4	0.1	2.2
Mixed		0.6	1.4	5.4	0.5	7.9
Other, None and Unknown	0.1	0.1	0.4	0.4		1.0
Total	2.2	7.8	22.5	51.8	15.7	100.0

Greatest Story Ever Told

Religion of Household	Social Class of Household					
	I	II	III	IV	V	Total
Catholic	0.4	3.0	9.7	25.4	10.8	49.3
Protestant	1.1	3.7	9.3	17.2	5.6	36.9
Jewish		0.4	1.5	1.1	0.4	3.4
Mixed		1.1	3.0	4.9	0.7	9.7
Other, None and Unknown				0.3	0.4	0.7
Total	1.5	8.2	23.5	48.9	17.9	100.0

What's Your Trouble?

Religion of Household	Social Class of Household					
	I	II	III	IV	V	Total
Catholic	1.9		7.5	15.2	11.3	35.9
Protestant		5.7	11.3	22.6	7.6	47.2
Jewish		3.7	3.8	1.9		9.4
Mixed			1.9	5.6		7.5
Other, None and Unknown						
Total	1.9	9.4	24.5	45.3	18.9	100.0

TELEVISION

Frontiers of Faith

Religion of Household	Social Class of Household					
	I	II	III	IV	V	Total
Catholic	2.6		10.2	17.9	2.6	33.3
Protestant	5.1		10.2	12.9	10.2	38.4
Jewish	2.6	2.6	2.6	5.0	2.5	15.3
Mixed			2.6	7.8		10.4
Other, None and Unknown					2.6	2.6
Total	10.3	2.6	25.6	43.6	17.9	100.0

This Is the Life

Religion of Household	Social Class of Household					
	I	II	III	IV	V	Total
Catholic			10.1	43.3	13.4	66.8
Protestant		3.3	3.3	6.8	3.3	16.7
Jewish	3.3		3.3			6.6
Mixed			3.3	3.3		6.6
Other, None and Unknown				3.3		3.3
Total	3.3	3.3	20.0	56.7	16.7	100.0

RADIO

The Catholic Hour

Religion of Household	Social Class of Household					
	I	II	III	IV	V	Total
Catholic	0.3	4.2	17.1	35.9	14.3	71.8
Protestant	1.0	1.4	3.2	5.9	3.1	14.6
Jewish		1.4	1.0	0.7		3.1
Mixed	0.4	0.7	2.1	5.2	1.1	9.5
Other, None and Unknown	0.4	0.3	0.3			1.0
Total	2.1	8.0	23.7	47.7	18.5	100.0

National Radio Pulpit

Religion of Household	Social Class of Household					
	I	II	III	IV	V	Total
Catholic			1.7	8.6		10.3
Protestant	10.3	17.3	13.8	31.1	5.2	77.7
Jewish			1.7			1.7
Mixed		1.7		6.9		8.6
Other, None and Unknown				1.7		1.7
Total	10.3	19.0	17.2	48.3	5.2	100.0

Table - continued   **RADIO**

Old Fashioned Revival Hour

Religion of Household	Social Class of Household					
	I	II	III	IV	V	Total
Catholic		2.4		7.1	4.8	14.3
Protestant			14.3	28.6	35.7	78.6
Jewish			2.4	2.4		4.8
Mixed					2.3	2.3
Other, None and Unknown						
Total		2.4	16.7	38.1	42.8	100.0

Billy Graham

Religion of Household	Social Class of Household					
	I	II	III	IV	V	Total
Catholic			2.7	2.7	2.7	8.1
Protestant		2.7	13.5	43.3	18.9	78.4
Jewish					2.7	2.7
Mixed			2.7	5.4		8.1
Other, None and Unknown					2.7	2.7
Total		2.7	18.9	51.4	27.0	100.0

The Art of Living

Religion of Household	Social Class of Household					
	I	II	III	IV	V	Total
Catholic			4.7	4.7	9.5	18.9
Protestant		19.0	28.6	14.3	4.8	66.7
Jewish				4.8		4.8
Mixed						
Other, None and Unknown		4.8	4.8			9.6
Total		23.8	38.1	23.8	14.3	100.0

APPENDIX E

Background Data of Respondents in Depth Interviews, Covering Various Socio- and Psychological Variables

TABLE 1. Comparison of distribution of respondents in depth interviews with distribution of households in 5 per cent sample of New Haven population

	Interview Respondents No.	Per Cent	5 Per Cent Sample No.	Per Cent
A. *Social Class*				
I	10	16.9	119	3.3
II	12	20.3	328	9.2
III	12	20.3	760	21.3
IV	19	32.2	1,723	48.5
V	6	10.2	629	17.7
Total	59	100.0	3,559	100.0
B. *Religion*				
Protestant	43	72.8	1,032	29.0
Roman Catholic	7	11.9	1,879	52.9
Jewish	3	5.1	315	8.8
Mixed	4	6.8	264	7.4
Other and None	2	3.4	69	1.9
Total	59	100.0	3,559	100.0
C. *Occupation of Head of Household*				
Housewife	3	5.1		
Higher executives, professionals and proprietors	13	21.9	187	5.3
Lesser executives, professionals and proprietors	9	15.3	209	5.9
Small independent business proprietors	2	3.4	151	4.2
Clerical and sales workers	7	11.9	564	15.8
Skilled laborers	9	15.3	949	26.6
Semiskilled laborers	7	11.9	874	24.5
Unskilled laborers	6	10.2	289	8.1
Students	1	1.7	31	1.0
Retired	2	3.4	35	1.0
Unknown	0	0	270	7.6
Total	59	100.0	3,559	100.0

Table 1 - continued

	Interview Respondents		5 Per Cent Sample	
	No.	Per Cent	No.	Per Cent
D. *Education of Head of Household: Years Completed*				
Graduate school	8	13.6	152	4.3
1-4 years college	19	32.2	447	12.6
•High school graduate	14	23.7	840	23.5
7-11 years	15	25.4	1,248	35.1
Under 7 years	1	1.7	428	12.0
Unknown	2	3.4	444	12.5
Total	59	100.0	3,559	100.0
E. *Age of Head of Household Compared to Age of Male Heads of Household in Sample*				
15-19	0	0	1	0.1
20-24	4	6.8	48	1.6
25-29	3	5.1	252	8.4
30-34	6	10.2	401	13.3
35-39	5	8.5	407	13.5
40-44	3	5.1	401	13.3
45-49	7	11.9	319	10.6
50-54	10	16.9	323	10.7
55-59	8	13.5	290	9.6
60-64	3	5.1	222	7.4
65 and over	9	15.3	353	11.7
Unknown	1	1.7		
Total	59	100.0	3,017	100.0
F. *Sex of Head of Household*				
Male	49	83.1	3,024	85.0
Female	10	16.9	535	15.0
Total	59	100.0	3,559	100.0
G. *Type of Household*				
Includes husband, wife and minor children	24	40.6	1,970	55.4
Includes husband, wife, no minor children	23	39.0	901	25.3
Broken families with minor children	0	0	248	7.0
Adults living alone	3	5.1	241	6.8
Other adult households	9	15.3	199	5.5
Total	59	100.0	3,559	100.0

Table 1 - continued

| | Interview Respondents | | 5 Per Cent Sample | |
	No.	Per Cent	No.	Per Cent
H. *Marital Status of Head of Household*				
Male married	47	79.6	2,890	81.3
Male widower	0	0	70	2.0
Male divorced	0	0	3	0.1
Male separated	1	1.7	7	0.2
Male unmarried	0	0	54	1.5
Female widowed	3	5.1	378	10.6
Female divorced	1	1.7	25	0.7
Female separated	0	0	23	0.6
Female unmarried	7	11.9	108	3.0
Female unknown	0	0	1	
Total	59	100.0	3,559	100.0
I. *Income*				
Over $15,000	7	11.9	48	1.3
$10,000-$14,999	3	5.1	52	1.5
7,501-10,000	4	6.8	151	4.2
5,001-7,500	10	16.9	470	13.2
3,501-5,000	19	32.2	1,165	32.7
2,001-3,500	9	15.3	1,220	34.3
Under $2,000	7	11.9	451	12.7
Unknown	0	0	2	0.1
Total	59	100.0	3,559	100.0
J. *Television and Radio Set Ownership*				
Families with radio and television sets	34	57.6	2,587	72.7
Families with television sets only	1	1.7	126	3.5
Families with radio sets only	24	40.7	819	23.0
Families with neither radio nor television	0	0	27	0.8
Total	59	100.0	3,559	100.0

Table 2. Interview respondents: number with stated primary or sole preoccupations in various socioreligious classes

	Family and Home	Self	Social Status	Work	Social Responsibility	Formal Religion	Total
A. Religion							
Protestant	14	14	I7	11	5	3	64
Roman Catholic	5					2	7
Jewish			2	2	1		5
None	6	5			2		13
Total	25	19	19	13	8	5	89
B. Social Class							
Median social class	III	III	III	II	I	IV	
C. Sex							
Male	10	5	8	9	4	3	39
Female	15	14	11	4	4	2	50
Total	25	19	19	13	8	5	89
D. Age of Head of Household							
Median age, head of household	39	68	37	50	46	50	
E. Income							
Median annual income	$3,501-$5,000	$2,001-$3,500	$3,501-$5,000	$5,001-$7,500	$10,001-$15,000	$3,501-$5,000	
F. Education of Head of Household							
Median years of schooling	12-plus Business College	10	14	15	16	12	

	Family and Home	Self	Social Status	Work	Social Responsibility	Formal Religion	Total
G. Occupation of Head of Household							
Housewife		3	1				4
Higher executives, professionals and proprietors	3	3	5	6	6	1	24
Lesser executives, professionals and proprietors	4					1	5
Small independent business proprietors	1		4	6	1	1	13
Clerical and sales workers	4	2	1			2	9
Skilled laborers	9	4	8	1			22
Unskilled laborers	2						2
Students		1			1		2
Retired	1	5					6
Institutionalized	1						1
Unknown		1					1
Total	25	19	19	13	8	5	89
H. Type of Household							
Includes husband, wife and minor children	16	2	10	5	6	3	42
Includes husband, wife, no minor children	8	9	7	6	2	1	33
Adults living alone		3				1	4
Other adult households	1	4	2	2			9
Other		1					1
Total	25	19	19	13	8	5	89
I. Television and Radio Set Ownership							
Families with radio and television sets	20	8	16	7	4	4	59
Families with radio sets only	5	11	3	6	4	1	30
Total	25	19	19	13	8	5	89

Table 3. New Haven interview chunk: median F-scale for preoccupational groups, by social class

| | Social Class | | | | | | | | | | | |
| | I | | II | | III | | IV | | V | | Total | |
Preoccupation	No.	Score	No.	Score	No.	Score	No.	Score	No.	Score	No.	Score
Family and home			5	3.87	7	3.42	3	4.24	5	5.41	20	4.10
Self			5	4.31	3	4.14	7	5.21			15	4.93
Social status	2	2.57			5	4.59	5	3.83			12	3.95
Work	1	2.55	4	2.98	2	4.87	1	3.97			8	3.28
Social responsibility	3	1.79	1	1.45	1	1.48					5	1.76
Formal religion							2	5.43			2	5.43

Table 4. New Haven interview chunk: percentage distribution of program uses by each preoccupation group in specified program classes

Religious Programs	Family and Home	Self	Social Status	Work	Social Responsibility	Formal Religion	Total
Sponsored by National Council of Churches:							
Total	22	50	32	35		20	31
Peale	13	29	16	13		13	17
Sockman	9	16	12	22		7	12
Bonnell		5	4				2
Roman Catholic Programs:							
Total	35	16	36	13	50	13	25
Sheen	28	16	36	13	50	13	23
What One Person Can Do	4						1
Rosary Hour	3						1
The Greatest Story Ever Told	28	5	24	30		13	20
Other Programs	15	29	8	22	50	53	24
Total Programs Used [a]	99	100	100	100	100	100	100

[a] Because of rounding adjustments, percentages in column will not always add precisely to 100.

Table 5. New Haven interview chunk: percentage distribution of audience for religious radio and television programs by specified prime or sole preoccupation groups

Religious Programs	Family and Home	Self	Social Status	Work	Social Responsibility	Formal Religion	Total
Sponsored by National Council of Churches:							
Total	21	40	16	16		6	99
Peale	23	42	15	12		8	100
Sockman	21	32	16	26		5	100
Bonnell		67	33				100
Roman Catholic: Total	41	15	23	8	8	5	100
Sheen	36	17	25	8	8	6	100
What One Person Can Do	100						100
Rosary Hour	100						100
The Greatest Story Ever Told	43	7	20	23		7	100
Other Programs	19	30	8	14	8	22	101
No Use of Religious Programs	22	11	33	11	22		99
Grand Total	28	23	19	15	6	9	100
Percentage Distribution of Groupings	6	21	28	21	15	9	100

Major Preoccupation of Respondents

Table 6. New Haven interview chunk: median F-scale scores for users
of specified religious programs, by social class

Religious Programs	I No.	I Score	II No.	II Score	III No.	III Score	IV No.	IV Score	V No.	V Score	Total No.	Total Score
Sponsored by National Council of Churches:												
Total	7	4.07	17	3.42	5	4.93					29	4.07
Peale	4	4.19	8	3.55	3	5.35					15	4.14
Sockman	3	3.00	8	3.55	1	4.93					12	3.55
Bonnell			1	2.66	1	4.93					2	3.80
Roman Catholic Programs:												
Total	3	4.31	7	4.07	5	4.93			3	5.52	18	4.72
Sheen	3	4.31	7	4.07	5	4.93					15	4.72
What One Person Can Do									2	5.69	2	5.69
Rosary Hour									1	4.38	1	4.38
The Greatest Story Ever Told			4	3.25	6	4.37	3	3.83	4	5.47	19	4.14
Other Programs			6	2.88	4	4.28	16	5.24	1	4.38	27	4.87
No Use of Religious Programs	6	2.28			6	4.04	4	4.42			16	3.40

Table 7. New Haven interview chunk: median authoritarian aggression scores for users of specified religious programs, by social class

Religious Programs	I No.	Score	II No.	Score	III No.	Score	IV No.	Score	V No.	Score	Total No.	Score
Sponsored by National Council of Churches:												
Total			7	3.63	17	3.38	5	6.00			29	3.63
Peale			4	4.07	8	3.44	3	6.00			15	4.12
Sockman			3	3.13	8	3.44	1	6.00			12	3.44
Bonnell					1	2.00	1	6.00			2	4.00
Roman Catholic Programs:												
Total			3	4.50	7	3.85	5	4.93	3	6.13	18	5.00
Sheen			3	4.50	7	3.85	5	4.93			15	4.63
What One Person Can Do									2	6.19	2	6.19
Rosary Hour Hour									1	5.00	1	5.00
The Greatest Story Ever Told			4	3.62	6	4.38	3	3.00	4	6.19	19	4.63
Other Programs			6	2.25	4	4.38	16	6.00	1	5.00	27	5.38
No Use of Religious Programs	6	1.94					6	3.76	4	4.62	16	3.13

Table 8. New Haven interview chunk: median F-scale scores for interest groups within the audiences of specified religious programs

Religious Programs	Family and Home		Self		Social Status		Work		Social Responsibility		Total	
	No.	Score	No.	Score	No.	Score	No.	Score	No.	Score	No.	Score
Sponsored by National Council of Churches:												
Total	9	3.42	14	4.62			6	4.87			29	4.07
Peale	5	3.42	8	4.62			2	4.87			15	4.14
Sockman	4	3.25	4	4.54			4	3.94			12	3.55
Bonnell			2	3.80							2	3.80
Roman Catholic Programs:												
Total	7	4.38	6	4.83	3	4.07	2	4.87			18	4.72
Sheen	4	3.78	6	4.83	3	4.07	2	4.87			15	4.72
What One Person Can Do	2	5.69									2	5.69
Rosary Hour	1	4.38									1	4.38
The Greatest Story Ever Told	9	4.72	2	3.40	4	4.33	2	3.47			19	4.14
Other Programs	5	3.52	9	4.93	1	2.79	5	3.97	1	1.45	27	4.87[a]
No Use of Religious Programs	4	4.37	1	4.52	6	3.39	1	2.55	4	1.78	16	3.40

[a] The "Formal Religion" interest group was omitted here because it contained only two individuals who used three "other" Protestant programs each. Their scores were 5.62 and 5.24, with median of 5.23.

Table 9. New Haven interview chunk: median scores on authoritarian aggression and authoritarian submission of members of interest groups who regularly use specified religious programs

Religious Programs	Family and Home No.	Score	Self No.	Score	Social Status No.	Score	Work No.	Score	Social Responsibility No.	Score	Total No.	Score
				A.	Authoritarian	Aggression						
Sponsored by National Council of Churches: Total	9	3.38	14	5.06			6	5.25			29	3.63
Peale	5	3.38	8	5.06			2	5.31			15	4.12
Sockman	4	2.82	4	4.87			4	6.31			12	3.44
Bonnell			2	4.00							2	4.00
Roman Catholic Programs:												
Total	7	3.85	6	5.38	3	4.63	2	5.31			18	5.00
Sheen	4	3.63	6	5.38	3	4.63	2	5.31			15	4.63
What One Person Can Do	2	6.19									2	6.19
Rosary Hour	1	5.00									1	5.00
The Greatest Story Ever Told	9	4.75	2	3.06	4	4.75	2	3.19			17	4.12
Other Programs	5	3.50	9	6.00	1	2.75	5	3.00	1	1.38	27	5.38[a]
No Use of Religious Programs	4	4.62	1	4.63	6	3.13	1	2.13	4	1.25	16	3.13
				B.	Authoritarian	Submission						
Sponsored by National Council of Churches: Total	9	5.14	14	4.86			6	5.29			29	5.14
Peale	5	5.14	8	4.86			2	5.43			15	5.14
Sockman	4	3.79	4	4.86			4	5.00			12	4.93
Bonnell			2	4.29							2	4.29
Roman Catholic Programs:												
Total	7	4.86	6	5.79	3	5.43	2	5.43			18	5.36
Sheen	4	4.36	6	5.79	3	5.43	2	5.43			15	5.29
What One Person Can Do	2	6.50									2	6.50
Rosary Hour	1	5.00									1	5.00
The Greatest Story Ever Told	9	4.86	2	3.86	4	5.43	2	3.86			17	5.00
Other Programs	5	4.43	9	5.86	1	4.00	5	5.29	1	1.29	27	5.29[a]
No Use of Religious Programs	4	4.50	1	5.43	6	4.57	1	2.29	4	1.93	16	4.07

[a] The two individuals, part of the audience for three "other" Protestant programs each, who were formal-religion-centered are not shown separately. Their authoritarian aggression scores were 6.63 and 5.50, and their authoritarian submission scores were 6.43 and 6.14.

APPENDIX F

Explanation of "Discriminatory Power" Used in Analysis of F-Scale

The three major items introduced into the F-scale to test attitudes toward religious authority were:

1. Most people who try to run their lives according to the teaching of the Bible find that Bible principles are not practical in real life.
2. The minister (or priest or rabbi) should be the final authority on the way we should act and what we should believe.
3. In order to obtain divine assistance in life's crises, it is necessary to get it through your church (or priest, pastor or rabbi).

The responses of as many individuals as possible (174 altogether, including, in addition to New Haven respondents, University of Illinois graduate and undergraduate students and ministers of the United Church of Canada) were analyzed for each of these items to determine the extent to which each accomplished its purpose i.e., provided an indicator of the internationalization of Protestant faith. The "discriminatory power" technique, developed originally by Rensis Likert and employed by the authors of *The Authoritarian Personality*,[1] was used in this analysis. It rests on reasoning that if an item produces results for an individual which agree with the results of his whole F-scale test, then it is efficient in placing him at a certain place on a possible continuum of attitudes and beliefs. The method produces results practically identical with those from the computation of coefficients of correlation and is much more economical of time and effort.

The discriminatory power method (hereafter referred to as "D.P.") uses the following procedure. Individuals whose total F-scale scores (based here on the items in the original F-scale only) fell in the highest 25 per cent of the chunk were considered high scorers; those whose total scores were in the lowest 25 per cent were regarded as low scorers. The average (mean) score on each of the three new items was computed for the individuals termed high scorers and for those termed low scorers. The larger the difference between the values of these means for high and low scorers, the greater the D.P. for the item. Whatever the meaning of the item was to the individuals in the chunk, it served to spread them out well, statistically, if this D.P. was large; or it failed to do so, if it was small. The significance of a particular sized D.P. rests in large part, however, on the mean score *for the whole chunk* on this item. If this mean was near 4.0, the chunk was obviously rather evenly divided pro and con on the issue touched by the item. If the item mean is less than 3.0, the whole chunk tends to disagree with the proposition; if the item mean exceeds 5.0 then the whole chunk tends

[1] Adorno, *op. cit.*, pp. 76–83.

to agree with the item. D.P.'s may be smaller and yet still quite useful in separating high from low scorers on a particular item, if the item mean is less than
3.0 or more than 5.0. The joint interpretation of item means and D.P.'s may be
guided by the following summary by the authors of *The Authoritarian Personality*:

> For items with group means in the approximate range 3.0 to 5.0, Discriminatory Pow-
> ers may be evaluated according to the following general standards: a D.P. of over 4.0 is
> very high and indicates almost uniform agreement by the high scorers, disagreement by
> the low scorers, with almost no overlap. D.P.'s of 3.0–4.0 are very satisfactory and indi-
> cate a clear-cut difference between high and low scorers. D.P.'s of 2.0–3.0, while statis-
> tically significant, indicate greater variability in the responses of low and high scorers
> and a fair amount of overlap. A D.P. between 1.0 and 2.0 involves considerable agree-
> ment by the low scorers and disagreement by the high scorers, but it still indicates a sta-
> tistically significant difference between the low mean and the high mean.* As the D.P.
> decreases below 1.0 the possibility of significance decreases rapidly.[2]

Table 1. Three questions on the internalization of religious experience:
analysis of item means and discriminatory powers with total
F-scale scores, by religion

		Religion		
	Protestant	Roman Catholic	Jewish	Other and None	Total
F-scale Scores					
Number	122	17	11	24	174
Means—total chunk	3.53	3.73	2.77	4.18	3.59
Means—lower quartile	2.25	2.29	1.78	1.97	2.18
Means—upper quartile	4.79	4.88	3.64	5.94	4.88
Bible Principles Are Not Practical					
Means—total chunk	2.61	2.82	2.64	4.04	2.83
Means—lower quartile	2.03	1.50	2.00	3.17	2.14
Means—upper quartile	3.27	5.50	3.67	5.67	3.84
Discriminating power	1.24	4.00	1.67	2.50	1.70
Minister — Final Authority					
Means—total chunk	1.79	2.53	1.64	2.61	1.97
Means—lower quartile	1.10	1.50	1.33	1.00	1.14
Means—upper quartile	2.77	2.50	1.67	5.50	3.05
Discriminating power	1.67	1.00	.34	4.50	1.91
Divine Assistance...Church					
Means—total chunk	2.87	3.82	3.18	3.26	3.04
Means—lower quartile	1.87	3.50	1.67	1.17	1.91
Means—upper quartile	3.63	3.75	4.33	5.17	3.79
Discriminating power	1.76	.25	2.66	4.00	1.88

* [From the source:] "While standard deviations have not been obtained for all
items, it can be shown that (with group N equal 100 to 150) the standard error of
the difference between the means for low and high scorers is almost never above .50,
seldom below .25. In terms of the critical ratio, then, a D.P. of over 1.0 is statistically
significant, that is, the means are different though the distributions are partially overlap-
ping."

[2] *Ibid.*, p. 80.

The results of the item analysis for our three new items are summarized in Table 1.

In comparison with the discriminating powers found for the items in the final form of the F-scale (by the authors of *The Authoritarian Personality*), none of our three items would be considered highly discriminating. Only one of the F-scale items had a D.P. as low as these three.[3] In further work along this line the item on the minister as the final authority should be reworded to tap a greater range of attitudes. Even this item, however, has a D.P. of 1.91, indicating a relatively clear separation of the low scorers and the high scorers. The other two items also have D.P.'s sufficiently large to be statistically significant in separating high and low scorers.

[3] *Ibid.*, p. 260.

INDEX

[The names printed in italic are fictitious names of persons interviewed in the study.]